iPad 2 Made Simple

Martin Trautschold
and
Gary Mazo

Apress®

iPad 2 Made Simple

ISBN-13 (pbk): 978-1-4302-3497-5

ISBN-13 (electronic): 978-1-4302-3498-2

President and Publisher: Paul Manning
Lead Editor: Steve Anglin
Development Editor: James Markham
Editorial Board: Steve Anglin, Mark Beckner, Ewan Buckingham, Gary Cornell, Jonathan Gennick, Jonathan Hassell, Michelle Lowman, Matthew Moodie, Jeff Olson, Jeffrey Pepper, Frank Pohlmann, Douglas Pundick, Ben Renow-Clarke, Dominic Shakeshaft, Matt Wade, Tom Welsh
Coordinating Editor: Kelly Moritz
Copy Editor: Patrick Meader
Compositor: MacPS, LLC
Indexer: BIM Indexing & Proofreading Services
Artist: SPi Global
Cover Designer: Anna Ishchenko

Distributed to the book trade worldwide by Springer Science+Business Media, LLC., 233 Spring Street, 6th Floor, New York, NY 10013. Phone 1-800-SPRINGER, fax (201) 348-4505, e-mail orders-ny@springer-sbm.com, or visit www.springeronline.com.

For information on translations, please e-mail rights@apress.com, or visit www.apress.com.

Apress and friends of ED books may be purchased in bulk for academic, corporate, or promotional use. eBook versions and licenses are also available for most titles. For more information, reference our Special Bulk Sales–eBook Licensing web page at www.apress.com/info/bulksales.

This book is dedicated to our families—to our wives, Julie and Gloria, and to our kids, Sophie, Livvie and Cece, and Ari, Dan, Sara, Billy, Elise and Jonah.

Without their love, support, and understanding, we could never take on projects like this one. Now that the book is done, we will gladly share our iPads with them— for a little while!

Contents at a Glance

Contents

About the Authors

Martin Trautschold is the founder and CEO of Made Simple Learning, a leading provider of Apple iPad, iPhone, iPod touch, BlackBerry, Android, and Palm webOS books and video tutorials. He has been a successful entrepreneur in the mobile device training and software business since 2001. With Made Simple Learning, he has helped to train thousands of Smartphone users with short, to-the-point video tutorials. Martin has now co-authored over twenty "Made Simple" guide books. He also co-founded, ran for 3 years, and then sold a mobile device software company. Prior to this, Martin spent 15 years in technology and business consulting in the US and Japan. He holds an engineering degree from Princeton University and an MBA from the Kellogg School at Northwestern University. Martin and his wife, Julia, have three daughters. He enjoys rowing with the Halifax Rowing Association in Daytona Beach, Florida and cycling with friends. Martin can be reached at martin@madesimplelearning.com.

Gary Mazo is Vice President of Made Simple Learning. Gary joined Made Simple Learning in 2008 and has co-authored the last nineteen books in the Made Simple series. Along with Martin and Kevin Michaluk from CrackBerry.com, Gary co-wrote CrackBerry: True Tales of BlackBerry Use and Abuse—a book about BlackBerry addiction and how to get a grip on one's BlackBerry use. Gary also teaches writing, philosophy, technical writing, and more at the University of Phoenix. He holds a BA in anthropology from Brandeis University. Gary earned his M.A.H.L (Masters in Hebrew Letters) as well as ordination as Rabbi from the Hebrew Union College-Jewish Institute of Religion in Cincinnati, Ohio. He has served congregations in Dayton, Ohio, Cherry Hill, New Jersey, and Cape Cod, Massachusetts. When not writing or teaching, Gary enjoys cycling and playing the piano. Gary is married to Gloria Schwartz Mazo; they have six children. Gary can be reached at gary@madesimplelearning.com.

About the Technical Reviewer

 **Rene Ritchie** is editor of TiPb.com, the iPhone, iPod touch, and iPad blog, which covers the full range of news; how-tos; and app, game, and accessory reviews. Part of the Smartphone Experts network, TiPb also provides a full range of help and community forums and has a thriving YouTube channel (www.youtube.com/theiphoneblog/), Facebook page (www.facebook.com/tipbcom/), and Twitter following (http://twitter.com/tipb). A graphic designer, web developer, and author, Rene lives and works in Montreal. He can be reached via rene@tipb.com or @reneritchie on Twitter

Acknowledgments

A book like this takes many people to put together. We would like to thank Apress for believing in us and our unique style of writing.

We would like to thank our Editors, Jim and Kelly, and the entire editorial team at Apress.

We would like to thank our families for their patience and support in allowing us to pursue projects such as this one.

Part I

Quick Start Guide

In your hands is one of the most exciting devices to hit the market since the original version: the new iPad 2. This Quick Start Guide will help get you and your new iPad 2 up and running in a hurry. You'll learn all about the buttons, switches, and ports. You'll also learn how to use the innovative and responsive touch screen, as well as multitask with the new App Switcher bar. Our App Reference Tables introduce you to both the built-in apps and some valuable additions from the App Store—and serve as a quick way to find out how to accomplish a task. We also show you some popular accessories that will help you get more out of your iPad.

Quick Start Guide

This Quick Start Guide is meant to be just that—a tool that can help you jump right in and find information in this book—and learn the basics of how to get around and enjoy your iPad right away.

We start with the nuts and bolts in the "Learning Your Way Around" section—what all the keys, buttons, switches, and symbols mean and do on your iPad. You'll see some handy features such as how to double-click the **Home** button to multitask; how to configure the **Rotation Lock/Mute** switch; and how to interact with the menus, submenus, and set switches—which you do in almost every application on your iPad. You'll also find out how to read your connectivity status and what to do when you travel on an airplane.

> **TIP:** Check out Chapter 2: "Typing Tips, Copy/Paste, & Search" for great typing tips and more.

In "Touch Screen Basics," we help you learn how to touch, swipe, flick, zoom, and more.

In "App Reference Tables," we've organized the app icons into general categories, so you can quickly browse the icons and jump to a section in the book to learn more about the app a particular icon represents. Here are the tables:

- Getting Started (Table 2)
- Staying Organized (Table 3)
- Being Entertained (Table 4)
- Staying Informed (Table 5)
- Networking Socially (Table 6)
- Being Productive (Table 7)

In "Other Fun Stuff," we show you the Electronic Picture Frame feature and how to enjoy videos on your iPad.

In "iPad Accessories," we give you a brief overview of some of the more common accessories you might find interesting.

So let's get started!

Learning Your Way Around

To help you get comfortable with your iPad, we start with the basics—what the buttons, keys, and switches do—then we move into how you start apps and navigate the menus. Probably the most important status indicator on your iPad, besides the battery, is the one that shows network status in the upper-left corner. You'll see how to quickly read the network status icons.

Keys, Buttons, and Switches

Figure 1 shows all the things you can do with the buttons, keys, switches, and ports on your iPad. Go ahead and try out a few things to see what happens. Try pressing the **Volume Down** key for two seconds, double-clicking the **Home** button, using the **Rotation Lock/Mute** switch, and pressing and holding the **Power/Sleep** key. Have some fun getting acquainted with your device.

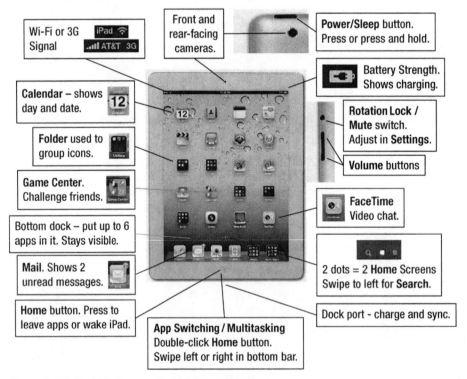

Figure 1. *The iPad 2 buttons, ports, switches, and keys*

Locking the Screen Rotation or Muting Your iPad

As soon as you start touching the iPad, you'll notice the screen rotates amazingly fast. There are times when you don't want it to rotate (called **Rotation Lock** or sometimes **Orientation Lock**)—for example, when you have it in your lap or on the table. The switch above the volume buttons on the upper-right edge of your iPad can be set to do two different functions. One function enables **Rotation Lock**, while the other enables you to **Mute** your device. (For example, you can mute rings from any incoming **FaceTime** video calls.) You can adjust which function you want to use for this side switch in the **Settings** app. In that app, select **General ➤ Use Side Switch to ➤ Rotation Lock** or **Mute**. Please see Chapter 8: "Multitasking and Mute/Lock Switch" for more details on how to use this switch.

Starting Apps and Using Soft Keys

Some apps have soft keys at the bottom of the screen, such as the **iPod** app shown in Figure 2.

For the soft keys to work in the **iPod** app, you must have some content (e.g., music, videos, and podcasts) on your iPad. See Chapter 3: "Sync with iTunes," for help syncing your music, videos, and more. Follow these steps to use the soft keys in the **iPod** app:

1. Tap the **iPod** icon to start the **iPod** app.

2. Touch the **Albums** soft key at the bottom to view your albums.

3. Touch the **Artists** soft key to view a list of your artists.

4. Try all the soft keys in **iPod** and other apps.

> **TIP:** You know which soft key is selected because it is highlighted—either with dark gray or with a color. The unselected soft keys are light gray or white.

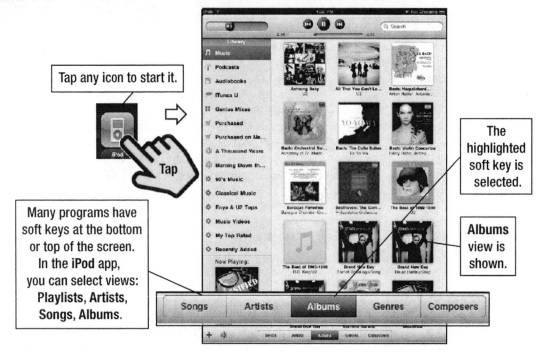

Tap any icon to start it.

Tap

The highlighted soft key is selected.

Albums view is shown.

Many programs have soft keys at the bottom or top of the screen. In the **iPod** app, you can select views: **Playlists, Artists, Songs, Albums.**

| Songs | Artists | Albums | Genres | Composers |

Figure 2. *Working with soft keys in apps*

Menus, Options, and Switches

Once you are in a program, you can select any menu item by simply touching it. In the **Settings** app, tap any item in the left column to see more options appear in the right column. Tap any item with a **Greater Than** symbol (**>**) to see another screen with options that you can adjust, such as **Show Each Photo For** (see Figure 3).

> **TIP:** You know there is a list of options if you see the **Greater Than** symbol (**>**) next to the menu item.

How do you get back to the previous screen or menu? Tap the button in the top left of the **Options** screen that shows the name of the previous screen. If you're in the **Show Each Photo For** screen, for example, you'd touch the **Picture Frame** button.

You'll see a number of switches on the iPad, such as the one next to **Zoom In on Faces** shown in Figure 3. To set a switch (e.g., from **ON** to **OFF**), just touch it.

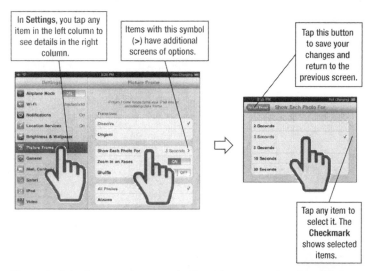

Figure 3. *Selecting menu items, navigating submenus, and setting switches*

Reading the Connectivity Status Icons

Since most of the functions on your iPad work only when you are connected to the Internet (e.g., email, the Web, the **App Store**, and **iTunes**), you need to know when you're connected. Understanding how to read the Status bar can save you time and frustration.

Cellular (3G) Data Signal Strength (1-5 bars):

Strong

Weak

Radio Off—
Airplane Mode

Wi-Fi Network Signal Strength (1-3 symbols):

Strong

Weak

Off

You can tell if you are connected to a network—and the general speed of the connection—by looking at the left end of your iPad's Top Status bar. Table 1 shows what you may see.

Table 1. *How to Tell When You Are Connected*

In the upper left corner, if you see letters and symbols...	Cellular Data Connection	Wi-Fi Connection	Speed of Data Transfer
...ıll AT&T 3G **..ıll Verizon 3G** (*will show your own carrier name*) **or** **iPad 🛜**	✓	✓	HIGH
...ıll AT&T E	✓	✗	MEDIUM
...ıll AT&T O **..ıll Verizon O**	✓	✗	LOW
✈ (Airplane Mode) **iPad**	✗	✗	No connection

Chapter 5: "Wi-Fi and 3G Connectivity" shows you how to connect your iPad to a Wi-Fi or 3G Cellular Data Network.

Traveling with your iPad—Airplane Mode and Wi-Fi

When you're flying on an airplane, the flight crew usually asks you to turn off all portable electronic devices for takeoff and landing. Then, when you get to altitude, they say "all approved electronic devices" can be turned back on.

You can turn off the iPad by pressing and holding the **Sleep/Wake** button on the top-right edge until the slider appears. Next, use the **Slide to Power Off** switch with your finger.

If you have a 3G/Cellular Data iPad, you can turn on **Airplane Mode** in the **Settings** icon as follows:

1. Tap the **Settings** icon.

2. Set the switch next to **Airplane Mode** in the top of the left column to **ON**.

> **TIP:** Some airlines do have in-flight Wi-Fi networks; in this case, you'll want to leave your Wi-Fi turned on.

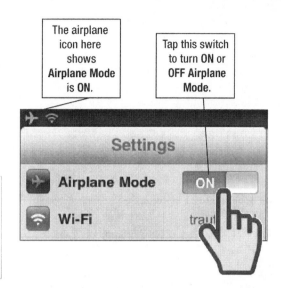

It's easy to turn off your Wi-Fi connection (see Figure 4):

1. Tap the **Settings** icon.

2. Tap **Wi-Fi** in the top of the left column.

3. Set the switch next to **Wi-Fi** in the top of the right column to **OFF**.

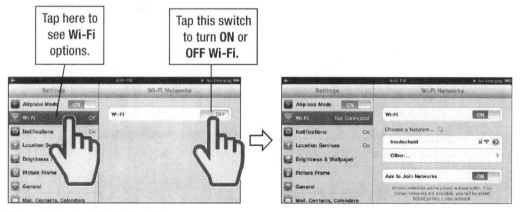

Figure 4. *Turning Wi-Fi OFF or ON*

Multitasking or App Switching

One of the great features on your iPad is the ability to *multitask*, or jump between applications, while leaving things like music playing in the background (see Figure 5).

Check out Chapter 8: "Multitasking and Mute/Lock Switch" for more information.

Double-click the **Home** button to bring up the **App Switcher** app at the bottom of the screen. Next, swipe right to see more icons of any app that is running. Tap the icon of any app you want to start. If you don't see the icon you want, then click the **Home** button to see the entire **Home** screen. Repeat these steps to jump back to the app you just left. The nice thing is that the app you just left is always shown as the first app on the **App Switcher** bar. Swipe to the left to see music controls and the opposite of the function you set for your side switch. For example, if you set your side switch to **Rotation Lock**, then you will see the **Mute** control here (and vice versa).

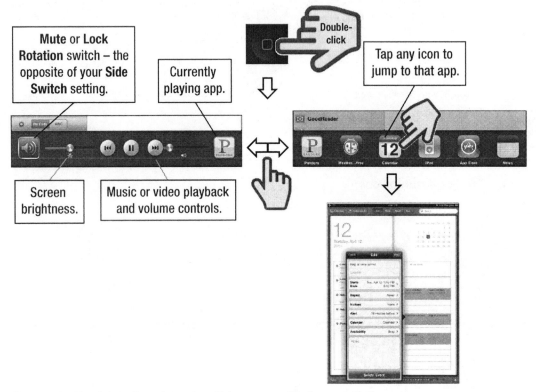

Figure 5. Double-click the **Home** button to switch apps or multitask on your iPad.

Touch Screen Basics

In this section, we describe how to interact with the iPad touch screen.

Touch Screen Gestures

The iPad has an amazingly sensitive and intuitive touch screen. Apple—renowned for making the iPhone, iPod touch, and iPod easy to use—has come up with an excellent larger touch-screen device.

If you are used to a physical keyboard and a trackball or trackpad, or an iPod's intuitive scroll wheel, this touch screen will take a little effort to master. With a little practice, though, you'll soon become comfortable interacting with your iPad.

You can do almost anything on your iPad by using a combination of the following:

- Touch screen *gestures*
- Touching icons or soft keys on the screen
- Tapping the **Home** button at the bottom

The following section describes the various gestures.

Tapping and Flicking

To start an app, confirm a selection, select a menu item, or select an answer, simply tap the screen. To move quickly through contacts, lists, and the music library in **List** mode, flick side to side or up and down to scroll through items (see Figure 6).

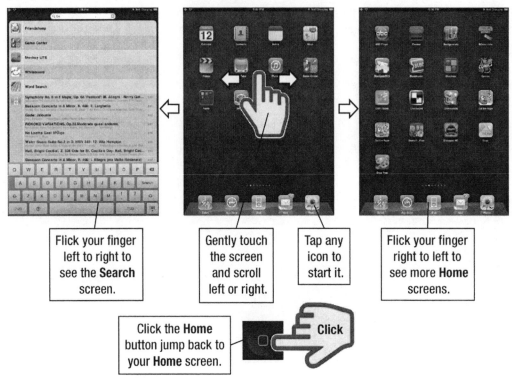

Flick your finger left to right to see the **Search** screen.

Gently touch the screen and scroll left or right.

Tap any icon to start it.

Flick your finger right to left to see more **Home** screens.

Click the **Home** button jump back to your **Home** screen.

Click

Figure 6. *Basic touch-screen gestures*

Swiping

To swipe, gently touch and move your finger (see Figure 7). You can also do this to move between open **Safari** web pages and pictures. Swiping also works in lists, such as the **Contacts** list.

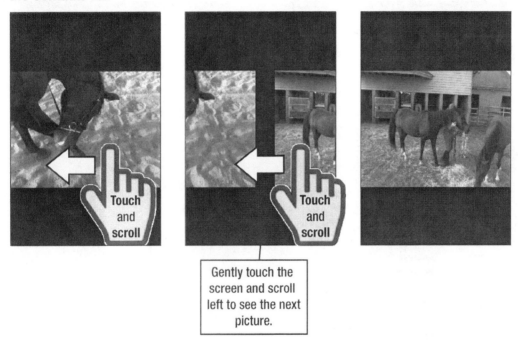

Gently touch the screen and scroll left to see the next picture.

Figure 7. *Touch and swipe to move between pictures and web pages.*

Scrolling

Simply tap and slide your finger to move or scroll around the screen (see Figure 8). You can use this gesture in messages (email), the **Safari** web browser, menus, and more.

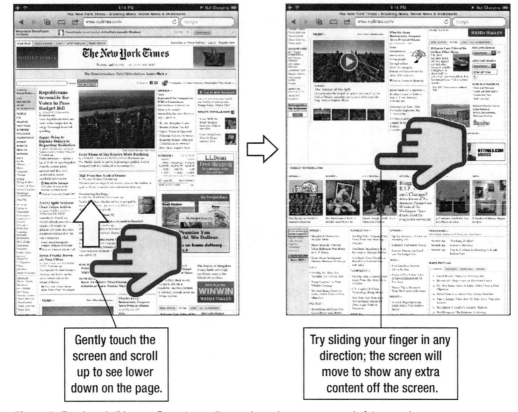

Gently touch the screen and scroll up to see lower down on the page.

Try sliding your finger in any direction; the screen will move to show any extra content off the screen.

Figure 8. *Touch and slide your finger to scroll around a web page, a zoomed picture, and more.*

Double-Tapping to Zoom In or Out

You can double-tap the screen to zoom in and then double-tap again to zoom back out. This works in many places, such as web pages, mail messages, and pictures (see Figure 9).

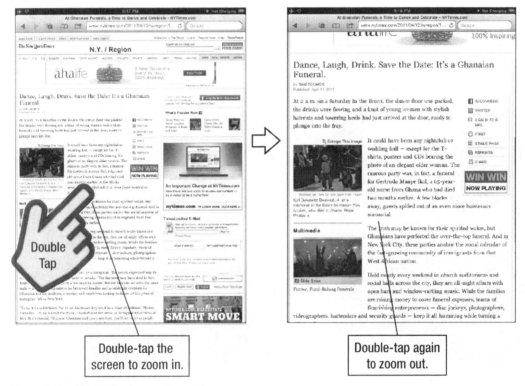

Double-tap the screen to zoom in.

Double-tap again to zoom out.

Figure 9. *Double-tapping to zoom in or out*

Pinching

You can also pinch open or closed to zoom in or out. This works in many places, such as web pages, mail messages, and pictures (see Figure 10). Follow these steps to use the pinching gesture:

1. To zoom in, place two fingers touching on the screen.

2. Gradually slide your fingers open. The screen zooms in.

3. To zoom out, place two fingers with space between them on the screen.

4. Gradually slide your fingers closed so they touch. The screen zooms out.

Pinch your fingers open to zoom in.

Lift your hands from the screen and then pinch open again to zoom in more.

At some point, you cannot zoom in any further.

Figure 10. *Pinch open to zoom in and pinch closed to zoom out.*

The Two-Finger Twist

This trick works in all the **iWork** apps (**Pages**, **Numbers**, and **Keynote**). This also works if you have turned on **Accessibility ➤ Web Rotor** or **Language Rotor**. Touch an image with two fingers at the same time, then rotate your hand on the screen to rotate the image (see Figure 11). It works temporarily in the **Photos** app, but the images rotate back to their previous orientation when you let go.

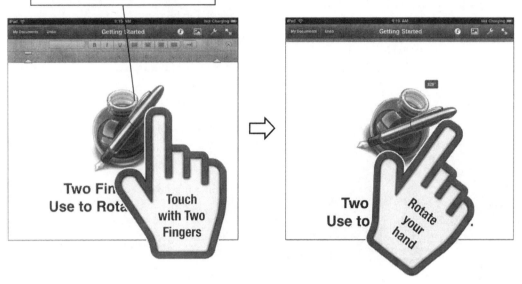

In some apps, like **Pages**, you can rotate images by touching them and rotating your hand.

Figure 11. *Twist with two fingures to rotate an image.*

App Reference Tables

This section gives you a number of tables that group the apps on your iPad, as well as other apps you can download, into handy reference tables. Each table gives you a brief description of the app and tells where to find more information about it in this book.

Getting Started

Table 2 provides some quick links to help you connect your iPad to the Web (using Wi-Fi or 3G), buy and enjoy songs or videos (**iTunes**, **iPod**, and **Videos**), get out of apps, sleep, power off, unlock your iPad, use the Electronic Picture Frame feature, and more.

Table 2. *Getting Started*

To Do This...	Use This...		Where to Learn More
Turn the iPad on or off		**Power/Sleep** button; press and hold this key on the top	Getting Started – Ch. 1
Adjust settings and connect to the Internet (via Wi-Fi or 3G)	Settings	**Settings ➤ Wi-Fi Network/ Cellular Data**	Wi-Fi & 3G – Ch. 5
Return to **Home** screen		**Home** button	Getting Started – Ch. 1
Unlock the iPad	slide to unlock	Slide your finger to unlock your iPad	Getting Started – Ch. 1
Enable the Electronic Picture Frame		Tap the **Flower** icon when locked	Personalize – Ch. 6
Completely power down your iPad	Press and hold the **Power** key	Then slide slide to power off	Getting Started – Ch. 1
Sync music, videos, pictures, addresses, calendar, email, and notes with your computer	**iTunes** (for Windows) and Apple Mac) MobileMe Sync Service Google/Exchange Sync		iTunes Sync – Ch. 3 Other Sync Methods – Ch. 4
Surf the Web	Safari	**Safari**	Safari – Ch. 11

Staying Organized

Table 3 gives you links to everything from organizing and finding your contacts to managing your calendar; from reading and responding to your email to getting driving directions; and more.

Table 3. *Staying Organized*

To Do This...	Use This...		Where to Learn More
Manage your contact names and numbers		**Contacts**	Contacts – Ch. 14
Manage your calendar		**Calendar**	Calendar – Ch. 15
View and send email		**Mail**	Email – Ch. 13
Find just about anything, get directions, avoid traffic, and more		**Maps**	Maps – Ch. 27

Being Entertained

You can have lots of fun with your iPad; Table 4 shows you how. You can buy or rent movies, check out free Internet radio with **Pandora**, and buy a book and enjoy it in a whole new way using **iBooks**. If you already use a Kindle, you can sync all your Kindle books to your iPad and enjoy them right away. Choose from over 350,000 apps from the App Store to make your iPad even more amazing, fun, and useful. Rent a movie from the Netflix or iTunes service and download it immediately for later viewing (say on an airplane or train). If you have a favorite ABC TV show, chances are you can find and watch it using the **ABC** app.

Table 4. *Being Entertained*

To Do This...	Use This...		Where to Learn More
Buy music, videos, podcasts, and more		**iTunes**	iTunes on the iPad – Ch. 20
Browse and download apps right to your iPad		**App Store**	App Store – Ch. 21
See playlists, artists, songs, albums, audiobooks, and more		**iPod**	Music – Ch. 9
Listen to free Internet radio		**Pandora**	Music – Ch. 9
Read a book anytime, anywhere		**iBooks**	iBooks & E-Books – Ch. 12

To Do This...		Use This...	Where to Learn More
Read your Kindle books		**Kindle**	iBooks and E-Books – Ch. 12
Look at, zoom in on, and organize your pictures		**Photos**	Photography – Ch. 16
Watch movies and music videos		**Videos**	Videos & TV – Ch. 10
Rent a movie		**Netflix**	Videos & TV – Ch. 10
Watch a TV show (Most are free and look amazing on the iPad screen.)		**ABC Player**	Videos & TV – Ch. 10
Play a game		**Games Icons**	Games – Ch. 22
Work on a crossword puzzle by tapping your finger		**Times Crosswords**	App Store – Ch. 21
Interact with a comic in a whole new way		**Marvel Comics**	New Media – Ch. 26

Staying Informed

You can also use your iPad to stay informed. For example, you can use it to read your favorite magazine or newspaper with up-to-the-minute and vibrant pictures and videos (see Table 5) or check out the latest weather like never before. You can do much more than simply browse the Web—you can interact with it using **Safari** on your iPad.

Table 5. *Staying Informed*

To Do This...	Use This...		Where to Learn More
Read a magazine		**Time Magazine**	New Media – Ch. 26
Read the newspaper		**New York Times**	New Media – Ch. 26
Check the weather		**The Weather Channel**	App Store – Ch. 21
Browse the Web		**Safari**	Safari – Ch. 11

Networking Socially

Your iPad also lets you connect and stay up to date with friends, colleagues, and professional networks using various social networking tools (see Table 6).

Table 6. *Networking Socially*

To Do This...	Use This...		Where to Learn More
Make calls with **Skype**		**Skype**	Social Networking – Ch. 23
Network on LinkedIn		**LinkedIn**	Social Networking – Ch. 23
Stay connected with friends on Facebook		**Facebook**	Social Networking – Ch. 23
Follow your favorites on Twitter		**TweetDeck**	Social Networking – Ch. 23

Being Productive

You can work with documents, spreadsheets, and presentation files using the **Pages**, **Numbers,** and **Keynote** apps—and the touch screen interface on the iPad. You can grab images to size, rotate, or move around in documents and presentations by just dragging, expanding, or rotating them with your fingers. You can access and read just about any PDF file or other document with the **GoodReader** app. You can also take notes with the basic **Notes** app or step up to the advanced **Evernote** app, which has amazing capabilities for integrating audio, pictures, and text notes, as well as syncing everything to a web site (see Table 7).

Table 7. *Being Productive*

To Do This...	Use This...		Where to Learn More
Write a letter, paper, or book		**Pages**	Productivity and File Transfer – Ch. 19
Calculate using a spreadsheet		**Numbers**	Productivity and File Transfer – Ch. 19
Develop and deliver a presentation		**Keynote**	Productivity and File Transfer – Ch. 19
Access and read almost any document		**GoodReader**	Productivity and File Transfer – Ch. 19
Transfer files (for free)		**Dropbox**	Productivity and File Transfer – Ch. 19

To Do This...	Use This...		Where to Learn More
Take notes, store your grocery list, and more		**Notes**	Notes – Ch. 24
Take and organize your notes in a whole new way		**Evernote**	Notes – Ch. 24

Other Fun Stuff

The iPad can be used as a fantastic electronic picture frame—we show you the basics here. And you'll love your iPad as a video player! In this section, we give you a few quick tips for getting around your video and music player, as well as for getting the most out of videos you see embedded in web pages.

The iPad as an Electronic Picture Frame

You may wonder what that little **Flower** icon next to the **Slide to Unlock** switch does when you lock your iPad. This starts the Electronic Picture Frame feature—a great way to share your pictures with others or simply enjoy your own pictures. To enjoy the Electronic Picture Frame feature, you need to do the following:

1. Load up your iPad with your pictures using **iTunes** (see the "Photos— Automatically Sync" section in Chapter 3: "Sync Your iPad with iTunes").

2. Tap the **Picture Frame** icon to turn on the Electronic Picture Frame feature.

3. Tap the icon again to turn it off.

The Electronic Picture Frame will cycle through all your pictures, or it can be customized to show only selected photo albums.

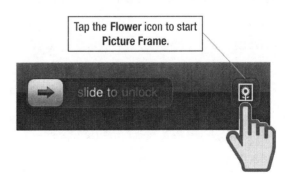

Tap the **Flower** icon to start **Picture Frame**.

> **TIP:** You can customize the way your picture frame operates, select specific albums, and more. See the "Personalize Your Picture Frame" section in Chapter 6: "Personalize & Secure Your iPad."

Navigating Around Your Music and Video Player

When playing a song or video, just tap anywhere in the middle of the screen to show or hide the controls at the top of the screen, as shown in Figure 12.

You will see controls appear at the top and bottom of the **iPod** app.

Tap the screen to show or hide the controls.

Figure 12. *Navigate around your music and video player.*

Watching Videos in Web Pages

A really fun thing to do is watch supported video formats right in their web pages. Unfortunately, the iPad does not support the Adobe Flash video format, which is used by many web sites. But there are many videos you can watch, such as the videos on the front page of the *New York Times* web page, as shown in Figure 13. Follow these steps to watch a video in a web page on this site:

1. Tap the **Safari** icon.

2. Tap the Address bar at the top and type in: www.nytimes.com.

3. Locate and tap any video; usually you'll see a **Play** icon like this in the middle of the picture.

4. The video will start playing right in the web page.

5. To expand the video to full screen, pinch open right inside the video. Put two fingers in the video and expand them while sliding them on the screen.

6. To watch the video in widescreen, tilt your iPad to **Landscape** mode.

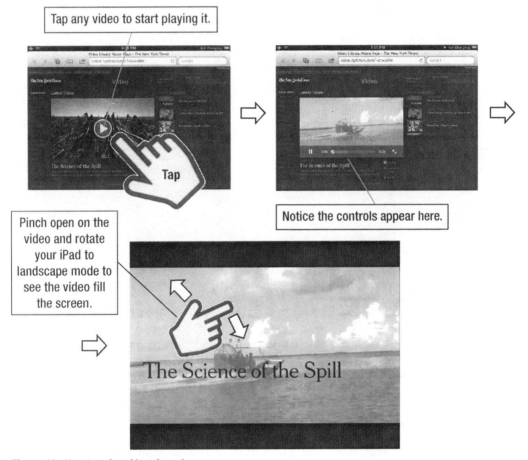

Tap any video to start playing it.

Tap

Notice the controls appear here.

Pinch open on the video and rotate your iPad to landscape mode to see the video fill the screen.

The Science of the Spill

Figure 13. *How to enjoy videos in web pages.*

iPad Accessories

Now let's take a brief tour of some of the accessories you might purchase to enhance the functionality of your iPad. You can buy most of these from any Apple store, Apple.com, or other accessory stores.

> **NOTE:** We show you more accessories, such as cases, in Chapter 1: "Getting Started."

Apple Keyboards

You should invest in one of Apple's two keyboards if you plan on doing a lot of typing on your iPad (see Figure 14). Each one costs about $70.00. We show you more about how to use these keyboards in Chapter 2: "Typing, Copy/Paste, & Search."

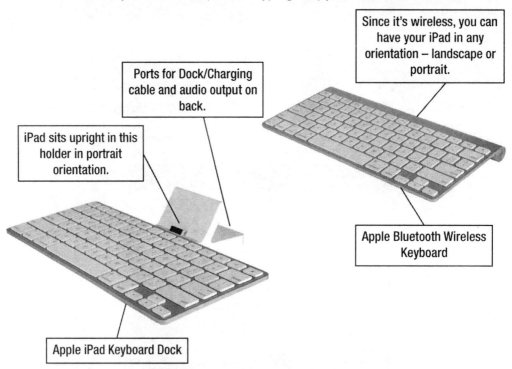

Since it's wireless, you can have your iPad in any orientation – landscape or portrait.

Ports for Dock/Charging cable and audio output on back.

iPad sits upright in this holder in portrait orientation.

Apple Bluetooth Wireless Keyboard

Apple iPad Keyboard Dock

Figure 14. *The Apple iPad Keyboard Dock and the Apple Wireless Bluetooth Keyboard*

The Apple iPad Dock

If you want to set up your iPad in a vertical orientation to use it as an electronic picture frame or have it held for you while you use it, check out the $29.00 iPad Dock. The iPad Dock also has a dock connector port in the back, so you can connect it to your computer or charger while the iPad is in sitting in the dock (see Figure 15).

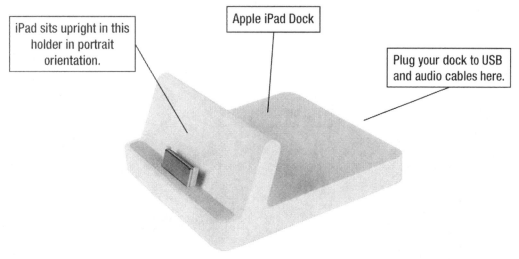

iPad sits upright in this holder in portrait orientation.

Apple iPad Dock

Plug your dock to USB and audio cables here.

Figure 15. *The Apple iPad Dock*

The Apple Camera Connection Kit

If you want to transfer your pictures from your digital camera to your iPad directly, but without first transferring them to your computer, you can do it with the Camera Connection Kit accessory. This $29.00 accessory gives you two small accessories—the one shown on the left of Figure 16 is the USB adapter; the other is the SD Card adapter. Both plug into the dock connector port on the bottom of your iPad.

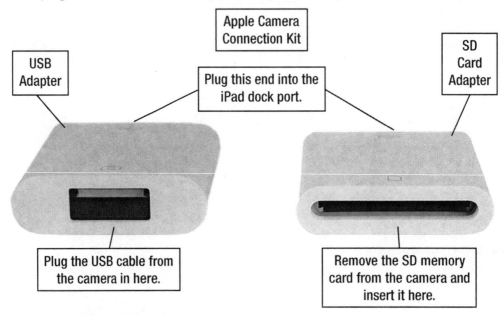

Apple Camera Connection Kit

USB Adapter

Plug this end into the iPad dock port.

SD Card Adapter

Plug the USB cable from the camera in here.

Remove the SD memory card from the camera and insert it here.

Figure 16. *The Apple Camera Connection Kit*

To import photos using these adapters, follow these steps:

1. Plug either the USB or the SD Card accessory into the dock port at the bottom of your iPad.

   a. If you are using the USB connector, plug the USB cable from your camera into the connector.

   b. If you are using the SD card connector, remove the SD memory card from your camera and insert it into the connector.

2. Your iPad should be turned on. If it is, it will immediately bring you to the **Import Photos** screen (see Figure 17).

3. To import all photos, tap the **Import All** button in the upper-right corner.

4. To import selected photos, begin by tapping pictures to select them. Next, tap the **Import** button and choose **Import Selected**.

5. You then have the option to **Keep** or **Delete** the photos on the camera or SD card.

6. The most recent imported photos will show up in the **Last Import** photo album. All imported photos will show up in the **All Imported** photo album.

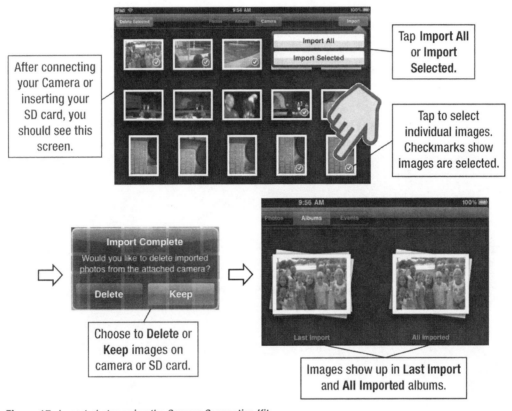

After connecting your Camera or inserting your SD card, you should see this screen.

Tap **Import All** or **Import Selected.**

Tap to select individual images. Checkmarks show images are selected.

Choose to **Delete** or **Keep** images on camera or SD card.

Images show up in **Last Import** and **All Imported** albums.

Figure 17. *Import photos using the Camera Connection Kit.*

VGA Adapter Cable

The VGA Adapter Cable is for you if you are using the **Keynote** app and want to play a presentation on a larger external VGA monitor from your iPad, or you want to play movies you rent or purchase from the iTunes Store.

> **CAUTION:** At the time of publishing, the VGA Adapter Cable accessory worked only in very limited apps and situations. For example, it worked only for the **Keynote** app in **Play** mode, and for certain movies purchased or rented from iTunes. However, it did not display the iPad screen as soon as you plugged it in.

This VGA Adapter Cable costs $29.00. You plug one end into your dock connector on the bottom of your iPad and connect the other end to the VGA cable going to the external monitor, as shown in Figure 18. When you play your presentation in **Keynote**, you can advance slides or jump between slides using your iPad.

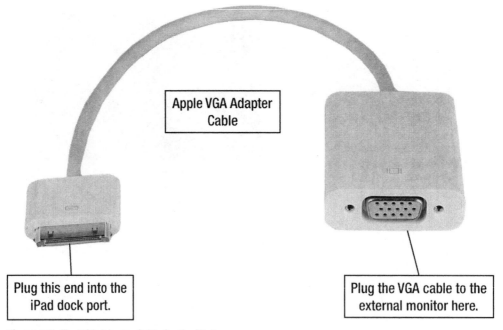

Apple VGA Adapter Cable

Plug this end into the iPad dock port.

Plug the VGA cable to the external monitor here.

Figure 18. *The VGA Adapter Cable for the iPad*

Part **II**

Introduction

Welcome to your new iPad 2—and to the book that tells you what you need to know to get the most out of it. In this part, we show you how the book is organized and where to go to find what you need. We even show you how to get some great tips and tricks sent right to your iPad 2 via short email messages, as well as where to find short, to-the-point video tutorials to learn more about your iPad.

Introduction

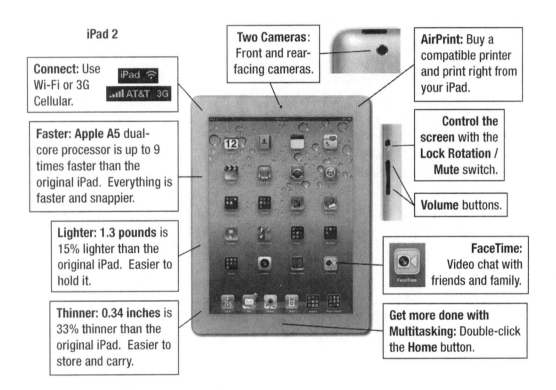

iPad 2

Two Cameras: Front and rear-facing cameras.

Connect: Use Wi-Fi or 3G Cellular.

AirPrint: Buy a compatible printer and print right from your iPad.

Faster: Apple A5 dual-core processor is up to 9 times faster than the original iPad. Everything is faster and snappier.

Control the screen with the **Lock Rotation / Mute** switch.

Volume buttons.

Lighter: 1.3 pounds is 15% lighter than the original iPad. Easier to hold it.

FaceTime: Video chat with friends and family.

Thinner: 0.34 inches is 33% thinner than the original iPad. Easier to store and carry.

Get more done with Multitasking: Double-click the **Home** button.

Congratulations on Your iPad 2!

In your hands is the newly enhanced iPad 2—smaller, thinner, and more powerful than the original iPad. It is arguably the most powerful and elegant media player, E-Book reader, gaming machine, life organizer, and just about everything else available today.

The iPad 2 can do close to 90% of what you already do on your computer—only better. The iPad 2 can also do virtually everything you can do on your smartphone. You can even make video calls from your iPad 2 with Apple's proprietary **FaceTime** app or the

Skype app. Yet the iPad is neither computer nor smartphone—it is nestled somewhere in between, where many of us live.

> **NOTE:** Take a look at Chapter 18: "FaceTime Video Messaging and Skype," where we show you how to use **FaceTime** and **Skype** on your iPad!

With your iPad, you can view your photos and interact with them using the same touch-screen gestures as an iPhone or iPod touch. You can pinch and zoom, rotate, and email your photos—all with simple taps gestures.

You can also interact with your content like never before. Newspapers look and read like newspapers and a web site all in one. You can flip through stories, videos, and pictures; and interact with your news.

And you can really feel like you are reading a book when you read on your iPad. Pages turn slowly or quickly (you can even see the words on the back of the pages as you turn them when you use the **iBooks** app).

You can manage your media library like never before. **iTunes** and the **iPod** app have a beautiful interface on the iPad. Choosing music, watching videos, organizing playlists, and more is effortless and fun on the large, high definition–quality screen.

Do you have a Netflix account? You can watch your favorite TV shows and movies on the beautiful iPad display. You can also manage your content and organize your queue right on the iPad.

You also no longer need to update your Facebook status on the tiny screen of your smartphone—with the iPad, you can see the web site on a large screen and have access to many of the features of your desktop version, yet also be able to interact with Facebook like never before, using the iPad's touch screen.

Finally, you can stay connected to the web and your email with the built-in Wi-Fi connection or the optional 3G connection of the iPad. All the latest high-speed protocols are supported, so you can always be in touch and get the latest content. There is even an almost "full-size" keyboard to type out emails when you use the iPad in **Landscape** mode.

Getting the Most Out of *iPad 2 Made Simple*

This book can be read cover-to-cover, but you can also peruse it in a modular fashion, by chapter or by topic within a chapter. Maybe you just want to check out the **App Store**, try the **iBooks** app, or get set up with your email or contacts. Or maybe you just want to load up your music. You can do all this and more with our book.

You will soon realize that your iPad 2 is a very powerful device. There are, however, many secrets "locked" inside that we help you "unlock" throughout this book.

Take your time—this book can help you on your way to learning how to best use, work, and have fun with your new iPad. Think back to when you tried to use your first Windows or Mac computer. It took a little while to get familiar with how to do things. It's the same with the iPad. Use this book to help you get up to speed and learn all the best tips and tricks more quickly.

Remember that devices this powerful are not always easy to grasp—at first.

You'll get the most out of your iPad if you read the book a section at a time and then try out what you read. We all know that reading and then performing an activity gives us a much higher retention rate than simply reading alone.

So, in order to learn and remember what you learn, we recommend you do the following:

Read a little, try a little on your iPad, and repeat!

How This Book Is Organized

Knowing how this book is organized will help you locate things that are important to you more quickly. Here we show you the main organization of this book. Remember to take advantage of our abridged table of contents, the detailed table of contents, and our comprehensive index to help you quickly pinpoint items of interest.

Day in the Life of an iPad User

Located inside the front and back cover, you'll find this excellent piece of information that is full of easy-to-access, cross-referenced chapter numbers. So if you see something you want to learn, simply thumb to that chapter and learn it—all in just a few minutes.

Part 1: Quick Start Guide

Part 1 of the Quick Start Guide touches on these topics:

Touch Screen Basics: A host of visual images helps you quickly learn to touch, swipe, flick, zoom, and more with your iPad touch screen.

App Reference Tables: Quickly peruse the icons or apps grouped by category. See a thumbnail of what all the apps on your iPad do next to a list of chapters where you can jump right to the details of how to get the most out of each app covered in this book.

Other Fun Stuff: Learn about the iPad as a music player, video player, and electronic picture frame.

iPad Accessories: Get a brief overview of some of the more common accessories, such as keyboards, cameras, and a new Digital AV adapter to connect your iPad to your HDTV. (Check out Chapter 1 for more accessory details.)

Part 2: Introduction

You are here now...

Part 3: You and Your iPad

This is the meat of the book, organized in 28 easy-to-understand chapters packed with loads of pictures to guide you every step of the way.

Part 4: The iPad's Soul Mate   iTunes

As a special bonus for our readers, we have provided an extensive iTunes User Guide in Chapter 29 that shows you how to really get around **iTunes** and explore all the possibilities of the desktop application. The more comfortable you can get with **iTunes**, the more you can arrange and use content from your computer on your iPad—making for a more enjoyable user experience.

Quickly Locating Tips, Cautions, and Notes

If you flip through this book, you can instantly see tips, cautions, and notes based on their formatting. For example, if you wanted to find all the Calendar tips, you would flip to the **Calendar** chapter and quickly find them.

> **TIPS, CAUTIONS,** and **NOTES** are all formatted like this, with a gray background, to help you see them more quickly.

The iPad Email Tips and Video Tutorials

Check out the authors' web site at www.madesimplelearning.com for a series of very useful "bite-sized" chunks of iPad tips and tricks. We have taken a selection of great tips out of this book and even added a few new ones. Click the "Free Tips" section and register for your tips in order to receive a tip right in your iPad inbox about once a week. Learning in small chunks is a great way to master your iPad!

Sometimes watching a video makes it much easier to understand a concept than reading about it. The authors understand this and are busy working on a series of video tutorials to accompany this book. Please visit www.madesimplelearning.com or email info@madesimplelearning.com to learn more about the iPad video tutorials.

You and Your iPad 2...

This is the heart of *iPad 2 Made Simple*. In this section, you'll find clearly labeled chapters—each explaining the key features of your iPad 2. You'll see that most chapters focus on an individual app or a specific type of application. Many of the chapters discuss applications that come with your iPad 2, but we also include some fun and useful apps you can download from the App Store. Sure, the iPad 2 is for fun, but it's for a whole lot more, too. We finish with some handy troubleshooting tips that can help if your iPad 2 isn't working quite right.

Chapter 1

Getting Started

In this chapter, we will take you on a step-by-step tour of your iPad 2, from charging it to activating the **iTunes** app for the first time. In the "iPad Basics" section at the end of this chapter, we will show you the basics of how to maneuver around on your iPad, so you can get up and running quickly.

Getting to Know Your iPad 2

In this section, we show you how to use everything you get in the box with your iPad 2. We also give you some iPad battery and charging tips, help you determine if your iPad has already been activated, and take a look at the **Slide to Unlock** feature.

What's in the Box

The cardboard box that contains your iPad 2 is barely larger than the iPad itself; indeed, it may seem skimpy if you're new to Apple products. However, it does contain everything you need to get started and enjoy your iPad 2—except for a good manual, which is why we wrote this book!

At the very top, as soon as you open the box, you see your new iPad 2.

Under the plastic holder for the iPad, you'll find a paper booklet with the text, "Designed by Apple in California." The box also includes the following:

- **A One Page Reference Guide**: One page?! Yes—it's just one page, front and back! The front shows the buttons, and the back tells you to download **iTunes** and connect your iPad to your computer to get started.

- **The iPad Product Information Guide**: This is a small booklet with a font that's way too small to read. It contains all the legal terms, conditions, warnings, and disclaimers related to your iPad.

- **Apple Logo Stickers**: You get two of those nice white Apple logos you sometimes see on car windows. Enjoy!

At the bottom of the box, you'll find the rest of your gear, as shown in Figure 1–1.

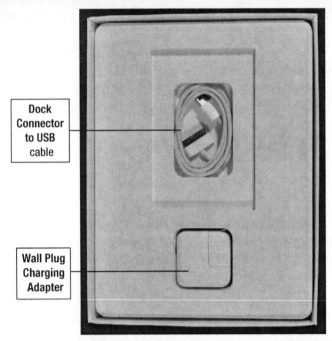

Figure 1–1. *The USB cable and wall plug charging adapter at the bottom of the box*

Dock Connector to USB Cable

Your iPad box ships with a Dock to USB cable. This is the cable you use to connect to your computer; it also doubles as your power cable.

Wall Plug Adapter (10 Watt)

The iPad also comes with a useful piece of hardware called a wall plug adapter (see Figure 1–1). This adapter lets you charge your iPad directly from a wall outlet without having your computer around. All you do is plug the Dock to USB cable into this wall adapter and the other end into your iPad.

> **TIP:** Buy an extra adapter, then keep one at home and one at the office. Current pricing for this plug adapter is less than US $10 at discount online stores.

Expected Battery Life and Charging Times

Apple says battery life for the new, faster iPad 2 with its advanced 25-watt rechargeable lithium-polymer battery should be the same as for the original iPad (see Table 1–1).

Table 1–1. *Battery Life Specifications from Apple*

Video and Audio Playback	10 hours
Surfing the Web	10 hours on Wi-Fi, 9 hours on 3G cellular
Charging Time	2 hour to get 80% in a fast charge, 4 hours to get fully charged

These battery life durations are in ideal conditions with a new, fully charged battery. You will notice that, over time, your actual battery life will diminish.

> **TIP:** If you find that your iPad battery is no longer holding a good charge or getting anywhere near the 10 hour expected life, you can have your battery replaced by Apple. Visit Apple's website at www.apple.com/batteries/replacements.html to learn how to get a new battery for your iPad. Cost at publishing time was $99 plus shipping.

Battery and Charging Tips

There's nothing worse than running out of juice just when you need it. The key question is this: how can you maximize your battery life and make sure your iPad is ready when you are? Here are a few tips that can help.

Getting More from Each Charge

To extend your battery life, try these tips:

- **Put the iPad into Sleep mode.** Tap the **Power/Sleep** button on the upper-right edge of the device to put it into **Sleep** mode.

- **Turn off Wi-Fi or 3G when not needed.** The Wi-Fi and 3G antennas use power even if you're not connected to a Wi-Fi or 3G network, so turn them off when you don't need them. Tap **Settings**, then set **Airplane Mode** to **ON.**

- **Lower your screen brightness**: Tap **Settings** and then **Brightness & Wallpaper**. Use the **Slider** bar to lower your brightness to a level less than halfway across that still works for you. Also, make sure **Auto-Brightness** is set to **ON.**

■ **Turn off Location Services**: If you don't need your actual location to be transmitted to your apps, you can turn this off. Tap **Settings**, then **Location Services**. Set **Location Services** to **OFF**. If you start an app that wants your location, you'll be reminded to turn it back on.

■ **Set a Shorter Auto-Lock**: Shortening the time your iPad takes to turn off the screen when not being used and go into **Sleep** mode can help save your battery. To do this, tap **Settings**, **General**, and **Auto-Lock**. Set **Auto-Lock** as short as possible—you can set this as short as **2 minutes** if you like.

■ **Turn off push email and push notifications:** Tap **Settings**, and then **Mail, Contacts, Calendars**. Next, tap **Fetch New Data** and set **Push** to **OFF.**

■ **Learn more about battery life** and get more cool iPad-related tips from the Apple website at www.apple.com/batteries/ipad.html.

Making the Battery Last Longer

A rechargeable battery loses its ability to maintain a charge over time, and it has only a limited number of cycles during its useful life. You can extend the life of your iPad battery by making sure you run it down completely at least once a month. The rechargeable battery will last longer if you perform this complete draining on a regular basis.

iPad Charging Accessories

No matter what you do, if you use your iPad a lot, you'll want to find more places and more ways to charge it. Table 1–2 lists some other options for charging your iPad besides using your power cord or connecting it to your computer.

Table 1–2. *Other Places and Ways to Charge Your iPad*

Airport Charging Station	Today most airports have wall sockets available where you can top off your iPad while waiting for your flight. Some airports have designated *charging stations*, while others just have wall sockets that may even be hidden behind chairs or other objects. You may have to do a bit of hunting to beat out all those other power-hungry travelers!
External Battery Pack	This accessory allows you to extend the life of your iPad battery by two to three times. You can buy such packs for about US $70–150. Search for "external iPad battery pack" on the Web to find the latest and greatest options.

Car Charger	If you are using your iPad heavily for phone calls during the day, you may want to invest in a car charger or another way to give it a little more juice in the middle of a long day. Some of these chargers give you powered USB outlets from your car cigarette lighter socket, while others give you a dock port connector to plug into the bottom of your iPad. Most run about US $15–30.
Car Power Inverter	If you are taking a long car trip, you can buy a power inverter to convert your 12V car power outlets into a power outlet where you can plug in your iPad charger. Do a Web search for "power inverter for cars" to find many options for US $50-100.
Other Accessories	As mentioned previously, you can also charge your iPad in many accessories designed to do other things, like play your music over speakers. Just look for the plug or lightning bolt icons to make sure your iPad is charging in such accessories.

Charging and Battery Tips

Your iPad may already have some battery life, but you might want to charge it completely, so you can enjoy uninterrupted hours of use after you get it set up. This charging time will give you a chance to check out the rest of this chapter, install or update iTunes, or browse all the cool iPad apps in the iTunes App Store (see Chapter 21: "The Amazing App Store").

The Dock to USB cable also doubles as your charger cable. It is located under the little white booklet beneath your iPad in the box that says, "Designed by Apple in California." Plug the wide end of the cable into the bottom of your iPad (next to the **Home** button), then plug the USB cable end into the small white box that has the fold-out plug for the electrical socket.

To make sure your device is plugged in correctly and getting charged, look for the small **Plug** icon inside the battery indicator in the upper-right corner of the iPad screen. If the screen is blank, tap the **Home** button once to light up the screen. You see the 100% next to the battery icon in this image to the right because we went into **Settings** ➤ **General** and set **Battery Percentage** to **ON**.

Will my iPad charge when connected to my computer?

The answer is: "It depends."

Your iPad *is* charging if you see the **Plug** icon inside the **Battery** icon when you connect your iPad to your computer with the USB cable. Most Mac computers, some Windows computers, and some powered USB hubs (an accessory that you can purchase that is plugged into the wall and has USB ports) provide enough power to charge your iPad while it is "awake" (the screen is on).

This is harder to determine when the iPad is in **Sleep** mode (screen off), and you see a "Not Charging" message next to the **Battery** icon on your iPad after you connect it to your computer. In this case, your iPad will probably be charging when it is in **Sleep** mode. You will have to experiment with your computer and iPad to make an accurate determination for a given condition. We discovered that, with a Windows laptop, the iPad definitely charged fine in **Sleep** mode, even though it said "Not Charging" when it was awake.

Your iPad Activation May Already Have Been Completed

For example, you may see a **Slide to Unlock** screen or a screen of icons on your **Home** screen when you turn on your iPad or tap the **Home** button (at the bottom of the device). If so, your iPad has already been activated. If you see a black screen showing a USB cable that needs to be plugged into iTunes (see Figure 1–3), then you still need to activate the device.

Slide to Unlock

When you first power on your iPad, you will see the **Slide to Unlock** screen. Just follow the path of the **Arrow** icon and gently slide the **Unlock** button to the right.

Once you do that, you will see your **Home** screen.

You will see four icons locked in the Bottom Dock (see Figure 1–2, bottom-right), while the rest of the icons can move back and forth in *pages* above this Bottom Dock. Learn how to move your favorite icons into the Bottom Dock in the "Moving Icons" section in Chapter 7: "Personalize and Secure Your iPad."

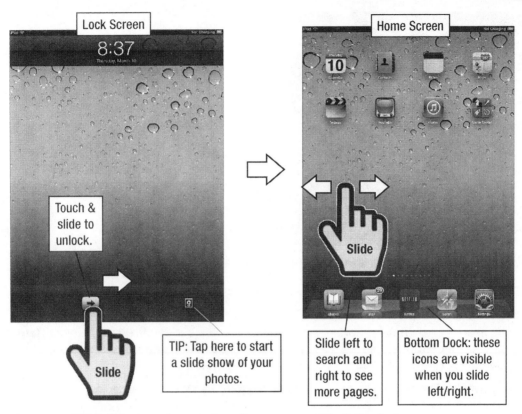

Figure 1–2. *Slide to Unlock, moving around your Home screen, and the Bottom Dock*

iTunes and Your iPad

To activate your iPad and load up your content (e.g., music, pictures, videos, and more), you will need to connect the device to the **iTunes** app on your computer. The **iTunes** app is also required to back up (and later restore) your iPad.

If you don't have the **iTunes** app, or you are not sure if you have the latest version, then you will have to upgrade. Connecting your iPad to the iTunes service for the first time will activate or tie your iPad to your Apple ID. Once you do that, you can buy songs, movies, books, and just about anything else right from your iPad or in iTunes on your computer.

Install or Update iTunes on Your Computer

If you see a screen on your iPad showing a USB plug pointing to iTunes, then you need to connect your iPad to the **iTunes** app on your computer (see Figure 1–3).

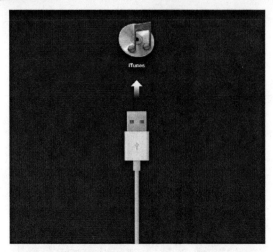

Figure 1–3. *An iPad screen showing the need to connect to iTunes to get started*

Generally, you will need to make sure you have the latest version of the **iTunes** program installed.

If you need to update the program, start **iTunes**. If you are a Windows user, select **Help** and then **Check for Updates**. If you are a Mac user, select **iTunes** and then **Check for Updates**. Follow the instructions provided to update **iTunes**.

Need detailed instructions? See our "iTunes Update" section in Chapter 29: "Your iTunes User Guide."

If you do not have the **iTunes** program loaded on your computer, then open a web browser and go to www.itunes.com/download. Download the software from the link provided.

Need detailed instructions? Again, see our "How to Download and Install iTunes" section in Chapter 29: "Your iTunes User Guide."

Connecting Your iPad to iTunes

Once you have installed or upgraded to the latest version of the **iTunes** program, you are ready to connect your iPad to the iTunes service on your computer.

> **TIP:** Using the **iTunes** app's Home Sharing feature, you can share your purchased content from the same iTunes account (music, apps, videos, iBooks, and more) on your iPad and across authorized computers on your home network. Also, you can sync any of the same content to any iPod/iPhone/iPad under the same iTunes account. Learn more about syncing content using iTunes in Chapter 3: "Sync Your iPad with iTunes" and learn about Home Sharing in Chapter 29: "Your iTunes User Guide."

By connecting your iPad to iTunes, you will register or associate your iPad (via the device serial number) to a particular iTunes Account (Apple ID).

> **TIP:** The bonus of this approach is that, if you have purchased apps and other content (e.g., music, videos, and more) for an iPhone or iPod touch, then you can run most of those apps on your iPad—although with a little smaller screen size. Note that you can authorize an iPad on more than one iTunes account; however, all content you sync to that iPad has to originate from a single computer. Therefore, you need to select your "main" computer to sync with your iPad.

If you do not yet have an iTunes account (Apple ID), don't worry—you can create one as you register your iPad.

Start iTunes

If the **iTunes** app isn't already running, double-click the **iTunes** icon on your desktop:

- Mac users: Click the **Finder** icon, select the **Go** menu, and then select **Applications** to look for **iTunes** (shortcut: **Shift+Command+A** for **Applications**).

- Windows users: Click the **Start** menu or **Windows** logo in the lower-left corner, select **All Programs**, and then choose **iTunes**.

Registering Your iPad the First Time

Once you have the **iTunes** app installed or updated and running on your computer, you are ready to connect your iPad for the first time and get it registered or activated. Once you do these things, you can start using your new iPad.

> **NOTE:** You can skip this registration section and jump to the "Set Up Your iPad" section later in this chapter if your iPad has already been registered. You know if your iPad is already registered if you see either **Slide to Unlock** at the bottom of the screen or a screen of icons when you tap the **Home** button on the bottom of your device.

Follow these steps to connect to your iPad and register or activate it:

1. Plug in the white USB connection cable that was supplied with your iPad to an available USB port on your computer.

> **NOTE:** When you connect your iPad to your computer the first time, your Windows computer should automatically install the necessary drivers. If you are on a Mac computer, depending on which version of operating system you have installed, Apple may recommend that you upgrade to the latest version of the operating system before using your iPad.

2. Click your **iPad** under **DEVICES** in the left column of iTunes in order to get started.

3. If you have not already registered your iPad, you should see a **Welcome** screen (see Figure 1–4). Click **Continue** to start registering your iPad.

Figure 1–4. *The iPad **Welcome** screen in **iTunes***

4. You will now see the **iPad Software License Agreement**.

5. Assuming you agree with the legal terms, check the box that says **I have read and agree to the iPad Software License Agreement** and click the **Continue** button.

6. Next, you will be given the opportunity to sign in using your Apple ID or to create a new Apple ID. Enter your Apple ID and password or click **I do not have an Apple ID** and select your country (see Figure 1–5).

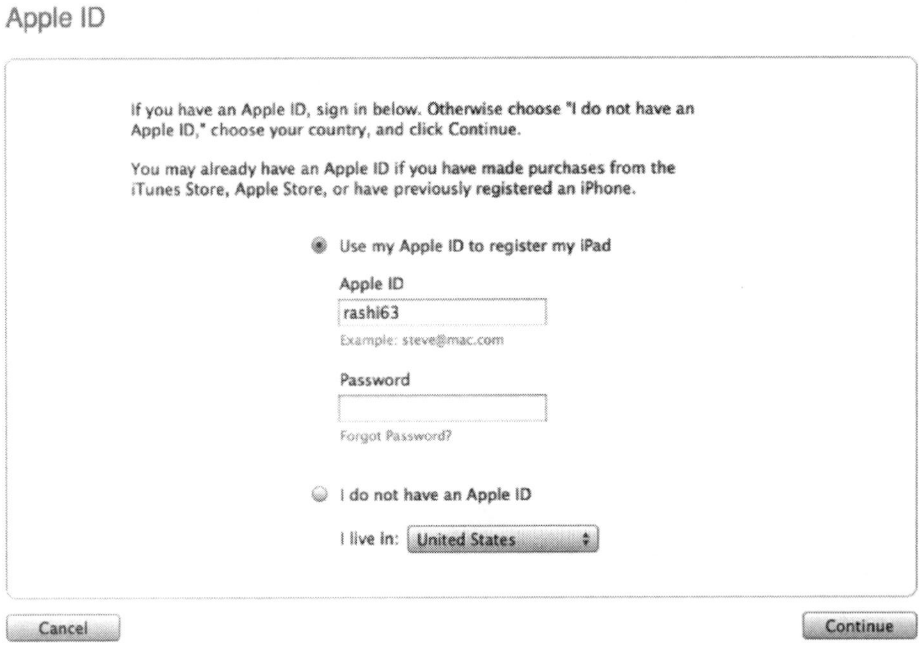

Apple ID

If you have an Apple ID, sign in below. Otherwise choose "I do not have an Apple ID," choose your country, and click Continue.

You may already have an Apple ID if you have made purchases from the iTunes Store, Apple Store, or have previously registered an iPhone.

⦿ Use my Apple ID to register my iPad

Apple ID

rashi63

Example: steve@mac.com

Password

Forgot Password?

◯ I do not have an Apple ID

I live in: [United States   ◆]

[Cancel]   [Continue]

Figure 1–5. *The **Apple ID** screen in **iTunes***

7. Click the **Continue** button.

▪ If you tried to enter your Apple ID and password and received an error message that "additional security information is required," read the "Troubleshooting: Fixing the Apple ID Security Error" section in Chapter 29: "Your iTunes User Guide."

8. You should now see the **Register your iPad** screen (see Figure 1–6).

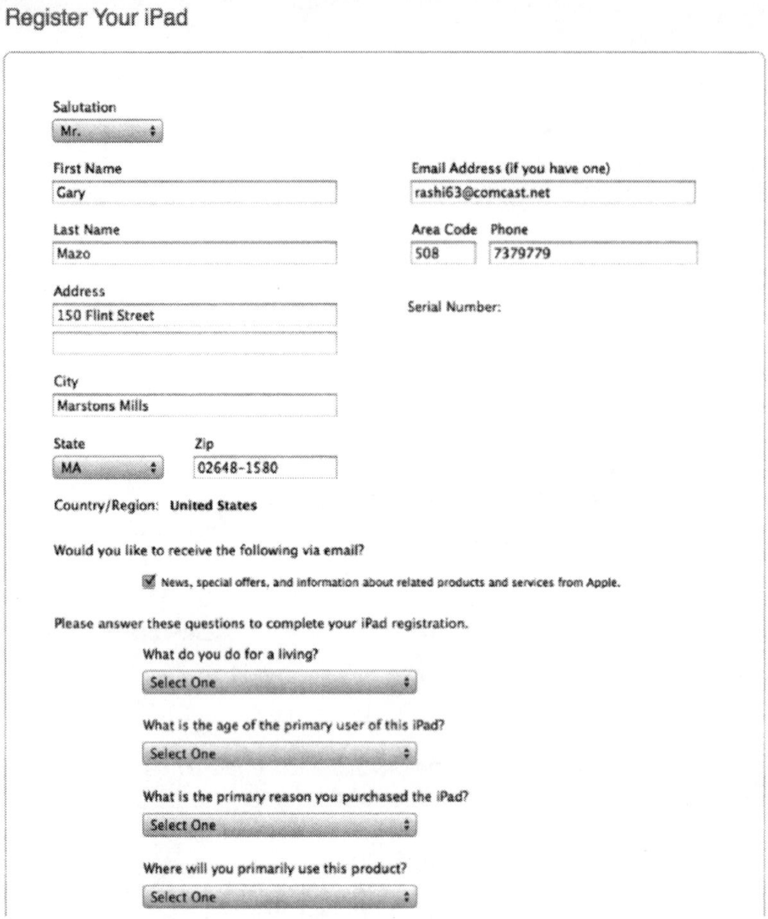

Register Your iPad

Figure 1–6. *The Register Your iPad screen in iTunes*

9. Type or verify that your information is correct and click **Submit** to complete your registration.

Setting up the Find My iPad Service

After you register your iPad, you may see a screen similar asking if you would like to set up the free Find My iPad service (see Figure 1–7). Click the **Set up Find My iPad** button and follow the on-screen instructions to get started. This service enables you to locate your iPad (whenever it is powered on and connected to the network) using the MobileMe Apple website (http://me.com).

> **TIP:** Please check out the MobileMe service detailed description in Chapter 4: "Other Sync Methods" to learn all about the various features of the service.

Figure 1–7. *Set up the Free Find My iPad service*

If you do not see this screen, follow these steps to get set up on your iPad:

> **TIP:** You can also watch a video and learn more on Apple's site here:
> www.apple.com/ipad/find-my-ipad-setup/.

1. Your iPad may be busy syncing with **iTunes** at this point. You'll have to wait until the sync is completed, and you see either the **Home** or **Slide to Unlock** screen; at that point, you can get started.

2. Tap the **Setup** app.

3. Tap **Mail, Contacts, Calendars**.

4. Tap **Add Account** and select **Mobile Me**.

5. Enter your **Apple ID** and **Password** and tap **Next** to login. You can click a link to create a free Apple ID if you don't have one. You may need to agree to the **Terms of Service** if this is the first time you are using your **Apple ID** with the Mobile Me service.

6. You should then receive an email message at your main email account connected to your Apple ID. You need to click the link in the email message you receive to **Verify** your account.

7. After a successful login, you should see a little pop-up window asking **Allow MobileMe to Use the Location of your iPad?** As you probably guessed, you definitely need to answer **OK** to have this service work correctly.

8. Make sure to set the **Find My iPad** to **ON**, as shown here. Then tap **Save** to complete the setup process.

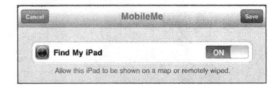

Disable or Adjust Find My iPad

You can also disable the service or change the MobileMe account used by returning to MobileMe's **Accounts** screen, as follows:

1. Tap the **Setup** app.

2. Tap **Mail, Contacts, Calendars**.

3. Tap the **Mobile Me** account under the **Accounts** screen in the right column.

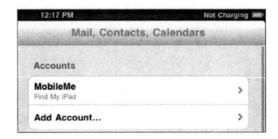

4. From this screen, you may:

   ■ Tap **Account** to adjust the account used.

   ■ Set **Find My iPad** to **ON** or **OFF**.

   ■ **Delete** your MobileMe account from this iPad.

5. Tap **Done** to save your changes.

Using Find My iPad from the Me.com Website

You can use the Find My iPad service from almost any web browser, whether it is on your computer or another mobile device. Follow these steps to use the service:

1. Open up a web browser and go to www.me.com.

2. Log in with your same Apple ID and password.

3. You should now see the **Find My iPad** (or iPhone) screen, which immediately shows the last known location of your device. Notice that, if you have multiple devices, you can select a different device in the left column to locate it.

> **NOTE:** A **Clock** icon next to the name of the device on the map
> Martin's iPad ⊙ indicates that it has been a little while since the last update. If your device has been powered off, then the last known location will be the location mapped when it was turned off.

4. Click the name of the device to see more options. You can do the following:

■ Click **Lock** to remotely lock your iPad. This protects your private information by adding a four-digit passcode.

- Click **Wipe** to remotely erase all your private information. Remember that you will have everything saved on your computer from the point of your last backup on iTunes, which is usually the last time you connected your iPad to iTunes on your computer. Check the box at the bottom and click **Erase All Data** to complete the process.

- Click **Display Message** or **Play Sound** to send a message to be displayed on your iPad or to play a sound for 2 minutes to help you locate your device. The sound is like the sonar sound on a ship, so it's pretty distinctive!

If you check this box, the message to the right will be displayed on your iPad and a sound will be played within a few seconds—a pretty nice feature!

Using Find My iPad from Another iOS Mobile Device

You can also access the Find My iPad service using a free app (called **Find My iPhone**) you download from the App Store. Follow these steps to use the app:

> **NOTE:** At the time of publishing, the app was called **Find My iPhone**, its original name. So, if that is the only app you find in the App Store, go ahead and download it for your iPad.

Find iPhone

1. Tap the **Find iPhone** app and log in using your **Apple ID** and **Password**.

2. Immediately you should be taken to the **Map** view showing your iPad.

3. Just as with the web-based version described previously, you can tap the name of the device to **Display a message/play a sound** on, remotely **Wipe** (erase), or remotely **Lock** (with a four-digit passcode) the device.

> **NOTE:** None of these options (i.e., **Display**, **Wipe**, or **Lock**) will work if you are using your iPad to view itself.

4. As on the me.com website, if you have more than one Apple device running iOS 4.2 or higher (e.g. iPhone or iPod touch), you can view these devices right from the app on your iPad. Simply tap the **Devices** button in the upper-right corner to see all your devices.

Apple's MobileMe Sync Service

After registering your iPad for the first time, you may see a screen advertising the MobileMe wireless sync service from Apple. To keep setting up your iPad, click the **No Thanks** button to continue to the next screen.

What is MobileMe?

As you saw in the earlier "Find My iPad" section, MobileMe provides the iPad location service for free. However, MobileMe does much more than that; it also provides a way to keep your email, contacts, calendar, and web bookmarks shared across all your computers and mobile devices. At publishing time, photo-sharing is limited to Mac computers with MobileMe **iPhoto** folders. MobileMe is free for a limited time (currently 60 days), and then it costs US $99.00 for a single user or US $149.00 for a family plan. See our "MobileMe Tour" section in Chapter 4: "Other Sync Methods."

Set Up Your iPad

The first time you connect your iPad, you have the chance to give it a name and select some other options (see Figure 1–8).

If you instead see a screen that asks about **Restoring from a backup**, then skip to the "Set up or Restore from Backup" section later in this chapter.

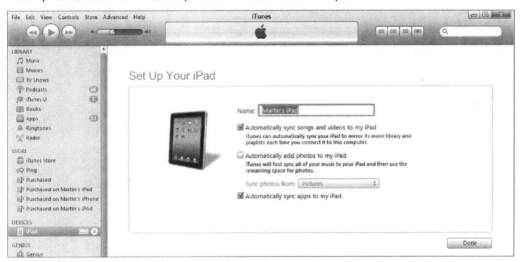

Figure 1–8. *Set up your iPad screen*

NOTE: If you are going to actively use two iPads, then we recommend you set up your second iPad as a new device and do not restore from a backup file. Otherwise, you might end up with two iPads with the same device name and cause confusion.

1. Give your iPad a **Name**. Each time you plug in your iPad—to this or any other computer—your iPad will show the name you choose here. In this case, we will call this one: **Martin's iPad**.

TIP: Setting up an iPad Quickly

To get moving quickly, uncheck all three boxes on the screen shown in Figure 1–9 and click **Done**. You can check or uncheck these boxes within the tabs you find in the **iTunes** app later. We show you the details in Chapter 3: "Sync Your iPad with iTunes" and in Chapter 29: "Your iTunes User Guide."

2. Check the box next to **Automatically sync songs and videos to my iPad** if you want all of your music and videos stored in your computer's iTunes library on your new iPad.

CAUTION: Your iPad does not have as much memory as your computer, so be careful when selecting automatically sync if you have thousands of songs, photos, or many videos in your computer's iTunes library.

3. Check the box next to **Automatically add photos to my iPad** if you want all your photos in specific folders on your computer synced to your new iPad.

4. Check the box next to **Automatically sync applications to my iPad** if you would like applications you purchase on your iPad backed up to your computer. This option allows you to update apps from the **iTunes** app on your computer; it also enables you to manage and arrange your app icons and **Home** screens using the **iTunes** app on your computer. We recommend you check this box.

5. Click **Done** to complete the **Set Up** screen.

Set up or Restore from Backup

If you have already synced a similar device such as an iPhone or iPod touch to your iTunes, then you will probably see the **Set Up Your iPad** screen with options to **Set Up as a new iPad** or restore from a backup (see Figure 1–9).

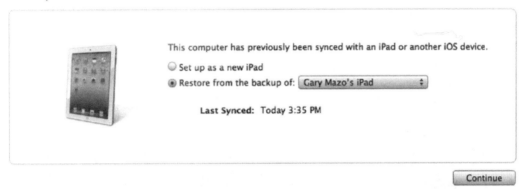

Set Up Your iPad

This computer has previously been synced with an iPad or another iOS device.

○ Set up as a new iPad
⦿ Restore from the backup of: [Gary Mazo's iPad   ⬍]

Last Synced: Today 3:35 PM

[Continue]

Figure 1–9. *Setting up or restoring an iPad*

1. Now you have several choices depending on your particular situation:

   a. If you are using an iPad for the first time, then select **Set up as a new iPad**. ⦿ Set up as a new iPad

   b. If you have previously synced your computer with another iPad and you want to restore from that backup file, select **Restore from the backup of** and then select the correct iPad backup file from dropdown list.

   c. If you have backed up another iOS device besides an iPad (e.g., an iPhone or iPod touch), we recommend you select **Set up as a new iPad**. ⦿ Set up as a new iPad You can later sync your apps, pictures, songs, and more to your iPad from iTunes; this approach is safer than using the backup file from a non-iPad device.

   > **CAUTION:** We have heard of people experiencing problems (lock-ups, lower battery life, and so forth) when they restore a backup from a non-iPad (iPhone/iPod touch) to the iPad. Also, selecting restore here assumes you have first made a backup of your old device (iPhone/iPod touch) in order to restore the latest information to your new iPad.

2. Click the **Continue** button.

> **NOTE:** If you want to keep your existing iPhone and/or iPod Touch and set up your new iPad, then you should select **Set up a New iPad**.

Setup Complete: The iPad Summary Screen

Once you confirm your choices and click **Done** (see Figure 1–8) or click **Continue** from the **Set up/Restore** screen (see Figure 1–9), you will be taken to the main **Summary** screen (Figure 1–10).

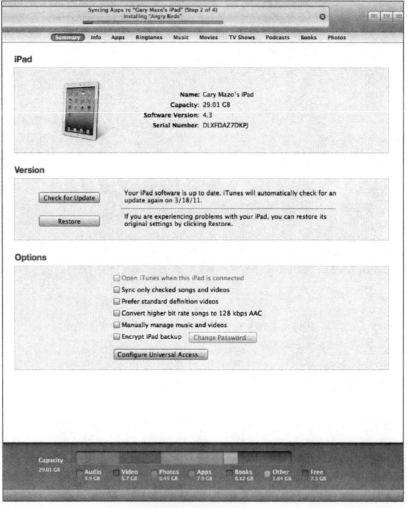

Figure 1–10. *The iPad Summary screen in iTunes*

Maintaining Your iPad

Now that you have set up your iPad, you will want to know how to safely clean the screen and then keep it protected with various cases.

Cleaning Your iPad Screen

After using your iPad a little while, you will see that your fingers (and possibly other fingers besides yours) have left smudges and oil on the formerly pristine screen. You will want to know how to safely clean the screen. One way to keep the screen cleaner throughout the day is to place a protective screen cover on the iPad, which may also have the added benefit of cutting down on glare (discussed in the next section).

We also recommend doing the following:

1. Turn off your iPad by pressing and holding the **Sleep/Power** key on the top edge, then use the **Slider** bar to turn it off.

2. Remove any cables, such as the USB Sync cable.

3. Rub the screen with a soft, dry, lint-free cloth (such as a cloth supplied to clean eyeglasses or something similar).

4. If the dry cloth does not work, then try adding a tiny bit of water to dampen the cloth. If you use a damp cloth, try not to get any water in the openings.

> **CAUTION:** Never use household cleaners, abrasive cleaners such as SoftScrub, ammonia-based cleaners such as Windex, alcohol, aerosol sprays, or solvents.

Cases and Protective Covers for Your iPad

Once you have your iPad in your hands, you will notice how beautifully it is constructed. You will also notice that it can be fairly slippery and could slip out of your hands or rock around a bit. It's also possible for the back of the iPad to get scratched when you are typing on it.

We recommend buying a protective case for your iPad. Average cases run about US $10-40 and fancy leather cases can run US $100 or more. Spending a little to protect your iPad that costs $500 or more makes good sense.

Where to Buy Your Covers

You can purchase your iPad protective cover at any of the following locations:

- Amazon.com (www.amazon.com)
- The Apple Accessory Store (http://store.apple.com)
- iLounge (http://ilounge.pricegrabber.com)
- TiPB – The iPhone + iPad Blog Store (http://store.tipb.com/)

You could also do a web search for "iPad cases" or "iPad protective covers."

> **TIP**: You *may* be able to use a case designed for another type of computer for your iPad; for example, a case for a netbook or small tablet computer might work well. If you go this route to try and save some money, however, just make sure your iPad fits securely in the case or cover.

What Cases to Buy

The following sections list some types of cases from which to choose and their price ranges.

Apple iPad Smart Cover (about $40 for plastic, $70 for leather)

Smart Cover image courtesy of Apple.com

What these do: Magnets on the case instantly draw the cover to the iPad for a solid fit. You can fold the cover back to create a nice, low stand.

Pros: Many colors, lightweight, and designed by Apple specifically for the iPad 2 — need we say more?

Cons: Will not protect the iPad as well from dings or dents (no protection on back of device).

Metal Case with Keyboard Built-in (about $100)

What these do: Provide a solid case and a built-in Bluetooth keyboard. If you are typing a lot on your iPad, this is a nice compact option.

Pros: Inexpensive compared to a separate case and keyboard. Easy to type with.

Cons: Add bulk and weight to the device.

ZAGGmate image courtesy Zagg.com

Rubber/Silicone Cases ($10-$30)

What these do: Provide a cushioned grip and should absorb iPad bumps and bruises.

Pros: Inexpensive, colorful, and comfortable to hold.

Cons: Not as professional in appearance as a leather case.

Waterproof Cases ($10-$40)

What these do: Provide waterproof protection for your iPad and allow you to safely use the iPad near water (in the rain, at the pool, at the beach, on a boat, and so forth).

Pros: Provide good water protection.

Cons: May make the touch screen harder to use; do not usually protect from drops or bumps.

Hard Plastic/Metal Case ($20-$100)

What these do: Provide hard, solid protection against scratches, bumps, and short drops.

Pros: Provide good protection.

Cons: Add some bulk and weight.

Leather Book or Flip Cases ($40-$100+)

What these do: Provide more of a luxury feel and protect the front and sides, as well as the back.

Pros: Provide leather luxury feel and protect the front and the back.

Cons: More expensive and add bulk and weight.

Screen and Back Cover Protectors ($5-$40)

What these do: Protect the screen and back of the iPad from scratches.

Pros: Help prolong life of your iPad and protect against scratches. Also, most such cases decrease screen glare.

Cons: Some may increase glare or affect touch sensitivity of the screen.

iPad Basics

Now that you have your iPad charged with a clean screen, registered, and decked out with a new protective case, let's take a look at some of the basics to help you get up and running.

Powering On/Off and Sleep/Wake

To power on your iPad, press and hold the **Power/Sleep** button on the top edge of the iPad for a few seconds (see Figure 1–11). Simply tapping this button quickly won't power on the iPad if it is completely off—you really need to hold it until you see the iPad power on.

When you are no longer using your iPad, you have two options: you can either put it into **Sleep** mode or turn it off completely.

Power/Sleep
button

Sleep/Wake: Tap quickly to sleep
or wake up the iPad.

Power On: Press & hold 4
seconds.

Power Off: Press & hold 4
seconds then **Slide
to power off**

Home button

Tap the **Home** button
once to wake the iPad.

TIP: Once awake,
double-tap the **Home**
button to multitask.

Figure 1–11. *The Power/Sleep and Home buttons*

The advantage of **Sleep** mode is that, when you want to use your iPad again, a quick tap of the **Power/Sleep** button or the **Home** button will bring your iPad back awake. According to Apple, the iPad has up to a month of stand-by power.

If you want to maximize your battery or if you know you won't be using your iPad for quite some time—say, when you go to sleep—you might want to turn it off completely. The way to do this is to press and hold the **Power/Sleep** button until you see the **Slide to Power Off** bar appear. Just slide the bar to the right and the iPad will power off.

The Home Button

The key you will use most often is your **Home** button (see Figure 1–11). This button will begin everything you do with your iPad. Press it once to wake up your iPad (assuming it is in **Sleep** mode.)

Pressing the **Home** button will take you out of any application program and bring you back to your **Home** screen.

> **TIP:** Double-tapping your **Home** button can be set to do different things, such as starting the iPad function, search, and more (see how to configure this button in the section that follows).

Multitask by Double-Clicking the Home Button

One of the nice features of the iPad (new in iOS 4.2and higher) is multitasking. This feature enables you to have more than one app open at a time. To multitask, simply double-click the **Home** button, then slide your finger back and forth to select an app to jump to.

> **TIP:** You'll find more details on multitasking in Chapter 8: "Multitasking and Voice Control."

Volume Keys

Located on the upper-right side of the iPad are simple **Volume Up/Volume Down** keys that you will find very handy (see Figure 1–12). In many places, you can also control the volume of the song, video, **FaceTime** call, or podcast playing by sliding your finger on the screen volume control.

FaceTime Ringer Volume

If you're not playing a song, video, or other content, pressing these **Volume** keys will adjust the volume of your **FaceTime** app's ringer.

> **Tip:** Hold down the **Volume Down** key for about two seconds to quickly mute the sound on the iPad.

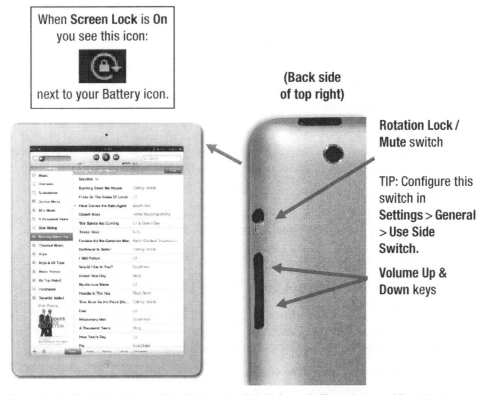

When **Screen Lock** is **On** you see this icon:

next to your Battery icon.

(Back side of top right)

Rotation Lock / Mute switch

TIP: Configure this switch in **Settings > General > Use Side Switch.**

Volume Up & Down keys

Figure 1–12. *The Mute / Screen Rotation Lock switch, Volume Up/Down keys, and Home button*

TIP: You can also adjust the volume of music playback using the **Slider** control in the upper-left corner of your **iPod** app.

Rotation Lock / Mute Switch

Just above the **Volume** keys, you will find the **Mute / Screen Rotation Lock** switch (see Figure 1–12).

This particular switch has had a varied life on the iPad. If you owned an original iPad, then you know that this switch started out as a **Screen Rotation Lock** switch. Then Apple changed it to be simply a **Mute** switch in IOS 4.2. With iOS 4.3 and later devices, you can now configure the function of this switch.

To change the function of this switch, follow these steps:

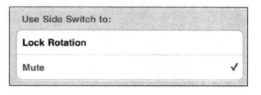

5. Tap **Settings**, then tap **General**.

6. In the **Use Side Switch to:** section, select **Lock Rotation** or **Mute**

Use this when you want to mute the iPad or force it to stop rotating the screen. The **Rotation Lock** is useful when you have your iPad sitting flat on your desk or in your lap, and you want to force it to stay in either **Portrait** or **Landscape** orientation.

> **TIP:** This is a great way to read iBooks in bed. Turn your iPad to **Landscape** mode, lock the screen rotation, and read your book. Check out Chapter 12: "iBooks and e-Books" for more.

Adjust or Disable the Auto-Lock Time Out Feature

You will notice that your iPad will Auto-Lock and go into **Sleep** mode with the screen blank after a short amount of time. You can change the time interval before this happens or even disable this feature altogether using the **Settings** icon:

1. Touch the **Settings** icon from your **Home** screen.

2. Touch **General** in the left column, then touch **Auto-Lock** in the right column.

3. You will see your current time interval next to **Auto-Lock** on this page (Figure 1–15). The default setting is that the iPad locks after five minutes of sitting idle (to save battery life). The choices you have for this setting range from two to fifteen minutes, or **Never**.

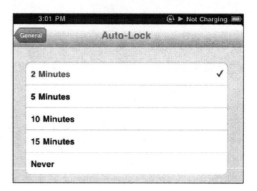

4. Touch the desired setting to select it — you know it's selected when you see the **Checkmark** icon next to it.

5. Then, tap the **General** button in the top row to get back to the **General** screen. You should see your change now reflected next to **Auto-Lock**.

> **BATTERY LIFE TIP:**
>
> Setting the **Auto-Lock** shorter (for example, 2 minutes) will help you save battery life.

Adjusting the Date and Time

Usually, the date and time is either set for you or adjusts when you connect your iPad to your computer, which we cover in Chapter 3: "Sync Your iPad with iTunes." You can, however, manually adjust your date and time quite easily. You may want to do this when you are traveling with your iPad and need to adjust the time zone when you land. Follow these steps to do so:

1. Touch the **Settings** icon.

2. Touch **General** in the left column and **Date & Time** in the right column to see the **Date & Time** settings screen.

3. If you prefer to see 09:30 and 14:30 instead of 9:30 AM and 2:30 PM, respectively, then tap the **24-Hour Time** setting switch to **ON**.

4. To set the date and time, touch the **Set Date & Time** button to see the pop-up window with the wheels that rotate as you touch and move them.

5. Touch and slide the **hour**, **minute**, and **AM/PM** wheels to move them up or down.

6. Similarly, to change the date, tap the **Date** (in this image **Wednesday, March 23, 2011**).

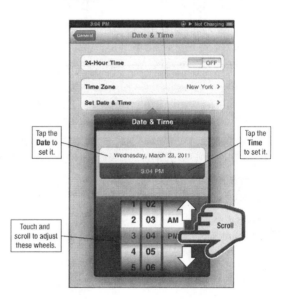

Setting Your Time Zone

Follow these steps to set the time zone:

1. Tap **Time Zone** on the same **Date & Time** screen shown in the previous section.

2. Start to type in the name of the desired city (see Figure 1–13).

3. Touch the name of the city to select it and the screen will automatically move back to the **Date & Time** screen.

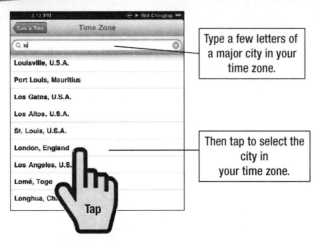

Type a few letters of a major city in your time zone.

Then tap to select the city in your time zone.

Figure 1–13. *Setting your time zone*

Adjusting the Brightness

Your iPad has an **Auto-Brightness** control available, which is usually set to **ON** by default (see Figure 1–14). This uses the built-in light sensor to adjust the brightness of the screen. Generally, we advise that you keep this set to **ON**.

If you want to adjust the brightness, you certainly can. From your **Home** screen, touch the **Settings** icon. Then touch the **Brightness & Wallpaper** tab, which is near the top of the left column, and move the **Slider** control to adjust the brightness.

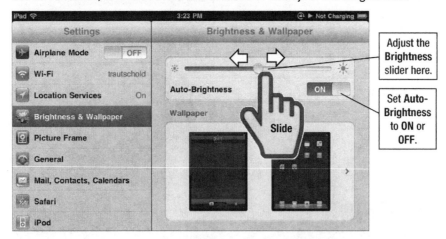

Adjust the **Brightness** slider here.

Set **Auto-Brightness** to **ON** or **OFF**.

Figure 1–14. *Setting the brightness of your iPad*

> **TIP**: Setting the brightness lower will help you save battery life. A little less than 1/2 way across seems to work fine.

Chapter 2

Typing Tips, Copy/Paste, and Search

In this chapter, we will show you some good ways to type and save valuable time typing on your iPad, whether you use the **Portrait** (vertical/smaller) keyboard or the **Landscape** (horizontal/larger) keyboard. We will show you how to select different language keyboards, how to type symbols, and other tips. We will also show you some tips and tricks when working with various external keyboard accessories for your iPad.

Later in this chapter, we will tell you about the **Spotlight Search** and the **Copy and Paste** function. **Copy and Paste** will save you lots of time, as well as increase your accuracy when working with your iPad.

Typing on Your iPad

You will quickly find two on-screen keyboards on your iPad: the smaller one visible when you hold your iPad in a vertical orientation, and the larger **Landscape** keyboard visible when you hold the iPad in a horizontal orientation. The nice thing is that you can choose whichever keyboard works best for you. And if you prefer a physical keyboard, we will show you the ins-and-outs of a few nice accessory keyboards from Apple and ZAGG (see Figure 2–1).

Apple iPad
Keyboard Dock

Apple Bluetooth
Wireless Keyboard

ZAGGmate w/Bluetooth
Keyboard Case

iPad fits in above the
ZAGGmate keyboard.

Figure 2–1. *Several keyboard accessories from Apple and ZAGG*

Typing on the Screen with the Portrait Keyboard

You will find when you first start out with your iPad that you can type most easily with one finger—usually your index finger—while holding the iPad with the other hand.

After a little while, you should be able to experiment with thumb typing (as you see so many people doing with their iPhone or BlackBerry smartphones). Once you practice a little, typing with two thumbs instead of a single finger will really boost your speed. Just be patient; it does take practice to become proficient at typing quickly with your two thumbs.

You will actually notice after a while that the keyboard touch sensitivity assumes you are typing with two thumbs. What this means is that the letters on the left side of your keyboard are meant to be pressed on the left side, and the keys on the right are meant to be pressed on the right side (see Figure 2–2).

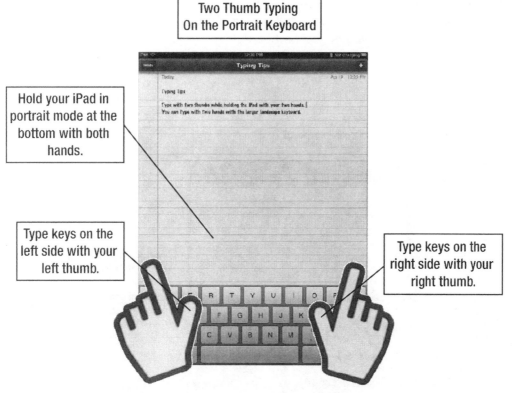

Two Thumb Typing On the Portrait Keyboard

Hold your iPad in portrait mode at the bottom with both hands.

Type keys on the left side with your left thumb.

Type keys on the right side with your right thumb.

*Figure 2–2. Typing with two thumbs while holding the iPad in **Portrait** mode*

TIP: If you have larger hands and find typing on the smaller vertical keyboard challenging, then flip your iPad on its side to get the larger **Landscape** keyboard (see Figure 2–3).

Typing on the Screen with the Larger Landscape Keyboard

Simply turn the iPad sideways in almost any app and the keyboard will change to a larger **Landscape** keyboard to make it easier to type (see Figure 2–3). Follow these steps to type on the **Landscape** keyboard:

1. It helps if you place the iPad at a slight incline as you type; this makes it easier to see the screen. You can also simply lay the iPad on a flat surface. It usually helps if you either have the iPad in a case (see Chapter 1: "Getting Started" to learn about various cases) or sitting on a soft surface so it does not rock as you are typing.

2. Type with two hands as you would on a normal computer keyboard. With some practice, you can almost type as fast on this larger keyboard as you do on a regular physical keyboard.

> **TIP:** Try recycling an old mouse pad to use as a rest for your iPad while you type.

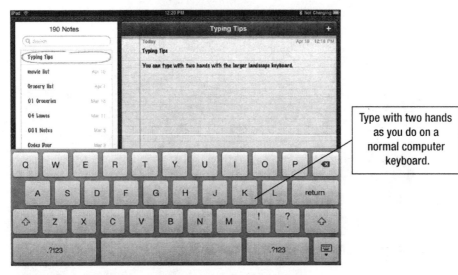

Full Hand Typing On the Landscape Keyboard

Type with two hands as you do on a normal computer keyboard.

Figure 2–3. *Typing with two hands when in **Landscape** orientation*

> **TIP:** For the frequent traveler, using the virtual keyboards on your iPad saves a ton of space in those cramped airline seats compared to any laptop computer!

Typing with External Keyboards (Purchase as Separate Accessories)

If you need to do a lot of typing or are simply uncomfortable with the "typing on glass" feel of the virtual keyboards, you can buy external keyboards that work with the iPad. We have tested two from Apple, but we know there are more keyboard dock and Bluetooth options available. We showed you, but have not tested, a keyboard/case combination called the ZAGGmate earlier in this chapter (see Figure –1). Check out the iPad/iPhone/iPod blogs or online stores (e.g., www.amazon.com) to find keyboards and other accessories. You can also do a quick web search for "iPad external keyboard" to find other options.

External Keyboard Shortcuts

Once you connect an external keyboard to your iPad, you can use many of the shortcuts on your keyboard that you have become familiar with on your computer keyboard. The following shortcuts should save you some time when typing on your iPad:

- **Select Text with Arrows :** Command-Shift-Arrow keys
- **Cut Selected Text:** Command + X
- **Copy Selected Text:** Command + C
- **Paste Selected Text:** Command + V
- **Undo:** Command + Z
- **Redo:** Command + Y

TIP: If you plan to do a lot of typing on your iPad, investing some money in one of these external keyboards can be worth its weight in gold! In our testing, we preferred the Apple iPad Keyboard Dock because it held the iPad at a very nice angle for typing. If you use the Bluetooth keyboard, you really need to invest in a case that will hold your iPad up at an angle, so that it is easier to read while typing.

CAUTION: A few iPad apps only work in **Landscape** orientation and will not work with the Keyboard Dock because the whole app will look sideways when in the vertical orientation—
Apple Keynote is one prominent example.

Apple Wireless Keyboard (Bluetooth)—About US $70

Besides being easier and faster to type on, external keyboards give you the added benefit of showing you more of the iPad screen because the virtual keyboard is gone.

TIP: If you own another Apple computer, you may already own the Wireless Keyboard—it is the same Wireless Keyboard that Apple has made for a while.

Getting Your iPad Connected

Your iPad uses a wireless Bluetooth connection, so you must first connect, or *pair*, this keyboard with your iPad (see Chapter 25: "Bluetooth" for more information). You can use these steps to connect virtually any wireless keyboard to your iPad:

1. Tap the **Settings** icon (see Figure 2–4).
2. Tap **General** in the left column.

3. Tap **Bluetooth** in the right column.

4. Make sure the Bluetooth receiver is set to **ON** by tapping the switch if it shows **OFF**.

5. Turn on your Apple Wireless Keyboard by pressing the **On/Off** button on the right edge of the round tube under the top of the keyboard. You will know when the keyboard is on and has batteries when the green light in the upper-right corner is on or flashing.

6. Once the Wireless Keyboard is powered on, you should see it listed under **Devices** in the **Bluetooth** screen on the iPad. Tap the keyboard listed under **Devices** to have the iPad generate a pairing number (see Figure 2–4).

7. Type in the pairing code number from the iPad on the Wireless Keyboard and press the **Enter/Return** key on the keyboard.

8. Sometimes it takes two or three tries to get the keyboard to pair with your iPad. Keep trying; it will work eventually!

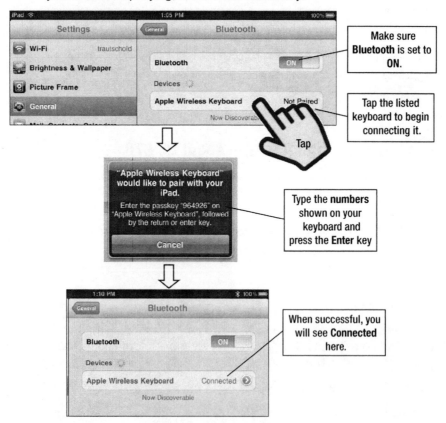

Figure 2–4. *Pairing a Bluetooth Wireless Keyboard with your iPad*

Switching Between the Wireless and On-Screen Keyboards

It's easy to switch between a wireless keyboard and the built-in on-screen keyboard—

and vice versa. Simply press the **Eject** key ▲ in the upper-right corner of the keyboard to temporarily disconnect the Wireless Keyboard and see the on-screen keyboard.

Press the **Eject** key again to reconnect the Wireless Keyboard and make the on-screen keyboard disappear.

Apple iPad Keyboard Dock—About US $70

Besides giving you the physical keyboard to type on, the Keyboard Dock also gives you the added benefit of holding your iPad up at an angle like a regular computer screen. It is very nice!

> **NOTE:** At the time of publishing, the original iPad dock had not been updated by Apple, so it will hold both the iPad and iPad 2 (if a little loosely). We believe there may be an updated iPad dock specifically designed for the iPad 2 released soon.

Other benefits of this keyboard are that it is designed by Apple specifically for the iPad, so you have specially designed keys, as shown in Figure 2–5. To the right of these keys, along the top, you also have media control keys: **Previous Track**, **Play/Pause**, **Next Track**, and **Volume**. You also have a **Lock** key.

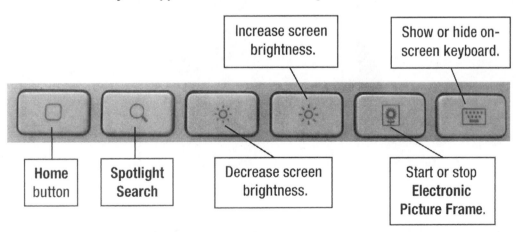

Keys on upper left corner of iPad Keyboard Dock

Increase screen brightness.

Show or hide on-screen keyboard.

Home button

Spotlight Search

Decrease screen brightness.

Start or stop **Electronic Picture Frame**.

Figure 2–5. *Special keys on the iPad Keyboard Dock*

> **TIP:** To wake up the sleeping iPad, you can simply tap any key on the iPad Keyboard Dock.

Unlike a laptop computer, the angle at which the iPad sits in the dock is fixed and cannot be adjusted; however, this angle seemed to work perfectly for us when we tested it.

> **CAUTION:** The iPad can be a little unstable in the Keyboard Dock. We recommend a good flat, stable surface. Also, be careful if you have little people (or really big dogs) running around they could easily knock the iPad off the dock by accident.

Connecting Your iPad to the Keyboard Dock

Connecting your iPad to the Keyboard Dock is very simple—just set it on the dock to plug it into the port on the bottom of your iPad, as shown in Figure 2–6.

Figure 2–6. *An iPad sitting in the Keyboard Dock—great for typing long documents*

> **NOTE:** If you have put your iPad in a case, you will most likely have to remove it before you connect the iPad to the Keyboard Dock. This has the added benefit of allowing the iPad to dissipate heat if you are charging it while it is in the dock.

You can then plug your USB sync and charging cable to the back of the Keyboard Dock to simultaneously connect the iPad to your computer or charge it in the wall socket.

Simply pull the iPad up and out of the Keyboard Dock to disconnect it.

> **CAUTION:** At the time of publishing, standard keyboard tricks such as **Command-C** for copy, **Command-V** for paste worked with the two keyboard accessories; however, the iPad auto-capitalization, auto-correction, and double-tapping the **Space** key for period shortcuts did not work.

Connecting Two Keyboards at Once

If you happen to have both the Wireless Keyboard and the Keyboard Dock, we have discovered that you can simultaneously type with both keyboards on the iPad. So, you could potentially take turns typing on the same document, have dueling keyboards, or even try duet typing. In any case, it's a strange but true capability of these keyboards.

Saving Time with Auto-Correction

When you have been typing for a while, you will begin to notice a little pop-up window directly below some of the words you are typing—this is called Auto-Correction. (If you never see this pop-up window, then you will have to enable Auto-Correction in your **Settings** icon on your iPad.) You can save yourself time when you see the correct word guessed by just pressing the **Space** key at the bottom of the keyboard to select that word.

In this example, we start typing the word "especially." When we get to the *c* in the word, the correct word—*especially*—appears below in a pop-up window. To select it, we simply press the **Space** key at the bottom (see Figure 2–7).

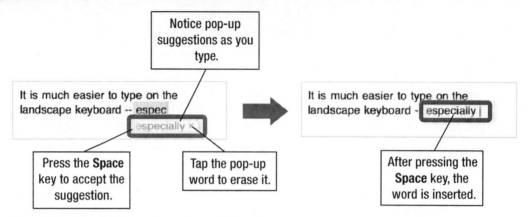

Figure 2–7. *Using Auto-Correction and suggested words*

Your first inclination might be to tap the pop-up word, but that simply erases it from the screen. It is ultimately faster to keep typing or press the **Space** key when you see the correct word, as there will be more situations in which the word is either correct or will become correct as you keep typing. This approach results in less finger travel in the long run.

After you learn to use the **Space** key, you will see that this pop-up guessing can be quite a time saver. After all, you were going to have to type a space at the end of the word, anyway!

Tip: With Auto-Correction, you can save time by avoiding typing the apostrophe in many common contractions, such as "won't" and "can't." Auto-Correction will show you a little pop-up window with the contraction spelled correctly; all you need to do to select the correction is to press the **Space** key.

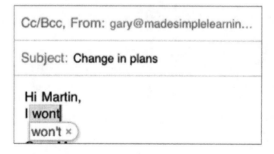

Hearing Auto-Correction Words Out Loud

You can set your iPad to speak the Auto-Text and Auto-Correction words as they appear. This might be helpful to you when selecting the correct word. Follow these steps to enable this type of speaking:

1. Tap the **Settings** icon.

2. Tap **General** in the left column.

3. Tap **Accessibility** near the bottom of the right column.

4. Set the switch next to **Speak Auto-text** to **ON**.

After you enable this feature, you will hear the Auto-Correction word that pops up whenever you are typing. If you like the word you hear, then press the **Space** key to accept it; otherwise, keep typing. This feature can save you some time by sparing you the need to look up from the keyboard.

Accessibility Options

There are a number of useful features on the iPad to help with accessibility. The **VoiceOver** option will read the text from the screen to you. It will tell you what you tap on, what buttons are selected, and all the options. It will read entire screens of text, as well. If you like to see things larger, you can also turn on the **Zoom** feature, as described in the next section.

Large Text

Sometimes, the standard font is just too small to be easily read. In these cases, the **Large Text** feature is a great help.

Tap **Large Text** from the **Accessibility** options to adjust the font size in **Contacts, Mail, and Notes**.

You can select from **Off** (the default is about 12-point text) all the way up to 56-point text.

VoiceOver   Getting Your iPad to Speak To You

One cool feature of the iPad is that you can turn on the **VoiceOver** feature, so that the iPad will speak anything shown on the screen. You can even get it to read to you from any email, text document, or even an iBook page.

Follow these steps to enable **VoiceOver**:

1. Tap the **Settings** icon.

2. Tap **General** in the left column.

3. Tap **Accessibility** near the bottom of the right column.

4. Tap **VoiceOver** in the left column.

5. Set the **VoiceOver** switch to **ON** and select **OK** from the pop-up window to confirm.

> **CAUTION:** As shown on the screen to the right, the **VoiceOver** gestures are different from the normal gestures. Tap the **Practice VoiceOver Gestures** button to get used to them.
>
> Notice that you can adjust the **Speaking Rate** from slow to fast and make other adjustments, such as **Typing Feedback**, **Use Phonetics**, and **Use Pitch Change**. Give some of these a try to see which options work best for you.

Tap **Braille** to connect your iPad to a Braille device with Bluetooth.

Tap **Web Rotor** to adjust the various web site features to include in the *web rotor* (you'll learn more about this momentarily).

Similarly, tap **Language Rotor** to select languages to include for use with **VoiceOver** (again, you'll learn more about this momentarily).

When you type with **VoiceOver** enabled, by default every character you type will be spoken. You can change this in the settings screen just mentioned. You can make it speak just words, just characters, or nothing.

To have an entire page read to you in the **iBooks** app, you need to simultaneously touch the bottom and top of the block of text on the screen. If you tap in the text with one finger, only a single line is read to you.

Tapping the top of a note in the **Notes** app will read the entire note to you.

Web Rotor and Language Rotor

Two interesting features when using **VoiceOver** are the Web Rotor and Language Rotor. You can customize what items appear in these rotors in the **VoiceOver** setting screen shown previously.

To use the Web or Language Rotors, you need to place two fingers on the screen and simultaneously rotate them around (as though you were turning a dial with your fingertips). Once you do this, a small **Rotating Dial** icon appears on the screen (see the image to the right with the **Rotating Dial** set to **Headings**).

Next, a simple swipe down with one finger on the screen will jump to the next item in the selected list.

For example, if you set the Web Rotor to **Headings**, then swipe down with a single finger, the **VoiceOver** will jump down to the next heading on the page. Swipe up to jump back to the previous heading.

To switch languages, first select a number of languages from the **VoiceOver** Language Rotor settings screen.

Put two fingers on the screen and rotate until you see the pointer set to **Language**.

Next, swipe down to select the next **VoiceOver** language. Swipe up to go back to a previously selected language.

Using Zoom to Magnify the Entire Screen

You may want to turn on the **Zoom** feature if you find that the text, icons, buttons, or anything on the screen is a little too hard to see. With the **Zoom** feature turned on, you can zoom the entire screen to almost twice the size. This makes everything much easier to read.

> **NOTE:** You cannot use **VoiceOver** and **Zoom** at the same time, you need to choose one or the other.

Follow these steps to enable **Zoom**:

1. Tap the **Settings** icon.

2. Tap **General** in the left column.

3. Tap **Accessibility** near the bottom of the right column.

4. Tap **Zoom** in the right column.

5. Set the switch next to **Zoom** to **ON**.

Similar to **VoiceOver**, **Zoom** uses the three-fingered gestures. Make sure to take note of them before you leave the screen.

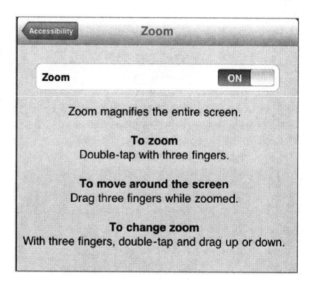

White on Black

If the contrast and colors are difficult to see, then you might want to turn on the **White on Black** setting. Follow these steps to change this setting:

1. Get into the **Accessibility** screen in the **Settings** app, as shown previously.

2. Set the **White on Black** switch to **ON**.

With this setting **ON**, everything that is light on the screen becomes black, and everything that is dark or black becomes white.

Triple-Click Home Button Options

You can set a triple-click of the **Home** button to do various things related to accessibility:

1. Get into the **Accessibility** screen in the **Settings** app, as shown previously.

2. Tap **Triple-click the Home Button** near the bottom of the right column.

3. Choose from **Off**, **Toggle VoiceOver**, **Toggle White on Black**, or **Ask**.

Magnifying Glass for Editing Text/Placing the Cursor

How many times have you been typing something and wanted to move the cursor precisely between two words or letters?

This can be hard to do until you figure out the magnifying glass trick. What you do is this: touch and hold your finger on the place where you want the cursor (see Figure 2–8). After a second or two, you will see the **Magnifying Glass** icon appear. Then, while you hold your finger on the screen, slide it around to position the cursor. When you let go, you will see the **Copy/Paste** pop-up menu, but you can ignore it.

Figure 2–8. *Touch and hold the screen to bring up the **Magnifying Glass** icon and place the cursor.*

Typing Numbers and Symbols

You might wonder how you type a number or a symbol using the on-screen keyboard on the iPad. When you are typing, tap the **.?123** key in the lower-left corner to see numbers and common symbols such as $! ~ & = # . - +. If you need more symbols, tap the **#+=** key from the number keyboard, just above the **ABC** key in the lower-left corner (see Figure 2–9).

TIP: You even get an **Undo** key when you press the **.?123** key—a nice addition to any keyboard!

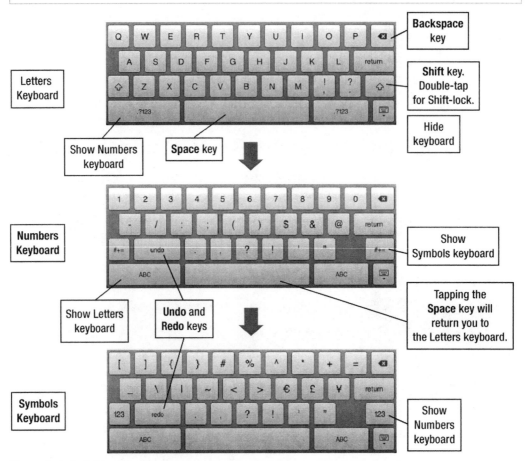

Figure 2–9. *Switching between the Letters, Numbers, and Advanced Symbol keyboards*

TIP: Notice that the **Numbers** and **Symbols** keyboards will stay active until you either hit the **Space** key or tap the key for another keyboard, such as **ABC**.

Touch and Slide Trick

The following tips are courtesy of Rene Ritchie from the iPhone/iPad Blog (www.tipb.com).

Typing Uppercase Letters

Normally, you would tap the **Shift** key and then tap the letter to type an uppercase letter.

Touch Shift then slide to the letter.

However, a faster way to type a single uppercase letter or symbol that requires the **Shift** key is to touch the **Shift** key, keep your finger on the keyboard, slide over to the key you want, and then release.

For example, to type an uppercase "M," touch the right **Shift** key, then slide over to the "M" key and release.

Rapidly Typing a Single Number

If you have to type just a single number, then touch the **.?123** key and slide your finger up to the number. However, to type several numbers in a row, it's best to tap the **.?123** key, let go, and then tap each number.

Typing Symbols that Require Shift

The same goes for the question and exclamation marks, which require you to press **Shift** on the Letters keyboard. Touch the **Shift** key, then slide over and let go on the **?** key.

Typing the Apostrophe

Press and hold the **Comma/Exclamation** key to see the apostrophe pop-up window.

The apostrophe is highlighted in blue, so simply let go of the key to type it.

> **TIP:** For most common contractions, your Auto-Correction dictionary should automatically insert the apostrophe. For example, type "dont" and then press the **Space** key to have the apostrophe inserted: "don't."

Press and Hold Keyboard Shortcut for Typing Symbols and More

You might also wonder how you type the symbols not shown on the keyboard.

> **TIP:** You can type more symbols than are shown on the screen.

All you do is press and hold a letter, number, or symbol that is related to the symbol you want; this will bring up a special context menu.

For example, if you want to type the EURO symbol (€), you press and hold the **$** key until you see the other options. Next, you slide up your finger to highlight, and then let go on the EURO symbol.

Touch and hold works on vowels and some symbols.

This tip also works with the **.com** key in the **Safari** web browser. You can get additional web site suffixes by pressing and holding this key.

The screen on the right shows the **.co.uk** and **.ie** keys among its options. These keys are not on the standard US keyboard, but they are present because we have installed the English (UK) international keyboard (refer to the earlier section in this chapter for help with international keyboards).

TIP: There is a good bullet point character (or degree sign, depending on how you look at it) on the **Numbers** screen. You access it by pressing and holding the **Zero** key (**0**). You can also press and hold the **?** and **!** keys to get their Spanish-inverted cousins.

Left and Right Arrows (International Languages)

If (and only if) you have activated an international language keyboard where typing is done from right to left (e.g., Hebrew or Japanese), you will notice a button with a pair of arrows appear in the right end of the pop-up window above the text. Clicking this

Arrows button  lets you adjust the way text is typed on your iPad—either from right to left or left to right.

Keyboard Options & Settings

There are a few keyboard options to make typing on your iPad easier. The keyboard options are located in the **General** tab of your **Settings**. Follow these steps to change your keyboard settings:

1. Touch the **Settings** icon.

2. Touch **General** in the right column.

3. Touch **Keyboard** in the left column to see this screen.

Auto-Capitalization

When you start a new sentence, the first word will automatically be capitalized if **Auto-Capitalization** is **ON**.

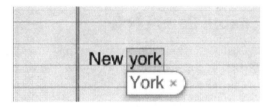

Also, common proper nouns will be correctly capitalized. For example, if you were to type "New york," you would be prompted to change it to "New York"—again, just pressing the **Space** key would implement the correction. If you backspace over a capital letter, the iPad will assume the new letter you type should be a capital, as well.

This feature is also set to **ON** by default.

Auto-Correction ON / OFF

Using the built-in dictionary, the Auto-Correction feature will automatically make changes to commonly misspelled words.

> **TIP:** If the Auto-Correction feature changes a word incorrectly, you can hit the **Backspace** key immediately to bring up to bring up a pop-up window with the original word (prior to Auto-Correction).

For example, if you type in "wont," Auto-Correction will change it to "won't" on the fly. You need to make sure Auto-Correction is **ON** if you want this feature to work (**ON** is the default setting).

Check Spelling

Your iPad will check your spelling automatically because the default setting for this option is **ON**. However, if you would prefer to disable spell check, simply switch **Check Spelling** to **OFF**.

> **TIP:** When spelling is turned on, any words that the spell checker thinks are misspelled will be underlined. Tap any underlined word to see a list of suggested corrections.

Enable Caps Lock

Sometimes when you type, you may want to lock the caps by pressing and holding the **Caps** key (**up-arrow** key)—just as you do on a computer keyboard. Enabling **Caps Lock** will allow you to do this.

This is set to **OFF** by default.

The "." Shortcut

If you are an iPhone user or BlackBerry user, you might be familiar with the feature that will automatically put in a period at the end of the sentence when you double-tap the **Space** key. This is exactly the same feature that you can enable on the iPad. By default, this is also set to **ON**.

Typing in Other Languages—International Keyboards

At the time of publishing, the iPad enables you to type in over a dozen different languages. Some of the Asian languages, such as Japanese and Chinese, offer two or three keyboards for different typing methods.

To enable various language keyboards, follow these steps:

1. Touch the **Settings** icon (see Figure 2–10).

2. Tap **General** in the left column.

3. Tap **Keyboard** near the bottom of the right column.

4. Tap **International Keyboards**.

5. Tap **Add New Keyboard** to add additional international keyboards.

6. Tap any keyboard/language listed to add that keyboard.

7. Now you will see that keyboard listed in the available keyboards.

8. To adjust keyboard options, tap the listed keyboard.

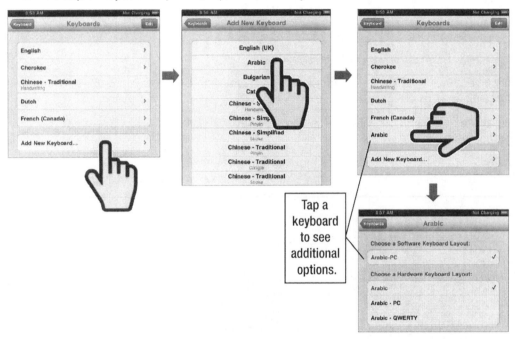

Figure 2–10. *Adding and customizing international keyboards*

Editing or Deleting International Keyboards

It's also easy to edit or delete international keyboards:

1. Return to the **Keyboards** screen showing the list of all the keyboards (see Figure –11).

2. Tap **Edit** in the top-right corner to change the keyboard order or delete a keyboard.

3. To change the order of the listed keyboards, drag the left edge of the listed keyboard up or down.

4. To delete a keyboard, tap the **Red Minus Sign** icon, then tap **Delete**.

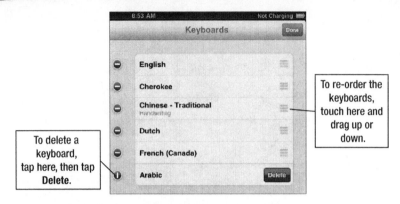

Figure 2–11. *Editing and deleting international keyboards*

Once you have enabled a number of keyboards, tap the **Globe** key to cycle between all the languages (see Figure 2–12).

Japanese and some other languages provide several keyboard options to meet your typing preferences.

In some of the languages (such as Japanese, shown in Figure 2–12), you will see the letters typed change into characters. You will also see a row of other character combinations above the keyboard. When you see the combination you want, tap it.

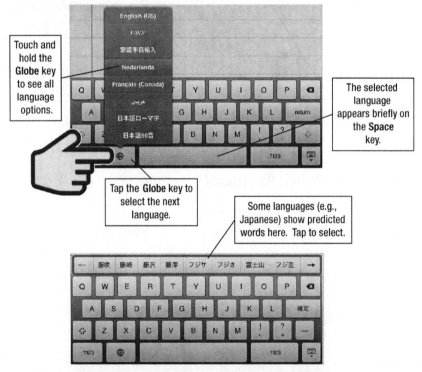

Figure 2–12. *Tap the **Globe** key to cycle between international keyboards.*

Copy and Paste

There are lots of ways to copy and paste text. For example, the **Copy and Paste** feature is very useful for taking text from your calendar and putting it in an email. It's also great for taking a note and placing it in an email or in your calendar. You can even copy text from your **Safari** web browser and paste it into a note or a mail message.

Selecting Text

If you are reading or typing text, you can select the text in a few ways. For example, you can tap or double-tap the text to start selecting text for the copy. This works in mail, messages, and notes.

Double-Tap and Drag Blue Handles

One way to select text is to double-tap a word then drag the blue handles.

You will see a box with blue dots (handles) at opposite corners. Just drag the handles to select the text you wish to highlight and copy, as shown in Figure 2–13.

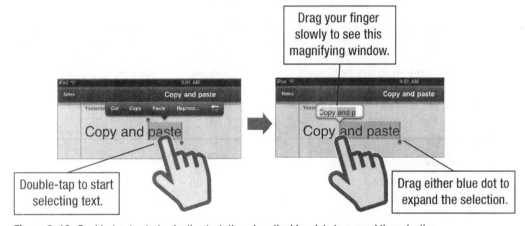

Figure 2–13. *Double-tap to start selecting text, then drag the blue dots to expand the selection.*

Using Select or Select All

The other way to select text while you are typing something is to tap the text once and then choose **Select** or **Select All** from the pop-up window. This same pop-up window will also appear if you double-tap anywhere on the screen, except on the text itself.

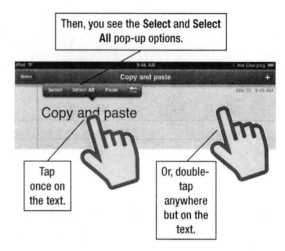

Then, you see the **Select** and **Select All** pop-up options.

Tap once on the text.

Or, double-tap anywhere but on the text.

Selecting Text with Two-Finger Touch

The other way to select text requires that you touch the screen simultaneously with two fingers. This seems to work best if you are holding your iPad with one hand and use your thumb and forefinger from your other hand to touch the screen. What you want to do is touch the screen at the beginning and end of the text you want to select. Don't worry if you cannot get the selection exactly on the first touch. After the first touch, use the blue handles to drag the beginning and end of the selection to the correct position (see Figure 2–14).

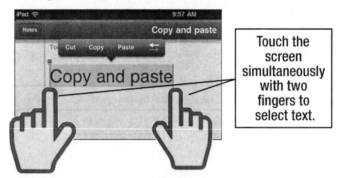

Touch the screen simultaneously with two fingers to select text.

Figure 2–14. *Select text by touching the screen at the same time with two fingers.*

Selecting Web Site or Other non-Editable Text with Touch and Hold

In the **Safari** web browser and other places where you cannot edit the text, you can hold your finger on some text and a word or the entire paragraph will become highlighted with handles at each of the corners.

Drag the handles if you want to select even more text.

> **NOTE:** Drag up or down to quickly select entire paragraphs or more. You can drag smaller than a paragraph to use the fine-text mode selector with the blue handles.

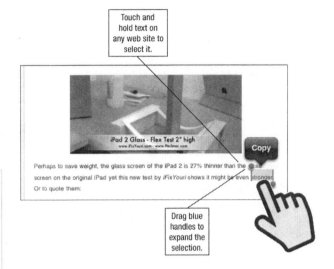

Touch and hold text on any web site to select it.

Drag blue handles to expand the selection.

Cut or Copy the Text

Once you have the text that you wish to copy highlighted, just touch the **Copy** tab at the top of the screen. The tab will turn blue, indicating that the text is on the clipboard.

> **NOTE:** If you have previously cut or copied text, then you will also see the **Paste** option, as shown here.

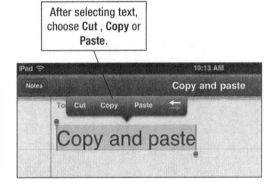

After selecting text, choose **Cut** , **Copy** or **Paste**.

Pasting the Text

Follow these steps if you are pasting the text into the same note or mail message:

1. Use your finger to move the cursor to where you want to paste the text. Remember the **Magnifying Glass** trick (described earlier in this chapter) to help you position the cursor.

2. Once you let go of the screen, you should see a pop-up window asking you to **Select**, **Select All**, or **Paste**.

3. If you don't see this pop-up window, then double-tap the screen.

4. Select **Paste** to paste your selection.

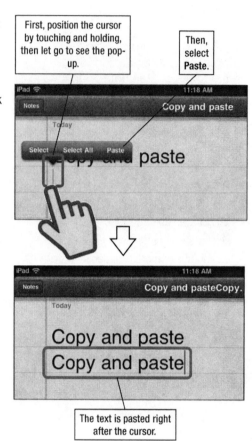

First, position the cursor by touching and holding, then let go to see the pop-up.

Then, select Paste.

The text is pasted right after the cursor.

Pasting Text or an Image into Another App

Follow these steps to paste the text or image you have copied into another app:

1. Press the **Home** button (see Figure –15).

2. Tap the app into which you want to paste the text. In this case, let's tap **Mail**.

3. Tap the **Compose** icon 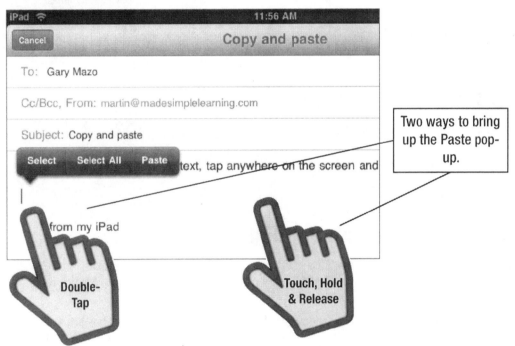 to write a new email.

4. Double-tap anywhere in the body of the message.

5. Tap **Paste**.

Figure 2–15. *Bring up the **Paste** command by either double-tapping or pressing, holding, and releasing.*

Move the cursor to the body of the text and either double-tap or touch, hold, and release your finger. This will bring up the **Paste** pop-up window. Tap **Paste** and the text on the clipboard will be pasted right into the body of the email.

Shake to Undo Paste or Typing

One of the great new features in the Copy and Paste feature is the ability to undo either typing or the text you just pasted.

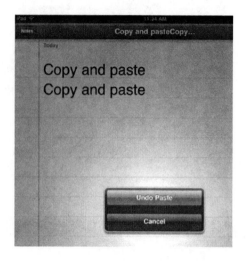

All you have to do is shake the iPad after the paste. A new pop-up window appears, giving you the option to undo what you have just done.

Tap **Undo Paste** or **Undo Typing** to correct the mistake.

> **TIP:** There is an **Undo** button on the keyboard as well. Just press the **.?123** key; it is in the lower-left corner.

> **TIP: Delete Text by Selecting It and Pressing Backspace**
>
> This tip is for you if you ever want to delete a number of lines of text, a paragraph, or even all the text you just typed with one or two taps. Use the techniques described previously to select the
>
> text you want to delete. Next, simply press the **Delete** key ⌫ in the lower-left corner of the keyboard to delete all the selected text.

Finding Things with Spotlight Search

A great feature on your iPad for finding information is the **Spotlight Search**, Apple's proprietary search method. This feature provides your iPad with a global search for a name, event, or subject.

The concept is simple. Let's say you are looking for something related to Martin. You cannot remember if it was an email, a note, or a calendar event; however, you do know it was related to Martin.

This is the perfect time to use the **Spotlight Search** feature to find everything related to Martin on your iPad.

Activating Spotlight Search

Begin by starting the **Spotlight Search**, which resides to the left of the first page of the **Home** screen.

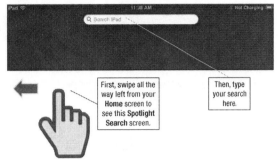

On the left side of the first circle (indicating the first page of your **Home** screen), you can see a very small **Magnifying Glass** icon.

Swipe to the right of this first page of icons to get to the **Spotlight Search** page.

Search for Apps

One great way to use the **Spotlight Search** is to quickly find your apps. If you have more than two or three pages of **Home** screens, you may want to use it.

Start the search and type a few letters of the app name, such as **Weather**. This will find all your weather-related apps.

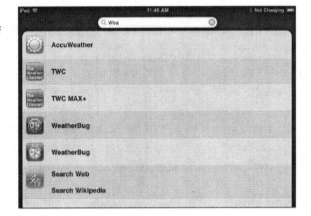

Search the Web or Wikipedia

If you know you want to search the web or Wikipedia, skip the step of going to the **Safari** web browser and typing the information into the **Search** bar. You can save even more time by skipping the step of going to the Wikipedia site.

For example, you might want to know where Zip Code 10708 is located in the US. Simply type "10708" into **Spotlight Search** and tap **Search Web** (see Figure –16).

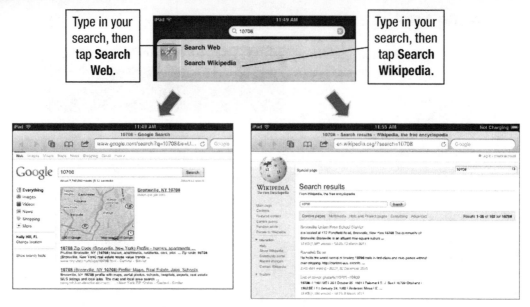

Figure 2–16. *Search the Web or Wikipedia from **Spotlight Search**.*

Search for Mail, Contacts, Videos, Songs, Appointments, and More

The beauty of the **Spotlight Search** is that it can search for virtually anything on your iPad. You may want to find a contact, video, song, calendar appointment, or other item. It's easy to use; just start typing in the **Search** page (see Figure –17).

> **TIP:** If you are looking for a person, type his full name to more accurately find items from only that person (e.g., "Martin Trautschold"). This will eliminate any other Martins who might be in your iPad and make sure you find items only related to Martin Trautschold.

In the search result, you'll see all emails, appointments, meeting invitations, and contact information the search finds. Tap one of the results in the list to view its contents.

Figure 2–17. *Search your iPad for all types of content with **Spotlight Search**.*

Your search results stay there until you clear them, so you can go back to **Spotlight Search** once again by swiping to the right from your **Home** screen.

To clear the **Search** field, just touch the **X** in the **Search** bar. To exit **Spotlight Search**, just press the **Home** key or swipe to the left.

Customizing Spotlight Search

There may be times you want to selectively search for only certain items. Other times, you may want to remove specific items (such as mail messages) from the search. You can do this by adjusting the options for **Spotlight Search** in your **Settings** app. Follow these steps to do so:

1. Tap the **Settings** icon.

2. Tap **General**.

3. Tap **Spotlight Search** in the right column to see the screen shown here.

4. Tap any item to check or uncheck it.

5. Touch and hold the icon on the right edge of each item to slide it up or down the list.

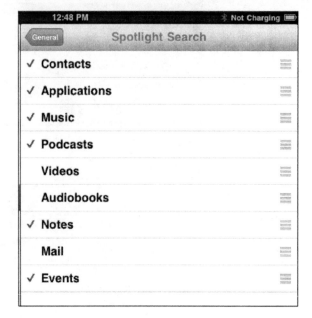

Chapter 3

Sync Your iPad with iTunes

In this chapter we will show you the steps to get set up to synchronize information between your iPad and your Windows or Mac computer. Besides syncing, iTunes can do so much more, like organize your music, create playlists, buy songs, videos; it also has Home Sharing and Genius features. To learn about these features, please check out Chapter 29.

> **NOTE:** If you do not maintain a calendar or contact list on your computer or elsewhere, nor have any photos, videos, music, audiobooks or pictures on your computer, you still need to connect your iPad to iTunes on your computer to at minimum backup your iPad as well as perform software updates when they become available.

We will also show you what to consider before you sync, how to set up the automatic sync of your personal information, and how to manually transfer information. With iTunes, you can sync or transfer contacts, calendar, notes, apps, music, videos, documents, and picture libraries. iTunes also has the added benefit that it automatically will backup your iPad whenever you connect it to your computer. We even show you a few simple troubleshooting tips if things are not working quite right. Finally, we show you how to check for updates and install updated operating system software for your iPad.

> **TIP:** If you are new to iTunes, we strongly recommend you check out Chapter 29, "Your iTunes User Guide," to help you get the most out of iTunes.

Before You Set Up Your iTunes Sync

There are a few things you need before you can start syncing using iTunes. We cover the prerequisites and answer a few common questions about the reasons to use iTunes. We also help you understand what happens if you own another Apple device, such as an iPhone or iPod, and start syncing with your iPad.

Prerequisites Before You Sync

There are just a few things you need before you start syncing your iPad with iTunes.

1. Make sure you have the latest version of iTunes installed on your computer. For how to install or update iTunes, see Chapter 29: "Your iTunes User Guide."

2. Create an iTunes account (Apple ID); see the "Create iTunes Account" section in Chapter 29.

3. Get the white sync cable that came with your iPad. One end plugs into the dock port in the bottom of your iPad near the **Home** button and the other plugs into the USB port on your computer.

Can I Sync iTunes with Another iPhone, iPod touch, or iPod and My iPad?

Yes! As long as you are syncing to the same computer, you can sync many Apple devices (Apple says up to five, but we have heard of people syncing more) to the same iTunes account on a single computer.

> **CAUTION:** You can't sync the same iPad, iPhone, or iPod to two different computers. When you attempt to do this, you will see a message similar to this: "Would you like to wipe this device (iPad, iPhone, iPod) and re-sync the new library?" If you select Yes, then all the music and videos on the device will be erased.

Other Sync Options: MobileMe and Exchange/Google

There are other ways to synchronize your personal information and email, such as Exchange/Google and MobileMe, which we cover in Chapter 4: "Other Sync Methods." Keep in mind, however, that even if you choose to go with these other ways to sync, you will still need to use iTunes to

*   Backup and restore your iPad.

*   Update the iPad operating system software.

- Sync and manage your applications, also known as "apps."
- Sync your music library and playlists.
- Sync movies, TV shows, podcasts, and iTunes U content .
- Sync books.
- Sync photos.

Considering Other Sync Options

Table 3–1 summarizes your other synchronization options. What you choose to use for synchronization should be driven by where you currently store your email, contacts, and calendar—your environment.

> **NOTE:** As you can see in Table 3–1, with some environments you can wirelessly sync your contacts and calendars to your iPad.

Table 3–1. *Synchronization Options for Your Personal Information*

Your Environment	Wireless Sync Using	Desktop Sync Using	Notes
Google for Email, Calendar, and Contacts	Settings ➤ Mail,Contacts,Calendar ➤ Add Account ➤ Microsoft Exchange	iTunes	This is free.
Google for Email (You don't want wireless sync with Google for Contacts and Calendar)	Settings ➤ Mail,Contacts,Calendar ➤ Add Account ➤ Gmail	iTunes required to sync Google Contacts and Calendar	This is free.
Email, Calendar, and Contacts on Microsoft Exchange Server	Settings ➤ Mail,Contacts,Calendar ➤ Add Account ➤ Microsoft Exchange	iTunes	This is free.
Email, Calendar, and Contacts in Yahoo!	Email only: Settings ➤ Mail,Contacts,Calendar ➤ Add Account ➤ Yahoo!	iTunes required to sync Yahoo! Contacts and Calendar	This is free.

Your Environment	Wireless Sync Using	Desktop Sync Using	Notes
Email, Calendar, and Contacts on various platforms. You are subscribed to MobileMe service.	Settings ➤ Mail,Contacts,Calendar ➤ Add Account ➤ MobileMe	MobileMe	This is free for 60 days, then US$99 for one user and US$149 for a family plan. ** *Pricing valid as of publication time.*
Email, Calendar, and Contacts in AOL	Email only: Settings ➤ Mail,Contacts,Calendar ➤ Add Account ➤ AOL	iTunes required to sync AOL Contacts and Calendar	This is free.
LDAP (Lightweight Directory Access Protocol) Contacts	Settings ➤ Mail,Contacts,Calendar ➤ Add Account ➤ Other ➤ Add LDAP Account	Not available.	This is free.
CalDAV Calendar Account	Settings ➤ Mail,Contacts,Calendar ➤ Add Account ➤ Other ➤ Add CalDAV Account	Not available.	This is free. You must have access to CalDAV account with a username and password in this format: cal.server.com
Subscribed Calendar at your work	Settings ➤ Mail,Contacts,Calendar ➤ Add Account ➤ Other ➤ Add Subscribed Calendar	Not available.	This is free. You must have access to a subscribed calendar (web address, username, and password). Access to server is in this format: myserver.com/cal.ics

Setup Your iTunes Sync

We show you all the steps to perform both automated syncs and manual transfers of information to your iPad using iTunes.

The iPad Summary Screen

Once you connect your iPad to your computer, you can see important information, like your iPad's memory capacity in GB, installed software version, and serial number. You can also check for updates to the software version or restore data to your iPad. There are several other options that are available on this screen.

iTunes Navigation Basics:

Get a feel for the left nav bar. Click on various items in this left nav bar and notice that the main display window changes (see Figure 3–1).

The top nav bar inside the main window also changes based on what you have selected in the left nav bar.

For example, when you click on your iPad in the left nav bar, you will see tabs across the top of the main window that show information related to your device.

When you click on the iTunes store in the left nav bar, you see tabs related to the store in the main window.

To see the **iPad Summary** screen:

1. Start up iTunes software on your computer.

2. Connect your iPad to your computer with the white USB cable supplied with the device. Plug one end into the bottom of the iPad near the **Home** button and plug the other end into a USB port on your computer.

3. If you have successfully connected your iPad, you should see your iPad listed under **DEVICES** in the left nav bar.

4. Click on your iPad in the left nav bar, then click on the **Summary** tab on the left edge of the main window (see Figure 3–1).

5. If you want to be able to drag and drop music and videos onto your iPad, you need to check the box next to **Manually manage music and videos**.

6. If you want to have iTunes open and sync your iPad automatically whenever you connect it to your computer, check the **Open iTunes when this iPad is connected** box.

NOTE: You may see the text and checkbox next to Open iTunes when this iPad is connected in the Options area on this Summary screen grayed out (not-clickable). This is because of a setting in the iTunes Edit Preferences ➤ Device tab screen, the checkbox next to **Prevent iPods, iPhones and iPads from syncing automatically** has been checked. If you uncheck this box in the Preferences ➤ Device tab, then you can make the **Open iTunes when this iPad is connected** a clickable item again.

☑ Prevent iPods, iPhones, and iPads from syncing automatically

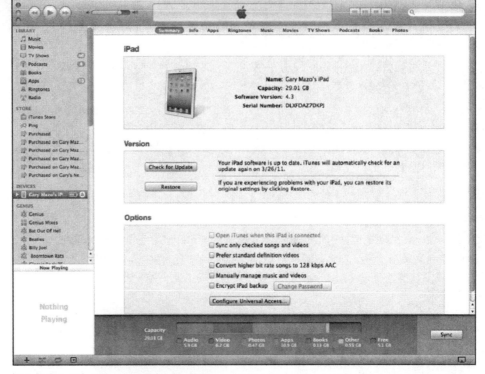

Figure 3–1. *The iPad summary screen in iTunes*

iTunes Navigation Basics

Get a feel for the left nav bar. Click various items in this left nav bar and note that the main display window changes.

The top nav bar inside the main window also changes based on what you have selected in the left nav bar. For example, when you click your **iPad** in the left nav bar, you'll see tabs across the top of the main window that show information related to your device. When you click the **iTunes store** in the left nav bar, you see tabs related to the store in the main window.

Getting to the Sync Setup Screen (Info Tab)

Your first step is to get to the setup screen for syncing your contacts, calendar, email, and so forth. You follow the same steps described previously for getting to the **Summary** screen, except now you click the **Info** tab at the top to see the Contacts (and other sync settings) in the main iTunes window.

Sync Your Contacts and Calendars

Let's start by setting up syncing of your contacts and calendars.

1. Check the **Sync Contacts with** box and adjust the pull-down menu to the software or service where your contacts are stored. At publication time, on a Windows computer these are Outlook, Google Contacts, Windows Contacts, and Yahoo! Address Book. See Figure 3–2. You can also select **All contacts** or **Selected groups**.

2. To sync Calendars, check the **Sync Calendars with** box and adjust the drop-down list to match the software where you store your calendar on your computer, as shown in Figure 3–2. You may also select **All calendars** or **Selected calendars**.

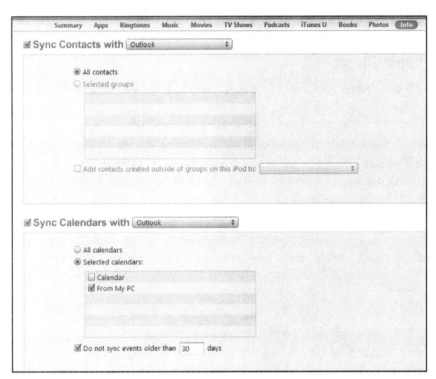

Figure 3–2. *Selecting software for syncing contacts (Windows)*

CAUTION: Whenever you switch between software and services in these Sync Settings screens (called the sync provider), it affects every one of the mobile devices connected to your iTunes account. For example, if you sync contacts to your iPhone or iPod touch (in addition to your iPad), these changes will also affect MobileMe. You will be changing the way contacts sync for any other devices connected to your iTunes account.

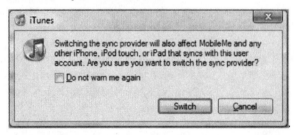

Google and Yahoo! Sync

If you select Google or Yahoo! sync, you'll be prompted to enter your Google ID or Yahoo! ID and password.

NOTE: The options you see in this and other drop-down boxes on the **Info** tab will vary slightly depending on the software installed on your computer. For example, on a Mac, the contacts sync does not have a drop-down list; instead the other services, such as Google Contacts and Yahoo!, are shown as separate check boxes.

To continue setting up your email accounts, bookmarks, and more, scroll down the page. If you don't want to set anything else up for syncing, click the **Apply** button in the lower-right corner of the iTunes screen to start the sync.

TIP: If you're a Mac user who uses Microsoft Entourage, you'll need to enable Entourage to sync with iCal. To do this, go into the Preferences settings in Entourage, then go to Sync Services and check the boxes for synchronizing with iCal and Address book, as shown in Figure 3–3. If you are a user of Office for Mac 2011, you will need to install SP1 (Service Pack 1) to allow syncing to your iPad through iTunes. As of writing this book, the SP1 update had not yet been released. Based on Microsoft's Office for Mac website, you should be able to use Apple Sync Services to sync Outlook calendar, contacts, notes and tasks.

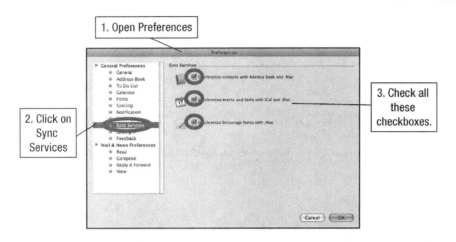

Figure 3–3. *Microsoft Entourage and Outlook settings (Apple Mac)*

Syncing Email Accounts, Browser Bookmarks, and Notes

Scroll down the page to sync email account settings, browser bookmarks, and notes.

> **NOTE:** After syncing the email account settings to your iPad, you'll still have to enter your password for each email account in the **Settings ➤ Mail, Contacts, Calendars** for each email account. You have to do this only once on your iPad for each account.

1. Scroll down below the Calendar settings on the same **Info** tab in iTunes to see the **Mail** account settings.

2. Check the **Sync Mail Accounts from** box and adjust the pull-down menu to the software or service that stores your email (Figure 3–4). This might be Outlook on a Windows computer or Entourage or Mail on a Mac.

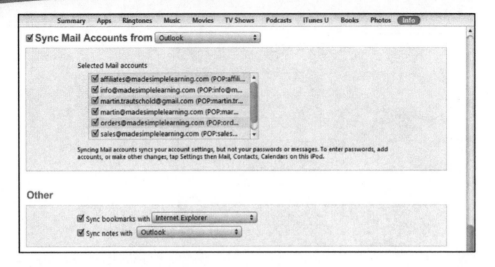

Figure 3–4. *Setting up email accounts, browser bookmarks, and notes to sync*

NOTE: As of publication time, iTunes supports only two web browsers for sync: Microsoft Internet Explorer and Apple Safari. If you use Mozilla Firefox or Google Chrome, you can still sync your bookmarks, but you'll have to install free bookmark sync software (such as xmarks from www.xmarks.com) to sync from Firefox or Chrome to Safari or Explorer. Then you can sync your browser bookmarks in a two-step process. The Firefox Homeapp is a nice option to sync bookmarks for Firefox users (visit http://itunes.apple.com/ca/app/firefox-home/id380366933?mt=8)

3. To sync your browser bookmarks, check the **Sync bookmarks with** box and adjust the pull-down menu to the web browser you use (see Figure 3–4). At this time, you can select only Internet Explorer or Safari.

4. To sync your notes, check the **Sync notes with** box and select the software or service where your notes are stored.

5. Click the **Apply** button in the lower-right corner of the iTunes screen to start the sync.

NOTE: Depending on how much information (especially contacts and calendar information) you have, the initial sync could take 15 minutes or more.

Syncing Your iPad with iTunes

The syncing is normally automatic when you plug in your iPad to your computer's USB port. The only exception is if you have disabled the automatic sync.

Keeping Track of the Sync

At the top of iTunes, inside the Status window, you can see what is happening with the sync. You may see **Syncing contacts with [your name here]'s iPad** or **Syncing calendars with [your name here]'s iPad**, which lets you see what is currently being synced.

Handling Sync Conflicts

Sometimes, the iTunes sync will detect conflicts between the data in your computer and on your iPad, such as the same contact entry with two different company names, or the same calendar entry with two different notes. Handling these conflicts is fairly straightforward.

1. In the **Conflict Resolver** window, click the information that is correct. This turns the background a light blue, while the side not selected is white. See Figure 3–5.

2. If there are any more conflicts, click the **Next** button until you finish resolving all conflicts.

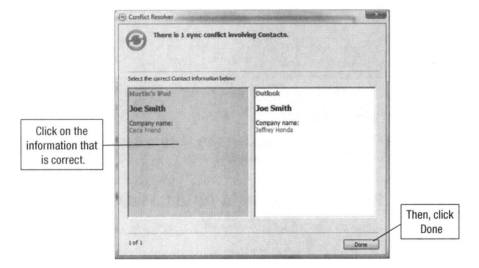

Figure 3–5. *iTunes sync Conflict Resolver*

3. Click **Done** to close the window.

4. All your selections will be applied to the next sync with your iPad. You are given the choice to **Sync Now** or **Sync Later**.

> **NOTE:** Conflicts can cause the sync to stop in mid-process. Contacts are synced first, then the Calendar. So if a Contacts sync conflict is found, the Calendar will not sync until the Contacts conflict is resolved. Make sure to resync your iPad after you resolve conflicts to complete the sync.

Cancelling a Sync in Progress

You can cancel a sync from iTunes or from your iPad.

To cancel the sync from iTunes on your computer:

Click the **X** inside the sync status window, as shown in Figure 3–6.

Figure 3–6. *Clicking the X in the status window in iTunes to cancel the sync*

To cancel the sync from the iPad:

Slide the slider bar at the bottom of the screen that says **Slide to Cancel.** This is in the same place as the normal **Slide to Unlock** message.

Why Would You Not Want iTunes to Automatically Sync?

There could be a few reasons to sync manually instead of automatically:

1. You don't want to fill up your iPad with too many music and video files.

2. The sync and backup process takes a long time, so you don't want it to happen every time you connect your iPad to your computer.

3. You plug your iPad into various computers to charge it up, but don't want to be asked if you want to erase and resync your music every time.

> **NOTE:** If you want to drag and drop music and videos, you need to make sure to check the **Manually manage music and videos** box in the **Summary** tab in iTunes.

Manually Stopping the Auto Sync Before It Starts

There may be times you want to connect your iPad to your computer without the auto sync starting up. This could be because you don't have much time and want to quickly drag and drop a few new songs to your iPad without syncing everything else.

To stop the normal auto sync of your iPad, you can press certain keys on your computer keyboard while connecting your iPad to your computer.

On a Windows PC:

Press and hold **Shift** + **Ctrl** while connecting your iPad to your computer.

On a Mac:

Press and hold **Command** + **Option** while connecting your iPad.

Turning Off the Auto Sync Permanently

You can turn off the auto sync permanently in iTunes. You might want to do this if you prefer to have manual control over all the sync processes.

> **CAUTION:** Turning off the auto sync also disables the automatic backup of your iPad every time you connect it to your computer. This setting is best for a secondary computer, which you might use to charge your iPad but would never want to sync.

To turn off the auto sync in iTunes, follow these steps:

1. From the iTunes menu, select **Edit** and then **Preferences**.

2. Click the **Devices** tab at the top.

3. Check the **Prevent iPods, iPhones, and iPads from syncing automatically** box (see Figure 3–7).

4. Click the **OK** button to save your settings.

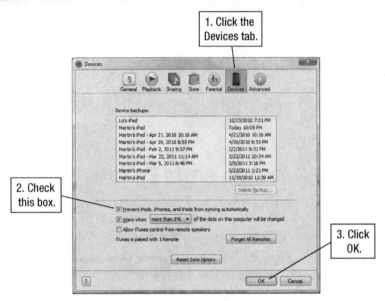

Figure 3–7. *Disabling auto sync in iTunes*

Getting a Clean Start with the Sync

Sometimes you'll have issues with the sync and just need to get a fresh start. There are a few things you can do in this regard with iTunes: you can erase or reset the sync history so iTunes thinks it is syncing for the first time with your iPad, and you can force all information on the iPad to be replaced with information from your computer.

Resetting Sync History (Make iTunes Think It Is Syncing for the First Time)

To reset your sync history in iTunes, follow these steps:

1. Select the **Edit** menu and then click **Preferences**.

2. Click the **Devices** tab at the top of the iTunes Preferences window.

3. Click the **Reset Sync History** button at the bottom, as shown in Figure 3–8.

4. Confirm your selection by clicking **Reset Sync History** in the pop-up window.

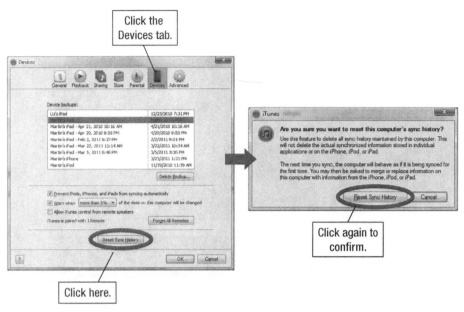

Figure 3–8. *Resetting sync history in iTunes*

Replacing All Information on the iPad (Next Sync Only)

Sometimes you may need to get a fresh start with your iPad information. For whatever reason, you want to get rid of all the information on your iPad in one or all the synced apps and just start over. Follow these steps:

1. As you did to set up the sync previously, connect your iPad to your computer, start iTunes, click your **iPad** in the left nav bar, and click the **Info** tab at the top of the main window.

2. Scroll all the way down to the **Advanced** section (see Figure 3–9).

3. Check one, some, or all of the boxes as you desire.

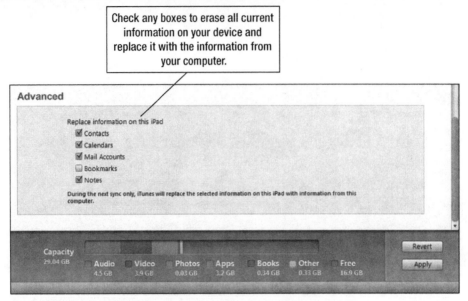

Figure 3–9. *In the Advanced area, select the information you want to replace.*

4. When you are ready, click the **Apply** button in the lower-right corner. The sync should happen immediately. All of the information for the apps you have checked will be erased from the iPad and replaced with the information from your computer.

Apps: Syncing and Managing Them

With iTunes, you can sync and manage your apps on your iPad. It's easy to drag and drop your app icons around on a particular **Home** screen page or even between pages on your iPad.

Syncing Apps in iTunes

Follow these steps to sync and manage apps:

1. As you did to set up the sync previously, connect your iPad to your computer, start iTunes, and click your **iPad** in the left nav bar.

2. Click the **Apps** tab on the top of the main window.

3. Check the **Sync Apps** box to see all apps stored on your iPad and your **Home** screens, as shown in Figure 3–10.

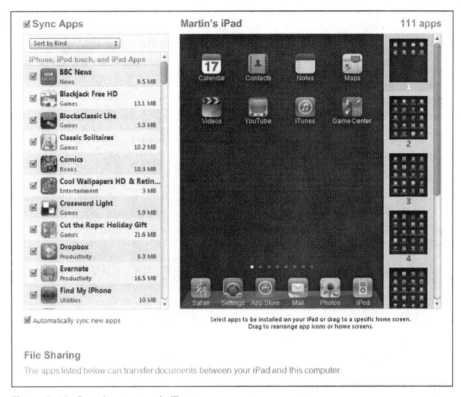

Figure 3–10. *Sync Apps screen in iTunes*

Moving Apps, Working with Folders, or Deleting App Icons

It is easy to move around and organize your application icons in this screen in iTunes.

To move an app within a screen: Click it and drag it around the screen.

To move an app between Home screen pages: Click and drag it to the new page in the right column. The new page expands; drop it on the new page.

To dock an app on the bottom dock: Remove one icon if there are already six icons. Then click and drag the icon to the dock.

To remove an icon: Hover over it to see the X and then click the X.

> NOTE: **You can't remove icons such as Contacts, Settings, Safari and other pre-installed core icons.**

To create a new folder: Drag and drop one icon onto another icon.

To move an app into an existing folder: Drag and drop the icon onto the Folder icon.

To move an app out of a folder: Click the folder to open it. Then drag and drop the icon outside of that folder.

To view another Home screen page: Click that page in the right column.

To delete a folder: Remove all apps from that folder (drag them out) and it will disappear.

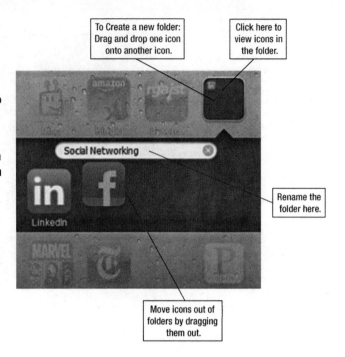

Removing and Reinstalling Apps

To remove an app from your iPad, simply uncheck the box next to it and confirm your selection, as shown in Figure 3–11. Don't worry—since you are syncing apps to your computer in iTunes, you still have a copy of the app inside iTunes.

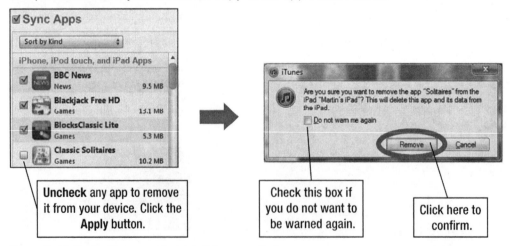

Figure 3–11. *Unchecking an app to delete it from your iPad*

> **TIP**: Even if you delete an app from your iPad, if you have chosen to sync apps as shown, you can still reinstall that app by rechecking the box next to it. The app will be reloaded onto your iPad during the next sync.

Getting Downloaded Items into iTunes to Sync Them

If you buy or download content from the iBookstore, iTunes store, or App Store within iTunes, it automatically appears in your own iTunes library. But how do you get content that you have downloaded from the Web into iTunes? (It does not automatically appear in iTunes.) What happens if something you downloaded is compressed in a .zip file, like an audiobooks? In this section, we help you understand the basic steps of downloading content from the Web to your computer and then getting it into iTunes so you can sync it to your iPad.

> **TIP**: You can also find great audiobooks (both free and paid) from **Audible.com**.

Step 1: Download the content to your computer

Go to the web site where you want to download content. In this case, we want a free audiobook from `http://librivox.org`. We have searched for titles by Mark Twain and want to download the entire set of chapters for *Roughing It*.

Click the link **Zip file of the entire book** in the left column of links. (This 488 MB file will take you between 15 minutes and 4 hours to download depending on the speed of your Internet connection.)

Step 2: Unzip the file, if necessary

Next, locate the file you just downloaded. It will usually be in your Downloads folder. Unzip or uncompress all the files.

This unzipping process will vary depending on what software you have installed on your PC or Mac. However, it usually involves double-clicking to open the zip file. Then select **Unzip**, **Unzip All**, **Extract**, or **Extract All**. Most often, all these files will be unzipped either directly into the **Downloads** folder, or a folder within the **Downloads** folder with the name of the zip file.

Step 3: Drag and drop the content into iTunes

Next, locate the files you extracted and highlight them all. You can select all files in a list by holding the Shift key on your computer keyboard and clicking the top file and then the bottom file in the list.

Then, drag the entire highlighted list over to iTunes and drop it on your library in the top of the left column. You can also use the File ➤ Add File to Library menu command instead of the drag-and-drop method.

Step 4: Select content to sync to your device

Use the steps shown in the sections later in this chapter to sync the downloaded content to your iPad.

How to make sure an Audiobook shows up as an Audiobook (not music)

TIP: some audiobook files appear in your Music Library. Here's how to correct this.

If you downloaded a free audiobook from Librivox.org, then the audiobook will probably appear in your **Music** library, but you can change this. In order to put the files into the correct **Audiobook** library, perform the steps listed below.

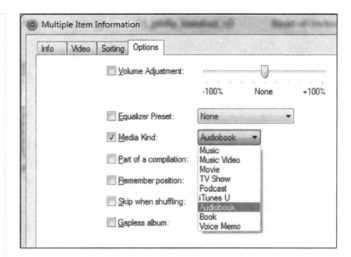

1. View your audio books in Album view to easily select all chapters or parts at once.

2. Then right-click on the audiobook album cover and select **Get Info** or press the shortcut keys **Command + I** (Mac) or **Control + I** (PC). Say **Yes** to the warning pop-up about edit information for multiple items, if you see it.

3. Click on the **Options** tab on the top of the **Multiple Item Information** window.

4. Click the checkbox next to **Media Kind** and select **Audiobook**. (See image above.)

File Sharing (File Transfer) Between Your iPad and Your Computer

As long as you have an app installed that works with files, such as GoodReader or Stanza, you can use iTunes to transfer files between your computer and your iPad. You perform this file transfer using the bottom of the **Apps** tab in iTunes—below all the application icon screens.

> **TIP:** Some apps, such as GoodReader, come with wireless methods for transferring and sharing files. Check out the GoodReader section in Chapter 27: "New Media: Reading Newspapers, Magazines, and More" for more information.

Copying Files from Your Computer to Your iPad

To copy files from your computer to your iPad, follow these steps:

1. As you did to set up the previous sync, connect your iPad to your computer, start iTunes, and click your **iPad** in the left nav bar.

2. Click the **Apps** tab on the top of the main window.

3. Scroll down to the **File Sharing** section below the apps, as shown in Figure 3–12.

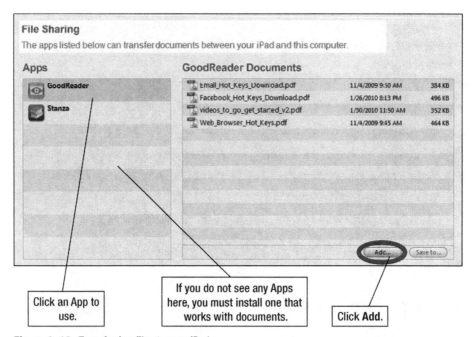

Figure 3–12. *Transferring files to your iPad*

4. Click any app in the left column, and then click the **Add** button in the lower-right corner.

5. A window will pop up. Select a file to transfer and click the **Open** button. The file will be transferred immediately to your iPad.

Copying Files from Your iPad to Your Computer

To copy files from your iPad to your computer, follow these steps:

1. Connect your iPad to your computer, start iTunes, and click your **iPad** in the left nav bar.

2. Click the **Apps** tab at the top of the main window.

3. Scroll down to the **File Sharing** section below the apps (see Figure 3–13).

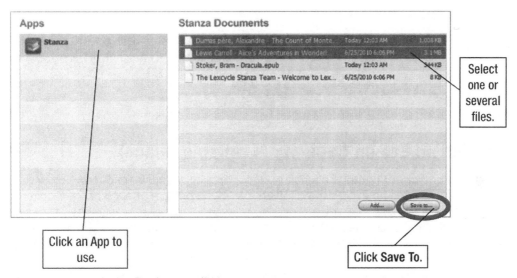

Figure 3–13. *Transferring files from your iPad*

4. Click any app from which you want to transfer the files in the left column.

5. Select one or several files using any of these methods:

   a. Click a single file.

   b. Hold the **Control** key (Windows) or **Option** key (Mac) and click any number of files.

   c. Hold the **Shift** key and click the top and bottom file in a list to select all files in that list.

6. After the file(s) are selected, click the **Save To** button in the lower-right corner.

7. A window will pop up asking you to select a folder on your computer to receive the files from your iPad. Locate and click the folder, and then click the **Select Folder** button. The file(s) will be transferred immediately to your computer.

Syncing Media and More

Now let's look at how to set up an automatic sync for music, movies, iBooks, iTunes U content, and more.

> **CAUTION:** Make sure you're logged into iTunes with the same iTunes account you want to use on your iPad, as Digital Rights Management (DRM)–protected content (music, videos, and more) won't sync unless both accounts match. You can log out and log in to iTunes on both your desktop and your iPad to make sure you are logged into the right accounts.

Keeping an Eye on Capacity (Available Space)

As you begin to select ringtones, music, videos, books, podcasts, and more to sync, you will want to keep an eye on the capacity bar at the bottom of each of the iTunes sync screens. If you see that you are nearing or exceeding capacity with any of your selections, you know you need to make a few adjustments. Sometimes you just can't take it all with you! Figure 3–14 shows that we currently have 15.6 GB (gigabytes) free on our iPad for more content—so we have plenty of free space.

Figure 3–14. *Watch the free space available as you make sync selections in iTunes*

Syncing Ringtones

When you click the **Ringtones** tab, you can choose to sync your entire ringtone library or selected items. Ringtones are used for **FaceTime** calls on the iPad.

1. Connect your iPad to your computer, start iTunes, and click your **iPad** in the left nav bar.

2. Click the **Ringtones** tab at the top of the main window.

3. Check the **Sync Ringtones** box, shown to the right.

4. The default is to sync all ringtones. To sync only specific ones, click the radio button next to **Selected ringtones**.

5. When you are done with your selections, click the **Apply** button to start the ringtone sync.

> **TIP**: Learn how to assign ringtones to your contacts, purchase custom ringtones, and create your own ringtones from your music in Chapter 18: "FaceTime Video Messaging and Skype."

Syncing Music

When you click the **Music** tab, you can choose to sync your entire music library or selected items.

> **CAUTION**: If you have manually transferred some music, music videos, or voice memos to your iPad already, you'll receive a warning message that all existing content on your iPad will be removed and replaced with the selected music library from your computer.

To sync music from your computer to your iPad, follow these steps:

1. Connect your iPad to your computer, start iTunes, and click your **iPad** in the left nav bar.

2. Click the **Music** tab on the top of the main window.

3. Check the **Sync Music** box (see Figure 3–15).

4. Click next to **Entire music library** only if you are *sure* your music library will not be too large for your iPad.

5. Click next to **Selected playlists, artists, and genres** if you are unsure whether your music library is too large, or if you want to sync only specific playlists or artists.

6. You can choose whether to include music videos and voice memos by checking those boxes.

7. You can also automatically fill free space with songs.

> **CAUTION:** We don't recommend checking this option because it will take up all the space in your iPad and leave no room for all those cool apps!

8. Now check off any of the playlists or artists in the two columns on the bottom of the screen. You can even use the search box at the top of the **Artists** column to search for particular artists.

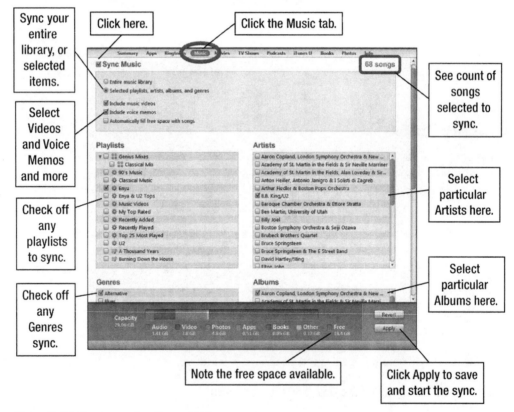

Figure 3–15. *Syncing music with your iPad*

Syncing Movies

When you click the **Movies** tab, you can choose to sync specific, recent, or unwatched movies, or all of them.

To sync movies from your computer to your iPad, follow these steps:

1. Connect your iPad to your computer, start iTunes, and click your **iPad** in the left nav bar.

2. Click the **Movies** tab on the top of the main window.

3. Check the **Sync Movies** box (see Figure 3–16).

4. If you'd like to sync recent or unwatched movies, check the **Automatically include** box and use the pull-down to select **All, 1 most recent, All unwatched, 5 most recent unwatched**, etc.

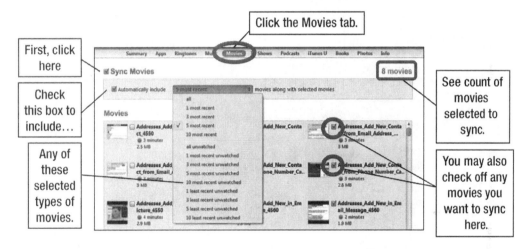

Figure 3–16. *Configuring movie sync to automatically include selections*

5. If you selected any item besides **All**, you have the choice to sync specific movies or videos to your iPad. Simply check the boxes next to the movies you want to include in the sync.

Syncing TV Shows

When you click the **TV Shows** tab, you can choose to sync specific, recent, or unwatched TV shows, or all of them.

To sync TV shows from your computer to your iPad, follow these steps:

1. Connect your iPad to your computer, start iTunes, and click your **iPad** in the left nav bar.

2. Click the **TV Shows** tab on the top of the main window.

3. Check the **Sync TV Shows** box (see Figure 3–17).

4. If you'd like to sync recent or unwatched TV shows, check the **Automatically include** box and use the pull-down to select **All, 1 newest, All unwatched, 5 oldest unwatched, 10 newest unwatched**, etc.

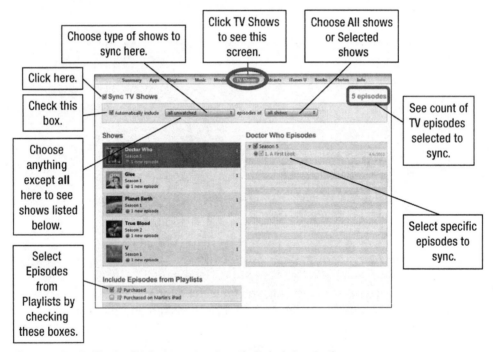

Figure 3–17. *Configuring TV show sync to automatically include selections*

5. Choose **all Shows** or **selected Shows** next to **episodes of**.

6. If you choose **Selected Shows**, you can choose individual shows and even individual episodes in the two sections in the middle of the screen.

7. If you have playlists of TV shows, you can select those for inclusion by checking the boxes in the bottom section of the screen.

Syncing Podcasts

When you click the **Podcasts** tab, you can choose to sync specific, recent, or unplayed podcasts, or all of them.

> **TIP:** Podcasts are audio or video shows that are usually regularly scheduled (e.g., daily, weekly, or monthly). Most are free to subscribe to in the iTunes store. When you subscribe and set up the auto sync as shown in this section, you'll receive all your favorite podcasts on your iPad.
>
> Many of your favorite radio shows are recorded and broadcast as podcasts. We encourage you to check out the **Podcast** section of the iTunes store to see what might interest you. You'll find podcasts of movie reviews, news shows, law school test reviews, game shows, old radio shows, educational content, and much more.

To sync podcasts from your computer to your iPad, follow these steps.

1. Connect your iPad to your computer, start iTunes, and click your **iPad** in the left nav bar.

2. Click the **Podcasts** tab on the top of the main window.

3. Check the **Sync Podcasts** box (see Figure 3–18).

4. If you'd like to sync recent or unplayed podcasts, check the **Automatically include** box and use the pull-down to select **All, 1 newest, All unplayed, 5 newest, 10 most recent unplayed**, etc.

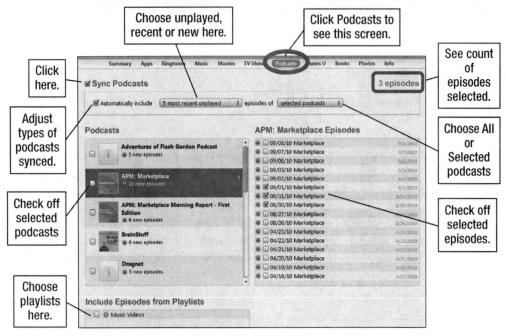

Figure 3–18. *Configuring podcast sync to automatically include selections*

5. Choose **All Podcasts** or **Selected Podcasts** next to **episodes of**.

6. If you choose **Selected Podcasts**, you can choose individual podcasts and even individual episodes in the two sections in the middle of the screen.

7. If you have playlists of podcasts, you can select those for inclusion by checking the boxes in the bottom section of the screen.

> **TIP:** After you sync these podcasts, you can enjoy them in the **Podcasts** section of the **Music** app on your device.

Syncing iTunes U

When you click the **iTunes U** tab, you can choose to sync specific, recent, or unplayed iTunes U content, or all content.

> **TIP**: iTunes U podcasts are similar to other audio or video podcasts, except that they focus on educational content and are mostly produced by colleges and universities. Most are free to subscribe to in the iTunes store. When you subscribe and set up the auto sync as shown in this section, you'll receive all your favorite iTunes U podcasts on your iPad.
>
> Be sure to check out the **iTunes U** section in the iTunes store. You may find your favorite college or university has shows to teach you biology, astronomy, or a whole lot more. There's even a Stanford University course on how to develop iPad apps! Many of the top universities broadcast class lectures from famous professors in iTunes U. Go ahead and check it out—what you'll find is amazing!

To sync iTunes U content from your computer to your iPad, follow these steps.

1. Connect your iPad to your computer, start iTunes, and click your **iPad** in the left nav bar.

2. Click the **iTunes U** tab on the top of the main window.

3. Check the **Sync iTunes U** box (see Figure 3–19).

4. If you'd like to sync recent or unplayed items, check the **Automatically include** box and use the pull-down to select **All, 1 newest, All unplayed, 5 newest, 10 most recent unplayed**, etc.

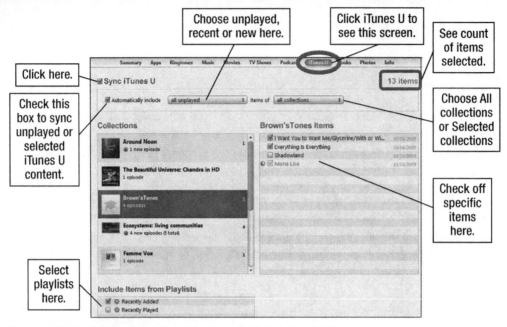

Figure 3–19. *Configuring iTunes U sync to automatically include selections*

5. Choose **All Collections** or **Selected Collections** next to **items of**.

6. If you choose **Selected Collections**, you can choose individual collections and even individual items in the two sections in the middle of the screen.

7. If you have playlists of iTunes U podcasts, you can select those for inclusion by checking the boxes in the bottom section of the screen under **Include Items from Playlists**.

Syncing iBooks, PDF files, and Audiobooks

When you click the **Books** tab, you can choose to sync all or selected books and audiobooks.

> **TIP:** Books on the iPad are electronic versions of their paper cousins. They are in a specific electronic format called *ePub*. You can buy them in the iBookstore on the iPad or acquire them from other locations and sync them to your iPad using the steps described here. Books you acquire elsewhere must be unprotected or "DRM-free" in order to sync them to your iPad. You read these books in the **iBooks** app or in other book reader apps on your iPad. See Chapter 12: "iBooks and E-Books" to learn more.

To sync books, PDF files, or audiobooks between your computer and your iPad, follow these steps:

> **TIP:** You can find free iBooks to download by doing a search for "project gutenberg" in the iBookstore. You can find free audiobooks to download by going to `http://librivox.org` from your computer web browser and downloading public domain audiobooks. (These free audiobooks are typically not read by professional actors but by volunteers, so the quality may vary.) See the section "Getting Downloaded Items into iTunes to Sync Them" in this chapter to see exactly how to download and sync free audiobooks.

1. Connect your iPad to your computer, start iTunes, and click your **iPad** in the left nav bar.

2. Click the **Books** tab on the top of the main window.

3. Check the **Sync Books** and **Sync Audiobooks** boxes (see Figure 3–20).

4. If you'd like to sync all books, leave the default **All books** selection.

5. Otherwise, choose **Selected books** and make your choices by checking specific books in the window.

> **TIP:** In order to sync iBooks, PDF files, and other similar documents to your iPad, you need to first drag and drop your file from your computer into your iTunes library. Grab the file from any folder on your computer, and drag and drop it right on your library in the upper left column in iTunes.

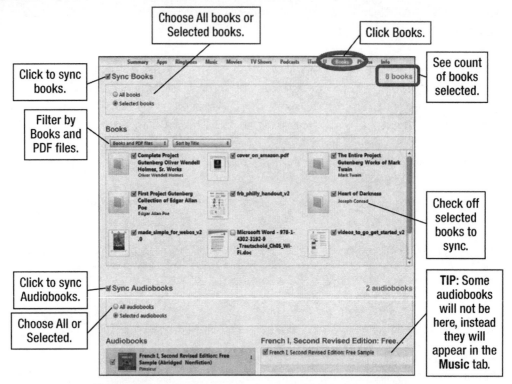

Figure 3–20. *Configuring books and audiobooks sync to automatically include selections*

6. If you would like to sync all audiobooks, leave the default **All audiobooks** selection.

7. Otherwise, choose **Selected audiobooks** and make your choices by checking off specific audiobooks in the window below this selection item.

TIP: After you sync these books, you can enjoy them in the **iBooks** app on your device. You can listen to audiobooks in the **iPod** app, where the **Audiobooks** tab is on the left side.

NOTE: Audiobooks from **Audible** require that you first authorize your computer with your **Audible** account before you can sync them to your iPad from your computer.

Syncing Photos

When you click the **Photos** tab, you can choose to sync photos from all folders or selected folders and you can even include videos.

> **TIP**: You can create a beautiful electronic picture frame and share your photos on the stunning iPad screen (see Chapter: 16 "iPad Photography"). You can even use your photos to set the background wallpaper and screen-lock wallpaper (see Chapter 7: "Personalize and Secure Your iPad" for more information).

To sync photos from your computer to your iPad, follow these steps:

1. Connect your iPad to your computer, start iTunes, and click your **iPad** in the left nav bar.

> **TIP**: Mac users can also sync photos using **iPhoto** or **Aperture**, including Events (time-based sync), Faces (person-based sync), and Places (location-based sync).

2. Click the **Photos** tab on the top of the main window.

3. Check the **Sync Photos from** box (see Figure 3–21).

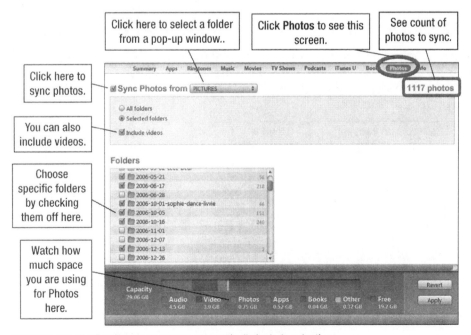

Figure 3–21. *Configuring photo sync to automatically include selections*

4. Click the pull-down menu next to **Sync Photos from** and select a folder where your photos are stored. If you want to grab all your photos, go to the highest folder level possible (e.g., C: on your Windows computer or "/" on your Apple Mac).

5. If you'd like to sync all photos from the selected folder on your computer, select **All folders**, shown in Figure 3–21.

> **CAUTION:** Because your photo library on your computer may be too large to fit on your iPad, be careful about checking **All folders**.

6. Otherwise, choose **Selected folders** and make your choices by checking specific folders in the window below, as shown in Figure 3–21.

7. You can also include any videos in the folders by checking the **Include videos** box, as shown in Figure 3–21.

8.   When you are done choosing your photos to sync, click the **Apply** button to save your settings and start the sync.

9. When the sync starts, you'll see the status in the middle-top status window in iTunes.

How to Know What Is New or Unplayed in iTunes

You may notice little numbers next to items in the left nav bar of iTunes (see Figure 3–22). There are similar little blue numbers in the upper-right corner of items in the main window. These numbers show how many items are unplayed, unwatched, or, in the case of apps, require updates.

Figure 3–22. *Quickly seeing the number of unplayed items*

Manually Transferring Music, Movies, Podcasts, and More on Your iPad (Drag-and-Drop Method)

The Auto Sync sections showed you how to automatically sync content to your iPad. Here you'll learn how to manually transfer songs, videos, books, audiobooks, and more. The process is the same for all types of content, so we'll show you how to do it for just one type.

> **TIP**: Use these same drag-and-drop techniques to add items to a playlist.

To manually transfer content from your computer to your iPad, follow these steps:

> **NOTE**: Be sure to check **Manually manage music and videos** on the **Summary** tab in iTunes before you try to drag and drop music or videos. If you've chosen to automatically sync content (e.g., music, movies, podcasts, etc.), you won't be able to use this drag-and-drop method to copy items to your iPad.

1. Connect your iPad to your computer, and start iTunes.

2. In the left nav bar, click your **iPad**. Then click the **Summary** tab at the top. Near the bottom of the screen, make sure the **Manually manage music and videos** box is checked. You may see a warning message if you have previously synced music or videos to your iPad, saying that all previously synced music and videos will be replaced with your iTunes library. This is OK.

    ☑ Manually manage music and videos

3. In the left nav bar, under the **LIBRARY** heading, click the type of content (**Music, Movies, TV Shows, Podcasts, iTunes U**, etc.) you'd like to transfer.

4. In the main window, you'll see your library of content. It's usually easiest to select **List View** from the top of iTunes, as shown in Figure 3–23. This allows you to see all the content in a list and easily select a single item or group of items.

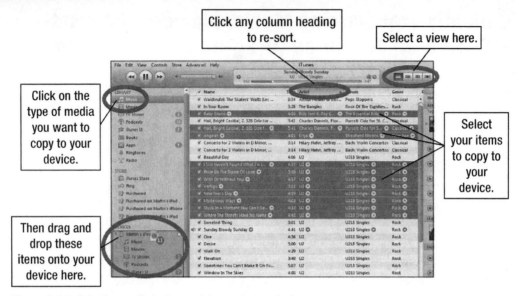

Figure 3–23. *Selecting media to drag and drop onto your device*

5. Here is how to select content individually, in a list or separated:

a. To select an individual item, simply click it to highlight it.

b. To select items that are not in a continuous list, Windows users press and hold the **Control** key while clicking items, and Mac users press and hold the **Command** key while clicking items.

c. To select items in a continuous list, press and hold the **Shift** key while clicking first the top item and then the bottom item in the list. All the items in between will be selected.

▶	Name		Time	Artist
☑	Hail, Bright Cecilia!, Z. 328 Ode fo...		3:41	Charles D
☑	Big Lie Small World	⊕	5:05	David Har
☑	Tomorrow We'll See	⊕	4:49	David Har
☑	Water Music Suite No.2 in D, H...	⊕	4:01	English Ba
☑	Canon and Gigue in D Major: I....	⊕	4:32	English Co
☑	Watermark	⊕	2:26	Enya
☑	Cursum Perficio	⊕	4:09	Enya
☑	On Your Shore	⊕	4:00	Enya
☑	Storms in Africa	⊕	4:05	Enya
☑	Exile	⊕	4:22	Enya
☑	Miss Clare Remembers	⊕	2:00	Enya
☑	Orinoco Flow	⊕	4:26	Enya
☑	Evening Falls...	⊕	3:49	Enya
☑	River	⊕	3:12	Enya
☑	The Longships		3:39	Enya
☑	Na Laetha Gael M'Óige		3:57	Enya

6. Then, to copy these items to your iPad, simply click and drag the selected item(s) over to your iPad and let go of the mouse button. All selected items will then be copied to your iPad in the left column under DEVICES.

Troubleshooting iTunes and the Sync

Sometimes iTunes does not behave exactly as you'd expect it to, so here are a few simple troubleshooting tips.

Check Out the Apple Knowledgebase for Helpful Articles

The first step when you're having a problem is to check out Apple's support pages, where you'll find lots of helpful information. On your iPad or computer's web browser, go to this web page and click a topic or device for help:

http://www.apple.com/support/ipad/

iTunes Locked Up and Will Not Respond (Windows Computer)

1. Bring up the **Windows Task Manager** by simultaneously pressing the **Ctrl** + **Alt** + **Del** keys on your keyboard. The **Task Manager** should look something like Figure 3–24.

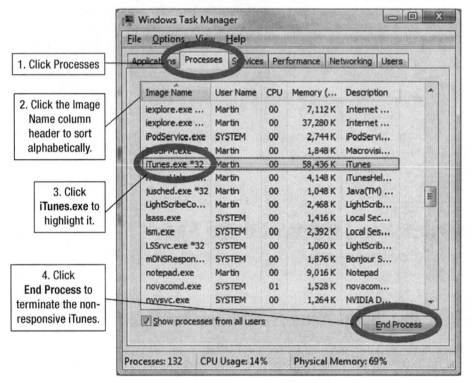

Figure 3–24. *Locating* iTunes.exe *in Windows Task Manager to terminate it*

2. Then, to end the process, click **End process** from the pop-up window.

3. Now, iTunes should be forced to close.

4. Try restarting iTunes.

5. If iTunes will not start or it locks up again, reboot your computer and try again.

iTunes Locked Up and Will Not Respond (Mac Computer)

> **TIP:** Pressing **Command** + **Option** + **Escape** is the shortcut to bring up the **Force Quit Applications** window shown in Figure 3–25.

1. Go up to the iTunes Menu at the top and click.

2. Click **Quit iTunes.**

3. If that doesn't work, go to any other program and click the small Apple in the upper left-hand corner.

4. Click **Force Quit** and the list of running programs will be displayed.

5. Highlight iTunes and click the **Force Quit** button.

6. If this does not help, try restarting your Mac.

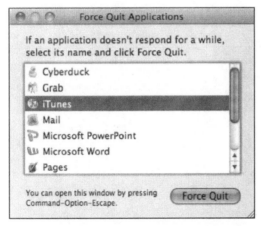

Figure 3–25. *Force Quit Applications window on Mac computers*

Updating Your iPad Operating System

You can check for updated software and install updated operating system (called "iOS") software using iTunes.

> **NOTE:** Do this update when you won't mind being without your iPad for 30 minutes or more, depending on the amount of information on your iPad and the speed of your computer and Internet connection.

Normally, iTunes will automatically check for updates on a set schedule, about every two weeks. If no update is found, iTunes will tell you when it will check for another update.

To manually check for updated iOS software in iTunes and install it, perform the following steps: and see Figure 3–26:

1.   Start iTunes.

2.   Connect your iPad to your computer.

3.   Click your **iPad**, listed under **DEVICES** in the left nav bar.

4.   Click the **Summary** tab in the top nav bar.

5.   Click the **Check for Update** button in the center of the screen in the **Version** section.

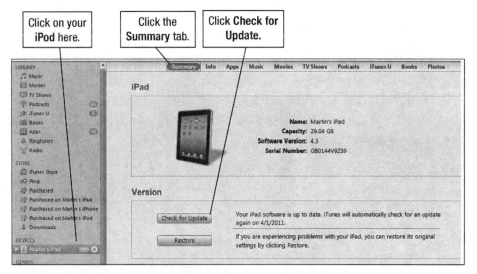

Figure 3–26. *Checking for updated software*

6.   If you have the latest version, you'll see a pop-up window saying something like "This version of the iPad software (4.x.x) is the current version." Click **OK** to close the window. You are done with the update process.

7. If you don't have the latest version, a window similar to the one shown to the right will tell you a new version is available and ask if you would like to update. Click **Download and Update**.

8. iTunes will take you through a few screens that describe the update and ask you to agree to the software license. If you agree, click **Next** and **Agree** to download the latest iOS software from Apple. This will take about 5–10 minutes.

TIP: We show you all the screens you might see in this update process in the "Reinstalling the iPad Operating System" section of Chapter 29: "Troubleshooting."

9. Next, iTunes will back up your iPad, which might take 10 minutes or more if your iPad is filled with data.

10. Now the new iOS will be installed and your iPad erased.

11. Finally, you'll be presented with the screen allowing you to set your iPad up as a new one or restore it from a backup.

   a. Choose **Set up as a new iPad** if you want to erase all your data after the update process

   b. Choose **Restore from the backup of**, and make sure you select the correct backup file (usually the most recent one).

Now your iPad will be restored or set up as you selected and your iPad OS update is complete.

Chapter 4

Other Sync Methods

In Chapter 3: "Sync Your iPad with iTunes," you learned how to connect your iPad to your computer and use iTunes to sync your personal information, music, videos, and more. In this chapter, we explore some alternative ways to wirelessly synchronize information to your iPad. The benefit of the wireless methods is that you don't need to connect your iPad to your computer to have the information updated. Everything happens over the air—automatically. The two methods we cover are Apple's MobileMe Service and Exchange/Google Sync.

> **NOTE:** If you use the Gmail account setting instead of Exchange (as we describe in this chapter) to set up your Gmail, you will be able to wirelessly sync your email, calendar, and notes, but not your Google contacts. So if you don't need Google Contacts synced, you can use the Gmail setting instead of Exchange.

Wireless Sync of Your Google, Hotmail or Exchange Information

Using the steps we describe here, your iPad can wirelessly sync your email, contacts, and calendar from a Microsoft Exchange account or a Google Account.

> **TIP:** You can now wirelessly sync multiple Exchange accounts on your iPad. If you have several Google, Hotmail,or Microsoft Exchange accounts, you can wirelessly sync all accounts at the same time to your iPad.

Why Do We Say Google/Exchange?

We use the words Google and Exchange interchangeably here because you set up your Google sync using the Exchange setting on your iPad. Google has licensed Microsoft

Exchange ActiveSync so you can now set up your Google account just like an Exchange account and enjoy the same push email, contacts, and calendar functionality. We know it is a little confusing, but you set up both your Google and Exchange accounts in the identical manner, using the Exchange settings on your iPad—so we say Google/Exchange.

Between the time of writing the original iPad book and this iPad 2 book, Hotmail has also added ActiveSync capabilities, so we have included information in this chapter about setting up Hotmail as well.

If You Want a Google Account, Create One

If you don't have a Microsoft Exchange account, but you still want a wireless sync, then you should set up a free Google account to store your contacts and calendar. The account will allow you to start using Google Mail (Gmail), Contacts, and Calendar.

To set up your Google account, follow these steps:

1. From your computer web browser (you can't create a Gmail account your iPad) type in: www.gmail.com.

2. Click the **Create an account** button.

3. On the next screen, enter the information requested and click the button at the bottom of the page that says **I accept. Create my account.**

4. If successful, you'll see a screen that says **Congratulations!** Click the **Show me my account** button to get started.

5. To see your Calendar, click the **Calendar** link in the upper left corner (see Figure 4–1).

6. To see your Contacts, click the **Contacts** link in the left side of the Gmail Inbox page.

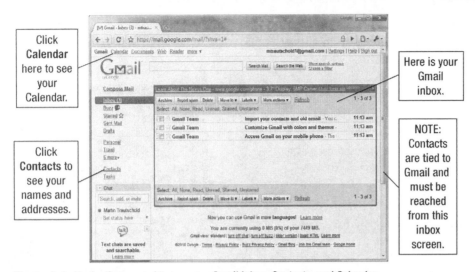

Figure 4–1. *Navigating around to see your Gmail Inbox, Contacts, and Calendar*

As soon as you set up the sync as shown in this chapter, you will begin to see all changes to your contacts and calendar from Google magically appear on your iPad. The same goes for any changes or additions from your iPad—they will automatically appear in Google in moments.

> **TIP**: It is extremely easy for your Google Contacts list grow into the thousands because it automatically includes everyone you have ever emailed from your Gmail account. You may want to clean up your list before you set up the sync to your iPad.

Set Up Your Google, Hotmail, or Exchange Account on Your iPad

The following steps show you how to set up the wireless sync for either your Exchange account or your Google contacts and calendar:

1. Touch the **Settings** icon on your iPad.

2. Touch **Mail, Contacts, and Calendars**.

3. In the right column, you'll see a list of your email accounts and, below that, the **Add Account** option.

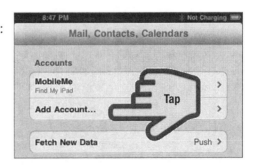

If you have no accounts set up, you will see only **Add Account**. In either case, tap **Add Account.**

4. On the next screen, choose **Microsoft Exchange**.

NOTE: You should choose Microsoft Exchange if you want to have the wireless sync with your Google Contacts and Calendar. If you select Gmail, you will not be able to wirelessly sync your Google Contacts and Notes, but not your Calendar.

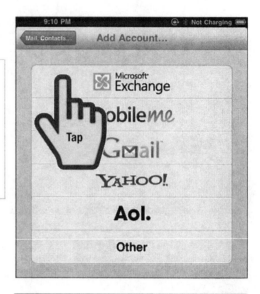

5. Type your email address.

TIP: To type the **.com** (or .net, .edu, .org, etc.) in the email address, press and hold the period key until you see the **.com** key appear above it. Slide over and press **.com**.

6. Many times, your email address is also your username. If so, it's easier to copy and paste than re-type. To copy your e-mail address into the Username field, follow these steps:

    a. Touch and hold the **email address** until you see the black pop-up appear above it. Tap **Select All**.

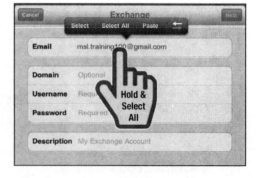

b. Tap **Copy**.

c. Double-tap in the **Username** field (you can also touch and hold) until you see the pop-up appear and tap **Paste**.

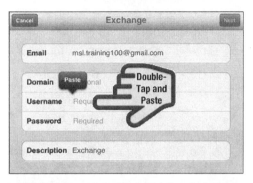

7. For Gmail, leave the **Domain** blank.

For Exchange email, you may need to enter the Domain name supplied by your administrator.
Type your **Password.**
If you want, you can adjust the **Description** of the account, which defaults to your email address.

8. Tap the **Next** button in the upper right corner.

9. You may see an **Unable to Verify Certificate** screen as shown. If you do see it, click **Accept** to continue.

10. For Gmail, type **m.google.com** in the **Server** field.
    For Hotmail, type **m.hotmail.com** In the **Server** field.
    For Exchange email, enter your server address. (Example: **mobile.servername.com**)

11. Click **Next** in the upper right corner.

12. On this screen you have the option to turn the **Mail, Contacts,** and **Calendars** wireless sync **On** or **Off**. For each sync you'd like to turn on, tap the switch to change it to **On**.

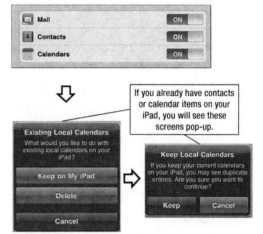

NOTE: If you already have contacts or calendar items on your iPad, you may see warning pop-up messages after you tap Yes next to Contacts and Calendar.

Your choices are to **Keep on My iPad** or **Delete**. If you choose **Cancel** it stops setting up your Exchange account.

Select **Keep on My iPad** to keep all existing contacts and calendar events on your iPad. These items will not end up on your Google or Exchange account—they will stay on your iPad.

You may end up with some duplicate contacts or calendar events on your iPad if the same ones already exist on your Google or Exchange account.

Select **Delete** if you already have these contacts or calendar items in your Exchange or Google account and do not want to duplicate them.

13. Tap **Save** to save your settings.

14. You're done with the initial setup of your account. You should see your new account listed under the **Accounts** heading on the **Mail, Contacts, Calendars** screen .

Edit or Delete Your Google, Hotmail, or Exchange Account

After you set up your Google, Hotmail, or Exchange account on your iPad, you may want to adjust some of the default settings, such as which mail folders are synced (only the inbox by default), number of days of mail to sync (default is three days), and other settings. You would also use the steps shown here to remove or delete the account.

1. Get into your Mail settings screen as you did when you first set up your account (tap the **Settings** icon, tap **Mail, Contacts, Calendars**).

2. Tap the mail account you wish to adjust or remove.

3. In order to change your account username, account name, or password, tap **Account** at the top. You will see the information you saw when you first set up this account.

4. If you want to remove this account from your iPad, tap **Delete Account** at the bottom and confirm your selection.

5. To enable or disable wireless syncing for **Mail**, **Contacts**, and **Calendar** items, tap the switches to set them **On** or **Off**.

> **NOTE**: If you set any switch to Off for these items, they will all be deleted from your iPad. For example, all synced contacts would immediately be deleted from your **Contacts** app.

6. To adjust how much mail is synced to your iPad, tap **Mail Days to Sync** and adjust to suit your needs (you can go from **1 Day** to **No Limit**, with 3 Days as the default).

    Tap the button with your **Email Account Name** in the upper left corner to save your choices and return to the previous screen.

7. **Tap Mail Folders to Push to** specify which mail folders should sync to your iPad.

   The default is just the **Inbox**, but you can tap to select any number of folders. (Each selected folder is shown with a check mark.)

   > **TIP:** You can only move mail between these folders on your iPad if you have selected them here to sync.

8. Tap the **Email Account Name** in the upper left corner to save your choices and return to the previous screen.

9. Then tap the **Done** button in the upper right corner to finish with this account and return to your **Settings**.

10. Press the **Home** button to return to the **Home** screen.

Working with Wirelessly Synced Data on Your iPad

Once you set up the wireless sync, your Contacts and Calendar information will flow quickly into your iPad. If you have thousands of contacts, it could take several minutes for the first sync to complete.

You may want to jump ahead and review Chapter 14: "Working with Contacts" and Chapter 15: "Your Calendar" for details about working with both apps.

> **NOTE:** Since the sync with Google or Exchange is wireless, you'll need to make sure you have an active network connection from your iPad. Check out Chapter 5: "Wi-Fi and 3G Connectivity" to learn more.

New Group for Google/Exchange Contacts

For each Google/Exchange account you add to your iPad, you will end up with a separate group in your **Contacts** app. If you've added some contacts to your iPad or synced it at least once with iTunes, you may end up with additional groups of contacts (see Figure 4–2).

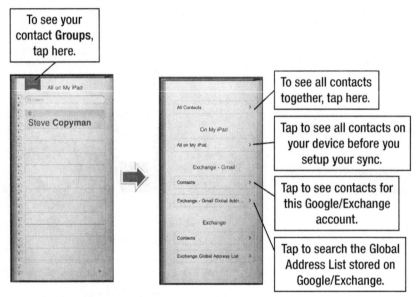

Figure 4–2. *You may see various groups in your Contacts.*

The default view in your **Contacts** list is to see all contacts from all synced accounts. You can selectively view contacts from various accounts. To view your Google or Exchange contacts, follow these steps:

1. Tap the **Contacts** icon.

2. Tap the **Groups** tab in the upper left corner.

3. If you've added new contacts or synced your address book, you'll see a **From My PC** or **From My Mac** group at the top. Under that you will see your Google or Exchange email address or the descriptive name assigned to that account when you set it up. **Exchange - Gmail** and **Exchange** are the two Google/Exchange accounts synced in our example (see Figure 4–2).

4. Tap the **Contacts** listed under your Google or Exchange email address/account name to see all your synced contacts.

Working with Contacts

To add, edit, or delete contacts in your Google or Exchange contacts group, do the following:

1. Follow the steps to view your Google or Exchange contacts group.

2. **To add a contact**: Tap the + button in the upper right corner of the **Contacts** list view. Add contact details (covered in Chapter 14: "Working with Contacts.") Touch **Done** in the upper right corner.

3. **To edit a contact**: Locate the contact in the list and tap the **Edit** button at the bottom under the contact details. Make any changes and press the **Done** button.

4. **To delete a contact**: Locate the contact you want to remove. Tap the **Edit** button under the contact details. Scroll to the bottom of the details and tap the **Delete Contact** button.

5. **To search for a contact on your iPad**:

    a. If you don't see the **Search** window at the top, drag your finger all the way up the right-side alphabet to the top.

    b. Tap in the **Search** window and type a few letters of someone's first name, last name, or company name to find them.

    c. Your **Contacts** list will immediately be filtered by what you type. If you see the name you want, tap it. Otherwise, tap the **Search** button in the lower right corner.

6. **To perform a global address list search:**

    a. Tap the **Groups** tab in the upper left corner (see Figure 4–2).

    b. Tap the second button under the Google/Exchange contacts group, the **Global Address List** search button. If your email address is long, then you will see only your email address on this button; however, if you have a short email address or have provided a short descriptive name, then you will see something like **Exchange - Global Address List** (see Figure 4–2).

    c. Tap in the **Search** window and type a few letters of someone's first name, last name, or company name to find them.

    d. Press the **Search** button to start searching.

The great thing is that any changes you make to your Google or Exchange contacts on your iPad are wirelessly communicated and appear in your Google or Exchange account in just a few seconds.

> **NOTE:** To add, edit, or delete contacts in your other group (not the Google or Exchange group), first go to that group (**From My PC** or **From My Mac**), then make the changes you want. These additions, edits, or deletions will not affect your Google or Exchange contacts—they are kept separate.

Working with the Calendar

After you set up the sync with the Google or Exchange calendar on your iPad, all the calendar events will appear on your iPad—no wires or sync cable required. You will also be able to invite people to meetings and respond to meeting invitations.

Any event you change or update on your iPad will be wirelessly synced with Google or Exchange.

Each Calendar Has a Different Color

You will also notice that every new Google or Exchange account you add to your iPad will create a separate calendar with a new color.

To see the color used for each calendar, tap the **Calendars** button in the upper left corner.

On this screen you can see the color for each calendar.

You can selectively show calendars by tapping on the **email address**.

To hide a calendar, tap the **email address** to remove the checkmark.

To show a calendar, tap the **email address** to add the checkmark.

Invite People to Meetings from Your iPad

Now you can invite people to your calendar events. Here are the steps to follow:

1. Tap your **Calendar** icon to start your calendar.

2. Touch the + button in the lower right corner to schedule a new event.

3. On the **Add Event** screen, enter the meeting title and location and adjust the starting and ending time as required.

4. Tap the **Invitees** tab to invite people (see Figure 4–3.)

5. In order to invite someone, you have a few options.

    a. Type his or her **email address** (all invitations are sent via email).

    b. Type a few letters of his or her first and last name separated by a space to instantly locate the person if he or she is in your contact list.

    c. Or, tap the **blue plus sign** to find someone by browsing your contact list.

6. Touch the **name** and **email address** you want to use. If someone has more than one email address, you'll need to select one.

7. Add more invitees if you desire, then tap **Done** to exit the **Add Invitees** window.

8. Adjust any other items in the **Add Event** screen and tap **Done** to save.

9. The meeting invitation(s) will be sent via email immediately to everyone you invited.

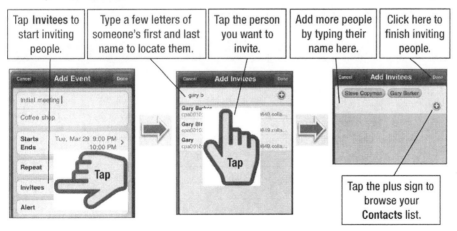

Figure 4–3. *How to invite people to meetings.*

Seeing the Status of Invitees on Your Calendar

You can see who has accepted, rejected, or not replied your invitations by viewing the status of the invitations in the left column of your Calendar.

You will see the status of each person's reply shown next to their status. The various status indicators you will see are:

- **No reply**
- **Accepted**
- **Maybe**
- **Declined**

● **Invitation: Initial meeting @ Tue Mar 29 9pm - 10pm (Martin Trautschold)**	9 PM to 10 PM
Coffee shop	
from	Martha Sanders
my status	Accepted
invitees	Steve Copyman, Gary Mazo, Martin Trautschold
alert	15 minutes before
notes	more details » <https://www.google.com/calendar/event?action=VIEW& more...

Responding to Exchange Meeting Invitations from Your iPad

When you are connected to an Exchange email server and the person who invited you to a meeting is also on the same Exchange server, you will be able to use the **Invitations** inbox inside your Calendar app.

You will receive notifications on your **Calendar** icon, shown here. In this image, there are four new meeting invitations.

Follow these steps to work with Exchange meeting invitations in your Calendar invitations inbox. You will also receive an alert pop-up on the iPad screen similar to the one shown in Figure 4–4. If you are ready to respond immediately to the meeting, tap **View** from the pop-up alert.

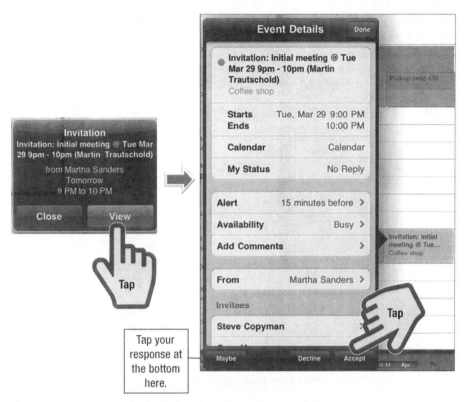

Figure 4–4. *Reply to meeting invitations from the pop-up alert window*

If you want to reply later, simply tap **Close** from the alert. Then you can use the **Invitations** inbox in your **Calendar** to reply.

1. Start your **Calendar** app.

2. Tap the **Invitations** inbox button in the upper left corner of the **Calendar** screen (see Figure 4–5).

3. If you only have one invitation, it will open. If you have multiple invitations, you will see all your invitations listed. Tap the invitation to which you wish to respond.

4. To respond to the invitation, tap one of the three buttons at the bottom of the Event screen: **Accept**, **Maybe**, or **Decline.**

5. If you select **Accept** or **Maybe**, the calendar event is added to your iPad calendar and the response is sent immediately via email to the meeting organizer. You're done.

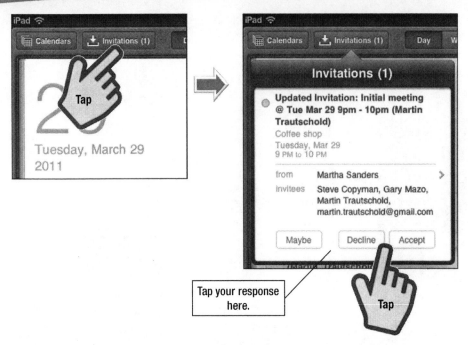

Figure 4–5. *Replying to Exchange meeting invitations using the calendar Invitations inbox*

Responding to Google or Hotmail Meeting Invitations from Your iPad

If you are using Google or Hotmail Calendar with Exchange sync, you will be able to reply to meeting invitations in the **Mail** app on your iPad.

1. Tap your **Mail** icon to start the program.

2. Navigate to the **Inbox**, which has the meeting invitation.

3. Locate the invitation.

Most invitations look something like the image shown here. Usually they start with the word **Invitation**.

> **TIP**: To quickly find all meeting invitations in your inbox, type the word **meet** or **invitation** in the search box. Tap the **Subject** button to search only the message subjects.

4. Tap the **Meeting Invitation** to open it.

5. Tap **Yes**, **Maybe**, or **No** next to **Going?** to reply to the invitation.

6. As soon as you tap one of the choices, your reply will be sent. You may be shown a Google or Hotmail Calendar web page to type optional details in your invitation reply.

Wireless Sync Using the MobileMe Service

Another option if you do not use Google or Exchange and still want to wirelessly sync your information is to use the MobileMe service from Apple. The MobileMe service provides a great service to wirelessly sync your personal information between your computer (PC or Mac) and your iPad and other mobile devices, such as an iPad.

The MobileMe Cloud: The MobileMe service uses what is sometimes called a cloud to sync all your information. The MobileMe Cloud is a term used to describe the web servers where all your MobileMe information is stored on the Internet. The servers and the associated software you install on your computer (PC or Mac) and your mobile devices (iPhone, iPad, etc.) help keep all your mobile devices in sync with your computer. The idea is that changed information (a new calendar event, a new contact name) gets sent from your iPad to the cloud. Then the cloud disperses the changed information to all the devices in your MobileMe account, such as your computer, iPhone, or iPad.

Once you set up MobileMe from your computer and then set up access from your iPad, all your personal information (contacts, calendar, even bookmarks) will be shared wirelessly between your computer and your iPad.

In addition to the wireless sync of personal information, MobileMe lets you do the following:

- Create a web-based photo gallery that you can access and add to from your iPad.

- Create an **iDisk** that allows you to share documents easily between your iPad and your computer. You can also use it to share files that are too large to email (some email systems block files larger than about 5MB).

- Find your lost iPad using the **Find My iPad** feature (described in Chapter 1: "Getting Started").

- Erase all of the personal data on your lost iPad remotely using the **Remote Wipe** feature.

- If you have multiple Macs in your home or business, MobileMe also allows you to sync **docks**, **settings**, **passwords**, and **other information** between your Macs, and use **Back to my Mac** remote desktop to retrieve files or share screens.

> **NOTE:** As of publishing time, after your 60-day free trial, Apple charges $99/year for individual MobileMe service and $149/year for a family plan.
>
> However, also at publishing time, there was a rumor floating around the web that Apple may make MobileMe a free service. Check with the MobileMe web site (www.mobileme.com) to find out the latest information.

Sign Up for the MobileMe Service (PC or Mac)

Apple makes it easy for you to learn about MobileMe from iTunes after you register your iPad or the first time you connect your iPad to your computer. You will most likely see an ad for MobileMe with a **Try It Free** button.

If you use iTunes to sync your iPad, you will also see a **Learn More** button at the top of the **Info** tab (see Figure 4–6).

1. Connect your iPad to your computer.

2. Click on **your iPad** in the left nav bar of iTunes.

3. Click the **Info** tab at the top.

4. Click the **Learn More** button in the MobileMe section.

Figure 4–6. *Get started with MobileMe from the iTunes Info tab*

You can also sign up for MobileMe directly from their web site.

1. Type your personal information to set up your account and click the **Continue** button. Then enter your billing information and click the **Sign Up** button at the bottom.

2. If everything was entered correctly, you'll see a **Signup Complete** screen similar to the one shown here.

You have now created your MobileMe account. Now you'll set up MobileMe on your Mac or PC and your iPad.

If you are a Windows PC user, skip to the "Set Up MobileMe on Your PC" section.

Set Up MobileMe on Your Mac

After you have created your MobileMe account, you are ready to set up the software on your Mac. The MobileMe software that runs on your Mac is included in the latest version of the Leopard (v10.5.8 or higher) or Snow Leopard (v10.6.3 or higher) operating systems.

If you don't have the latest version of the Mac system software, you'll have to install it and configure the MobileMe software to sync to the MobileMe cloud to get started.

1. Click on the **Apple menu** and select **Software Update** as shown.

   > **TIP:** You'll find extensive step-by-step instructions showing you how to install or upgrade software on your Mac in Chapter 30: "Your iTunes User Guide."

Click here to get the latest software for your Mac.

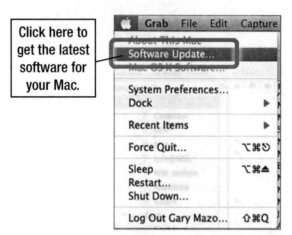

2. Follow the steps to complete the software update.

Click here to locate the MobileMe software.

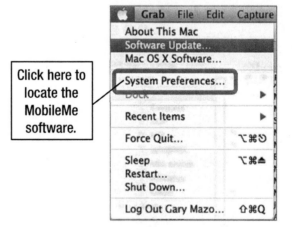

3. After you have successfully installed the software update, click on the **Apple menu** and select **System Preferences**.

4. Click on the **MobileMe** icon in the Internet & Wireless section of System Preferences.

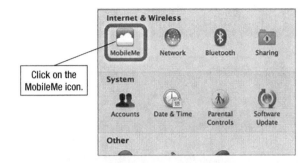

5. Enter your MobileMe **Member Name** and **Password**.

6. Click **Sign In**.

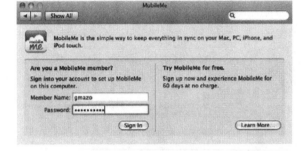

7. Click the **Sync** tab at the top to see the screen shown here.

8. Check the box next to **Synchronize with MobileMe.**

9. Next to this check box is a drop-down for configuring the sync frequency. The default is **Automatically**, but you can sync every **Hour**, **Day**, **Week**, or **Manually**.

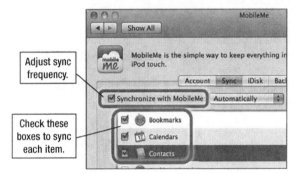

10. To sync bookmarks, check the box next to **Bookmarks** and select your **web browser**.

11. To sync contacts, check the box next to **Contacts**.

12. To sync calendars, check the box next to **Calendars.**

13. You can also sync various other items by checking them. After you have set up syncing, you can configure your iDisk by clicking the **iDisk** tab and completing the screen (see Figure 4–7).

14. When you are done, close the **MobileMe** control panel.

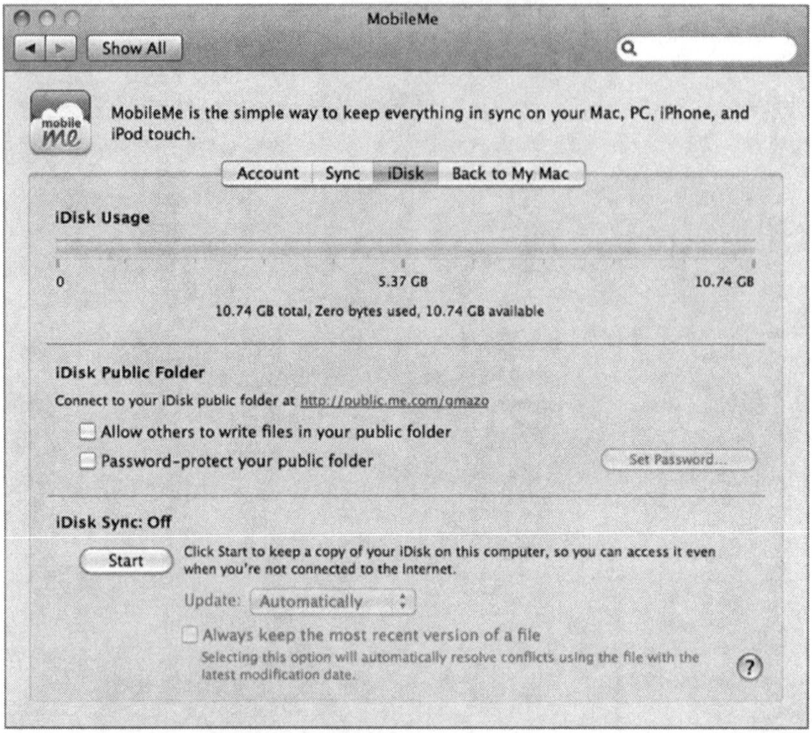

Figure 4–7. *MobileMe control panel showing the iDisk tab*

As soon as you close the MobileMe control panel, MobileMe will start sending your selected items—Contacts, Calendars, and Bookmarks— to the MobileMe web site.

Now you can skip to the "Multiple Ways to Access MobileMe" section while we discuss how Windows users configure MobileMe.

Set Up MobileMe on Your Windows PC

After creating your MobileMe account, you need get the software set up on your PC. You will install the latest version of iTunes and the MobileMe software on your PC and then configure it to sync to the MobileMe cloud to get started.

1. In your web browser, go to www.apple.com/mobileme/setup/pc.html.

2. If you don't have iTunes version 10 or later, click the **iTunes** link to download it.

> **TIP:** We provide step-by-step instructions for installing or upgrading iTunes in Chapter 30: "Your iTunes User Guide."

Click the link to download the MobileMe Control Panel for Windows.

3. Click the **Download** button on this screen to download the installation file.

4. Follow the steps on the screen to install the software on your computer.

5. Once the software is installed, start it up by one of these two methods:

   - Clicking on the **MobileMe** icon on your Windows desktop

   - Starting it from your **Start** button or searching for via the **Windows** icon in the lower left corner. Type **MobileMe** and the icon should appear at the top of the Start menu under **Programs**. Click it.

6. Click the **Sync** tab at the top.

7. Check the box next to **Sync with MobileMe.**

8. Next to this check box is a drop-down for the sync frequency. The default is **Automatically**, but you can choose to sync every **Hour**, **Day**, **Week**, or **Manually**.

9. To sync contacts, check the box next to **Contacts** and select where your contacts are stored (such as **Outlook**, **Google Contacts**, **Yahoo!**, or **Windows Contacts**). For Google and Yahoo!, you will need to enter your username and password by clicking the **Options** button that appears (see Figure 4–8).

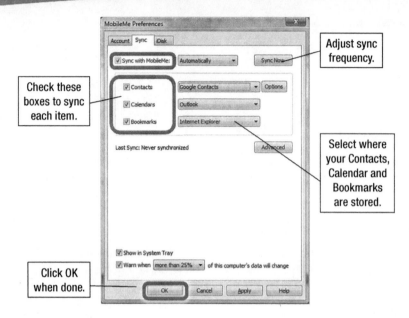

Figure 4–8. *MobileMe for Windows preferences control panel showing the Sync tab*

10. To sync calendars, check the box next to **Calendars** and select where your Calendars are stored (e.g., **Outlook** or elsewhere).

11. To sync bookmarks, check the box next to **Bookmarks** and select your computer's web browser (only Safari and Internet Explorer were supported for syncing bookmarks at publishing time).

12. Click **OK** when done.

As soon as you click **OK**, MobileMe will start sending your selected items—Contacts, Calendars, and Bookmarks—to the MobileMe web site.

Multiple Ways to Access MobileMe

After the first sync, you will have at least the following three ways to access your synced information:

■ The computer where you originally stored your contacts and calendar

■ The MobileMe web site

■ Your iPad (or other mobile device)

Since you already know how to get to the information on your computer, we will focus on how to access information from the MobileMe web site and your iPad.

A Quick Tour of the MobileMe Web Site

You can do many useful and amazing things from the MobileMe web site. You can locate your iPad, send messages to it, make it beep loudly, and remotely lock or erase it. Here's a quick tour.

1. Go to the **MobileMe** from a web browser on your computer by typing www.me.com.

2. Type your username and password and click **Log In**.

3. To view your mail, click the **Cloud** icon in the upper left corner, then click the **Mail** icon.

4. This will show your MobileMe **inbox** for all email going to your Mobile Me email address: (membername)@me.com.

5. To view your contacts, click the **Cloud** icon then click the **Contacts** icon.

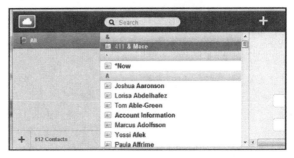

6. To view your calendar, click the **Cloud** icon then the **Calendar** icon. Note that there are various buttons at the top for the calendar views: Day, Week, Month and List.

7. To view your photo albums, click the **Cloud** icon then the **Gallery** icon.

8. To create a new album, click the **+** in the lower left corner.

9. Enter your **Album Name**, and check the **Allow** and **Show** settings you want. Also, for Mac users, decide whether you want to sync with **iPhoto** or **Aperture**.

10. Click the **Create** button to create your new album.

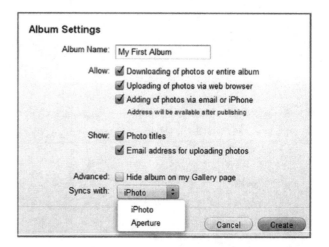

11. Click the **Upload Arrow** to select photos or videos to upload to your MobileMe album.

12. Navigate to the folder on your computer where your pictures are stored, click the picture or video to select it, and then click the **Open** button.

NOTE: The following image file formats are supported: .png, .gif, .jpg, .jpeg. The following video types are supported: .mov, .m4v, .mp4, .3gp, .3g2, .mpg, .mpeg, .avi.

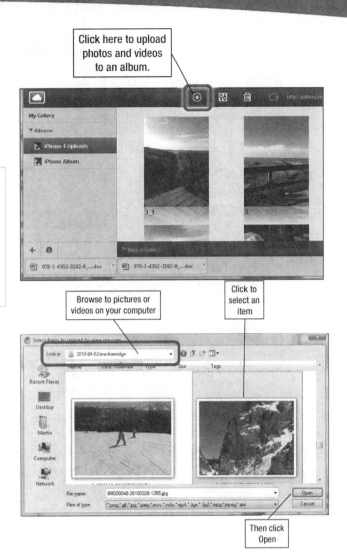

13. Click the **Cloud** icon 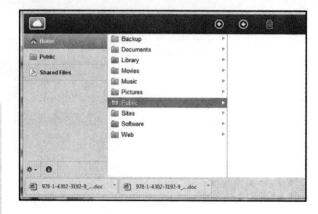 then the **iDisk** icon to view the files located on the MobileMe iDisk.

> **TIP**: You can easily store and retrieve files on this iDisk from your computer and your iPad. You can even share files that are too large to email or that you'd like to print from your iPad using the **Public** folder.

14. Click the **Cloud** icon  then the **Find My iPad** icon to locate your iPad. You will need to re-enter your password for security purposes. This feature assumes you have already logged into MobileMe from the **Settings** app on your iPad.

15. Click your name in the upper right corner, then select **Account** from the drop-down list. In your account page, you can adjust the options, see your account type and trial expiration date (if you are on a free trial), get help, or check whether the MobileMe service is running.

Setting Up Your iPad to Access Your MobileMe Account

Now that you've set up your MobileMe account, you are ready to sign into it from your iPad. We show you how to do this in the "Find My iPad" section of Chapter 1: "Getting Started."

1. Tap your **Settings** icon.

2. Tap **Mail, Contacts, Calendars**.

3. Tap **Add Account**.

4. Tap **MobileMe** for the account type.

5. Enter your **Name** and your MobileMe **Email Address** and **Password,** then tap **Next**.

6. Now you'll see the MobileMe configuration screen showing your sync options.

7. To turn any synced item **On** or **Off**, tap the switch.

8. To turn on **Find My iPad**, which will show your iPad on a map on the MobileMe web site, move the switch to **On**.

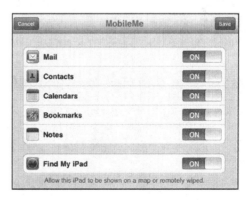

> **NOTE:** If you have any existing contacts, calendars, or other information on your iPad, these will be kept separate from your MobileMe contacts and calendars.

9. When you are done, tap **Save.** You should be brought back to the Settings screen and see your MobileMe account listed with the selected items turned on for syncing.

Using MobileMe After Setup

Using MobileMe is fairly seamless once you get it set up. You update your contacts and calendar on your iPad and the changes just appear on your computer. And, if you've set up other mobile devices such as an iPad on the same account, the changes appear there as well. Everything is kept in sync wirelessly and automatically.

MobileMe has a few very cool features that we will highlight next.

Find My iPad, Send Messages, and Remote Wipe

From any web browser, you can locate your iPad using the **Find My iPad** feature in MobileMe. You can send a message and play a loud sound to alert someone on your iPad, even if it is locked. You can remotely lock your iPad using a four–digit code and remotely erase all information on your iPad.

Please refer to the "Find My iPad" section of Chapter 1: "Getting Started."

Additional Settings for Google/Exchange or MobileMe

Once you set up the Google/Exchange or MobileMe sync, you may notice a few new options on your Settings screen in addition to the ones shown in Chapter 14: "Working with Contacts" and Chapter 15: "Your Calendar."

1. Tap the **Settings** icon.

2. Tap **Mail, Contacts, Calendars** in the left column.

3. Scroll down the right column to the bottom to see the image shown here.

4. The new option in the Contacts section is the **Default Account**. You can set this to be either your Exchange/Google account or your computer's account.

5. Notice that you can turn your **New Invitation Alerts On** or **Off.**

6. The new option in the Calendars section is **Sync,** which allows you to set how much of your calendar to sync (**2 weeks**, **1 month**, **3 months**, **6 months**, or **All events**).

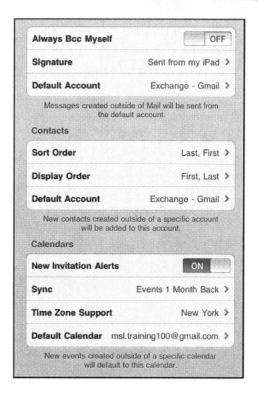

7. You can also select which is your **Default Calendar** for new events you add to your iPad. You can change this calendar when you create a new event.

Chapter 5

Wi-Fi and 3G Connections

We live in a connected world. Wireless Internet (Wi-Fi) access has become the rule, not the exception—chances are you're already using Wi-Fi at your home or office. Now you can use it to connect your iPad. And if your iPad has a 3G radio, you can also connect to the Internet anywhere you have cellular data coverage—a much wider area than Wi-Fi networks.

In this chapter, we'll talk about the differences between the two types of connections for your iPad: Wi-Fi (wireless local area network) and 3G (cellular service—the wide area data network used by your mobile phone). We'll show you all the ways to get connected or disconnected from these two types of networks. There may be times you want to disable or turn off your 3G connection and only use Wi-Fi to save money in data connection charges.

The beauty of the iPad is that it has wireless Internet access built in. Once you connect your iPad to a wireless (Wi-Fi or 3G) network, you can be sending email and surfing the Web in minutes. And once you discover all the great apps and books available, you'll never want to be disconnected again.

> **NOTE:** Your iPad may not have a 3G connection. Some iPads come with only the Wi-Fi connection and do not have the ability to connect to a 3G cellular network.
>
> How do you know which iPad you have? A 3G-enabled iPad will have a black plastic strip along the top edge that shows more prominently along the back side of the iPad; this strip aids in data reception (see Figure 5 1).

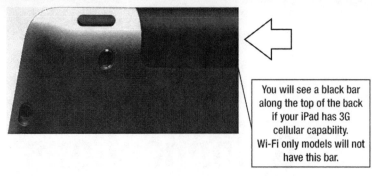

You will see a black bar along the top of the back if your iPad has 3G cellular capability. Wi-Fi only models will not have this bar.

Figure 5–1. *How to tell if your iPad has 3G cellular capabilities*

What Can I Do When I'm Connected to a Wi-Fi or 3G Network?

What follows are some of the things you can do when connected to a Wi-Fi or 3G network:

- Access and download apps (programs) from the App Store.

- Access and download music, videos, podcasts, and more with the **iTunes** app on your iPad.

- Browse the Web using **Safari**.

- Send and receive email messages.

- Use social networking sites that require an Internet connection like Facebook, Twitter, and so on.

- Use your iPad as a phone with the **Skype** app (see Chapter 22: "Social Networking").

- Play games that use a live Internet connection.

- Anything else that requires an Internet connection.

Wi-Fi Connections

Every iPad comes with Wi-Fi capability built in. If you have a 3G model then you have both 3G and Wi-Fi. So let's take a look at getting connected to the Wi-Fi network. Things to consider about Wi-Fi connections include:

- There is no additional cost for network access and data downloads (if you are using your iPad in your home, office, or a free Wi-Fi hotspot).

- Wi-Fi tends to be faster than a cellular data 3G connection.

- More and more places, including airplanes, provide Wi-Fi access, but you may have to pay a one-time or monthly service fee.

Setting Up Your Wi-Fi Connection

To set up your Wi-Fi connection, follow these steps:

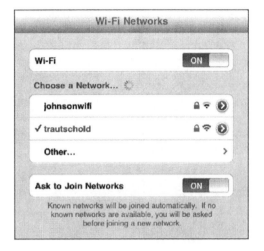

1. Tap the **Settings** icon.

2. Tap **Wi-Fi** in the left column to see the screen shown at the right.

3. Make sure the **Wi-Fi** switch is set to **ON**.

4. Once Wi-Fi is **ON**, the iPad will automatically start looking for wireless networks.

5. The list of accessible networks is shown below the **Choose a Network...** option. You can see in this screenshot that we have two networks available.

To connect to any network listed, just touch it. If the network is unsecure—that is, it does not require a password—you will be connected automatically.

NOTE: Some places, like coffee shops, use a web-based login instead of a username/password screen. In those cases, when you click a network (or try to use **Safari**), the iPad will slide up a browser screen, and you'll see the web page along with your login options.

Secure Wi-Fi Networks—Entering a Password

Some Wi-Fi networks require a password to log in. This is set when the network administrator creates the wireless network. You will have to know the exact password, including whether it is case-sensitive.

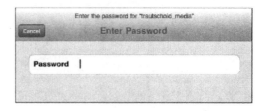

If the network does require a password, you will be taken to the password-entry screen. Type the password exactly as given to you and press the **Enter** key on the on-screen keyboard (which is now labeled **Join**).

On the **Choose a Network...** screen, you'll see a **Checkmark** icon showing that you are connected to the network.

TIP: You can paste text into the password dialog. Thus for longer or random-character passwords, you can transfer your passwords to your iPad (in an email message) and just copy and paste them. Just remember to delete the email immediately after you do this to keep things secure.

Switching to a Different Wi-Fi Network

At times you may want to change your active Wi-Fi network. This might occur if you are in a hotel, apartment, or other place where the network selected by the iPad is not the strongest network, or you want to use a secure network instead of an unsecure one.

To switch from the currently selected Wi-Fi network, tap the **Settings** icon, touch **Wi-Fi** in the left column, and then touch the name of the Wi-Fi network you want to join. If that network requires a password, you'll need to enter it to join the network (see Figure 5–2).

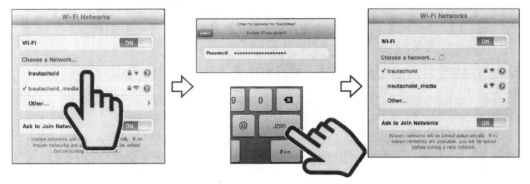

Figure 5–2. *Switching to a different Wi-Fi network*

Once you type the correct password (or touch an open network), your iPad will join that network.

Verifying Your Wi-Fi Connection

To verify that you are connected to a Wi-Fi network, look for the network name with the **Checkmark** icon next to it.

When you go back to the **Settings** screen, you should now see the name of your Wi-Fi network with a **Checkmark** icon next to it in the list under **Choose a Network...**

Advanced Wi-Fi Options (Hidden or Undiscoverable Networks)

Sometimes you may not be able to see the network you want to join because the name has been hidden by the administrator. In the next section, you will learn how to join such networks on your iPad. Once you do so, the next time you come into contact with that network, your iPad will join it automatically, without asking. You can also tell your iPad to ask every time it joins a network; we will show you how to do that, as well. Sometimes you may want to erase or forget a network. For example, assume you are at a one-time convention and you want to get rid of the associated network—you'll learn how to do that, too.

Why Can't I See the Wi-Fi Network I Want to Join?

Sometimes, for security reasons, people don't make their networks discoverable, and you have to manually enter the name and security options to connect.

As you can see in Figure 5–3, your list of available networks includes **Other**... Touch the **Other** tab, and you can manually enter the name of a network you would like to join.

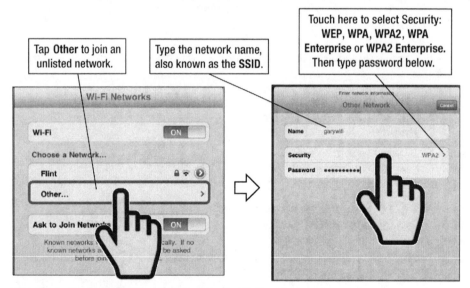

Figure 5–3. *You can manually enter the name of a Wi-Fi network.*

Type in the Wi-Fi network name, touch the **Security** tab, and then choose which type of security is being used on that network. If you are unsure, you'll need to find out from the network administrator.

When you have the information you need, enter it along with the proper password. This new network will be saved to your network list for future access.

Reconnecting to Previously Joined Wi-Fi Networks

The nice thing about the iPad is that, when you return to an area with a Wi-Fi network you have previously joined (whether it was an open or a secure, password-protected network), your iPad will automatically join the network without prompting you for a password or other connection information. However, you are free to turn off this automatic-joining feature, as described in the next section.

Ask to Join Networks

By default, the **Ask to Join Networks** switch is set to **ON,** which means you will join known or visible Wi-Fi networks automatically. If networks are available that are not known to you, you will be asked before being connected.

If the switch is set to **OFF**, you will be automatically connected only to known networks, and you'll have to follow the procedures we described previously for manually joining unknown networks.

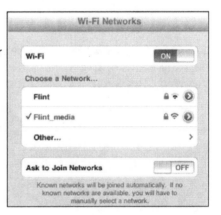

Why might someone turn off automatically joining a network? This could be a good security measure if, for example, you don't want your kids to be able to join a wireless network on the iPad without your knowledge.

Forget (or Erase) a Network

If you find that you no longer want to connect to a network on your list, you can "forget" it—i.e., take it off your list of networks. Follow these steps to do so:

1. From the **Wi-Fi** screen in the **Settings** app, tap the small **Blue** arrow next to that network. The screen that follows shows the network details of that particular connection (see Figure 5–4).

2. Tap **Forget this Network** at the top of the screen.

3. You will be prompted with a warning. Tap **Forget Network** and the network will no longer show up on your list.

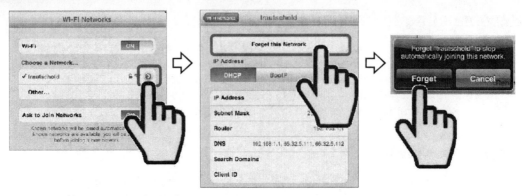

Figure 5–4. *How to forget a Wi-Fi network*

3G Cellular Data Connection

If you have a 3G iPad, you will also be able to connect to a cellular data network; this is the same network you connect to with an iPhone or other mobile phone. Here are some things to consider about cellular data connections:

- A 3G cellular network has wider availability than a Wi-Fi connection—you can connect to 3G in a car or away from a city, whereas Wi-Fi is not typically be available in these locations.

- You face extra monthly service fees for access to the cellular data network.

- In the US, you have two options for cellular data, depending on which iPad you purchased: AT&T and Verizon.

    - AT&T's current plans are $15 for 250MB per month and $25 for 2GB (about 2,000 MB) data.

    - Verizon's current plans are $20 for 1GB, $35 for 3GB, $50 for 5GB, and $80 for 10GB of data.

Here are some things you can do with 1GB of wireless data:

- Browse 6,500 web pages

- Download 300 songs

- Watch 65 YouTube videos

- Download 2,000 photos

NOTE: Orange UK, Vodafone UK, O2, Rogers Canada, and other international carriers may have different pricing plans.

Setting Up Your 3G Connection

Before you can connect to the 3G cellular network, you have to purchase a cellular data plan from your wireless carrier. As mentioned previously, your carrier choices for the iPad in the US are currently AT&T and Verizon.

> **TIP:** You might be able to spare yourself some money on your cellular data plan by doing the following:
>
> - Always use Wi-Fi when possible.
> - Start with a lower cost, lower capacity cellular data plan.
> - Monitor your cellular data usage throughout the month to make sure you are not going to exceed the lower cost data plan.
>
> You may find that you can live with the lower cost plan if you use Wi-Fi for most of your data needs.

Follow these steps to connect to a cellular data network:

1. Tap the **Settings** icon on your iPad.

2. Tap **Cellular Data** in the left column.

3. Set the switch next to **Cellular Data** to **ON** (see Figure 5–5).

4. The first time you do this, you will see a pop-up window asking you to set up your account:

    a. Enter your personal information, a username, and a password that are specific to this new cellular data plan. This account is not connected your email account, cell phone plan, or any other account, so you can enter the same information or make it different.

> **NOTE:** At the time of publishing, the wireless carriers in the US (AT&T and Verizon) offer recurring billing plans. This means that you set up the plan once, and you are billed every month until you cancel the plan.

    b. Scroll down to see the rest of the screen and select your data plan by tapping the screen.

    c. Enter your credit card information.

5. Tap the **Next** button.

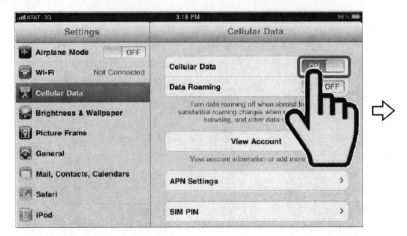

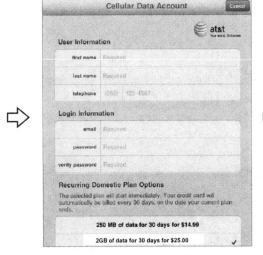

Figure 5–5. *Buying a cellular data plan*

6. On the next screen, you will need to swipe to the bottom of the
agreement and tap **Agree** to continue—assuming you agree, of course.

7. If you are traveling with your iPad, then tap **Add International Data** and follow the steps in the next section.

8. If you do not want to add the international plan at this time (you can always add it later), then tap **Submit** to finish.

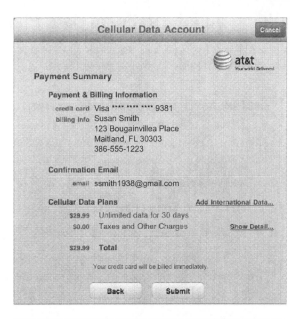

9. After tapping **Submit**, you will see a window similar to this one. Tap **OK** to close the window.

10. Finally, when your new cellular data plan is set up, you will see a pop-up message similar to this one.

Adding an International Data Plan

If you plan on taking a trip, you may want to add an international data plan to your iPad. It is easy to do so by following these steps:

> **CAUTION:** Not all carriers provide international roaming plans for your iPad. Please check with your carrier to make sure you can purchase a plan. If not, then you may want to consider turning off your 3G connection while you are out of the country and using Wi-Fi only, which is free.

1. Tap the **Settings** icon.

2. Tap **Cellular Data** in the left column.

3. Tap **View Account** in the right column.

4. Log in to the account by entering the cellular data username and password you used when you created this account.

5. Tap **Add International Plan** (see Figure 5–6).

6. Do the following on the **International Data Plan** window:

   a. Select your **One-Time International Plan**.

   b. Adjust your plan **Start Date** to match your travel needs.

   c. Tap the **View Full List of Countries** link at the bottom to verify the plan will support the countries you need.

   d. Tap **Done**.

   e. You may need to confirm your selection on the following screen.

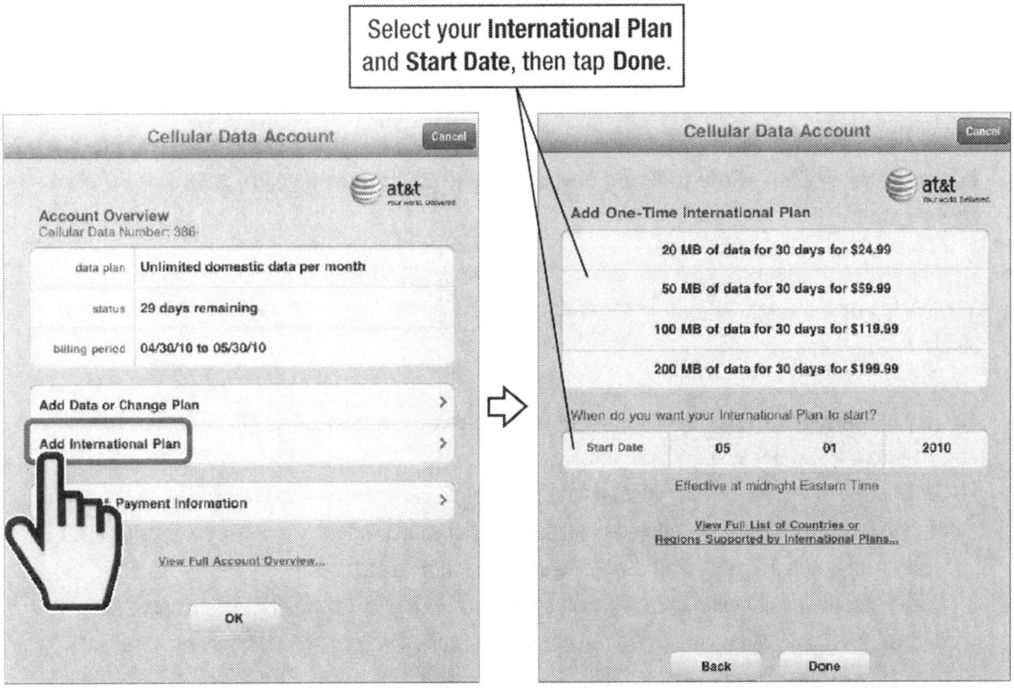

Figure 5–6. *Buying an international cellular data plan*

Monitoring Your Cellular Data Usage and Changing Your Plan

If you purchase the limited-use data plan (the $15 plan for 250MB/month), you will want to check periodically to see how much data you are using on a daily basis.

To do this, follow these steps:

1. Tap the **Settings** icon.

2. Tap **Cellular Data** in the left column.

3. Tap **View Account** in the right column.

4. Log in to the account by entering the cellular data username and password you used when you created this account (see Figure 5–6).

5. Look at your **data plan**, **status**, and **billing period** listed in the **Account Overview** section at the top. You will only see actual data usage in megabytes (MB) if you have purchased a plan that limits the amount of data you can use (e.g., 250 MB).

6. If you want to change your plan or add data, then tap **Add Data or Change Plan** and follow the steps presented to adjust your plan.

NOTE: Your iPad will notify you when you have 20%, 10%, and 0% of data usage left on your 250MB plan. You'll also have the option to renew that plan for another $14.99 or upgrade to the $30 unlimited plan.

International Travel—How to Avoid Large Cellular (3G) Data Roaming Bills (for 3G iPad Models Only)

We've heard of people who traveled to another country being surprised with $300 or $400 of monthly roaming charges after their trip. You can avoid these charges by taking a few easy steps before and during your trip:

1. Try to use your Wi-Fi connection at free Wi-Fi networks overseas; this will keep your cellular data roaming charges to a minimum.
2. Sign up for a one-time international data plan, as explained earlier in the "Adding an International Data Plan" section. In most cases, activating the international data plan allows you to save some money over the standard data roaming charges.
3. Learn about any potential data roaming charges. Check with your cellular data supplier about any data roaming charges. You can try searching on your phone company's web site, but usually you'll have to call the help desk and specifically ask what the iPad data roaming charges are for the country or countries you'll be visiting. If you plan to use email, mapping, web browsing, or any other data services, you should specifically ask about whether any of these services are charged separately.

Explore buying and using a foreign SIM Card (MicroSIM format).

Your iPad cellular data supplier may not offer special deals on international data roaming plans or may have rates that are unreasonably high. In such cases, you can insert a SIM card that you'll purchase in the foreign country.

CAUTION: The iPad uses a MicroSIM, and almost all other phones use a MiniSIM. This may make it hard to find an international carrier with a SIM card that will fit.

Often, inserting a SIM card for the country you're in will eliminate or greatly reduce data roaming charges. However, do carefully check the cost of data on that foreign SIM card. Using a foreign SIM card may save you hundreds of dollars, but it's best to do some Web research or try to talk to someone who recently traveled to the same country to make sure.

Airplane Mode—Turn Off 3G and Wi-Fi

Often when you are flying on an airplane, the flight crew will ask you to turn off all portable electronic devices for takeoff and landing. Then, when you get to altitude, the crew will say "all approved electronic devices" can be turned back on.

You can turn off the iPad by pressing and holding the power button on the top right edge, then **Slide to Power Off** with your finger.

If you have a 3G/cellular data iPad, then you can turn on **Airplane Mode** in the **Settings** icon as follows:

1. Tap the **Settings** icon.

2. Set the switch next to **Airplane Mode** in the top of the left column to **ON**.

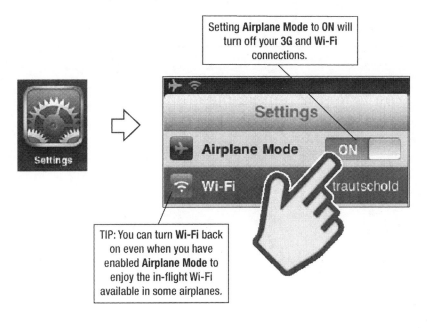

Setting **Airplane Mode** to **ON** will turn off your **3G** and **Wi-Fi** connections.

TIP: You can turn **Wi-Fi** back on even when you have enabled **Airplane Mode** to enjoy the in-flight Wi-Fi available in some airplanes.

TIP: Some airlines have in-flight Wi-Fi networks; in that case, you will want to leave your Wi-Fi turned **ON**.

You can turn your **Wi-Fi** connection **OFF** or **ON** by following these steps (see Figure 5–7):

1. Tap the **Settings** icon.

2. Tap **Wi-Fi** in the top of the left column.

3. Set the switch next to **Wi-Fi** in the top of the right column to **OFF**.

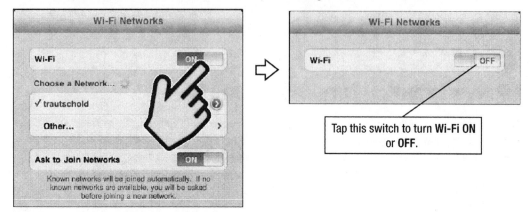

Figure 5–7. *How to Turn Wi-Fi **OFF** or **ON**.*

Chapter 6

Organize Your iPad Icons and Folders

Your new iPad is very customizable. In this chapter, we'll show you how to move icons around and put your favorites just where you want them. You've got up to 11 pages of icons to work with, and you can adjust the look-and-feel of those pages so it suits your tastes.

Like a Mac computer or an iPhone, the iPad has a *Bottom Dock* where you can put the icons for your favorite apps. Your iPad comes with four standard icons in the Bottom Dock, but you can replace these with others so your favorite apps are always available at the bottom of your screen. You can also add two more icons for a total of six items in the Bottom Dock. You can even move an entire folder of apps to the Bottom Dock.

> **TIP:** You can also move or delete icons using iTunes on your computer. Check out Chapter 29: "Your iTunes User Guide" for more information.

Moving Icons to the Bottom Dock—Docking Them

When you turn your iPad on, you'll notice the four icons locked to the Bottom Dock: **Safari**, **Mail**, **Photos**, and **iPod**.

It is possible that your icons may be different, but you can easily change them.

Suppose you decide you want to swap out one or more of the existing icons for apps you use more often. Fortunately, moving icons to and from the Bottom Dock is easy.

If you prefer, you can keep the standard four and add two more for a total of six icons in the **Bottom Dock**.

Keep up to 6 icons that you want to see all the time. These icons will always remain visible even when you slide the other icon screens left/right.

Bottom Dock

Starting the Move

Press the **Home** button to get to your **Home** screen. Now, touch and hold any icon on the **Home** screen for a couple of seconds. You'll notice that all the icons start to shake.

Try moving just a couple of icons around at first. You'll see that when you move an icon down, the other icons in the row move to make space for it.

Once you have a feel for how the icons move, you're ready to replace one of the Bottom Dock icons with one of your choosing. While the icons are shaking, take the icon you want to replace from the Bottom Dock and move it up to an area covered by other icons. If you move it to a large blank area, it will jump back to the dock.

> **NOTE:** You can have up to six icons in the Bottom Dock; if you already have six icons there, you'll have to remove one to replace it with a new one.

Suppose you want to replace the standard **iPod** icon with your **App Store** icon. The first thing to do is hold the **Music** icon and move it up a row—out of the Bottom Dock, as shown in Figure 6–1.

To stop the icons from shaking, tap your **Home** button.

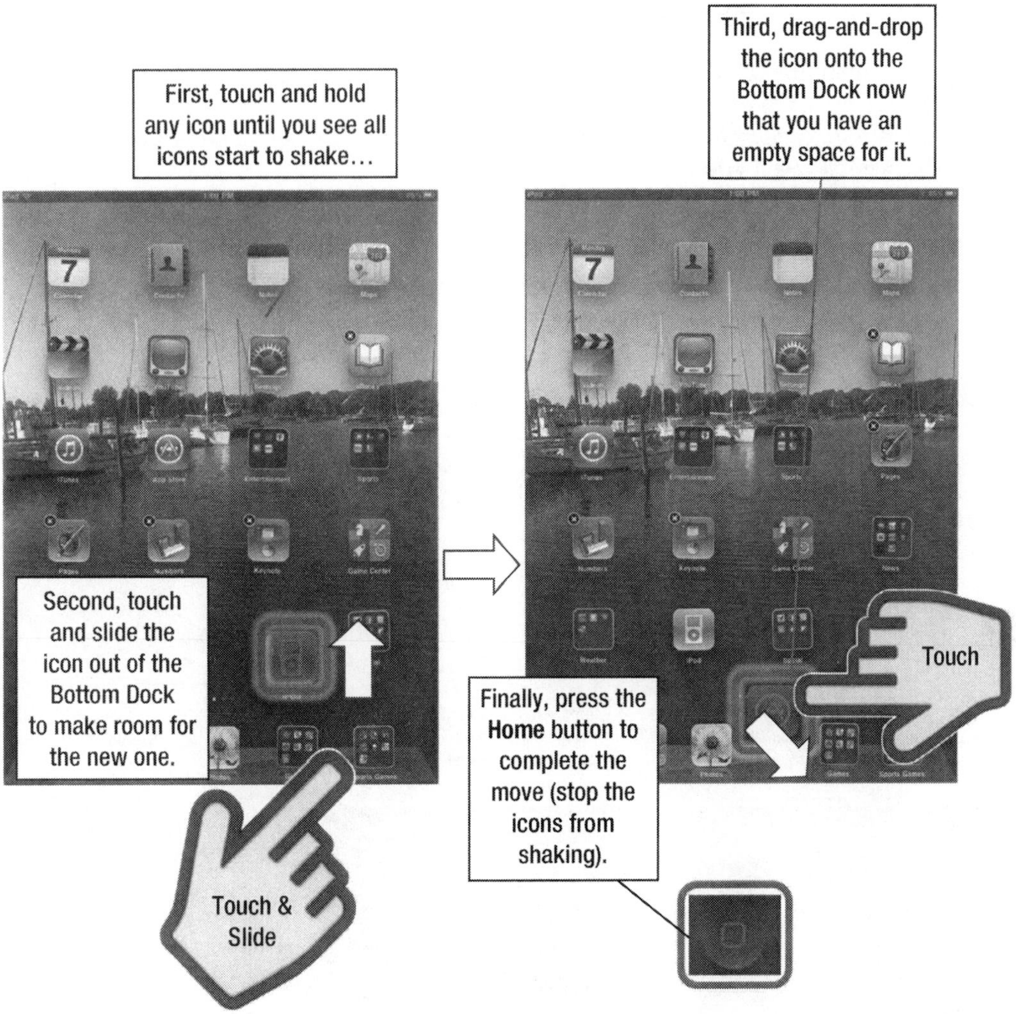

First, touch and hold any icon until you see all icons start to shake…

Third, drag-and-drop the icon onto the Bottom Dock now that you have an empty space for it.

Second, touch and slide the icon out of the Bottom Dock to make room for the new one.

Touch

Finally, press the **Home** button to complete the move (stop the icons from shaking).

Touch & Slide

Figure 6–1. *Swapping icons in the Bottom Dock*

Next, locate your **App Store** icon and move it to the Bottom Dock. As you do this, the icon will become sort of transparent until you actually set it into place.

When you are sure you have the icons just where you want them, press the **Home** button once and the icons will lock into place. Now you have the **App Store** icon in the Bottom Dock, where you want it.

Moving Icons to a Different Page

The iPad can hold 20 icons on a page (not including the dock), and you can find these pages by *swiping* (right to left) on your **Home** screen. With all the cool apps available, it is not uncommon to have five, six, or even more pages of icons. You can have up to 11 pages filled with icons if you're the adventurous type!

> **NOTE:** You can also swipe from left to right on any screen except the **Home** screen. On the **Home** screen, swiping left to right takes you to **Spotlight Search**; see Chapter 2: "Typing Tips, Copy/Paste, and Search" for more information.

Assume you may have an icon you rarely use on your first page, and you want to move it way off to the last page. Or you may want to swap the icon for an app you often use from the last of the icon pages to the first. Both tasks are very easy to accomplish; moving icons between pages is very much like moving icons to the Bottom Dock. Follow these steps to move icons between pages:

1. Touch and hold any icon to initiate the moving process.

2. Touch and hold the icon you wish to move. For example, let's say you want to move the **iBooks** icon to the first page (see Figure 6–2).

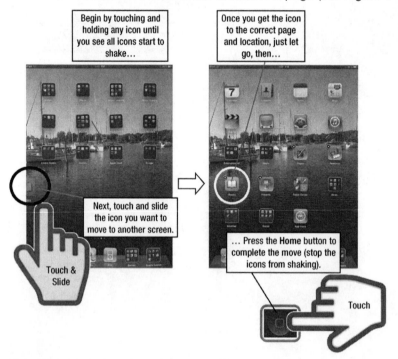

Figure 6–2. *Moving icons from one page to another*

3. Now drag and drop the icon onto another page. To do this, touch and hold the **iBooks** icon and drag it to the left. You'll see all of your pages of icons move by. When you get to the first page, release the icon. Doing so will place it at the very beginning.

4. Press the **Home** key to complete the move and stop the icons from shaking.

Deleting Icons

Be careful—it's as easy to delete an icon as it is to move it. However, when you delete an icon on the iPad, you are actually deleting the program it represents. This means you won't be able to use the program in the future without reinstalling it or redownloading it.

> **NOTE**: You can set a parental control (**Restriction** in **Settings**) to prevent accidental app deletion. This is handy if you have young kids who think deleting apps is a fun game.

Depending on your **Application Sync** settings in iTunes, the program may still reside in your **Applications** folder in iTunes. In that case, you would be able to easily reinstall the deleted app if you wanted to by checking that application in the list of apps to sync in iTunes. If not, you can always download it again onto your device from the same account at no charge.

As Figure 6–3 shows, the deleting process is similar to the moving process. Touch and hold any icon to initiate the deleting process. As before, touching and holding makes the icons shake, allowing you to move or delete them.

> **NOTE**: You can delete only programs you have downloaded to your iPad; the preinstalled icons and their associated programs can't be deleted. You can tell which programs can be deleted because the icons that can be deleted contain a small black **x** in the upper-left corner.

Just tap the **x** on the icon you'd like to delete. You'll be prompted to either delete or cancel the delete request. If you select **Delete**, the icon and its related app will be removed from your iPad.

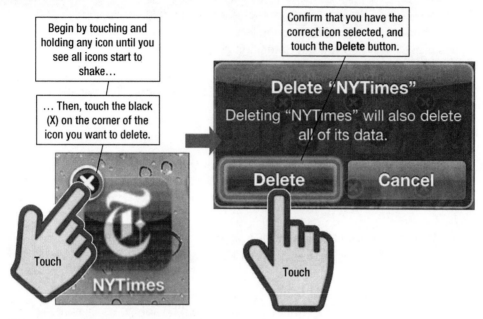

Figure 6–3. *Deleting an icon—and its associated program*

Chapter 7

Personalize and Secure Your iPad

In this chapter, you will learn some great ways to personalize your iPad, as well as how to protect your iPad with passcode security. For example, you will learn how to download some great free wallpaper and change the wallpaper for your **Lock** and **Home** screens. You will learn how to personalize the sounds your iPad makes by adjusting whether you hear a sound when you receive or send e-mail, lock the iPad, type using the keyboard, or are alerted before an event on your calendar. You will also learn how to customize the **Picture Frame** settings (this is the app that shows your pictures when the device is locked). You can vary times, transitions, and even select which albums of pictures are shown. Many aspects of the iPad can be fine-tuned to meet your needs and tastes, enabling you to give your iPad a more personal look and feel.

Changing Your Lock Screen and Home Screen Wallpapers

There are actually two screens you can personalize on your iPad by changing the wallpaper.

The first is the **Lock** screen, which appears when you first turn on or wake up your iPad. The wallpaper for this screen image is shown behind the **slide to unlock** slider bar.

The second is the **Home** screen. The wallpaper for this is shown behind the icons.

You can use the wallpaper pictures that come with the iPad, or you can use your own images.

> **TIP:** You may want the wallpaper for your **Lock** screen to be less personal than your **Home** screen wallpaper. For example, you might choose to put a generic landscape image on your **Lock** screen and a picture of a loved one on your **Home** screen.

There are a couple of ways to change the wallpaper on the iPad. The first way, changing the wallpaper from your settings, is very straightforward.

Changing Wallpaper from Your Settings

Touch the **Settings** icon, then touch the **Brightness & Wallpaper** tab in the left-hand column. The settings for brightness and wallpaper will appear in the right-hand column.

To begin selecting wallpaper, touch the images of your currently selected wallpaper under **Wallpaper** on the right side of the screen, as shown in Figure 7–1.

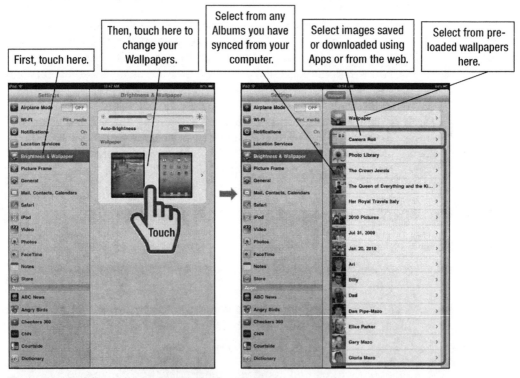

Figure 7–1. *Changing wallpaper from the **Settings** icon*

On the right side of the screen (see the right image in Figure 7–1), you'll see some albums or image folders. You have several choices:

- Tap the **Wallpaper** tab at the top to see all the preloaded wallpaper pictures for the iPad.

- Tap the **Saved Photos** album, which contains any images you've saved from the Web, from screenshots (which you take by pressing and holding the **Home** button and **Power/Sleep** key simultaneously), or even from wallpaper apps or pictures you take with the iPad's cameras.

- Tap any of the albums displayed below **Saved Photos**. These additional albums will be visible only if you have synced photos from iTunes.

Once you tap any of the albums, you'll see all the images within that album, as shown in Figure 7–2.

Tap any of the images in the album to see it on the full screen.

When previewing the image on the full screen, you can accomplish the following:

- Zoom in or out by pinching your fingers open or closed.

- Tap the **Cancel** button to return to the album if you don't like the image.

- Tap the **Set Lock Screen** button to set the image only for your **Lock** screen.

- Tap the **Set Home Screen** button to set the image only for your **Home** screen.

- Tap the **Set Both** button to set the image for both your **Lock** and **Home** screens.

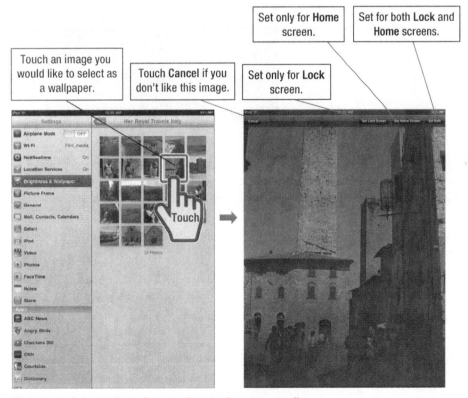

Figure 7–2. *Select a picture from an album to change your wallpaper.*

Changing Wallpaper from Any Picture

The second way to change your wallpaper is to view any picture in your **Photos** collection and select it as your wallpaper.

Tap the **Photos** icon to get started. To learn more about working with photos, check out Chapter 16: "iPad Photography."

Touch the photo album you want to look through to find your wallpaper.

When you find a photo you want to use, touch it. It will open on your screen.

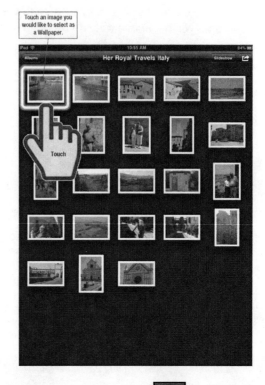

After you preview the image (see Figure 7–3), tap the **Set As** icon on the top-right corner of the screen and select **Use As Wallpaper**. Zoom in or out as you desire and then set the image as either your **Lock** or **Home** screen (or both), as just described.

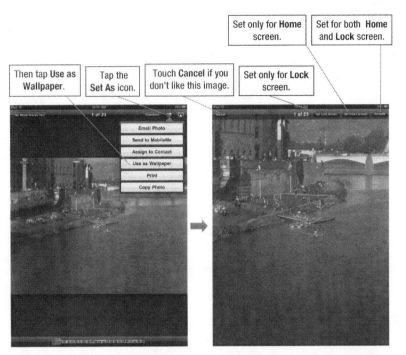

Figure 7–3. *Start from the **Photos** app to use an existing photo or image as wallpaper.*

If you decide you'd rather use a different picture, choose **Cancel** and pick a different one.

Download Great Wallpaper from Free Apps

Go to the App Store and do a search for **Backgrounds** (see Chapter 20: "App Store" for more information). You'll find a number of free and low-cost apps designed specifically for your iPad. One app that we like is called **Backgrounds HD,** which has hundreds of beautiful background images you can download for free to your iPad.

> **NOTE:** With **Backgrounds HD,** as with most wallpaper apps, you will need a live Internet connection—either Wi-Fi or 3G. Because image files tend to be quite large, you should probably stick with Wi-Fi unless you have an unlimited monthly data plan for your 3G cellular data network.

Adjusting Sounds on Your iPad

You can fine-tune your iPad so that it does or does not make sounds when you receive new mail, send mail, the calendar alarm rings, the keyboard clicks, or your iPad is locked. To adjust sounds, follow these steps:

1. Tap your **Settings** icon.

2. Tap **General** in the left column.

3. Tap **Sounds** in the right column.

4. Tap any of the switches to turn **ON** or **OFF** the sound when the event occurs.

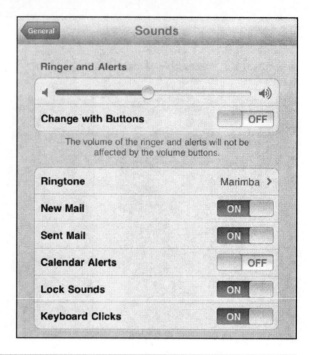

TIP: To use the **Volume** buttons on the side of the iPad to adjust your alert volume, just move the toggle under **Change with Buttons** to the **ON** position.

Personalize Your Picture Frame

Picture Frame is the app that lets you display a slideshow of photos on your locked iPad. We'll describe the many ways you can customize the display.

Starting or Stopping the Picture Frame App

You may have noticed the little icon next to the **slide to unlock** slider bar when your iPad is locked. This is the **Picture Frame** icon.

Tap this icon to turn on the electronic picture frame.

Tap the icon again to turn it off.

Picture Frame will cycle through all your pictures, or you can customize it to show only selected photo albums.

Tap this icon to turn your iPad into an electronic Picture Frame.

CAUTION: If you have private pictures stored on your iPad, it could get quite embarrassing if **Picture Frame** accidentally displays these photos while in **Locked** mode. This section shows you how to restrict the albums that are used for the slideshow.

NOTE: You can disable **Picture Frame** by setting a passcode security lock on your iPad. We show you how later in this chapter.

Customizing Your Picture Frame

Depending on the types of pictures you have stored on your iPad, you will almost certainly want to set up your **Picture Frame** to display just the albums or photos you want. Follow these steps to do so:

1. Tap the **Settings** icon.

2. Tap **Picture Frame** in the left column. Now, you can adjust various settings for the picture frame (see Figure 7–4).

3. If you want to show only one picture on the screen at a time, select **Dissolve**. If you want to show two to four images at once, select **Origami**. **Origami** will show two to four images on the screen and have them fold over on each other, as though you were folding paper.

4. **Zoom in on Faces** is selectable only if you've chosen the **Dissolve** transition. This is a neat feature that will zoom in on any faces detected in the individual photos,

5. Set **Shuffle** to **ON** if you want **Picture Frame** to display the selected photos randomly.

6. If you want all your photos to be included in the slideshow (the default setting), select **All Photos**.

7. People often want to keep some photos private. To do so, select **Albums**, then tap or check the albums to include. (The check indicates that an album will be included.)

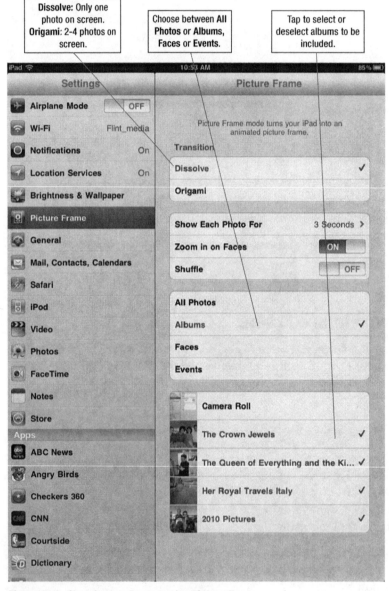

Dissolve: Only one photo on screen. Origami: 2-4 photos on screen.

Choose between **All Photos** or **Albums**, **Faces** or **Events**.

Tap to select or deselect albums to be included.

Figure 7–4. *Choosing how to customize* ***Picture Frame***

TIP: To really control what **Picture Frame** displays, set up an album on your computer with only the images you are happy to have everyone see when the device is locked. Next, sync that album to your iPad using iTunes. For help with this, check out Chapter 3: "Sync Your iPad with iTunes."

Keyboard Options

You can fine-tune your keyboard by selecting various languages and changing settings such as **Auto-Correction** and **Auto-Capitalization** (see Chapter 2: "Typing Tips, Copy/Paste, & Search" for keyboard options and how to use the various features).

How to Secure Your iPad with a Passcode

Your iPad can hold a great deal of valuable information. This is especially true if you save information such as the Social Security numbers and the birth dates of your family members. It is a good idea to make sure that anyone who picks up your iPad can't access all that information. Also, if your children are like ours, they'll probably pick up your cool iPad and start surfing the Web or playing a game. You might want to enable some security restrictions to keep your kids safe.

Setting a Passcode to Lock Your iPad

Touch the **Settings** icon and then the **General** tab in the left column. Now scroll down and tap the **Passcode Lock** item.

Here you have the option of setting a four-digit passcode that prevents unauthorized access to your iPad and your information. If the wrong passcode is entered, however, even you won't be able to access your information. So it is a good idea to use a code you'll remember easily or to write it down somewhere secure (see Figure 7–5).

Use the keyboard to enter a four-digit code. You will then be prompted to enter your code once more.

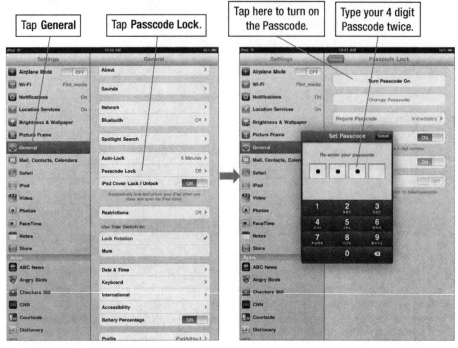

Figure 7–5. *Enabling security by setting a passcode*

Passcode Options:

Once you have set your passcode, you will be presented with a few options:

Turn Passcode Off
Change Passcode
Require Passcode (Immediately, 1 min., 5 min., 15 min., 1 hour, 4 hours)

> **NOTE**: You can also turn off **Simple Passcode**. This enables you to set a longer, more secure password with letters, numbers, symbols, and so on.

NOTE: Setting a shorter time for **Require Passcode** is more secure. Setting the time to **Immediately** (the default) is the most secure option. However, using a setting of one minute may save you the headache of retyping your passcode if you accidentally lock your iPad.

Picture Frame (the default is **ON**): Set this to **OFF** to prevent the pictures from being seen in **Locked** mode.

Erase Data (the default is **OFF**): If this is set to **ON,** all data will be erased after ten unsuccessful attempts to enter the passcode.

CAUTION: You may want to set **Erase Data** to **OFF** if you have young children who like to bang away at the security to unlock the keyboard when it comes out of **Sleep** mode and is locked. Otherwise, you may end up with your iPad being erased frequently.

Setting Content Restrictions

You might decide you don't want your kids listening to explicit lyrics in music on your iPad. You may also not want them to visit YouTube and watch content you find objectionable. Setting content restrictions is quite easy on your iPad.

Once again, touch the **General** tab under **Settings** and tap **Restrictions**.

You will see a large button that says **Enable Restrictions**.

When you touch this, you'll be prompted to enter a **Restrictions Passcode**—just pick a four-digit code you will remember.

NOTE: The **Restrictions Passcode** is a separate passcode from your main iPad passcode. You could set it so it's the same as your main iPad passcode to make it easy to remember; however, that could be problematic if you let your family know the main passcode, but do not want them adjusting the restrictions. You will need to enter this passcode to turn off restrictions later.

Note that you can use the content restrictions to control whether certain apps run at all, such as **Safari**, **YouTube**, **iTunes**, **Installing Apps**, or **Location**.

Also, you should keep in mind that **OFF** = **RESTRICTED**.

You might think that **ON** means something is restricted, but it is the opposite. To disable or restrict something, you need to touch the slider next to it and set it to **OFF**. If you look at the word **Allow:** above all the tabs, then this approach makes sense.

As you can see, you can restrict access to lyrics for **Music & Podcasts** to what is **Clean**.

You can also use ratings-based restrictions to control the content of **Movies**, **TV Shows**, and **Apps** that can be played on your iPad.

In the example in the image to the right, only movies with ratings up to PG-13 can be played. Movies with ratings of R and NC-17 can't be played.

Chapter 8

Multitasking and Mute/Lock Switch

In this chapter, we will describe how to use the **App Switcher** bar to multitask, or jump between apps on your iPad. Multitasking is a new and very welcome feature on the iPad, one that was not available when the first iPad launched. This feature means you can leave one app running in the background while you do something else. For example, you might take a quick break from a game to go and update your status on Facebook or send a tweet on Twitter, and then jump back to your game.

The **App Switcher** bar provides another nice piece of functionality that we'll cover in this chapter. On the first iPad, there was a hardware button that locked the screen orientation. When the software was updated, that switch became a **Mute** key. With the new iOS 4.3, you can use the **App Switcher** bar to dictate how you want that switch to behave as well as make adjustments in the **Settings** app for the **Lock/Rotation** switch.

Multitasking or App Switching

With *multitasking*, or *App Switching*, you can leave many of your apps running in the background as you switch over to another without stopping the current app.

> **NOTE**: Developers have to implement multitasking on their end. While more and more multitasking-aware apps and updates are appearing every day, some apps still don't do it or don't do it fully.

Why might you want to use multitasking? Here are a few scenarios where you might want to use multitasking on your iPad:

- Copy and paste from one app (**Mail**) to another (**Calendar**).
- Answer a **FaceTime** call or reply to an **Email** message, and then jump back into the game you were playing without missing a beat.

- Continue listening to Internet radio (such as **Pandora** or **Slacker**) while playing your favorite game or browsing the Web.

- You no longer have to wait for photos to upload to **Facebook** or **Twitter**—they can be uploading in the background while you go and do other things on your iPad.

- If you use **Skype** to call people, you can now leave it running in the background to receive incoming calls; this was not possible before.

- You can also now keep turn-by-turn navigation running in the background and get voice directions while on a call or in another app. Like VoIP and streaming audio, navigation got a dedicated API.

How to Jump Between Apps

In order to multitask, you need to bring up the **App Switcher** bar at the bottom of the screen. Follow these steps to do so:

1. From any app or even the **Home** screen, double-click the **Home** button to bring up the **App Switcher** at the bottom of your screen (see Figure 8–1).

2. All open apps will be shown on the **App Switcher** bar.

3. Swipe right or left to find the app you want and tap it.

4. If you don't see the app you want on the **App Switcher** bar, press the **Home** button and start it from the **Home** screen.

5. Double-click the **Home** button again and tap the app you just left to jump back to it.

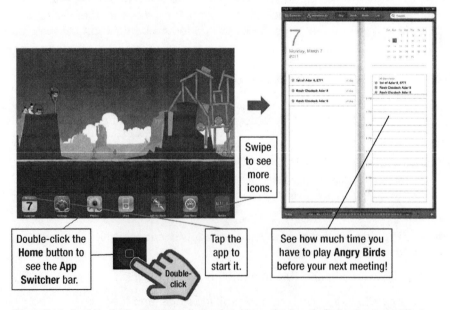

Swipe to see more icons.

Double-click the **Home** button to see the **App Switcher** bar.

Double-click

Tap the app to start it.

See how much time you have to play **Angry Birds** before your next meeting!

Figure 8–1. *Double-clicking the **Home** button to bring up the **App Switcher** bar to multitask*

How to Close Apps from the App Switcher

If you exit an app using a single click of the **Home** button, that app will stay running in the background, unless it is an active VOIP call, a location/navigation app, or some sort of upload.

> **NOTE**: Technically, any app other than VoIP, streaming audio, and location-aware apps will save state and suspend–or it will finish Internet activity such as uploading, and then save state and suspend. This takes up resources, however, and the iOS will shut apps when it determines memory is low. If there is a rogue process or an app that isn't killed quickly enough and chokes the iPad's memory, manually killing that process or app can fix things.

There are times when you want to completely close an app. For example, sometimes you may find your iPad running a little slower than you might like. In such cases, it can be a good idea to close apps completely and free up memory. Follow these steps to do so:

1. Double-click the **Home** button to bring up the **App Switcher** bar.

2. Press and hold any icon in the **App Switcher** bar until they all shake. You will notice that a **Red Circle** icon with a minus sign appears in the upper-left corner of each icon.

3. Tap the **Red Circle** icon to completely close the app.

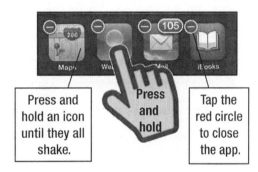

Press and hold an icon until they all shake.

Press and hold

Tap the red circle to close the app.

> **NOTE**: The preceding steps kill running apps or flush the saved state. Any app you close this way must restart the next time you tap it. Built-in apps like **Mail** will restart automatically, so you won't miss any emails.

iPod Controls and Lock Rotation/Mute Key

You can accomplish one other thing on the **App Switcher** bar if you swipe from left to right: see the iPod controls and the screen **Orientation Lock/Mute** icon.

The first generation iPad only let you adjust the **Orientation Lock**; after a subsequent software update, however, you could mute the iPad with the **Side** switch.

With the new iOS 4.3, you can change the function of the **Side** switch to **Lock Rotation** or **Mute**. Whichever is *not* chosen for the **Side** switch will be available in the **App Switcher** bar.

For example, if you have the **Side** switch set to **Lock Rotation**, the **App Switcher** bar will give you an icon to **Mute** the iPad.

> **NOTE:** The **Lock Rotation** feature is very useful is you are in an app like **iBooks** and don't want the book you are reading to keep changing between **Portrait** and **Landscape** modes if you shift positions or accidentally turn the iPad.

Follow these steps to set the function of the **Side** switch:

1. Tap the **Settings** icon.

2. Tap the **General** icon on the left-hand side.

3. Scroll down the right-hand side until you see the **Use Side Switch to**: option.

4. Choose either **Lock Rotation** or **Mute**. The other option will now be available in the **App Switcher** bar, as shown in Figure 8–2.

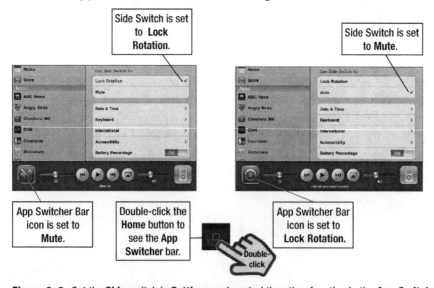

Figure 8–2. *Set the* **Side** *switch in* **Settings** *and control the other function in the* **App Switcher** *bar.*

Once you choose your preferred settings, changing the **Lock Rotation** or **Mute** function is easy:

1. From any app or even the **Home** screen, double-tap the **Home** button to bring up the **App Switcher** at the bottom of your screen.

2. Swipe left to right to see the iPod controls and the **Lock Rotation/Mute** icon.

3. Tap the **Lock Rotation** icon to lock the screen in **Portrait**, or **Vertical**, orientation. This orientation will be maintained even if you turn the iPad on its side. You know it is locked when you see a **Lock** icon inside the button and a **Lock** icon in the top status bar.

4. You can also use the **Previous Track**, **Play/Pause**, and **Next Track** buttons in the middle. If you hold down the **Previous Track** or **Next Track** buttons, they become **Rewind** or **Fast-Forward** buttons.

5. Or, you can tap the **iPod** icon to jump to the **iPod** app. If you were controlling background audio with another app like **Pandora**, you would see that icon instead.

6. You will also see control buttons for **AirPlay** (see Chapters 9 and 10), **Brightness**, and **Volume** (see Figure 8–3).

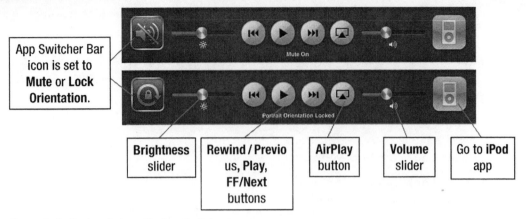

Figure 8–3. *iPod* controls on the *App Switcher* bar

Chapter 9

Playing Music

In this chapter, we show you how to turn your iPad into a great music player. The iPad comes from Apple, which popularized electronic music players, so you can bet it has some great capabilities. We will show you how to play and organize the music you buy from iTunes or sync from your computer. We will also show to view playlists in many ways and quickly find songs. Plus we will show you how to use the Genius feature to have the iPad locate and group similar songs in your library—it's sort of like a radio station that plays only music you like.

> **TIP:** Learn how to buy music right on your iPad in Chapter 20: "iTunes on the iPad." Find out how to buy music using iTunes on your computer or load your music CDs onto iTunes so you can sync them with your iPad in the "iTunes User Guide" in Part 4.

We will also show you how to stream free music using a free app called **Pandora**. With **Pandora**, you can select from a number of Internet radio stations or create your own by typing in your favorite artist's name.

Finally, we will discuss the **Home Sharing** feature, introduced in the latest version of software on the iPad 2. This software allows you to browse and play any content from your home network on your iPad while connected to the network.

Your iPad As a Music Player

Your iPad is probably one of the best music players on the market today. The generous screen size really allows you to interact with your music, playlists, cover art, and the organization of your music library. You can even connect your iPad via Bluetooth to your home or car stereo, so you can listen to beautiful stereo sound from your iPad!

> **TIP:** Check out Chapter 25: "Bluetooth" to learn how to hook up your iPad to your Bluetooth stereo speakers or car stereo.

Whether you use the built-in **iPod** music app or an Internet radio app like **Pandora**, you will find that you have unprecedented control over your music on the iPad.

The iPod App

Most music is handled through the **iPod** app—its icon is right on the **Home** screen. This icon is usually in the Bottom Dock of icons—the last one on the right.

Touch the **iPod** icon and, as Figure 9–1 shows, you'll see five soft keys across the bottom:

- **Songs:** See an alphabetical list of songs (also searchable).
- **Artists:** See an alphabetical list of artists (searchable like your Address Book).
- **Albums:** See an alphabetical list of albums (also searchable).
- **Genres:** See your music organized by musical genres.
- **Composers:** See an alphabetical listing of musical composers.

Figure 9–1. *The iPod **Home** screen layout*

TIP: You can turn the iPad sideways if that makes it easier to hold. Everything functions exactly the same on this screen, regardless of the orientation of the screen.

Playlists View

> **Note:** A playlist is a list of music you create. It can be made up of any genre, artist, year of recording, or collection of songs that interests you.

Many people group together music of a particular genre, like classical or rock. Others may create playlists with fast-beat music and call it "workout" or "running music." You can use playlists to organize your music just about any way you please.

Playlists are created either in iTunes on your computer and then synced to your iPad (see the "iTunes Guide"). You can also create a playlist right on your iPad, as we describe in the next section.

Once you've synced a playlist to your iPad or created one on your iPad, it shows up on the left-hand side of the iPod screen, under **Library**.

In this example, we touch our **Beatles** playlist, and all the songs from that playlist are listed.

To go to a different playlist, we just touch a different playlist along the left-hand side.

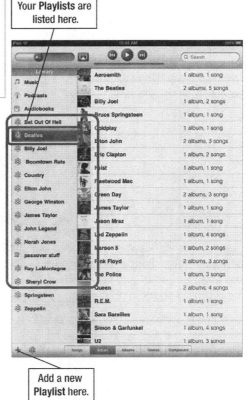

Your **Playlists** are listed here.

Add a new **Playlist** here.

> **NOTE:** You can edit the contents of some of your playlists on your iPad. However, Genius playlists that are created on your computer or iPad can't be edited on the iPad itself.

Creating Playlists on the iPad

The iPad lets you create unique playlists on the device that can be edited and even synced with your computer. Let's say you want a new selection of music in your iPad playlist. Just create the playlist—we'll show you how later in the chapter—and add songs. Whenever you want, you can remove those songs and add new ones—it couldn't be easier!

To create a new playlist on the iPad, touch the **Plus Sign** in the lower-left corner.

Give your playlist a unique name (we'll just call this one "iPad playlist"), and then touch **Save**.

The iPad then displays the **Add Songs** screen. Touch anywhere in the song name for any song you want to add to the new playlist.

You know a song is selected and will be added to the playlist when it turns gray.

> **NOTE:** Don't get frustrated trying to remove or deselect a song you tapped by mistake. You can't remove or deselect songs on this screen; you have to click **Done**, then remove them on the next screen. (We show you how in a moment.)

Select **Done** at the top right and the contents of the playlist will be displayed.

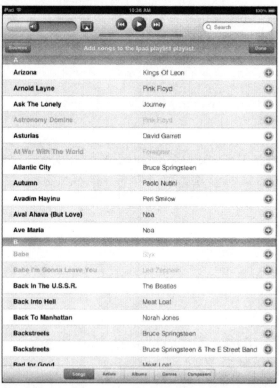

If you tapped a song or two by mistake or changed your mind, after you click **Done** you can remove songs on the next screen.

Follow these steps to delete a song:

1. Tap the **Red Circle** to the left of the song name.

2. Tap the **Delete** button to the right of the song.

Follow these steps to move a song up or down in a playlist:

1. Touch and hold the three gray bars to the right of the song.

2. Drag the song up or down and then let go.

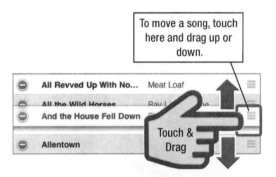

To move a song, touch here and drag up or down.

Touch & Drag

When you are sure you are done, just touch **Done** in the upper-right corner and your playlist will be set.

To change the playlist later, touch the **Edit** button and follow the steps described previously.

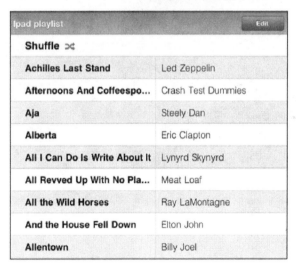

Searching for Music

Almost every view from your **iPod** app (i.e., **Playlists**, **Artists**, **Videos**, and **Songs**) has a **Search** window in the upper-right corner, as shown in Figure 9–2. Tap once in that **Search** window and type a few letters of the name of an artist, playlist, video, or song to instantly see a list of all matching items. This is the best way to quickly find something to listen to or watch on your iPad.

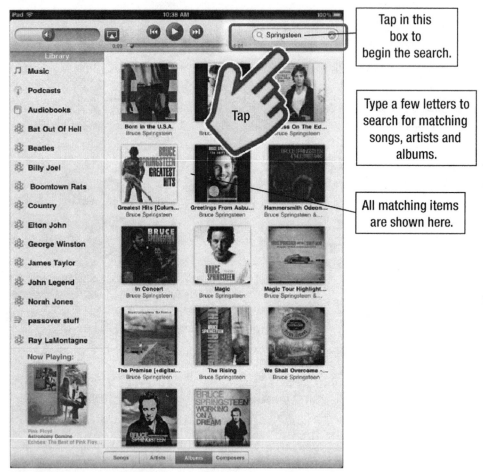

Figure 9–2. *Searching for music*

Changing the View in the iPod App

The **iPod** app is very flexible when it comes to ways to display and categorize your music. Sometimes, you might want to look at your songs listed by the artist. Other times, you might want to see a particular album or song. The iPad lets you easily change the view to help manage and play just the music you want at a given moment.

Artists View

The **Artists** view lists all the artists on your iPad; or, if you are in a playlist and select **Artists**, it will list the artists in that playlist.

Flick through the list to move to the first letter of the artist's name you are looking for.

When you find the artist's name, touch that name and all the songs by that artist will be listed, with a picture of the album art to the left.

> **TIP:** Use the same navigation and search features as you do with your **Contacts** app (the address book).

Aerosmith	1 album, 1 song
America	1 album, 1 song
Billy Joel	1 album, 3 songs
Boston	1 album, 4 songs
Bruce Hornsby & The Range	1 album, 1 song
Bruce Springsteen	1 album, 1 song
Crosby, Stills, Nash & Young	1 album, 1 song
The Doobie Brothers	1 album, 4 songs
The Eagles	1 album, 1 song
Elton John	2 albums, 2 songs
Eric Clapton	1 album, 1 song
Fleetwood Mac	1 album, 2 songs
Foreigner	2 albums, 3 songs
Green Day	1 album, 1 song
Jackson Browne	2 albums, 2 songs
James Taylor	1 album, 1 song
Joe Cocker	1 album, 1 song
Journey	1 album, 3 songs
KANSAS	1 album, 1 song
Led Zeppelin	1 album, 4 songs
Lynyrd Skynyrd	1 album, 1 song

Artists   Albums   Genres   Composers

Songs View

Touching the **Songs** tab shows you a list of every song on your iPad.

If you know the exact name of the song, flick through the list or touch the first letter of the song in the alphabetical list to the right.

Albums View

The music on your iPad is also organized by albums, which you'll see when you touch the **Albums** tab at the bottom.

Again, you can scroll through the album covers or touch the first letter of the album name in the alphabetical list, and then make your selection.

Once you choose an album, all the songs on that album will be listed.

To close the pop-up window with the list of songs, simply tap anywhere outside that window.

Genres

The **Genres** tab arranges your music into music types. This can be an easier way to find your music and to have more of a "themed" listening experience.

At times, you may want to hear a rock or jazz mix; you could select those particular genres and start playing some or all of your songs that fit those genres.

In this image, we touched **Rock**, and the iPad popped up a little window showing us how many albums and songs we have in that particular genre.

Composers

As with the other views, touching the **Composers** tab at the bottom lists your music in a specific way.

Sometimes you forget the title of the song, but you know the composer. Browsing the **Composers** on your iPad can help you find just what you are looking for.

Similar to other views, the **Composer** view tells you how many albums and songs you have by each composer.

Allen Collins	1 album, 1 song
Bruce Springsteen	3 albums, 3 songs
David Gilmour, Roger Waters,...	1 album, 1 song
don henley/glenn frey/joe walsh	1 album, 1 song
don henley/glenn frey/john da...	1 album, 1 song
Eric Clapton, Jim Gordon	1 album, 1 song
Freddie Mercury	1 album, 1 song
Graham Nash	1 album, 2 songs
Gregg Allman & Stephen Alai...	1 album, 1 song
James Robert Robinson 1943-...	1 album, 2 songs
Jim Steinman	1 album, 2 songs
Johnston, Tom	1 album, 1 song
Pete Townshend	1 album, 1 song
Simmons, Patrick	1 album, 1 song
Tom Scholz	1 album, 1 song

Viewing Songs in an Album

When you're in **Albums** view, just touch an album cover and the cover will flip, showing you the songs on that album (see Figure 9–3).

> **TIP**: When you start playing an album, the album cover may expand to fill the screen. Tap the screen once to bring up (or hide) the controls at the top and bottom. You can use these controls to manage the song and screen, as we'll describe in the next section.

To see the songs on an album that is playing, tap the **List** button. The album cover will turn over, revealing all the songs on that album. The song that is playing will have a small **Blue Arrow** next to it.

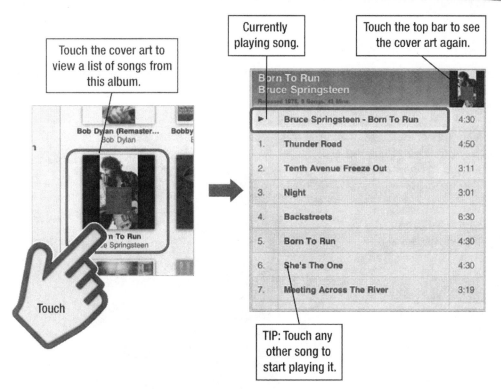

Figure 9–3. *Touch the album cover to see the songs on it.*

Tap the **Title Bar** above the list of songs and the album cover will return to its place in your music library.

> **NOTE:** This only works when you are in **Album** view. If you touch an album cover in **Artists** view, the song associated with that album cover will start to play.

Playing Your Music

Now that you know how to find your music, it is time to play it! Find a song or browse to a playlist using any of the methods listed previously. Simply tap the song name and it will begin to play.

This screen shows a picture of the album from which the song originates and the name of the song at the top.

Along the top of the screen, you'll find the **Volume** slider bar and the **Previous Song**, **Play/Pause**, and **Next Song** buttons.

If you want to see other songs on the album, just double-tap the album cover, and the screen will flip to show the other songs on that album.

To just view a list of songs in the album, touch the **List** button in the lower-right corner.

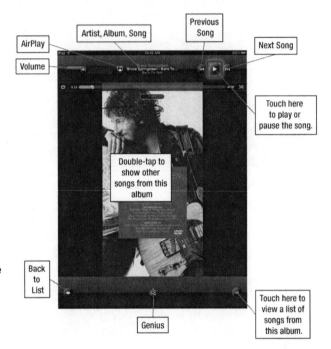

Pausing and Playing

Tap the **Pause** symbol (if your song is playing) or the **Play** arrow (if the music is paused) to play or resume your song.

Playing the Previous or Next Song

If you are in a playlist, touching the **Next** arrow (to the right of the **Play/Pause** button) will advance you to the next song in the list. If you are searching through your music by album, touching **Next** will advance to the next song on the album. Touching the **Previous** button will do the reverse.

NOTE: If you're at the beginning of a song, **Previous** will take you to the previous song. If the song is already playing, **Previous** will go to the beginning of the current song (and a second tap will take you to the previous song).

Adjusting the Volume

There are two ways to adjust the volume on your iPad: using the external **Volume** buttons or using the **Volume** slider control on the screen.

The external **Volume** buttons are on the upper-right side of the device. Press the **Volume Up** key (the top button) or the **Volume Down** key to raise or lower the volume. You'll see the **Volume** slider control move as you adjust the volume. You can also just touch and hold the **Volume** slider key to adjust the volume up or down.

TIP: To quickly mute the sound, press and hold the **Volume Down** key for about two seconds. You can also double-click the **Home** key and slide the **App Switcher** bar to the right to reveal the Music controls. If the **Side** switch is set to **Lock Rotation** (see Chapter 7), then there will be a soft key to mute the iPad.

Repeating, Shuffling, and Moving Around in a Song

In **Play** mode, you can activate additional controls by simply tapping the screen anywhere on the album cover. You'll then see an additional slider (the Scrubber Bar) at the top, along with the symbols for **Repeat** and **Shuffle.**

Moving to Another Part of a Song

Slide the Scrubber Bar to the right and you'll see the elapsed time of the song (displayed to the far right) change accordingly. If you are looking for a specific section of the song, drag the slider, then let go and listen to see if you are in the right place.

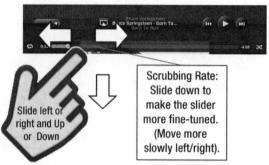

Slide left or right and Up or Down

Scrubbing Rate: Slide down to make the slider more fine-tuned. (Move more slowly left/right).

TIP: To make the slider move more slowly (i.e., to fine-tune it), drag your finger down the screen. This is called the *scrubbing rate*.

Repeat One Song and Repeat All Songs in Playlist or Album

To repeat the song you are listening to, touch the **Repeat** symbol at the left of the top controls twice until you see it turn blue with a 1 on it.

To repeat all songs in the playlist, song list, or album, touch the **Repeat** icon until it turns blue (and does not have a 1 on it).

To turn off the **Repeat** feature, press the icon until it turns white again.

Shuffle

If you are listening to a playlist, album, or any other category or list of music, you might decide you don't want to listen to the songs in order. Touching the **Shuffle** symbol rearranges the music to play in random order. You know **Shuffle** is set to **ON** when the icon is blue and set to **OFF** when it is white.

Genius

Apple has a feature for iTunes called Genius Playlists. If the Genius feature is activated in **iTunes**, You will see the **Genius** symbol shown on the bar to the right.

Genius Playlist:
Tap here to create a new playlist based on this song.

> **NOTE:** You must use **iTunes** on your computer to enable Genius Playlists. Check out "Chapter 29: Your iTunes User Guide "to learn how.
>
>

What the Genius feature does is create a playlist by associating similar songs with the one you're listening to. Unlike a random "shuffle" of music, Genius will scour your music library and then create a new playlist of 25, 50, or 100 songs (you set the Genius features in **iTunes** on your computer).

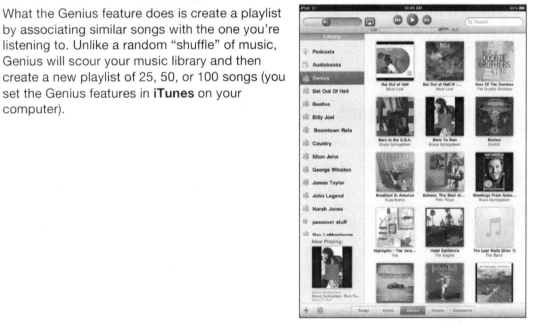

Genius is a great way to mix up your music and keep it fresh. The simple act of playing the type of music you like enables Genius to find some buried songs that may not be part of your established playlists.

> **TIP:** To create permanent Genius playlists, just create them in **iTunes** on your computer and sync them to your iPad. The Genius playlists you sync from **iTunes** can't be edited or changed on the iPad itself, but you can save, refresh or delete Genius playlists created on the iPad.

Now Playing

Sometimes you're having so much fun exploring your options for playlists or albums that you get deeply buried in a menu, and then find yourself just wanting to get back to the song you're listening to. Fortunately, this is always very easy to do because at the bottom left of most of the music screens, there is a **Now Playing** icon you can touch.

> **TIP:** To get back to the small album cover view in the bottom-left corner, tap the screen to bring up the controls, and then press the **Left Arrow** in the lower-left corner to get back to the previous view.

Viewing Other Songs on the Album

You may decide you want to listen to another song from the same album, rather than going to the next song in the playlist or genre list.

In the lower-right corner of the **Now Playing** screen, you'll see a small button with three lines on it. (If you don't see any controls, tap the screen once to bring them up.)

Tap that button and the view switches to a small image of the album cover. The screen now displays all the songs on that album.

Touch another song on the list and that song will begin to play.

NOTE: If you were in the middle of a playlist or a Genius Playlist and you start listening to another song from an album, you will not be taken back to that playlist. Instead, you'll need to either go back to your playlist library or tap **Genius** to make a new Genius Playlist.

Blue Triangle: Shows currently playing song.

Touch any other song to start playing it.

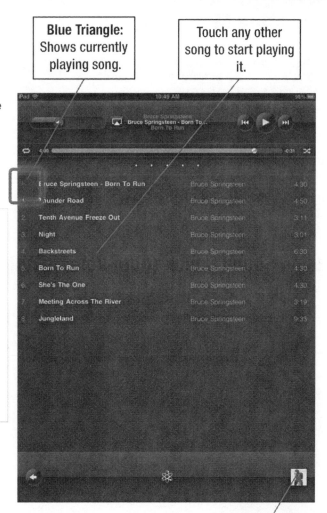

Touch **Album** icon to switch back to album cover.

Adjusting Music Settings

There are several settings you can adjust to tweak your music-playing to suit your tastes. You'll find these in the **Settings** menu. Just touch the **Settings** icon on your **Home** screen to bring up the menu.

In the middle of the **Settings** screen, touch the **iPod** tab to go to the **iPod** music settings screen. There are four settings you can adjust on this screen: **Sound Check**, **EQ**, **Volume Limit**, and **Lyrics & Podcast Info**.

Using Sound Check (Auto Volume Adjust)

TIP: Because songs are recorded at different volumes, sometimes during playback a particular song might sound quite loud compared to another. **Sound Check** can eliminate this. If **Sound Check** is set to **ON**, all your songs will play back at roughly the same volume.

EQ (Sound Equalizer Setting)

Sound equalization is very personal and subjective. Some people like more bass in their music, some like more treble, and some like more of an exaggerated mid-range. Whatever your music tastes, there is an **EQ** setting for you.

> **NOTE:** Using the **EQ** setting can diminish battery capacity somewhat.

Just touch the **EQ** tab and then select either the type of music you most often listen to or a specific option to boost treble or bass. Experiment, have fun, and find the setting that's perfect for you.

Volume Limit (Safely Listen to Music at Reasonable Volumes)

The **Volume Limit** screen provides a great way for parents to control the volume on their kids' iPads. It is also a good way to make sure you don't listen too loudly through headphones, so you don't damage your ears. You just move the slider to a volume limit and then lock that limit.

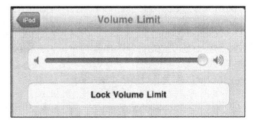

To lock the volume limit, touch the **Lock Volume Limit** button and enter a four-digit passcode. You will be prompted to put your passcode in once more and the volume limit will then be locked.

Showing Music Controls When Your iPad Is Locked

You can control your music even if your iPad is locked. Just double-click the **Home** button (when iPad is locked) and the controls for adjusting the music show up on the top locked screen. There is no reason to unlock the screen and then go to the **iPod** app to find the controls.

Notice that the screen is still locked in the image to the right—yet the music controls are now visible along the top. You can pause, skip, go to a previous song, or adjust the volume without actually unlocking the iPad.

Home Sharing

New to the iPad this year is the ability to share your home iTunes library via Apple's proprietary Home Sharing function.

Essentially, Home Sharing allows you to browse and play anything from your home library (usually on your desktop or network drive) on your iPad.

One great advantage of this feature is that you aren't constrained by the limited storage on the iPad; this feature gives you access to your entire library whenever you are connected to your home network.

Follow these steps to enable Home Sharing:

1. Tap the **Settings** icon on the **Home** page.

2. Touch the **iPod** icon in the left-hand column.

3. Input your **Apple ID** and **Password** under the **Home Sharing** heading on the right. Make sure you enter the same Apple ID and password as the computer on the network that has Home Sharing enabled (see Chapter 29).

4. Touch the **Done** button on the keyboard.

5. Start up the **iPod** app and notice the new category in the top left entitled **Library**.

6. Touch **Library** and see the available network libraries to browse.

7. Choose your **Network** library and now browse and play any item from your home network on the iPad (see Figure 9–4).

Figure 9–4. *Using Home Sharing on the iPad*

AirPlay

The **AirPlay** program is another Apple proprietary function built into the iPad. **AirPlay** is available across a wide range of apps, but here we will just look at **AirPlay** and the **iPod** app.

AirPlay essentially is built-in wireless streaming of your music to an **AirPlay**-compatible device, such as an Apple TV or wireless speaker system.

With an Apple TV hooked up, you can choose **AirPlay** and have whatever is playing on your iPad stream automatically to your home theater setup.

Using **AirPlay** is easy; follow these steps to do so:

1. Start your iPod app.

2. Play any song or album.

3. Touch the **AirPlay** icon.

4. Choose the **AirPlay** device to which you wish to send your music (see Figure 9–5).

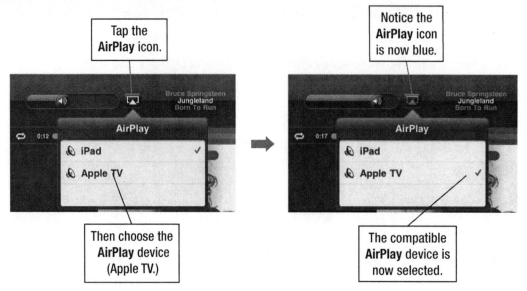

Figure 9–5. *Using AirPlay on the iPad*

Listening to Free Internet Radio (Pandora)

While your iPad gives you unprecedented control over your personal music library, there may be times when you want to just "mix it up" and listen to some other music.

> **TIP:** A basic Pandora account is free and can save you considerable money compared with buying lots of new songs from the iTunes Store.

Pandora grew out of the Music Genome Project. This was a huge undertaking. A large team of musical analysts looked at just about every song ever recorded, and then developed a complex algorithm of attributes to associate with each song.

> **NOTE:** Pandora may have some competition by the time you read this book. Right now there's one other competitor called **Slacker Personal Radio**, but there will probably be more. If you want to find more options, try searching the App Store for "iPad Internet Radio." Please also note that **Pandora** is a US-only application. **Slacker** is available only in the US and Canada, while **Spotfly** is big in Europe. Hopefully, more options will begin to pop up for international users.

Getting Started with Pandora

Pandora lets you design your own unique radio stations built around artists you like. Best of all, it is completely free!

Start by downloading the **Pandora** app from the App Store. Just go to the App Store and search for "Pandora."

Now just touch the **Pandora** icon to start the app.

The first time you start **Pandora**, you'll be asked to either create an account or to sign in if you already have an account. Just fill in the appropriate information—an email address and a password are required—and you can start designing your own music-listening experience.

Pandora is also available for Windows or Mac computers, as well as for most smartphone platforms. If you already have a Pandora account, all you have to do is sign in.

Pandora's Main Screen

Your stations are listed along the left-hand side. Just touch one of your stations and it will begin to play. Usually, the first song will be from the actual artist chosen and the next songs will be from similar artists.

The large screen of the iPad lets you see lots of information.

In the middle of the page, you'll see a nice bio of the artist, which changes with each new song.

There will also be a small advertisement in the window in the lower-left corner—if you upgrade to **Pandora One**, you will see a different window very much like the **Now Playing** album cover in the **iPod** music app.

Thumbs Up or Thumbs Down in Pandora

If you like a particular song, touch the **Thumbs Up** icon and you'll hear more from that particular artist.

Conversely, if you don't like an artist on this station, touch the **Thumbs Down** icon and you won't hear that artist again.

You can also pause the song and come back later, or skip to the next selection on your station.

NOTE: With a free Pandora account, you are limited with the number of skips per hour you can make. You also will occasionally hear advertising. To get rid of these restrictions, upgrade to a paid Pandora One account, as explained momentarily.

Pandora's Menu

Above the bio to the right is a **Menu** button. Touch this and you can bookmark the artist or song, or go to the iTunes Store to buy music from this artist.

Creating a New Station in Pandora

Creating a new station couldn't be easier.

Just touch the **Search** window where you see **Artist, Song or Composer** in the upper-left corner and type in the name of an artist, song, or composer.

When you find what you are looking for, touch the selection and **Pandora** will immediately start to build a station around your choice.

You'll then see the new station listed with your other stations.

You can build up to 100 stations in Pandora.

> **TIP:** You can organize your stations by pressing the **By Date** or **ABC** buttons in the bottom-left corner of the screen.

Adjusting Pandora's Settings—Your Account, Upgrade, and More

You can sign out of your Pandora account, adjust the audio quality, and even upgrade to **Pandora One** (which removes advertising) by tapping the **Settings** icon in the lower-left corner of the screen (see Figure 7–5).

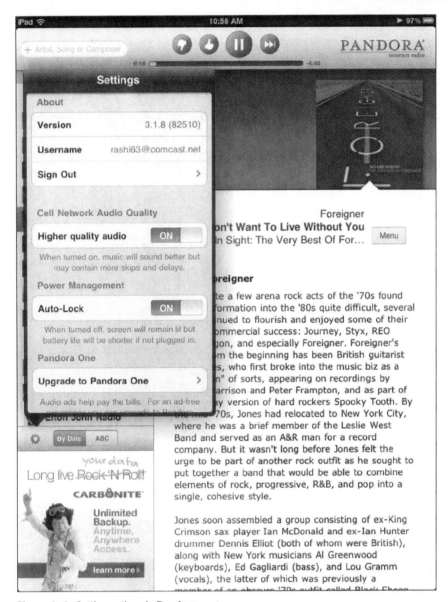

Figure 9–6. *Setting options in **Pandora***

To sign out, tap your account name.

To adjust the sound quality, move the switch under **Cell Network Audio Quality** to either **ON** or **OFF**. When you are on a cellular network, setting this to **OFF** is probably better; otherwise, you may hear more skips and pauses in the playback.

NOTE: You can only adjust the **Cell Network Audio Quality** on the iPad + 3G models.

When you are on a strong Wi-Fi connection, you can set this to **ON** for better quality. See Chapter 5: "Wi-Fi and 3G Connections" to learn more about the various connections.

To save your battery life, you should set the **Auto-Lock** to **ON**, which is the default. If you want the force the screen to stay lit, then switch this to setting to **OFF**.

To remove all advertising, tap the **Upgrade to Pandora One** button. A web browser window will open, and you'll be take to Pandora's web site to enter your credit card information. At the time of publishing, the annual account cost is $36.00, but that may be different by the time you read this book.

Using AirPlay in Pandora

You can magically "send" your music from **Pandora** to any **AirPlay** compatible device, just as you did earlier from the **iPod** app. The only difference is that, in order to access the **AirPlay** controls, you need to access the **App Switcher** bar.

Follow these steps to do so:

1. Double click the **Home** button to bring up the **App Switcher** bar.

2. Slide the **App Switcher** bar from left to right to show the **Music** controls. If you have many apps open, you may need to slide a couple of times.

3. Touch the **AirPlay** icon in the **Music** controls and select the **AirPlay**-compatible device to send your music to.

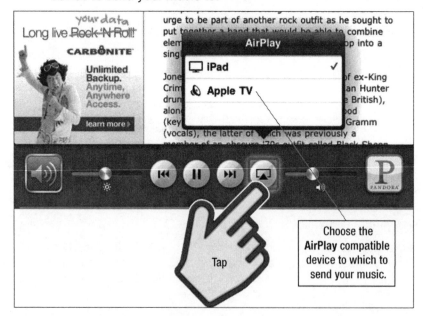

Figure 9–7. *Using Airplay in Pandora*

Chapter 10

Viewing Videos, TV Shows, and More

The iPad is an amazing "media consumption" device. Nowhere is this more apparent than in the various video-viewing applications available.

In this chapter, we will show you how to watch movies, TV shows, podcasts, and music videos on your iPad. You can buy or download such content for free from the iTunes store or iTunes University (iTunes U). You can also link your iPad to your Netflix account (and most likely other video rental services soon), allowing you to watch streaming TV shows and movies.

With your iPad, you can also watch YouTube videos and videos from the Web on your Safari browser and through various apps like the **ABC** app from the App Store.

> **NOTE:** Some apps, such as Canada's **Global**, are exclusive in each region. Video apps can vary by region, so check your local App Store and be sure to search for local TV network names like ABC or Global.

Using Your iPad As a Video Player

The iPad is more than a capable music player; it is also a fantastic, portable video-playing system. Its wide screen, fast processor, and great operating system make watching anything from music videos to TV shows and full-length motion pictures a real joy. The size of the iPad is perfect for watching shows while sitting back in a chair or while on an airplane. It is also great for the kids in the back seat of long car trips. The ten-hour battery life means you can even go on a coast-to-coast flight and not run out of power! You can also buy a *power inverter* for your car to keep the iPad charged even longer (see the "Charging Your iPad and Battery Tips" section in Chapter 1 for more information).

Loading Videos onto Your iPad

You can load videos on your iPad just as you do your music, using iTunes from your computer or right from the **iTunes** icon on your iPad.

If you purchase or rent videos and TV shows from iTunes on your computer, then you can manually or automatically sync them to your iPad.

Watching Videos on the iPad

To watch videos on your iPad, click the **Videos** icon, which is usually on the first page of icons on your **Home** screen.

> **NOTE:** You can also watch videos from the **YouTube** icon, the **Safari** icon, and other video-related apps you download from the App Store.

Video Categories

You can see several category buttons along the top of the **Videos** screen: **Movies, TV Shows, Podcasts,** and **Music Videos.**

> **NOTE:** If you enabled Home Sharing (see Chapter 9), you will also see a button for **Shared**.

The default view is the **Movies** view; if you have any movies loaded on the iPad, they will be visible.

You may see more or fewer categories depending on the types of videos you have loaded on your iPad. If you have only **Movies** and **iTunes U** videos, then you will see only those two category buttons. Touch any of the other categories to show the corresponding videos in each category.

Playing a Movie

Movies

Just Simply touch the movie you wish to watch, and it will begin to play (see Figure 10–1). Most videos take advantage of the iPad's relatively large screen, playing in **Widescreen** (also known as **Landscape**) mode. Just turn your iPad to watch them.

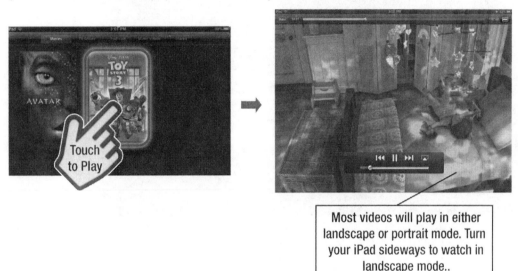

Most videos will play in either landscape or portrait mode. Turn your iPad sideways to watch in landscape mode..

Figure 10–1. *Playing a video*

When a video starts to play, you will see only that video; you won't see any menus, controls, or anything else on the screen.

To Pause or Access Controls

Touch anywhere on the screen, and the control bars and options will become visible (see Figure 10–2). Most controls are similar to those in the **Music Player** app. Tap the **Pause** button, and the video will pause.

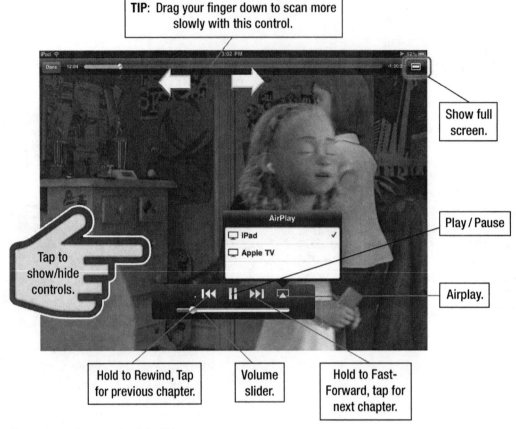

Move to a different section of the video.
TIP: Drag your finger down to scan more
slowly with this control.

Show full
screen.

Play / Pause

Tap to
show/hide
controls.

Airplay.

Hold to Rewind, Tap
for previous chapter.

Volume
slider.

Hold to Fast-
Forward, tap for
next chapter.

Figure 10–2. *The controls of the **Videos** app*

Fast-Forward or Rewind the Video

You can see the expected **Fast-Forward** and **Rewind** buttons of the **Videos** app on
either side of the **Play/Pause** button. To jump to the next chapter-specific part of the
video, just touch and hold the **Fast-Forward** button (to the right of the **Play/Pause**
button). When you get to the desired spot in the video, release the **Fast-Forward**
button. The video will begin playing normally.

To rewind to the beginning on the video, tap the **Rewind** button. To rewind to a specific
part or location, touch and hold the **Rewind** button, just as you did when fast-
forwarding the video.

> **NOTE:** If you're viewing a full-length movie with several chapters, tapping either **Reverse** or
> **Fast-Forward** will move either back or ahead one chapter.

Using the Time Slider Bar

At the top of the video screen is a slider that shows you the elapsed time of the video. If you know exactly (or approximately) which point in the video you wish to watch, just hold and drag the slider to that location. Some people find this to be a little more exact than holding down the **Fast-Forward** or **Rewind** buttons.

> **TIP:** Drag your finger down to move the slider more slowly. In other words, start by touching the **Slider** control, then drag your finger down the screen—notice that the further down the screen your finger is, the slower the slider moves left or right.

Changing the Size of the Video (Widescreen vs. Fullscreen)

Most of your videos will play in widescreen format. However, if you have a video that was not converted for your iPad or is not optimized for its screen resolution, you can touch the **Expand** button, which is to the right of the upper **Status** bar.

You will notice that there are two arrows. If you are in **Fullscreen** mode, the arrows point in, towards each other. If you are in **Widescreen** mode, the arrows point out, away from each other.

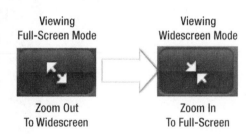

Viewing Full-Screen Mode   Viewing Widescreen Mode

Zoom Out To Widescreen   Zoom In To Full-Screen

In a widescreen movie that is not taking up the full screen of the iPad, touching the **Expand** button will zoom in a bit. Touching it again will zoom out.

> **NOTE:** You can also *double-tap* the screen to zoom in and fill the screen. Be aware that, just like on your widescreen TV, forcing a non-widescreen video into widescreen format can sometimes cause you to lose part of the picture.

Using the Chapters Feature

Most full-length movies purchased from the iTunes store, and some movies that are converted for the iPad, will give you a Chapters feature. This feature makes watching a movie on your iPad very much like watching a DVD on your home TV.

Just bring up the controls for the video by tapping the screen, and then select **Done**.

This will bring you back to the main page for the movie.

Touch the **Chapters** button in the upper-right corner, scroll to the chapter you wish to watch, and then touch it.

Viewing the Chapters

You can scroll or flick through quickly to locate the scene or chapter that you wish to watch.

You will also notice that the exact time that the chapter begins (relative to the start of the movie) displays to the right of each chapter image.

In addition to the chapter menu mentioned previously, you can also quickly advance to the previous or next chapter in a movie by tapping the **Rewind** or **Fast-Forward** buttons. One tap moves you one chapter in either direction.

> **NOTE:** The Chapters feature usually works only with movies that are purchased from the iTunes store. Movies that are converted and loaded onto your iPad usually will not have chapters.

Watching a TV Show

TV Shows

The iPad is great for watching your favorite TV shows. You can purchase TV shows from the iTunes store. You can also download sample shows from some iPad apps, like the **ABC** app.

Just touch the **TV Shows** tab at the top to see the shows you have downloaded on your iPad. Scroll through your available shows and touch **Play**. The video controls work just like the movie controls.

Watching Podcasts

Podcasts

We normally think of podcasts as being audio-only broadcasts that can be downloaded through iTunes. Video podcasts are now quite prevalent and can be found on any number of sites, including many public broadcasting websites and on iTunes U. The latter provides a listing of university podcasts and other school-related information through iTunes.

Consider this iTunes U story from Gary Mazo:

"Recently, I was browsing the **iTunes U** section inside the **iTunes** app on the iPad with my son, who had just been accepted to Caltech. We were wondering about the housing situation and, lo and behold, we found a video podcast showing a tour of the Caltech dorms. We downloaded it, and the podcast went right into the podcast directory for future viewing. We were able to do a complete virtual tour of the housing without flying out to the school's location in California from the East Coast."

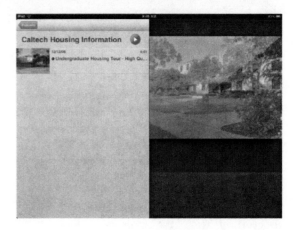

Watching Music Videos

Music videos are available for your iPad from a number of sources. Often, if you buy a *Deluxe* album from iTunes, it might include a music video or two. Music videos can also be purchased from the iTunes store, and many record companies and recording artists make them available for free on their websites.

Music videos will automatically get sorted into the **Music Videos** section of your **Videos** app.

Touch the **Music Videos** tab and start playing the video. The controls work just as they do in all other video applications.

Video Options

As in your music player, there are a few options that you can adjust for the video player. These options are accessed through the **Settings** icon from your **Home** screen.

Touch the **Settings** icon and then scroll down to touch the **Video** options.

Start Playing Option

Sometimes, you will have to stop watching a particular video. The **Start Playing** option lets you decide what to do the next time you want to watch the video. Your options are to either watch the video from the beginning or from where you left off. Just select the option that you desire and that will be the action your **Videos** app takes from now on.

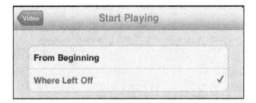

Closed Captioned

If your video has closed-captioned capabilities, closed captioning will be shown on your screen when this switch is turned to **ON**.

TV-Out: Widescreen

There are many third-party gadgets out there that allow you to watch the video from your iPad on some external source, such as a TV or computer screen, or even an array of video glasses that simulate watching on a very large-screen monitor. Most of these options require that your **Widescreen** setting under the **TV Out** option be set to **ON**. By default, it is set to **OFF**.

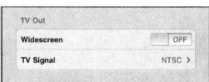

> **TIP:** You can purchase a VGA adapter to plug your iPad into a VGA computer monitor to watch movies. There is now an HDMI adapter available from Apple, as well.
>
> See the "Accessories" section of the Quick Start Guide for more information.

TV Signal

There are some advanced ways of taking content from your iPad and playing it on your TV or DVR with the right cable. You also need to have the right TV signal setting. This is typically changed only if you use your iPad in another country. If you live in the U.S., your TV works with the NTSC standard.

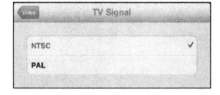

However, most European countries use PAL. If you are not sure which standard you use, contact your TV, cable, or satellite company.

Deleting Videos

To delete a video (to save space on your iPad), just choose the category from which you wish to delete the video—as you did at the start of this chapter (see Figure 10–3).

> **NOTE:** If you're syncing videos from iTunes, make sure to uncheck it there as well, or iTunes just might sync it right back to the iPad on the next sync!

Next, touch and hold on a particular video you wish to delete. Just as when deleting an app, a small black **x** will appear in the top left-hand corner. Touch the **x** and you will be prompted to delete the video.

Touch the **Delete** button, and the video will be deleted from your system.

> **NOTE:** This deletes the video only from your iPad—a copy will still remain in your video library in iTunes if you want to load it back onto your iPad at a later date. However, if you delete a rented movie from the iPad, it will be deleted permanently!

Figure 10–3. *Deleting a video*

AirPlay

AirPlay is another Apple proprietary function built into the iPad. **AirPlay** is available across a wide range of apps, but here we will just look at **AirPlay** and the **Videos** app.

AirPlay essentially is built-in wireless streaming of your music to an AirPlay-compatible device, such as an Apple TV or a wireless-speaker system.

With an Apple TV hooked up, you can choose **AirPlay** and have whatever is playing on your iPad stream automatically to your TV or home theater setup.

Using **AirPlay** is as simple as following these steps:

1. Start your **Videos** app.

2. Play any movie, TV show, or podcast.

3. Touch the **AirPlay** icon.

4. Choose the **AirPlay** device to which you wish to send your music (see Figure 10–4).

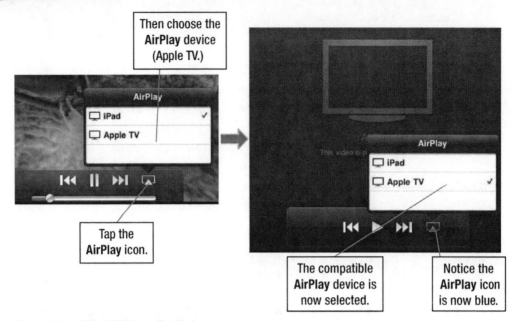

Figure 10–4. *Using **AirPlay** on the iPad*

Home Sharing

New to the iPad this year is the ability to share your home iTunes library via Apple's proprietary **Home Sharing** function.

Essentially, **Home Sharing** allows you to browse and play anything from your home library (usually on your desktop or network drive) on your iPad.

Begin by following the instructions for setting up **Home Sharing** as described in Chapter 9. At this point, the **Shared** button will appear as described previously. Touch the **Shared** button, and you will see all videos stored on your network drive available for viewing on your iPad.

YouTube on Your iPad

Watching YouTube videos is certainly one of the most popular things for people to do on their computers these days. YouTube is as close to you as your iPad.

You can find a **YouTube** icon right on your **Home** screen. Just touch the **YouTube** icon and you will be taken to the **YouTube** app.

Searching for Videos

When you first start the **YouTube** app, you will usually see the **Featured** videos on YouTube for that day.

You can now scroll through the video choices, just as you do in other apps.

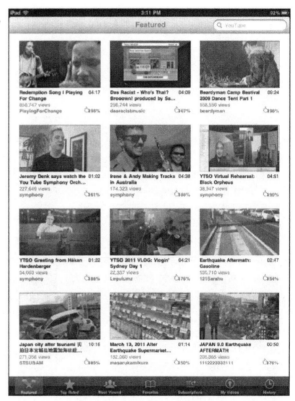

Using the Bottom Icons

You can see seven icons along the bottom of the **YouTube** app: **Featured**, **Top Rated**, **Most Viewed**, **Favorites**, **Subscriptions**, **My videos**, and **History**. Each is fairly self-explanatory.

To see the videos that YouTube is featuring that day, touch the **Featured** icon. To see those videos that are most-viewed online, touch the **Most Viewed** icon.

After you watch a particular video, you will have the option to set it as a favorite on **YouTube** for easy retrieval later on. If you have set bookmarks, they will appear when you touch the **Favorite** icon.

You can also search the huge library of YouTube videos. Touch the search box just as you have in previous apps, and the keyboard will pop up. Next, type in a phrase, topic, or even the name of a video.

In this example, I am looking for the newest Made Simple Learning video tutorial. I type in "Made Simple Learning" to see a list of videos to watch.

When I find the video I want to watch, I can touch it to see more information. I can even rate the video by touching the video during playback and selecting the **Thumbs up** or **Thumbs down** (like and dislike) buttons available in **Portrait** mode.

Playing Videos

Once you make your choice, touch the video you want to watch. Your iPad will begin playing the YouTube video in **Portrait** or **Landscape** mode (see Figure 10–5).

> **NOTE**: You will see an **AirPlay** icon on YouTube videos, as well. Just touch the **AirPlay** icon and you can send the video right to your Apple TV or other **AirPlay** device.

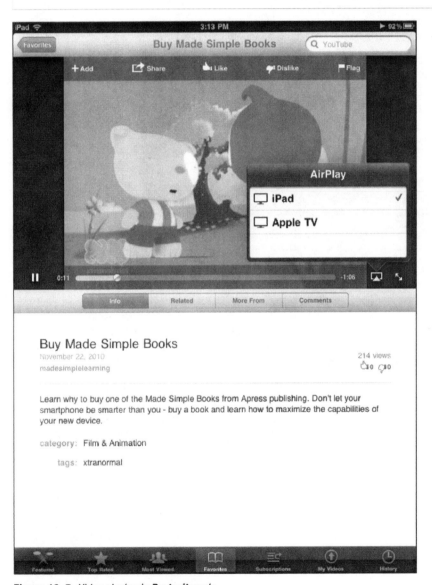

Figure 10–5. *Video playing in **Portrait** mode*

Video Controls

Once the video begins to play, the on-screen controls disappear, so you see only the video. To stop, pause, or activate other options while the video is playing, just tap the screen (see Figure 10–6).

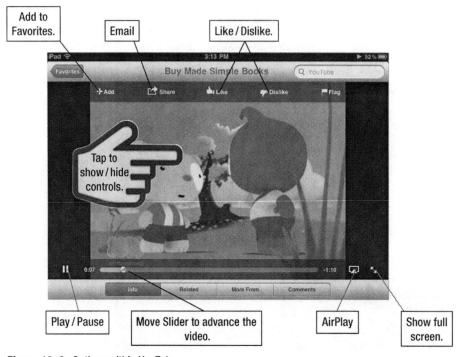

Figure 10–6. *Options within YouTube*

The on-screen options are very similar what you see when watching any other video. Along the bottom is the **Slider** control, which shows your place in the video. To move to another part in the video, just drag the slider.

To fast-forward through the video, just touch and hold the **Fast-Forward** arrow. To quickly move in reverse, touch and hold the **Reverse** arrow. To advance to the next video in the YouTube list, tap the **Fast-Forward/Next** arrow. To watch the previous video in the list, tap the **Reverse/Back** arrow.

To set a favorite, touch the **Favorite** icon.

To email the video, touch the **Share** icon. Your email will start with a link to the video in the body of the email. Next, type the recipient; you will learn more about sending email and attachments via email in Chapter 13.

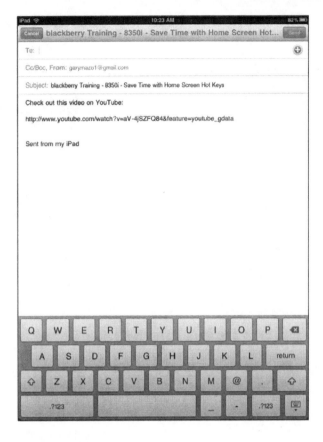

Checking and Clearing Your History

Touch the **History** icon

in the lower right-hand corner of the page. Your recently viewed videos will appear.

If you want to clear your history, just touch the **Clear** button in the upper-left corner.

To watch a video from your history, touch it and it will start to play.

Netflix on the iPad

In recent years, Netflix has grown to become a leading source of video rentals for consumers. Most recently, Netflix added video *streaming* of content that is delivered wirelessly to computers and other set-top boxes for your TV.

Now Netflix is available to iPad users through the **Netflix** app in the App Store.

Go to the App Store, as shown in Chapter 21: "The Amazing App Store," and search for the Netflix app.

Choose the **Download** button (the app is free) and you are on your way.

You need an active Netflix account to use this service, so either create one when you start the app or just sign into your Netflix account if you already have one.

The beauty of the **Netflix** app is that you can add DVDs to your queue and have them sent out to you. You can also watch TV shows and movies instantly—streaming them right to the iPad.

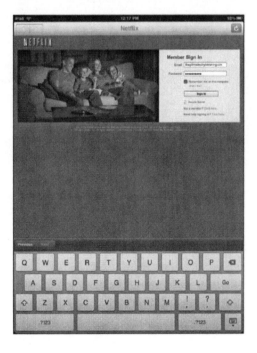

Navigating Netflix is very easy and just like using Netflix on your computer. You have a top bar with tabs for **Watch Movies Instantly**, **Watch TV Shows Instantly**, **Browse DVDs**, and **Your Queue.**

When you make your selection, you will see what you have recently watched (so you can resume watching), as well as video categories based on the preferences you selected when you established your Netflix account.

Each row of videos has a **See More** tab to show you more options. If you don't find what you are looking for, just touch the **Search** button at the bottom and type in the name of a movie, actor, director, or genre.

Once you find the movie or TV show you want to watch, touch **Play Now** and the movie will begin to stream to your iPad. The video controls are similar to those in all the other video-playing apps for theiPad; however, there is no **AirPlay** option for Netflix at this time.

> **CAUTION:** Netflix uses a great deal of data, so make sure you have a strong Wi-Fi signal if you are streaming over Wi-Fi. Alternatively, if you are using 3G cellular data, make sure you have an adequate data plan.

Watching Other TV Shows

New apps are introduced all the time, as are new options for watching other network shows and movies. This continues to change quickly; and, by the time you read this, even more TV shows will be available, with more to be added every month.

One of the best options at launch time was the **ABC** app, which is available as a free download in the App Store.

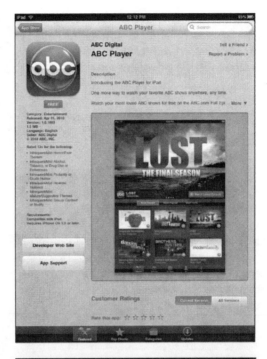

Once the app is downloaded, your favorite ABC TV shows will be available for streaming. ABC streams its most popular shows, making several full episodes available. The **ABC** app also uses large amounts of data, so make sure you have a good Wi-Fi connection or an unlimited 3G plan before you stream TV shows.

Hulu on the iPad

In recent years, Hulu has become a leading source of video streaming of content delivered wirelessly to computers and other set-top boxes for your TV.

Hulu Plus

Just after launch of the original iPad, the **Hulu Plus** app was released in the App Store. Hulu Plus is a subscription-based service of $7.99 a month, but there is also free content available.

With a full subscription to this service, pretty much every episode of every TV show you watch or have ever watched is now available to stream to your iPad.

Launch the app and you will see five icons at the top: **Free Gallery**, **Main**, **TV**, **Movies**, and **Search**.

Scroll through the **Free Gallery** to see which shows are available now for free viewing.

Touch a show and it immediately begins playing. Hold the iPad in **Landscape** mode to make the video fill the screen.

Searching for Videos

Touch the **Search** icon at the bottom and type in the name of a particular TV show. You can also browse the **Featured** or **Popular** categories. When you find your show, all the videos available will be available to watch.

NOTE: If you do not have a Hulu Plus subscription, you will not be able to view the videos.

Choosing What to Watch

Touch any one of the middle row of icons to see the **Featured**, **Most Popular**, or **Recently Added** videos.

Touch the **All** tab to choose between **Episodes**, **Movies**, or **Clips**.

Video Controls in Hulu Plus

The video controls are a bit different in the **Hulu Plus** app. Touch the screen when watching a show and, as when watching any other video, the video controls appear as shown in Figure 10–7.

There is a **Play/Pause** button at the left, as well as a timeline for the video. Simply drag your finger along the timeline to advance to another part of the video.

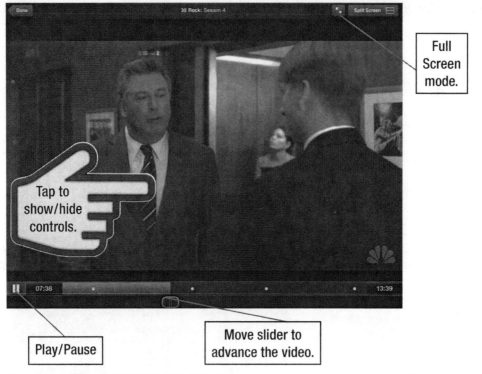

Figure 10–7. *Video controls in the **Hulu Plus** app*

NOTE: You cannot advance through commercials in **Hulu Plus**. During a commercial, an icon will appear in the upper right-hand corner that resembles the **Share** icon. If you touch this icon, you will go to the website of the advertiser.

CAUTION: Hulu Plus uses a great deal of data, so make sure you have a strong Wi-Fi signal.

Chapter 11

Surf the Web with Safari

Now we'll take you through one of the most fun things to do on your iPad: surfing the web. You may have heard web surfing on the iPad is a more intimate experience than ever before—we agree! We'll show you how to touch, zoom around, and interact with the Web like never before with Safari on your iPad. You'll learn how to set and use bookmarks, quickly find things with the search engine, open and switch between multiple browser windows, and even easily copy text and graphics from web pages.

Web Browsing on the iPad

You can browse the web to your heart's content via Wi-Fi or with your iPad's 3G connection (on Wi-Fi + 3G models.) The iPad has what many feel is the most capable mobile browsing experience available today. Web pages look very much like web pages on your computer. With the iPad's ability to zoom in, you don't even have to worry about the smaller screen size inhibiting your web browsing experience. In short, web browsing is a much more personal experience on the iPad.

You can browse in portrait or landscape mode, whichever you prefer. You can also quickly zoom into a video by double-tapping it or pinching open on it, which is natural to you because those are the motions to zoom in text and graphics.

Why Do Some Videos and Sites Not Appear? (Flash Player Required)

> ## Flash version 9,0 or greater is required
>
> ## You have no flash plugin installed
> Click here to download latest version

Some web sites are designed with Adobe Flash player, and as of publishing time, the iPad does not support Adobe Flash. Apple seems to have made a decision to not support the Flash Player. If you tap on a video and the video does not play, or you see something like "Flash Plugin Required," "Download the Latest Flash Plugin to view this video," or "Adobe Flash Required to view this site," you will not be able to view the video or web page.

There are now browsers in the App Store like **Skyfire** and **iSwifter** that transcode Flash into H.264 video on the server side so they work on iPad.

An Internet Connection Is Required

You do need a live Internet connection on your iPad—either Wi-Fi or 3G (cellular data)—in order to browse the web. Check out the "Connectivity" section in Chapter 5 to learn more.

Launching the Web Browser

You should find the **Safari** icon on your **Home Screen**; this is your web browser. Usually, the **Safari** icon is in the lower left of the **Bottom Dock**.

Touch the **Safari** icon and you will be taken to the browser's home page. Most likely, this will be Apple's iPad page.

As you find web sites you like, you can set bookmarks to easily jump to them at a later date. We will show you how later in this chapter.

Layout of Safari Web Browser Screen

Figure 11–1 shows how a web page looks in Safari, and the different actions you can take in the browser.

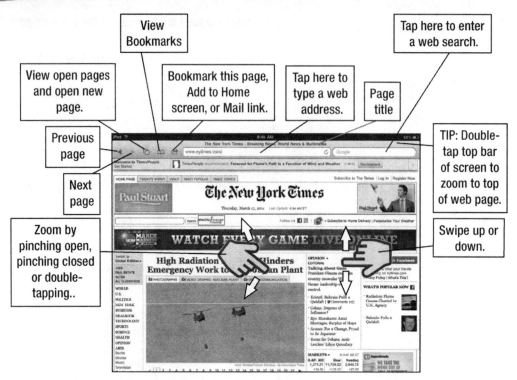

Figure 11–1. *Safari web browser page layout*

As you look at your screen, notice that the **Address Bar** is in the upper left side of the screen. This displays the current web address. To the right is the **Search** window. By default, this is set to Google search, but you can change it if you want.

At the top of the screen are five icons; **Back**, **Forward**, **Open Pages**, **Bookmarks**, and the **Action** button.

Typing a Web Address

The first thing you'll want to learn is how to get to your favorite web pages. Just as you would on your computer, you type in the web address (URL) into the browser. To start, tap the **Address Bar** at the top of the browser, as shown in Figure 11–2. The keyboard will appear and the window for the browser will expand. Start typing and press the **Go** key to go to that page.

> **TIP:** Remember to use the colon, forward slash, underscore, dot, and .com keys at the bottom to save time.

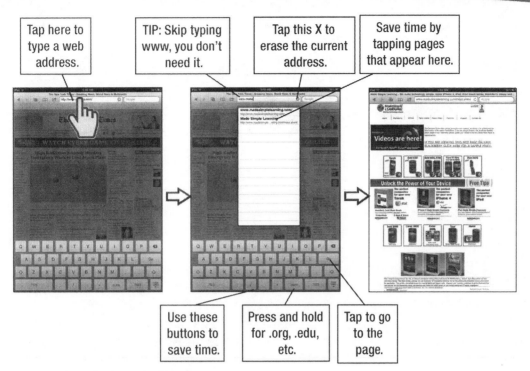

Figure 11–2. *Typing in a web address*

> **TIP:** Press and hold the .com key to see all the options: .org, .edu, .net, .de, etc.

Moving Backward or Forward Through Open Web Pages

Now that you know how to enter web addresses, you'll probably be jumping to various web sites. The **Forward** and **Back** arrows make it very easy to go to recently visited pages in either direction, as Figure 11–3 shows. If the **Back** arrow is grayed out, the section below about using the **Open Pages** button can help.

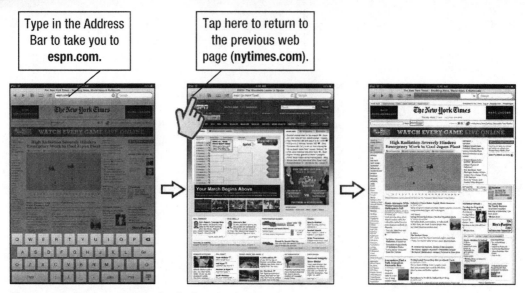

Figure 11–3. *Returning to a previously viewed web page*

Let's say you were looking at the news on the New York Times web site, then you jumped to ESPN to check sports scores. To go back to the New York Times page, just hit the **Back** arrow. To return to the ESPN site again, touch the **Forward** arrow.

Moving Between Web Pages

Sometimes when you click a link, the web page you were viewing moves to the background and a new window pops up with new content (another web page, a video, etc.). In such cases, the **Back** arrow in the new browser may not work!

Instead, you have to tap the **Open Pages** icon (just to the right of the arrows) to see a list of open web pages and then tap the one you want. In Figure 11–4, we touched a link that opened a new browser window. The best way to get back to the old one is to tap the **Open Pages** icon and select the desired page.

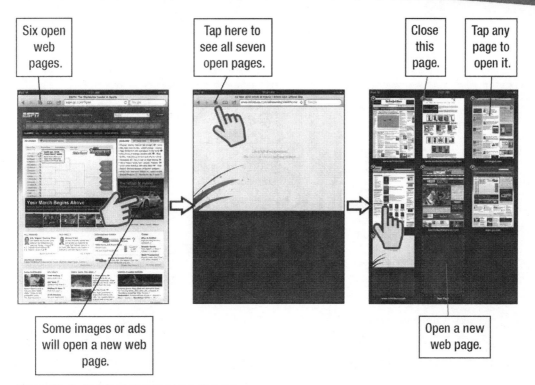

Six open web pages.

Tap here to see all seven open pages.

Close this page.

Tap any page to open it.

Some images or ads will open a new web page.

Open a new web page.

Figure 11–4. *Jumping between open web pages*

Jumping to the Top of the Web Page

Sometimes web pages can be quite long, which can make scrolling back to the top of the page a bit laborious. One easy trick is to just tap on the black title bar of the web page and you'll automatically jump to the top of the page, as shown in Figure 11–5.

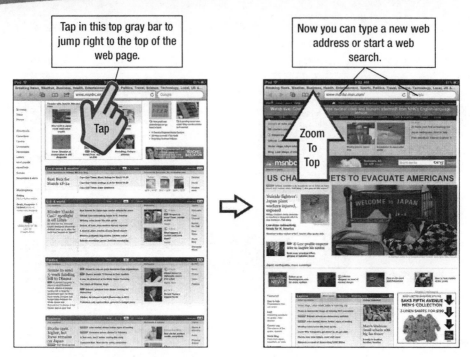

Figure 11–5. *Jump quickly to the top of a web page by tapping at the top*

Emailing a Web Page

Sometimes you find a page so compelling that you just have to send it to a friend. Touch the **Action** button next to the **Address Bar** and select **Mail Link to this Page** (see Figure 11–6). This creates an email message with the link that you can send.

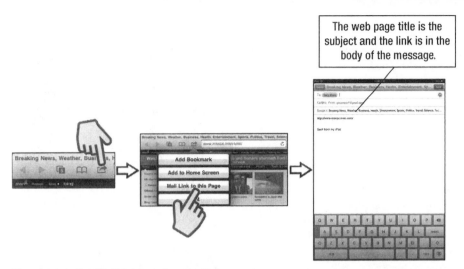

Figure 11–6. *Email a link to a web page*

How to Print a Web Page

The iPad now comes with a built-in **Print** command. If you have an **AirPrint** compatible printer (a full list of compatible printers can be found at www.apple.com/ipad/features/airprint.html) just connect your printer to your home network and select **Print** from the menu displayed when you touch the **Action** button. If you don't have an AirPrint-compatible printer, you still have a few options, but none of them are quite as simple as AirPrint.

> **NOTE:** Both the iPad and the printer need to be on the same Wi-Fi network. In other words, the iPad can't be on 3G.

Option 1: Email yourself or a colleague the web page link and print it from that printer. If you are traveling and staying at a hotel with a business center, you may be able to send it to someone at the business center or front desk to print the page.

Option 2: Buy a network printing app from the App Store that allows you to print to a networked printer. Of course, this only works if you have access to a networked printer. It's usually best if you do this from your home or office network and can get help setting up, as it can be quite challenging.

Adding Bookmarks

Just like on your home computer, you can set bookmarks on your iPad. To add a new bookmark, simply touch the plus sign (**+**) at the top of the web screen.

After touching 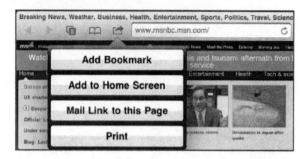 you'll see three options. Choose **Add Bookmark** to add a new bookmark.

After adding the new bookmark, you can edit its name (the web address is shown underneath the editing window). You can also choose the folder where you'd like the bookmark to appear. By default, it will go in your **Bookmarks** folder, but you can place it in any folder available to you, such as News or Popular.

Press **Save** to save your changes.

> **TIP:** If you add a bookmark to the Bookmark Bar, it will appear when you activate the URL field. Similar to desktop Safari, it gives you a drop-down menu of sites—very handy for quickly finding where you want to go.

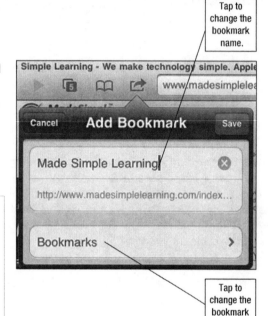

Tap to change the bookmark name.

Tap to change the bookmark folder.

Using Your Bookmarks

Once bookmarks are set, simply touch the **Bookmarks** icon from any web page to see them.

When you touch the **Bookmarks** icon, you'll find tabs for your **History, Bookmarks Bar,** and **Bookmarks Menu.** Under that you'll see preinstalled bookmarks for your iPad.

Bookmarks you add will, by default, go into your **Bookmarks Bar** unless you specify another spot.

> **TIP:** When you are creating your bookmarks, adjust the folder where the bookmark is stored by tapping the **Folder** name under the name of the Bookmark.

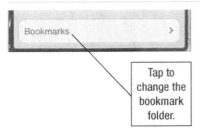

Tap to change the bookmark folder.

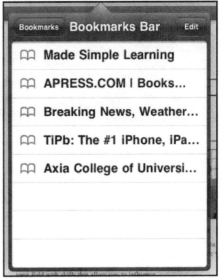

Searching the Web

Sometimes, you need to search for a particular topic, item, or web page. Searching the web couldn't be easier on the iPad.

The following steps show you how to set your default search engine in the **Safari** settings. When you first get your iPad, the default search engine is Google.

The **Search bar** is right next to the Web Address Bar. To perform a web search, follow these steps:

1. Touch the **Search bar** and the keyboard will appear.

2. Type in the name, web site, or topic you wish to search.

3. If a match pops up, just touch it to jump to the page or touch the **Search key** on the keyboard.

4. Your search results will be displayed using the default search engine (see Figure 11–7).

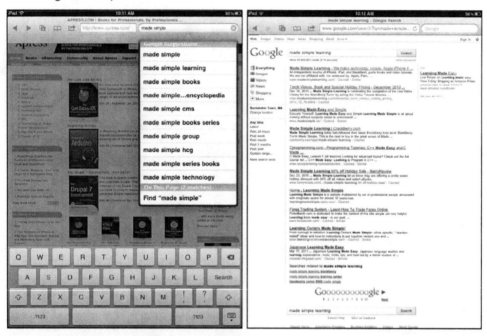

Figure 11–7. *Perform a web search using the Search bar in Safari*

> **TIP:** There's also the "On this page" listing at the bottom of the search results which lets you find words on the web page currently loaded in Safari (like cmd/ctl+F on the desktop).

Adding a Web Page Icon to Your Home Screen

If you love a web site or page, it's very easy to add it as an icon to your **Home Screen**. That way, you can instantly access the web page without going through the **Safari ➤ Bookmarks ➤** select bookmark process. You'll save lots of steps by putting the icon on your **Home Screen** (see Figure 11–8). This is especially good for quickly launching web apps, like Gmail or Buzz from Google, or web app games.

Here's how to add the icon:

1. Touch the **Action** button ⬆️ next to the address bar in the top of the browser.

2. Touch **Add to Home Screen**.

3. Adjust the name. You may want to put in the name of the site, but keep it short because there's not much room below the icons.

4. Tap the **Add** button in the upper right corner.

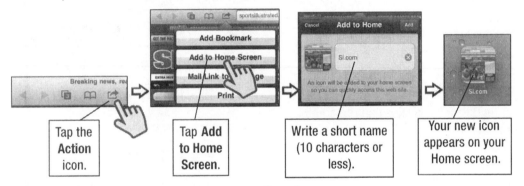

Figure 11–8. *How to add an icon for a web page to your Home Screen*

Browsing from Web History

A very useful tool on your iPad is the ability to browse the web from your **History**, just as you would on a computer.

Touch the **Bookmarks** icon and you'll see a tab marked **History**.

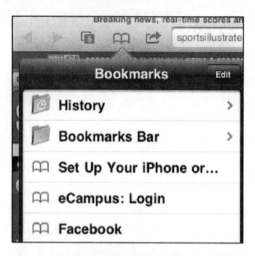

Touch the **History** tab and your recent web travels will be listed. If you haven't cleared your history lately, you may see one tab that says **Earlier Today** and another for other dates with stored history.

Just touch the name of a web site on the list, and Safari will load that page in the browser window.

To remove all the sites in your **History**, touch the **Clear History** button in the upper right, then the red **Clear History** button.

Adding Folders, Editing and Deleting Bookmarks

It's very easy to accumulate quite a collection of bookmarks since it's so easy to set them up. You may find you no longer need a particular bookmark, or you may want to organize them by adding new folders.

To manage your bookmarks, tap the **Edit** button at the bottom left corner of your Bookmarks menu.

You will notice that a red **minus sign** (-) appears to the left, and each bookmark turns into a tab that can be touched (see Figure 11–9).

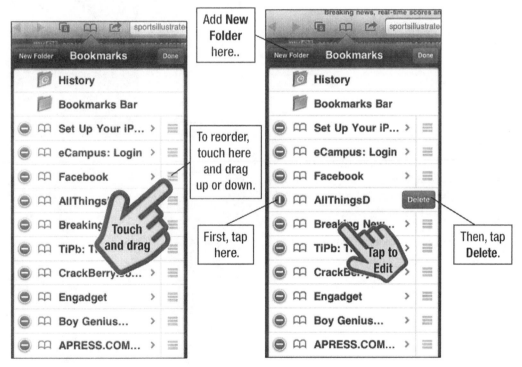

Figure 11–9. *Reorder and delete bookmarks*

To delete the bookmark, just touch the red **minus sign** and you'll see the **Delete** button pop up. Touch **Delete**, confirm the delete, and the bookmark will disappear from your menu.

To reorder bookmarks, just touch the icon at the right edge of each bookmark and drag up or down as you like.

To add a new folder, touch the **New Folder** button in the upper left corner. Type the name of the folder, select the location (folder) in which to place your new folder, and click **Done**.

Using the New Pages Button

On our home computers, many of us have come to rely on tabbed browsing— it allows us to have more than one web page open at a time so we can quickly move from one to another. The iPad has a similar feature you can access by touching the **New Page** icon at the top left of the of the web status bar. (This is the same icon you used to move through open pages earlier in this chapter.)

When you first touch this button, the web page you are currently viewing becomes small and moves to the left side of the screen.

Touch the **New Page** button and the browser will load a blank page, ready for you to input a new web address.

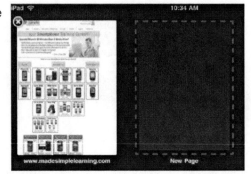

Now, just add a web address by touching the **Address Bar**, which brings up the keyboard. Type in the web address you want. Notice that there's no space bar on this keyboard—just touch the period (.) for the dot, or the .com button to fill out the address if the site has "com" at the end of the name.

Now when you touch the **New Page** icon, you can just touch the page you wish to view and it will load into the screen. As you did before, you can also touch the **New Page** button to load yet another new page into the browser window.

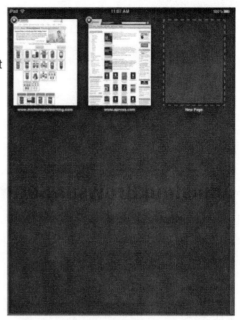

Zooming In and Out in Web Pages

Zooming in and out of web pages is very easy on the iPad. There are two primary ways of zooming—double-tapping and pinching.

Double-tapping: If you tap twice on a column of a web page, the page will zoom in on that particular column. This lets you home in on exactly the right place on the web page, which is very helpful for pages that aren't formatted for a mobile screen.

To zoom out, just double-tap once more. See how this looks graphically in the Quick Start Guide.

Pinching: This technique lets you zoom in on a particular section of a page. It takes a little bit of practice, but will soon become second nature. Take a look in the Quick Start Guide to see how it looks graphically.

Use your thumb and forefinger and place them close together at the section of the web page you wish to zoom into. Slowly pinch out, separating your fingers. You will see the web page zoom in (note that it may takes a couple of seconds for the web page to focus).

To zoom out to where you were before, just start with your fingers apart and move them slowly together; the page will zoom out to its original size.

Activating Links from Web Pages

When you're surfing the Web, often you'll come across a link that will take you to another web site. Because Safari is a full-function browser, you can just touch the link and you will jump to a new page.

If you want to return to the previous page, just press the **Back** arrow as shown earlier.

Adjusting Browser Settings

As with other settings you've adjusted so far, the settings for Safari are found in the **Settings** app.

To access this app, touch the **Settings** icon and then touch **Safari**.

Changing the Search Engine

By default, the search engine for the Safari browser is **Google**. To change this to **Yahoo**, just touch the **Search Engine** tab and then choose **Yahoo**. You can also choose **Bing** as your default search engine.

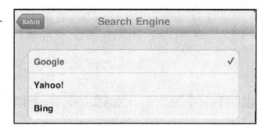

Adjusting Security Options

Under the **Security** heading,
JavaScript, and **Block Pop-ups** should,
by default, be set to **ON**. You can modify
either of these by just sliding the switch
to **OFF**.

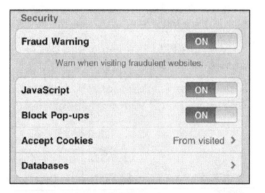

> **NOTE:** Many popular sites like Facebook
> require JavaScript to be **ON**.

You'll also see the **Accept Cookies** tab
here, which you can adjust to accept
cookies **Always**, **Never,** or **From
visited**.

Speed Up Your Browser: Clear History and Cookies

On the bottom of the Safari **Settings** screen,
you can see the **Clear History** and **Clear
Cookies** buttons.

If you notice your web browsing getting
sluggish, it's probably a good time to clear
out both your **History** and **Cookies**.

> **TIP:** This is also a good privacy measure as it
> prevents others from seeing where you've
> been browsing.

To preempt that sluggishness, it's a good idea to clear out your history and cookies on a fairly regular basis.

AutoFill Name, Password, Email, Address, and More

AutoFill is a convenient way to have the browser automatically fill out web page forms that ask for your name, address, phone number, or even username and password.

To enable **AutoFill**, touch the **AutoFill** tab in the Safari **Settings**. To use AutoFill to input your contact information, move the slider next to **Use Contact Info** to the **On** position.

To have **AutoFill** fill in names and passwords, move the slider next to **Names and Passwords** to **On**.

To set the correct **Contact Info**, touch the **My Info** tab and your contact list will be displayed. Choose your own contact information, as shown in Figure 11–10.

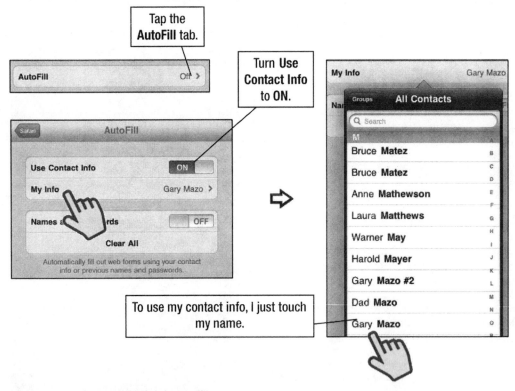

Figure 11–10. *Setting up My Info in AutoFill*

Once **AutoFill** is enabled, just go to any web page that has a field to fill out. As soon as you touch the field, the keyboard will come up at the bottom of the screen. At the top of the keyboard, you will see a small button that says **AutoFill**. Touch it and the web form should be filled out automatically (Figure 11–11).

CAUTION: Setting your name and password to be entered automatically means that anyone who picks up your iPad will be able to access your personal sites and information.

Touch the **AutoFill** button and web forms will be filled out automatically.

Figure 11–11. *Using AutoFill to automatically enter an email address and password*

Saving or Copying Text and Graphics from a Web Site

From time to time you may see text or a graphic you want to copy from a web site. We tell you briefly how to do this in this section, but to see graphically how to get it done, including using the **Cut** and **Paste** functions, please see the "Copy and Paste" section in Chapter 2. Here's a quick look:

To copy a single word, touch and hold the word until you see it highlighted and the **Copy** button appears. Then tap **Copy.**

To copy a few words or entire paragraph, touch and hold a word until it is highlighted. Then drag the blue dots left or right to select more text. You can flick up or down to select an entire paragraph. Then tap **Copy**.

TIP: Selecting a single word puts it in **Word Selection** mode where you can drag to increase or decrease the number of words selected. If you go past a single paragraph, it will typically switch to **Element Selection** mode where instead of corners you get edges that you can drag out to select multiple paragraphs, images, etc.

To **Save** or **Copy** a graphic, touch and hold the picture or image until you see the pop-up asking if you would like to **Save** or **Copy** the image.

Using Browsing History to Save Time and Find Sites

The advantage of keeping your frequently visited sites in history is that you can load them from the **History** tab when you go into the browser menu (see Figure 11–12). Also, sometimes you want to go back to a certain site, but you can't remember the name; checking your history will show you the exact site you wish to visit.

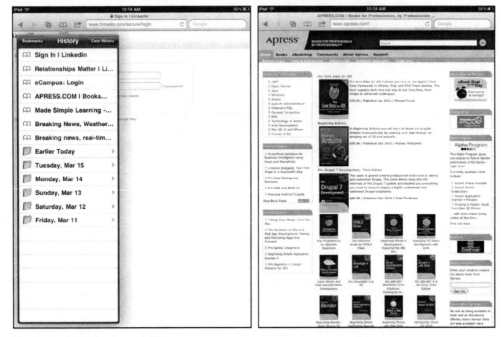

Figure 11–12. *Using Browser History*

iBooks and E-Books

Ever since the iPad was announced, one of its most touted features has been its ability as an E-Book reader. In this chapter, we will show you that what has emerged is an unparalleled book-reading experience. We will cover the **iBooks** app, how to buy and download books for it, and how to find some great free classic books. We will also show you some other E-Book reading options on your iPad, including the third-party **Kindle** and **Kobo** readers.

The iPad uses Apple's proprietary E-Book reader, **iBooks**. In this chapter, we will show you how to download the **iBooks** app, how to shop for books in the iBooks store, and how to take advantage of all the features in the **iBooks** app.

With **iBooks**, you can interact with a book like never before. You can turn pages, adjust font sizes, look up words in the built-in dictionary, and search through your text.

In the App Store, you can also find apps for Amazon's **Kindle** reader and other popular E-Book readers.

Download iBooks

The first time you open the App Store on your iPad, you will be prompted to download the free **iBooks** app. Select **Download** and **iBooks** will be downloaded and installed on your iPad.

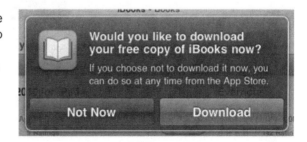

The iBooks Store

Before you can start enjoying your reading experience, you need to load up your iBooks library with titles. Fortunately, many books can be found for free in the iBooks store, including the complete Gutenberg Collection of classics and public domain titles.

Just touch the **Store** button in the upper left-hand corner of your bookshelf, and you will be taken to the iBooks store.

The iBooks store is arranged much like the App Store. There is a **Categories** button in the top left, next to the **Library** button. Touch this to see all the available categories from which you can choose your books.

Featured books are highlighted on the front page of the store, with **New** and **Notable** titles displayed for browsing.

At the bottom of the store are five soft keys: **Featured**, **NYTimes**, **Top Charts**, **Browse,** and **Purchases**. Touch the **NYTimes** button

to see the charts for the NYTimes bestsellers in fiction and non-fiction categories.

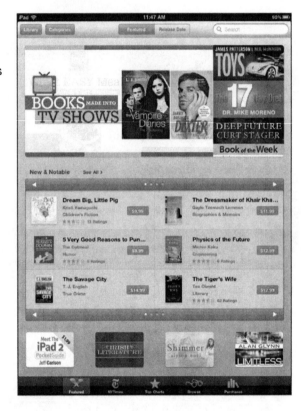

Touch the **Top Charts** button

 to see all the bestselling and top free books in the store.

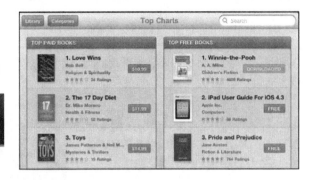

Touch the **Purchases** button to see all the books you have purchased or downloaded for your library.

Purchasing a book is much like purchasing an app. Touch the book title that you are interested in and browse the description and customer reviews. When you are ready to purchase the title, touch the **Price** button.

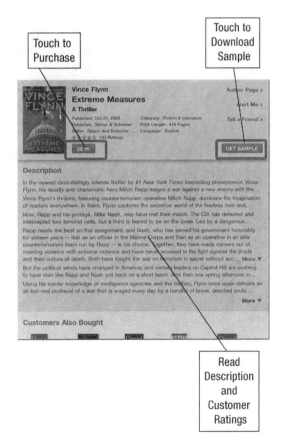

Touch to Purchase

Touch to Download Sample

Read Description and Customer Ratings

NOTE: Many titles have a sample download. This is a great idea if you are not sure whether you want to purchase a book. Downloading a sample is a great way to preview a book; you can always purchase the full book from within the sample.

Once you decide to download a sample or purchase a title, the view shifts to your bookshelf. At this point, you can see the book being deposited onto your bookshelf. Your book is now available for reading.

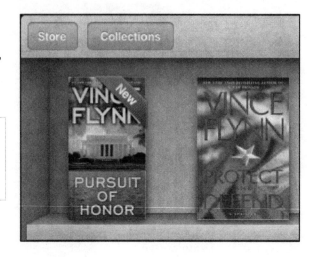

NOTE: New downloads will have the word "New" along the top of the right-hand corner.

Using the Search Window

Just like iTunes and the App Store, iBooks gives you a **Search** window into which you can type virtually any phrase. You can search for an author, title, or series. Just touch the **Search** window and the on-screen keyboard pops up. Type in an author, title, series, or genre of book.

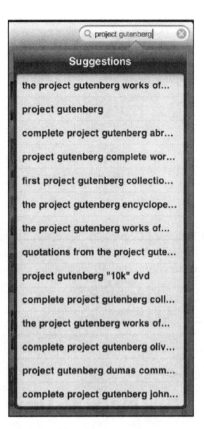

NOTE: You can also use the **Browse** button at the bottom for searching. For example, you can browse by author or category or use the **Search** box.

TIP: To search for lots of free books, perform a search for "Gutenberg Project" to see the thousands of free public domain titles.

You will see suggestions pop up that match your search; touch the appropriate suggestion to go to that title.

Reading iBooks

Touch any title in your bookshelf to open it for reading. The book will open to the first page, which is often the title page or other front matter in the book.

There is a **Table of Contents** button in the upper left-hand corner, next to the **Library** button (see Figure 12–1). To jump to the table of contents, touch either the **Table of Contents** button or simply turn the pages until you see these pages.

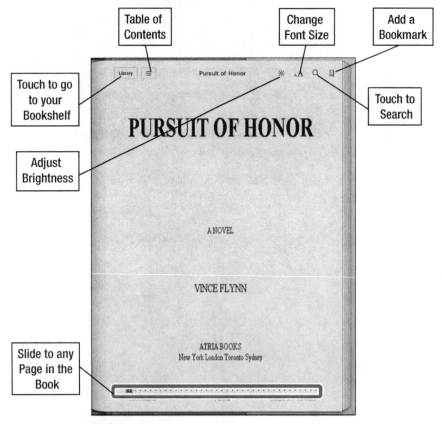

Figure 12–1. *The iBooks page layout*

You can turn pages in one of three ways:

- Touch the right-hand side of the page to turn to the next page.

- Slowly touch and hold the screen on the right-hand edge of the page. While still touching the screen, gently and slowly move your finger to the left.

Touch and "Turn"

Touch the right-hand side of the page and "Turn" it, just as you would in a real book.

TIP: If you move your finger very slowly, you can actually see the words on the backside of a page as you "turn" it—a very cool visual effect.

- The last way to turn pages is to use the **Slider** control at the bottom of the page. As you slowly slide from left to right, you will see the page number on top of the **Slider** control. Release the **Slider** control and you can advance to that particular page number.

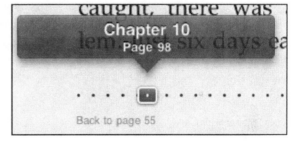

Customizing Your Reading Experience: Brightness, Fonts, and Font Sizes

In the upper right-hand corner of the book, there are three icons available to help make your reading experience more immersive (see Figure 12–2).

Touch the **Brightness** icon and you can adjust the brightness of the book.

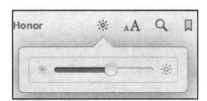

If you are reading in bed in a very dark room, you might want to slide it all the way down to the left. If you are out in the sunlight, however, you may need to slide it all the way to the right. Keep in mind that turning up the screen brightness is one of the more power-intensive things you can do on an iPad, so remember to turn it back down when you don't need the screen to be so bright anymore.

> **NOTE:** The preceding example adjusts the brightness only within the **iBooks** app. To adjust the global brightness of the iPad, use the control in the **Settings** app, which you can access by clicking the **Settings** icon and then choosing **Brightness & Wallpaper**.

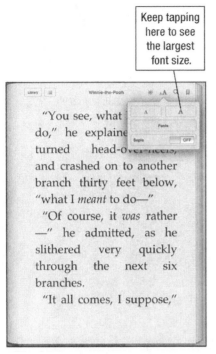

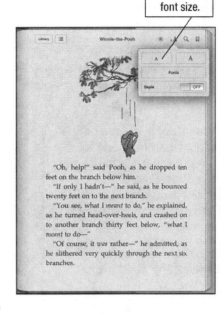

Figure 12–2. *Adjusting font sizes in the* **iBooks** *app*

The next **Text Size** icon lets you adjust the font size and type. After selecting this icon, you can increase the font size by tapping the large **A** button multiple times.

To decrease the font size, tap the small **A** button multiple times.

There are five available font styles. (There may well be more fonts when you read this book.)

Have fun and try out some of the various fonts. The default selection is the Palatino font; however, all of the fonts look great, and the larger font sizes can make a difference for some. The goal is to manipulate the fonts to make this reading experience as comfortable and as enjoyable as possible.

Grow Your Vocabulary Using the Built-in Dictionary

iBooks contains a very powerful built-in dictionary, which can be quite helpful when you run across a word that is new or unfamiliar.

> **TIP:** Using the built-in dictionary is an easy and fantastic way to build your vocabulary as you read. Instead of thumbing through a dog-eared dictionary to find the word, you will see the definition instantly appear in the pop-up window!

Accessing the dictionary could not be easier. Just touch and hold any word in the book. A pop-up will appear with the following options: use the **Dictionary**, set a **Bookmark**, or use **Search** to find other occurrences of this particular word.

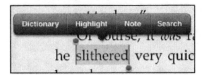

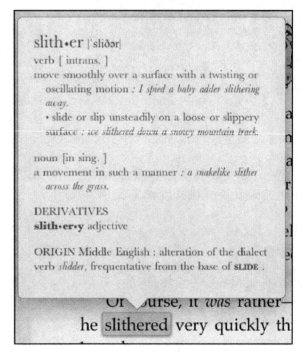

Touch **Dictionary**, and a pronunciation and definition of the word will be displayed.

Setting an In-Page Bookmark

There may be times when you wish to set an in-text bookmark for future reference.

The upper right-hand corner includes a **Bookmark** icon. Touch the **Bookmark** icon and it will change to a red bookmark on the page.

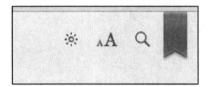

To view your bookmarks, touch the **Table of Contents** icon at the top left of the screen (next to the **Library** icon) and then touch **Bookmarks**. Touch the bookmark highlighted and you will jump to that section in the book.

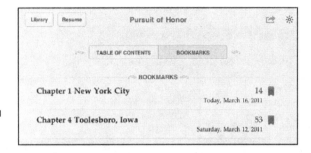

TIP: You do not need to set a bookmark every time you leave **iBooks**. **iBooks** will automatically remember where you left off in your book. Even if you jump to another book, you will return to exactly where you left off when you return to the book you were just reading. iBooks will now also sync with your iPhone or iPod touch **iBooks** app, so you can move back and forth between devices and keep your place.

Using Highlighting and Notes

There are some very nice "added touches" to the **iBooks** app. There may be times when you want to highlight a particular word to come back to at another time. There may be other times you want to leave yourself a note in the margin.

Both of these tasks are very easy to accomplish in the **iBooks** app. This feature is not yet available when viewing PDF files in **iBooks**.

Highlighting Text

Follow these steps to highlight text in a book you're reading:

1. Touch and hold any word to bring up the menu options.

2. Choose **Highlight** from the menu options.

3. To remove the highlight, touch and hold the highlighted section, and then select **Remove Highlight**.

To change the color of the highlight, do the following:

1. Touch and hold the highlighted word.

2. Choose **Colors** from the menu.

3. Choose a new color (see Figure 12–3).

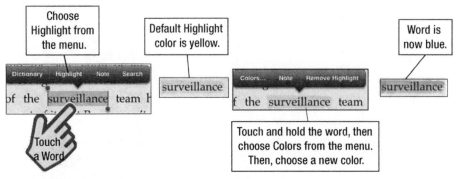

Figure 12–3. *Using the highlighting feature in* **iBooks**

Adding Notes

Do the following to add a note in the margin:

1. Touch and hold any word, as you did previously.

2. Choose **Note** from the menu.

3. Type in your note and then touch **Done**.

4. The note now appears on the side of the page in the margin (see Figure 12–4).

> **TIP**: Your notes will also appear under your bookmarks on the title page. Touch the **Title Page** button and then touch **Bookmarks**. The notes you write will be at the bottom of the page.

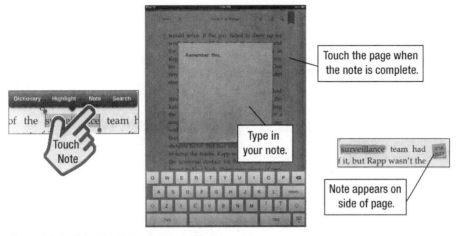

Figure 12–4. *Using the **Notes** feature in **iBooks***

Using Search

The **iBooks** app contains a powerful search feature built right in. Just touch the **Search** bar (as in other programs on the iPad) and the built-in keyboard will pop up. Type in the word or phrase for which you are searching and a list of chapters is shown where that word occurs.

Simply touch the selection desired and you will jump to that section in the book. You also have the option of jumping right to Google or Wikipedia by touching the appropriate buttons at the bottom of the **Search** window.

> **NOTE:** Using the Wikipedia or Google search will take you out of **iBooks** and launch **Safari**.

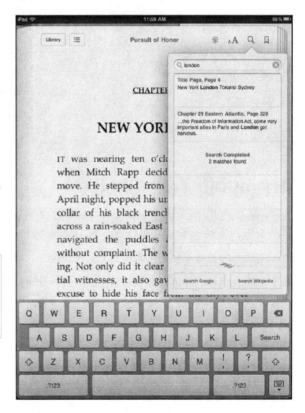

Deleting Books

Deleting books from your **iBooks** library is very similar to deleting applications from the iPad.

In the **Library** view, just touch **Edit** in the top right-hand corner.

Once you touch the **Edit** button, touch any book and a small blue check mark will appear.

Now touch the **Delete** button at the top and you will be prompted to **Delete** the book. Once you touch **Delete**, the book will disappear from the shelf.

Arranging Your Shelf

The upper right-hand corner of the bookshelf has two icons: **Cover** view and **List** view. The default arrangement for your bookshelf is to use the **Cover** view.

Follow these steps to change to **List** view:

1. Touch the **List** view icon to the right of the **Cover** view icon.

2. Choose whether you wish your books to be listed by **Bookshelf**, **Titles**, **Authors**, or **Categories**.

3. Touch the corresponding button at the bottom and your view of the shelf will change to reflect your choice.

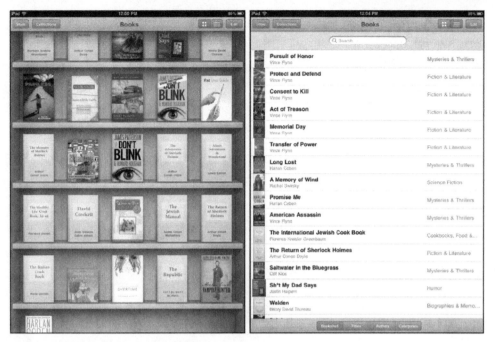

Figure 12–5. *Arranging books in either* **Cover** *or* **List** *view*

Collections

New to iBooks is the ability to store various collections. The two most common collections are **PDFs** and **Books**.

When you receive a PDF in an email (see the example in the next section) or transfer a PDF file via iTunes (see Chapter 29), you can choose to **Open** the PDF in **iBooks**. It will then be stored in your PDF collection.

Reading PDF Files in iBooks

One very cool feature of **iBooks** is the ability to read PDF files that are sent to you via email or synced via iTunes (see Chapter 3: "Sync Your iPad with iTunes").

In this example, a PDF file has arrived in our email, and we want to save it and view it in **iBooks**.

Follow these steps to open a PDF received via email:

1. Open the PDF file from the email.

2. In the upper right-hand corner, choose **Open in...** and then choose **iBooks**. The PDF file will now go into the PDF category of **iBooks**.

3. The PDF is saved in the PDF section. Just touch the file to open it and read it like any other iBook.

4. To delete a PDF file, follow the earlier instructions for deleting an iBook.

> **NOTE**: When you select **Open in...** in the upper right-hand corner of the PDF from the email, all available PDF reading apps will be listed. Choose **iBooks** from the list to open the file in **iBooks** or choose another reader to open the file in that app.

Until you save your first PDF file, you will see **Collections** listed, but you won't have any files stored. After you save your first PDF file, you will have PDF files in the **Collections** next to the **Store** button.

You can touch the **Collections** button to switch between the **Books** and **PDFs** categories.

Other E-Book Readers: Kindle and More

As we have noted, the **iBooks** app offers an unparalleled E-Book reading experience. There are, however, other E-Book reader apps available for the iPad that are worth checking out.

Many users already have a Kindle and have invested in a Kindle library. Others use the **Kobo** E-Reader software (formerly called **Shortcovers**) and have invested in a library of books for that platform.

Fortunately, both E-Book platforms have apps in the iPad App Store. When either program is downloaded and installed, you can sign in and read your complete library on your iPad.

> **NOTE:** No matter which of these other E-Readers you choose, you can always just sign in to the appropriate service to see your complete library and pick up just where you left off in your last book—even if you started reading on a different device.

Download E-Reader Apps

Go to the App Store. Touch **Categories** and then touch **Books**. You will find the **Kindle** and **Kobo** readers among the list of apps displayed. Both are free apps, so just touch the **Free** button to initiate the downloads.

> **TIP:** It is usually faster to just *search* by the name of the app if you know which one you are looking for.

Once the desired E-Reader software is installed, touch its icon to start the app.

Kindle Reader

Amazon's **Kindle** reader is the world's most popular E-Reader. Millions of people have Kindle books; the **Kindle** reader allows them to read their Kindle books on their iPad.

> **TIP:** If you use a Kindle device, don't worry about signing in from your iPad. You can have several devices tied to your single account. You will be able to enjoy all the books you have purchased for your Kindle right on the **Kindle** reader installed on the iPad.

Just touch the **Kindle** reader and either sign in to your Kindle account or create a new account with a user name and password.

Once you sign in, you will see your Kindle books on the **Home** page. You can either touch a book to start reading it, or you can touch the **Shopping Cart** to start shopping in the Kindle store.

NOTE: Touching the **Shopping Cart** will start your **Safari** browser. From there, you can purchase Kindle books. Once you are done, you will need to exit **Safari** and restart the Kindle reader.

To read a Kindle book, touch its cover. The options for reading can be found along the bottom row of icons.

You can add a bookmark by touching the **Bookmark** icon in the top right-hand corner. Once the bookmark is set, a small bookmark appears–just like in the **iBooks** app.

You can go to the cover, table of contents, or specify any location in the book to jump to (such as the beginning) by touching the **Goto** button.

The font, as well as the color of the page, can be adjusted. One very interesting feature is the ability to change the page to **Black**, which is great when reading at night.

To advance pages, either swipe from right to left, or touch the right-hand side of the page. To go back a page, just swipe from left to right or touch the left-hand side of the page.

Tap the screen and a **Slider** control appears at the bottom. You can adjust this control to advance to any page in the book.

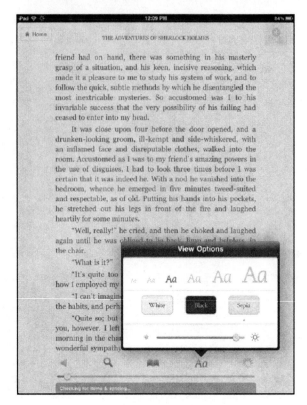

Kobo Reader

Like the **Kindle** reader, the **Kobo** reader you begins by asking you to sign in to your existing Kobo Books account. All of your existing Kobo Books will then be available for reading.

Kobo uses a "bookshelf" approach, similar to the one in **iBooks**. Tap the book cover for whichever book you wish to open.

Or you can touch the **I'm Reading** tab to pick up with what you were reading last. You can also go directly to the Kobo store to purchase books by touching the **Store** tab.

You can find three buttons along the top of the **Kobo** reader: **Table of Contents**, **Overview**, and **Bookmarks**.

Touch any button to advance to the particular feature desired.

You can also find four icons along the bottom: **Font**, **Brightness**, **Add Bookmark**, and **Display Settings**. Touch any of the buttons to make adjustments to your viewing.

To advance pages in the **Kobo** reader, touch the right-hand side of the page. To go back a page, just touch the left-hand side of the page. You can also use the **Slider** control at the bottom to advance through the pages.

Chapter 13

Email on Your iPad

In this chapter, we will help you explore the world of email in the **Mail** app on your iPad. You will learn how to set up multiple email accounts, check out all the various reading options, open attachments, and clean up your Inbox.

You will be pleased with the unified inbox feature that lets you see all your email in a single inbox. You also have the option to view threaded messages, where all messages related to a single topic (replies, forwards, and so on) are kept together in a single group. Or, if you prefer, you can turn off this feature in the **Settings** app.

And for cases when your email is not working quite right, you will learn some good troubleshooting tips to help you get back up and running.

Getting Started with Mail

Setting up email on your iPad is fairly simple. You can sync email account settings from **iTunes** (see the "Sync Email Account Settings" section in Chapter 3: "Sync Your iPad with iTunes"), or you can set up email accounts directly on your iPad. You do need a network connection to get email up and running.

A Network Connection Is Required

Mobile email is certainly all the rage today. You can view, read, and compose replies to emails already synced to your iPad without a network connection; however, you will need to have Wi-Fi network connectivity to send and/or receive email from your iPad. Check out Chapter 5: "Wi-Fi and 3G Connectivity" to learn more. Also check out the "Reading the Top Connectivity Status Icons" section in the Quick Start Guide in Part 1.

> **TIP:** If you are taking an airline trip, simply download all your email before you get on the airplane; this lets you read, reply, and compose your messages while offline. One important point here you may only have the email header downloaded before you go offline unless you tap the message to open and view it. In other words, before you take off, make sure you tap to open all important email messages to make sure the full messages get downloaded to your iPad. Any emails you compose on your iPad while offline will be sent after you land and re-establish your connection to the Internet.

Setting up Email on the iPad

You have two options for setting up your email accounts on the iPad:

- Use the **iTunes** app to sync email account settings.
- Set up your email accounts directly on the iPad.

If you have a number of email accounts that you access from an email program on your computer (e.g., **Microsoft Outlook**, **Entourage**, and so on), then the easiest approach is to use **iTunes** to sync your accounts. See the "Sync Email Account Settings" section in Chapter 3: "Sync Your iPad with iTunes" for more information on this topic.

If you only have a few accounts, or you do not use an email program on your computer that **iTunes** can sync with, then you will need to set up your email accounts directly on the iPad.

Entering Passwords for Email Accounts Synced from iTunes

In the "Sync Email Account Settings" section of Chapter 3, we showed you how to sync your email account settings to your iPad. After this sync completes, you should be able to view all of the email accounts on your iPad by opening the **Settings** app. All you will need to do is enter the password for each account.

The easy way is to enter account passwords is to type them into the pop-up window as you see the window appear.

Type your **Password** and tap **OK** to save it.

You can also enter your email account passwords and adjust other account details in the **Settings** app. To enter your password for each synced email account, follow these steps (see Figure 13–1):

1. Tap the **Settings** icon.

2. Tap **Mail, Contacts, and Calendars** in the left column.

3. Under **Accounts** in the right column, you should see all your synced email accounts listed.

4. Tap any listed email account, then tap **Account** to get to the **Account** details screen.

5. Type the account **Password** and click **Done**.

6. Repeat for all listed email accounts.

Figure 13–1. *Entering passwords for each email account synced from the **iTunes** app*

Adding a New Email Account on the iPad

To add a new email account on your iPad, follow these steps:

1. Tap the **Settings** icon.

2. Tap **Mail, Contacts, and Calendars**.

3. Tap **Add Account** below your email accounts.

> **TIP:** To edit any email account, just touch that account.

4. Choose which type of email account to add on this screen:

   ■ Tap **Microsoft Exchange** if you use a Microsoft Exchange email server, use Hotmail or Gmail, and you want to sync your contacts and calendar wirelessly.

   ■ Tap **Gmail** if you use Gmail and do not want your contacts synced wirelessly.

   ■ Tap **MobileMe, Yahoo**, or **Aol** if you use these services.

   ■ Tap **Other** to set up a different type of account.

> **TIP:** Learn more about **Google/Hotmail/Microsoft Exchange** and **MobileMe** in Chapter 4: "Other Sync Methods."

5. If you select **Other** from the account type, then you will see this screen, where you can add the following types of accounts: Mail, Contacts, and Calendars.

- To add an account to Mail, tap **Add Mail Account**.

- To add an account to Contacts, tap **Add LDAP Account** or **Add CardDAV Account**.

- To add an account to Calendars, tap **Add CalDAV Account** or **Add Subscribed Calendar**.

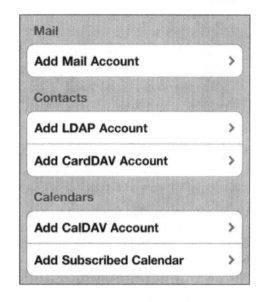

6. Now you will be able to enter your login credentials. Type your name as you would like others to see it when they receive mail from you into the **Name** field. If you selected a Contacts or Calendars type of account, then you would be need to enter the **Server** name, **User Name**, **Password**, and **Description**.

7. Next, add the appropriate information into the **Address**, **Password**, and **Description** fields.

8. Tap the **Next** button in the upper-right corner.

Specifying Incoming and Outgoing Servers

Sometimes, the iPad will not be able to automatically set up your email account. In these cases, you will need to type in a few more settings manually to enable your email account.

TIP: You may be able to find the settings for your email provider by doing a web search for your email provider's name and "email settings." For example, if you use Windows Live Hotmail (formerly known as Hotmail), then you might search for "Microsoft Exchange, POP, or IMAP email settings for Windows Live Hotmail." If you cannot find these settings, then contact your email provider for assistance.

If the iPad is unable to log into your server with only your email address and password, then you see a screen similar to this one.

Under **Incoming Mail Server**, type the appropriate information into the **Host Name**, **User Name**, and **Password** fields. Usually, your incoming mail server is something like **mail.***name of your isp***.com**.

To adjust the name of your outgoing server, tap **Outgoing Mail Server.** You can adjust the outgoing mail server on the following screen. These server names usually look like either **smtp.***name of your isp***.com** or **mail.***name of your isp***.com**.

You can try to leave the **Server Name** and **Password** fields blank. If that doesn't work, you can always go back and change them.

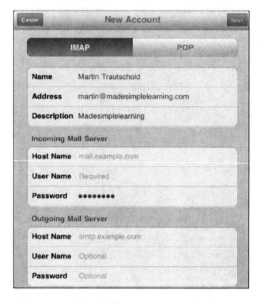

You may be asked if you want to use SSL (secure socket layer), a type of outgoing mail security that may be required by your email provider. If you don't know whether you need it, just check the required mail settings with your email provider.

TIP: The authors recommend that you use SSL security whenever possible. If you do not use SSL, then your login credentials, messages, and any private information is sent in plain text (unencrypted), leaving it open to snoopers.

Verifying that Your Account Is Set Up

Once all the information is entered, the iPad will attempt to configure your email account. You may get an error message; if that happens, you need to review the information you input.

If you are taken to the screen that shows all your email accounts, look for the new account name.

If you see it, your account was set up correctly.

Fixing the Cannot Get Mail Error

If you tap **Mail** icon and you receive an error that says "Password Incorrect," you will need to enter your password and click OK to see your email.

Review this chapter's "Enter Passwords for Email Accounts Synced from iTunes" section for additional help.

Email Basics

In this section, we give you a guided tour around your **Mail** app. We explain how to use it in both **Portrait** and **Landscape** modes, as well as how to perform the basics of reading, replying, filing, printing, and deleting messages.

Portrait and Landscape Mail Screens

Now that you have set up your email accounts on your iPad, it's time to take a brief tour of the **Mail** app. To better understand how to get around your **Mail** program, it helps to have a picture of how your **Mail** app looks in **Portrait** and **Landscape** views (see Figure 13–2).

In **Landscape** view, you always see your Inbox or Mailboxes in the left column with the email message in the right.

In **Portrait** view, you see the entire email message fill the screen. To see the **Inbox** or **Mailboxes** in a vertical pop-up window on the left side of the page, tap the **Inbox** button in the upper-left corner of the page.

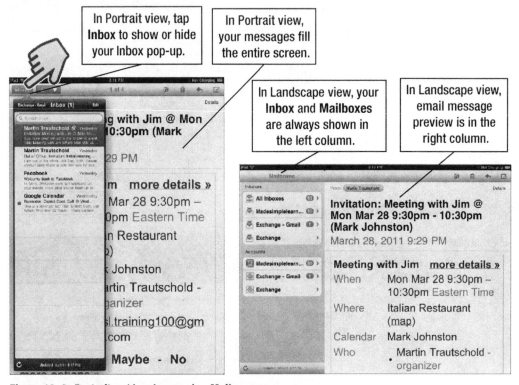

Figure 13–2. *Portrait* and *Landscape view Mail screens*

> **TIP:** If you are setting your iPad down on a desk or holding it in your lap, then you may want to use the **Portrait Lock** icon to lock your view in **Portrait** (vertical) mode. This will prevent the image from flipping around unnecessarily. To lock the view, follow these steps:
>
> 1. Double-tap the **Home** button and swipe left to right.
>
> 2. Tap the **Portrait Lock** button to lock the screen in **Portrait** mode.

Viewing Messages and the Unread Message Blue Dot

Tap any email message to view it In the main window.

Any unread messages are marked with a

Blue Dot icon ● to the left of the message.

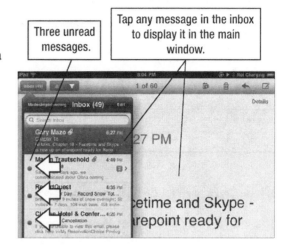

Three unread messages.

Tap any message in the inbox to display it in the main window.

Adjusting Mail Font Size

While we're on the topic of email, let's look at a useful tip on how to increase the font size of your email messages. You can go from the default of 10 or 12 points all the way up to 56 points (see Figure 13–3).

1. Tap **Settings**.

2. Tap **General**.

3. Tap **Accessibility** (right column).

4. Tap **Large Text** and then select the font size you desire.

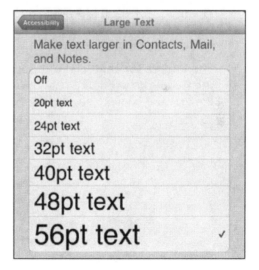

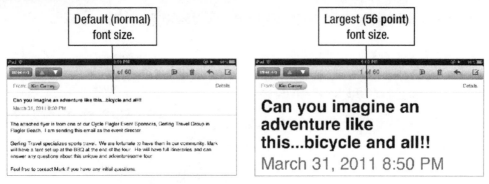

Figure 13–3. *Various font sizes in an email*

Viewing Your Mailboxes (Inboxes and Account Folders)

The top-level screen is your **Mailboxes** screen. You can always get to it by tapping the button in the upper-left corner. Keep tapping this button until you see no more buttons. When that happens, you are in the **Mailboxes** screen.

From the **Mailboxes** screen, you can access the following items:

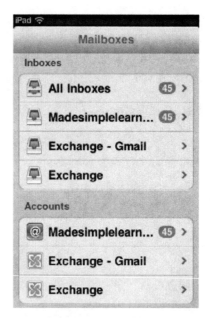

- **The unified inbox:** Do so by tapping **All inboxes**.

- **The inbox for each individual account:** Do this by tapping that email account name in the Inboxes section.

- **The folders for each email account in the Accounts section:** Do so by tapping the account name to see all folders.

You can view your mail in a unified inbox that shows all your email accounts in a single inbox or lists each account separately. You can also choose to view any mail account folders that are synced to your iPad.

It's good to get a mental picture of your various email accounts. Your **Mailboxes** screen sits at the top an upside-down tree. You can access each inbox can by clicking **Inboxes** at the top, or you can dig into the various synced mail folders (including your inboxes) by tapping the **Accounts** listed at the bottom (see Figure 13–4).

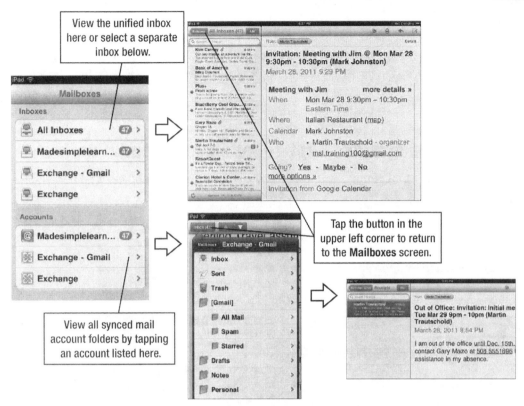

Figure 13–4. *Navigating to various inboxes and mail account folders*

Unified Inbox

From the **Mailboxes** screen, tap **All Inboxes** to view a single inbox that contains email from every one of your accounts together.

> **TIP:** Here's how you get to the **Mailboxes** screen.
>
> If you happen to be viewing an inbox or another mail folder, you will have to tap the button in the upper-left corner of the screen once or twice.

> **NOTE:** You will only see those mail folders you have chosen to sync during the mail setup process. For example, you might have 20 mail folders on your main mail account, but you might only see a few folders on your iPad. The default synced mail folders are **Inbox**, **Sent**, **Draft**, and **Deleted Items**.

Related Messages Are Kept Together in Threads

You will also notice that some messages show a number and a right-facing **Arrow** icon

(>) to the right of the message, like this: **2** >

This shows that there are two related messages (replies and forwards) to the message shown.

Tap any message to open it. The only time it will not open is if there are related messages. In that case, you will first see a screen with all the related messages. Tap any of those messages to open and view it (see Figure 13–5).

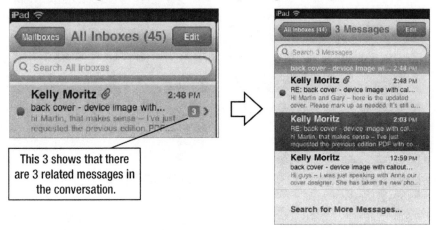

Figure 13–5. *Related messages are kept together in groups called* threads.

> **TIP:** You can disable this **Threaded** view in your **Settings** app. Tap **Settings** ➤ **Mail, Contacts, Calendars**, and set **Organize by Thread** to OFF.

Zooming In or Out

As when reading other text on your iPad, you can zoom in to see your email in larger text. You can do this by double-tapping the screen. You can also use the **Pinch** open or closed gesture to zoom in or out (see the "Zooming" section in our Quick Start Guide in Part 1 of this book for more information on these features).

Go to Next Message or Previous Message

In **Portrait** view, tap the **Up Triangle** icon or **Down Triangle** icon next to the **Inbox** button in the upper-right corner.

In **Landscape** view, you can simply tap the message in the left column to view it in the main (right column) preview window.

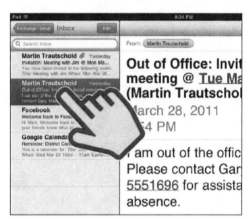

Copy and Paste

Here are a few tips to select text or pictures and then copy them from an email message:

- Double-tap the desired text to select a word, and then drag the blue handles up or down to adjust the selection.

  Next, select **Copy**.

- Press and hold the text, and then choose **Select** or **Select All**.

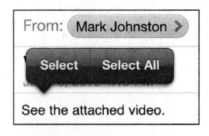

- Press and hold an image, and then select **Save Image** or **Copy**.

For a more complete description, please check out the "Copy and Paste" section in Chapter 2: "Typing Tips, Copy/Paste, and Search."

Move (File) a Message

Sometimes, you may want to organize your email for easy retrieval later. For example, you might receive an email about an upcoming trip and want to move it to the **Travel** folder. Sometimes you receive emails that require attention later, in which case you can move them to the **Requires Attention** folder. This can help you remember to work on such emails later.

To start moving a message, tap the **Move** icon in the upper-right corner of the screen.

The list of folders for your current mail account will appear in the left side of the screen.

Tap the folder to which you want to move the message.

> **TIP:** While you can move messages to the Spam folder, we recommend instead that you simply delete these messages.

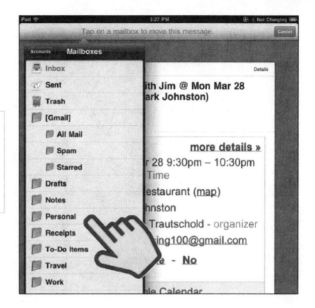

Move (File) a Bunch of Messages

To move many messages at once, open up the Inbox and follow these steps:

1. Tap the **Edit** button in the upper-right corner of the Inbox (see Figure 13–6).

2. Tap any message to select it—you see a **Red Checkmark** icon appear next to a message when it is selected.

3. Tap the **Move** button at the very bottom of the screen.

4. Now a list of folders will appear that you have synced from your Mail account. In Figure 13–6, we have a number of folders; however, you may only see two (depending on how your iPad is set up): Mail and Trash.

> **TIP:** You may be able to set up additional mail folders to sync in your **Settings** app. Tap **Mail, Contacts, Calendars**, then tap the account you wish to adjust. If you see a **Mail Folders to Push** option, then tap that and make adjustments. If you do not see that option, then you cannot sync additional mail folders with your particular account.

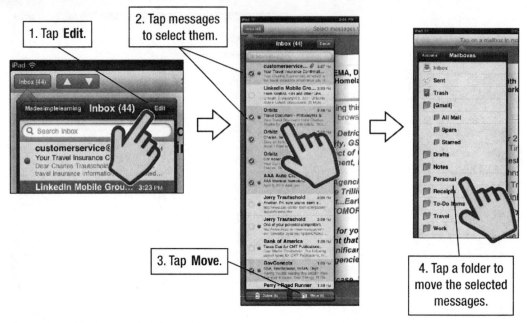

Figure 13–6. *Moving a number of messages at once*

Delete a Single Message

There are a few ways to delete a message.

While viewing a message, tap the **Trash**

Can icon 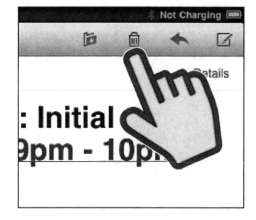 in the upper-right corner
of the screen.

The message will shrink, the garbage can
lid will open, the message will fly into the
can, and the lid will close. It's sort of fun—
give it a try!

The other way to delete an individual message is from the Inbox.

Simply swipe left or right over the message until you see the **Delete** button appear.

Then, tap the **Delete** button.

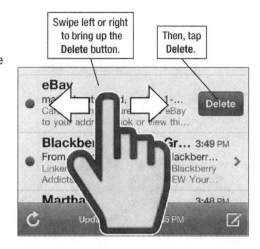

TIP: You can use the **Settings** app to make your iPad ask you before deleting email. To do so, tap **Mail, Contacts, Calendars** and set the switch next to **Ask Before Deleting** to **Yes**.

Deleting a Bunch of Messages

To delete many messages at once, open up the Inbox and use the techniques previously described to move a number of messages into a different mail folder:

1. Tap the **Edit** button in the upper-right corner of the Inbox (see Figure 13–7).

2. Tap any message to select it—you will see a **Red Checkmark** icon appear next to the message when it is selected.

3. Tap the **Delete** button at the very bottom of the screen.

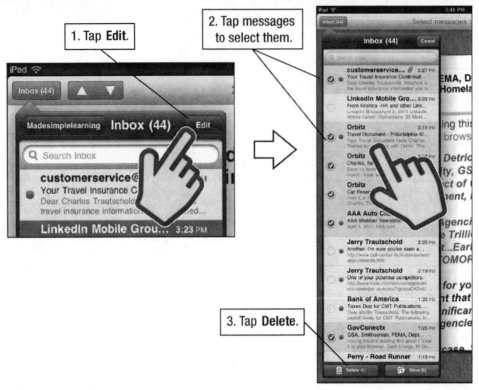

Figure 13–7. *Moving a number of messages at once*

Reply to Messages

You will probably use the **Reply** command most frequently. Follow these steps to respond to an email on your iPad:

1. While reading the mail message, touch the **Rounded Arrow** icon in the upper-right corner.

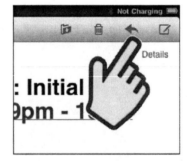

2. Tap **Reply** or **Reply All** from the dropdown list of buttons.

3. Type your reply and press **Send** in the upper-right corner.

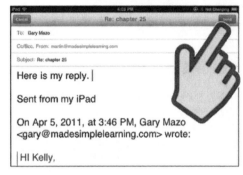

Using Reply All

Using the **Reply All** option is just like using the **Reply** function, except that all of the original recipients of the email and the original sender are placed in the address lines. The original sender will be in the **To:** line, while all other recipients of the original email will be listed on the **Cc:** line. You will only see the **Reply All** option if more than one person received the original email.

> **CAUTION:** Be careful when you use **Reply All**. This can be dangerous if some of the recipients are not shown on the original email because they stretch off the edge of the screen. If you do use **Reply All**, then make sure you check the **To:** and **Cc:** lists to make sure everyone should be receiving your reply.

Forward Messages

Sometimes, you get an email that you want to send to someone else. The **Forward** command will let you do that (see the "Email Attachments" section in this chapter for more about working with attachments).

> **NOTE:** You need to forward attachments to send them to others. If you want to send someone an attachment from an email you receive, you must choose the **Forward** option. (Note that choosing the **Reply** and **Reply All** options will not include the original email attachment(s) in your outgoing message.)

Just as when using **Reply**, you first tap the **Rounded Arrow** icon in the upper-right corner, then tap **Forward** from the dropdown list of buttons.

You may be prompted to address whether you want to include attachments (if there were any) from the original message.

At this point, you follow the same steps described previously to type your message, add recipients, and send it.

Print Messages

You can now print messages from your iPad, as long as you have an Apple **AirPrint**-compatible printer or a printer that can receive email messages and print the attachments. In this section, we will show you the way to print a message using Apple's **AirPrint**. Here is a list of **AirPrint**-compatible printers at the time of publishing (see Table 14–1). Our testing was done with the HP Photosmart e-AiO (D110a) printer.

Table 13–1. *A List of **AirPrint**-Compatible Printers*

HP Envy eAll-in-One series (D410)	HP LaserJet Pro CM1415fnw Color Multifunction Printer
HP Photosmart Plus e-AiO (B210)	HP LaserJet Pro CP1525n Color Printer
HP Photosmart Premium e-AiO (C310)	HP LaserJet Pro CP1525nw Color Printer
HP Photosmart Premium Fax e-AiO (C410)	HP Officejet 6500A e-AiO
HP Photosmart e-AiO (D110)	HP Officejet 6500A Plus e-AiO
HP Photosmart Wireless e-AiO (B110)— Europe and Asia-Pacific	HP Officejet 7500A Wide Format e-AiO
HP Photosmart eStation (C510)	HP Officejet Pro 8500A e-AiO
HP LaserJet Pro M1536dnf Multifunction Printer	HP Officejet Pro 8500A Plus e-AiO
HP LaserJet Pro CM1415fn Color Multifunction Printer	HP Officejet Pro 8500A Premium e-AiO

Step 1: Connect Your AirPrint-Compatible Printer to the Network

Before you can print to your printer, you need to connect it to the same wireless Wi-Fi network as your iPad. Wi-Fi network securities vary, so we did not include detailed steps to do so in this book. Please use the instructions that came with your printer to connect it to your network.

Step 2: Print from your iPad

Printing is easy and straightforward. Follow these steps to do so:

1. Open the mail message you wish to print.

2. Tap the **Rounded Arrow** icon in the upper-right corner and select **Print**.

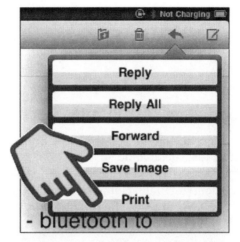

3. Tap **Printer** to select your printer from the network. (You'll only need to do this once because the iPad remembers your selection.)

4. Once selected, the printer name will appear. Adjust the number of copies using the **Plus** (+) and **Minus** (-) buttons.

5. When you are ready to print, tap **Print** and your document will be printed wirelessly on your printer.

Checking on Your Printing Documents

You can check on the status of your printing documents using the **Print Center** app. Follow these steps to do so:

1. Double-tap the **Home** button until you see the gray bar **(multitasking window)** of icons appear at the bottom of the screen.

2. You can see the active print jobs and, if you desire, stop the printing using the **Cancel Printing** button.

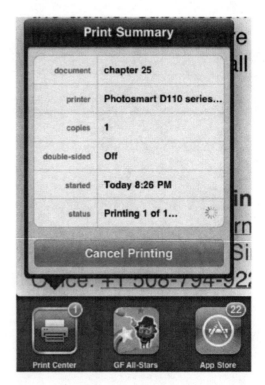

Compose a New Message

From any mail screen, tap the **Compose** icon in the upper-right corner to start writing a new email message.

Address the Message

You have a few options for selecting recipients, depending on whether the person is in your **Contact** list on your iPad:

Option 1: Type a few letters of someone's first name, then hit the **Space** key and then type a few letters of that person's last name. The person's name should appear in the list; tap that person's name to select that contact.

Option 2: Type an email address. Notice the **@** and **Period** (.) keys on the keyboard, which help your typing.

> **TIP:** Press and hold the **Period** key to see `.com`, `.edu`, `.org`, and other email domain name suffixes.

Option 3: Hit the **Plus** (+) sign to view your entire **Contact** list and search or select a name from it.

If you want to use a different contact group, tap the **Groups** button in the upper-left corner.

Deleting a Recipient

If you need to delete a name from the recipients list (**To:**, **Cc:**, or **Bcc:**), tap the name to select it and hit the **Backspace** key.

> **TIP:** If you want to delete the last recipient you typed (and the cursor is sitting next to that name), hit the **Delete** key once to highlight the name and hit it a second time to delete it.

Adding a CC or BCC Recipient

To add a carbon copy (**Cc:**) or blind carbon copy (**Bcc:**) recipient, you need to tap the **Cc:/Bcc:** field just under the **To:** field at the top of the email message. Doing so opens up the tapped field.

Changing the Email Account to Send From

If you have more than one email account set up, the iPad will use whichever account is set as the default account. (This is set in **Settings ➤ Mail, Contacts, Calendars ➤ Default Account** at the bottom of the **Mail** section.)

Follow these steps to change the email account you send from:

1. Tap an email's **From:** field to highlight it.

2. Tap a new email account to select it.

Type Your Subject

Now you need to enter a subject for your email. Follow these steps to do so:

1. Touch the **Subject:** line and enter text for the **Subject:** field of the email.

2. Press the **Return** key or tap the **Body** section of the email to move the cursor to the **Body** section.

Typing Your Message

Now that the cursor is in the body of the email (under the subject line), you can start typing your email message.

Email Signature

The default email signature is shown in the image to the right: **Sent from my iPad**.

> **TIP:** You can change this signature to be anything you want; see the "Changing Your Email Signature" section later in this chapter.

> **TIP:** If you have larger hands, it might be easier to type when the keyboard is larger. Once you get the hang of typing on the larger keyboard with two hands, you will find that it is much faster than typing with one finger. Also, you will see auto-capitalization and auto-correction happening. Learn more about typing in Chapter 2: "Typing Tips, Copy/Paste, and Search" for more typing tips.

Send Your Email

Once you have typed your message, tap the blue **Send** button in the top-right corner. Your email will be sent, and you should hear the iPad's sent mail sound, which confirms that your email was sent. You can learn how to enable or disable this sound in the "Adjusting Sounds on your iPad" section of Chapter 7: "Personalize and Secure your iPad."

Save As Draft to Send Later

If you are not ready to send your message, but want to save it as a draft message to send later, follow these steps:

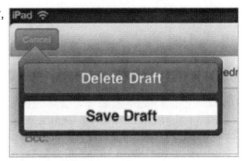

1. Compose your message, as described earlier.

2. Press the **Cancel** button in the upper-left corner.

3. Select the **Save Draft** button at the bottom of the screen.

Later, when you want to locate and send your draft message, follow these steps:

1. Open the **Drafts** folder in the email account from which you composed this message. See the "Moving Around in Mail Folders" section earlier in this chapter for help getting into the **Drafts** folder.

2. Tap the email message in the **Drafts** folder to open it.

3. Tap anywhere in the message to edit it.

4. Tap the **Send** button.

Checking Sent Messages

Follow these steps to confirm that the email was sent correctly:

1. Tap the **Email account name** button in the upper-left corner to see the mail folders for the account you just used to send your message.

2. Tap the **Sent** folder.

3. Verify that that the top email you see in the list is the one you just composed and sent.

> **NOTE:** You will only see the **Sent** and **Trash** folders if you have actually sent or deleted email from that account on the iPad. If your email account is an IMAP account, you may see many folders other than those described in this chapter.

Working With Email Attachments

Some email attachments are opened automatically by the iPad, so you don't even notice that they were attachments. Examples of these include Adobe's portable document format (**PDF**) files (used by **Adobe Acrobat** and **Adobe Reader,** among other apps) and some types of image, video, and audio files. You may also receive other documents as attachments, such as Apple's **Pages, Numbers,** and **Keynote** files or Microsoft's **Word, Excel,** and **PowerPoint** files. You will need to open these manually.

> **NOTE:** You can preview many types of files for example, word processing and spreadsheet documents using the **Quick View** function. However, if you want to edit a file, you need to open it in an app that allows for editing using the **Open In** feature.

Knowing When You Have an Attachment

Any email with an attachment will have a little **Paperclip** icon next to the sender's name, as shown to the right. When you see that icon, you know you have an attachment.

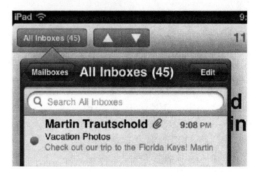

Receiving an Auto-Open Attachment

Now assume you received a few pictures or a one-page PDF file. (Multipage PDF files require that you tap to open them.)

Once you open the mail message with this kind of attachment, you will see it directly below the message.

In this example, there were several photos attached to this message that automatically opened. We just need to swipe down to see all the photos.

Saving Pictures You Receive

Say you liked one or more of the pictures you received. In order to save a photo on your iPad, press and hold any picture until you see a pop-up window appear.

In this example, we have four pictures, so we see **Save Image**, **Save 4 Images**, and **Copy**.

These images will be in your **Photos** app in the **Saved Photos** album. See Chapter 16: "iPad Photography" for more information about your **Photos** app.

Opening Email Attachments

Instead of immediately opening in the body of the email as we just described, other types of attachments, such as spreadsheets, word processing documents, and presentation files, will need to be opened manually.

Tap for Quick Look Mode

Follow these steps to open attachments in **Quick Look** mode:

1. Open the message with an attachment (see Figure 13–8).

2. Quickly tap the attachment to instantly open it in **Quick Look** mode. You can navigate around the document. Remember you can zoom in or out and swipe up or down.

3. If you open a spreadsheet with multiple tabs or spreadsheets, you will see tabs across the top. Touch another tab to open that spreadsheet.

4. When you are done looking at the attachment, tap the document once to bring up the controls, and then tap **Done** in the upper-left corner.

5. If you have apps installed that can open the type of attachment you are viewing (in this case, a spreadsheet), then you will see an **Open In** button in the upper-right corner. Tap the **Open In** button to open this file in another app.

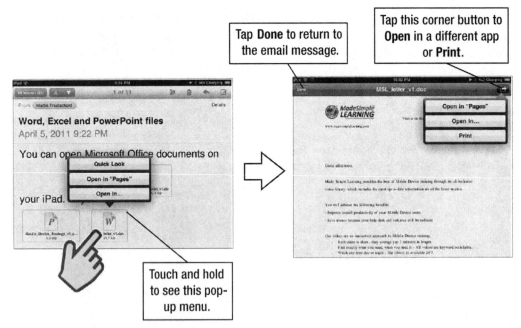

Tap **Done** to return to the email message.

Tap this corner button to **Open** in a different app or **Print**.

Touch and hold to see this pop-up menu.

Figure 13–8. *Quickly viewing attachments by tapping them*

Opening Docs in Other Apps

You may want to open the attachment in another application. For example, you might want to open a **PDF** file in **iBooks, Stanza,** or **GoodReader.** Follow these steps to do so:

1. Open the email message.

2. Press and hold the attachment until you see the pop-up window.

3. Select the **Open In** option.

4. Select the application you would like to use from the list (see Figure 13–9).

5. Finally, you can edit the document, save it, and email it back to the sender.

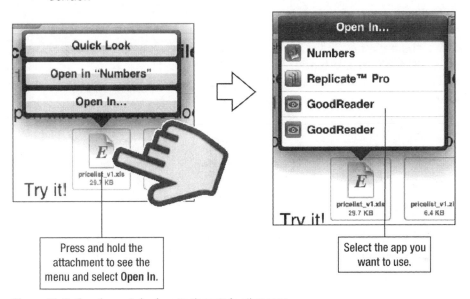

Figure 13–9. *Opening and viewing attachments in other apps*

Viewing a Video Attachment

You may receive a video as an attachment to an email. Certain types of videos can be viewed on your iPad (see the "Supported Email Attachment Types" section later in this chapter for a list of supported video formats). Follow these steps to open a video attachment:

1. Tap the video attachment to open it and view it in the video player.

2. When you are done viewing the video, tap the screen to bring up the player controls.

3. Tap the **Done** button in the upper-left corner to return to the email message.

Opening and Viewing Compressed .zip Files

Your iPad will not be able to open and view a compressed file of `.zip` format unless you install an app such as **GoodReader**. At the time of publishing, **GoodReader** was still a free app and well worth installing. Follow these steps to use **GoodReader**:

> **TIP:** Learn how to install and use **GoodReader** in Chapter 26: "New Media: Reading Newspapers, Magazines, and More."

1. Install the free **GoodReader** from the App Store.

2. Open the email message with the `.zip` file attachment.

3. Touch and hold the `.zip` attachment until you see a pop-up window at the bottom with a button that says, **"Open in GoodReader."** Tap that button to open the `.zip` in **GoodReader**.

> **CAUTION:** Do not just quickly tap the attachment to open it. At the time of publishing, this resulted in a blank white or black screen with nothing happening. Make sure to touch and hold the attachment until you see the button pop-up.

4. **GoodReader** should now open, and your `.zip` file should be at the top of the list of files. To open or uncompress the `.zip` file, tap the file and select the **Unzip** button.

5. Now you should see the uncompressed file—in this case, an Adobe .pdf file in the list of files above the .zip file.

6. Tap that uncompressed file to view it.

7. When you are done reading the attachment, double-click your **Home** button and tap the **Mail** icon to return to your reading your email.

Issues When Opening Email Attachments

Some types of attachments cannot be opened on your iPad. Such attachments show up with a **Question Mark (?)** icon. In this image, we tried to click an attachment of the type **winmail.dat**, which failed.

Supported Email Attachment Types and Audio/Video Formats

Your iPad supports the following file types as attachments:

- .doc and .docx (**Microsoft Word** documents)
- .htm and .html (web pages)
- .key (a **Keynote** presentation document)
- .numbers (an **Apple Numbers** spreadsheet document)
- .pages (an **Apple Pages** document)
- .pdf (Adobe's portable document format, used by programs such as **Adobe Acrobat** and **Adobe Reader**)
- .ppt and .pptx (a **Microsoft PowerPoint** presentation document)
- .txt (a text file)
- .vcf (a contact file)
- .xls and .xlsx (a **Microsoft Excel** spreadsheet document)
- .mp3 and .mov (audio and video formats)

- .zip (compressed files). Note that these are only readable if you have an app installed that can read them, such as **GoodReader** (see the "Opening and Viewing Compressed .zip Files" section in this chapter.

Your iPad also supports the following audio formats:

- HE-AAC (V1)
- AAC (16 to 320 Kbps)
- Protected AAC (from iTunes Store)
- MP3 (16 to 320 Kbps)
- MP3 VBR
- Audible (formats 2, 3, and 4)
- Apple Lossless
- AIFF
- WAV

Your iPad also supports the following video formats:

- H.264 video up to 720p at 30 frames per second
- Main Profile level 3.1 with AAC-LC audio up to 160 Kbps, 48kHz
- Stereo audio in .m4v, .mp4, and .mov file formats
- MPEG-4 video, up to 2.5 Mbps, 640 by 480 pixels, and at 30 frames per second
- Simple Profile with AAC-LC audio up to 160 Kbps, 48kHz, stereo audio in .m4v, .mp4, and .mov file formats
- Motion JPEG (M-JPEG) up to 35 Mbps, 1280 by 720 pixels, 30 frames per second, and audio in ulaw
- PCM stereo audio in .avi file format

Searching for Email Messages

The iPad has some good built-in search functionality to help you find your emails. You can search your **Inbox** by the **From**, **To**, **Subject**, or **All** fields. This helps you quickly locate exactly the messages you want to find.

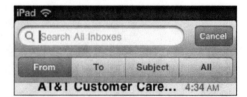

Activating Email Search

You can search an individual inbox, or search all inboxes together by going to the universal inbox (**All Inboxes**).

If you scroll up to the top, you will now see the familiar **Search** bar at the top of your **Inbox** (see Figure 13–10).

If your email account supports the feature, you can also search the server for email messages. At the time of writing, a few of the supported types of searchable email accounts include **Exchange**, **MobileMe**, and **Gmail IMAP**. Follow these steps to search through your email on a server:

1. Touch the **Search** bar to see a new menu of soft keys under the **Search** bar.

2. Type the text you wish to search for.

3. Touch one of the soft keys under the **Search** window:

   a. **From**: Searches only the sender's email addresses.

   b. **To**: Searches only the recipients' email addresses.

   c. **Subject**: Searches only message **Subject** fields.

   d. **All**: Searches every part of the message.

For example, assume I want to search my Inbox for an email I received from Martin. I would type Martin's name into the **Search** box and then touch **From**. My Inbox would then be filtered to show only the emails from Martin.

> **NOTE:** If you have multiple email accounts, you will not be able to search all of your inboxes at the same time because your iPad only lets you search one inbox at a time. For a more global search on your iPad, use the **Spotlight Search** feature shown in the "Finding Things with Spotlight Search" section of Chapter 2: "Typing Tips, Copy/Paste, and Search."

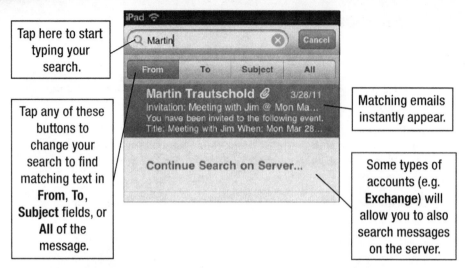

Tap here to start typing your search.

Tap any of these buttons to change your search to find matching text in **From, To, Subject** fields, or **All** of the message.

Matching emails instantly appear.

Some types of accounts (e.g. **Exchange**) will allow you to also search messages on the server.

Figure 13–10. *Searching for email using the From, To, Subject, or All text fields*

Fine-Tuning Your Email Settings

You can fine-tune your email accounts on your iPad with the myriad options available in the **Settings** app.

Follow these steps to change these settings:

1. Tap the **Settings** icon.

2. Tap **Mail, Contacts, Calendars**.

The sections that follow explain the adjustments you can make.

Automatically Retrieve Email (Fetch New Data)

In addition to the options under **Advanced**, you can use the **Email** settings to configure how often your email is fetched, or *pulled*, to your iPad. By default, your iPad automatically receives mail or other contact or calendar updates when they are *pushed* from the server.

You can adjust this setting by taking the following steps:

1. Touch the **Settings** icon.

2. Touch **Mail, Contacts, Calendars**.

3. Touch **Fetch New Data** under the email accounts listed.

4. Set **Push** to **ON** (default) to automatically have the server push data. Turn It **OFF** to conserve your battery life.

5. Adjust the timing schedule to pull data from the server. This is how frequently applications should pull new data from the server.

NOTE: If you set this option to **Every 15 Minutes**, you will receive more frequent updates, but sacrifice battery life compared to a setting of **Hourly**.

Having automatic retrieval is very handy if you just want to turn on your iPad and see that you have messages; otherwise, you need to remember to check.

Advanced Push Options

At the bottom of the **Fetch New Data** screen, below the **Hourly** and **Manually** settings, you can touch the **Advanced** button to see a new screen with all your email accounts listed.

Tap any email account to adjust its settings.

Most accounts can be **Fetched** on the schedule you set or set to **Manual**. The **Manual** option requires that you retrieve data using the **Update** button. This screen gives you the ability to adjust **Fetch**, **Manual**, or in some cases **Push** settings for each account you have set up.

Adjusting Your Mail Settings

Under the **Accounts** section, you can see all the email settings listed under **Mail**. The **Default** settings may work well for you; but if you need to adjust any of these, you can follow these steps.

Show: This sets how many emails are pulled from the server. You can specify anywhere from 25 to 200 messages (the default is 50 recent messages).

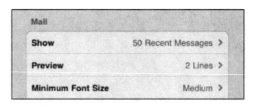

Preview: This option lets you set how many lines of text in addition to the **Subject** are shown in the **Inbox** preview. You can adjust this value from **None** to **5 Lines** (the default is **2 Lines**).

Minimum Font Size: This is the default font size shown when opening an email for the first time. It is also smallest font size

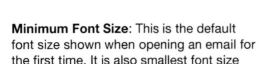

that you are allowed to zoom out to when viewing an email. Your options are **Small**, **Medium**, **Large**, **Extra Large**, and **Giant** (the default is **Medium**).

Show To/Cc Label: With this option **ON**, you will see a small **To** or **Cc** label in your Inbox before the subject. This label shows which field your address was placed in (the default state of this option is **OFF**).

Ask Before Deleting: Turn this option **ON** to be asked every time you try to delete a message (the default is **OFF**).

Load Remote Images: This option allows your iPad to load all the graphics (remote images) that are placed in some email messages (the default value for this option is **ON**).

Organize by Thread: This option groups related emails together. It shows only one message, with a number next to it. That number indicates how many related emails exist. This feature gives you a good way to keep all discussions together in one place (the default value of this option is **ON**).

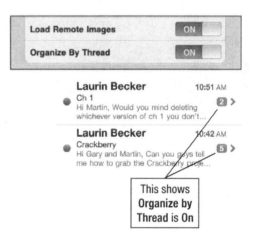

Always Bcc Myself: This option sends a blind carbon copy (**Bcc:**) of every email you send from your iPad to your email account (the default value of this option is **OFF**).

Changing Your Email Signature

By default, emails you send will say "Sent from my iPad." Follow these steps to change the **Signature** line of the email:

1. Tap the **Signature** tab.

2. Tap the **Clear** button and type in the new email signature you would like to appear at the bottom of all emails sent from your iPad.

3. When you are done editing the **Signature** field, tap the **Mail, Contacts...** button in the upper-left corner. This will return you to the **Mail** settings screen.

Changing Your Default Mail Account (Sent From)

If you have multiple email accounts set up on your iPad, you should set one of them—usually, the one you use most—as your **Default Account**. When you select **Compose** from the **Email** screen, the default account is always chosen. Also, if you click an email address in any other app to compose a new message, this **Default Account** will be selected. Follow these steps to change the email account you send from by default:

1. Tap the **Default Account** option, and you will see a list of all your email accounts.

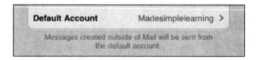

2. Tap the one you wish to use as your **Default Account** choice.

3. When you are done, touch the **Mail, Contacts...** button to return to the **Mail** settings menu.

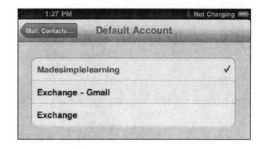

Toggling Sounds for Receiving and Sending Email

You may notice a little sound effect every time you send or receive email. What you hear is the default setting on your iPad.

If you want to disable this option or change it, you do so in the **Settings** program:

1. Tap your **Settings** icon.

2. Tap **General** in the left column.

3. Tap **Sounds** in the right column.

4. You will see various switches to turn sound effects on or off. Tap **New Mail** and **Sent Mail** to adjust the **ON** or **OFF** options.

Advanced Email Options

> **NOTE:** Email accounts set up as Exchange, IMAP, or MobileMe will not have this **Advanced** email settings screen. This only applies to POP3 email accounts.

To get to the **Advanced** options for each email account, follow these steps:

1. Touch the **Settings** icon.

2. Touch **Mail, Contacts, Calendars**.

3. Touch an email address listed under **Accounts**.

4. At the bottom of the mail settings pop-up window, tap the **Advanced** button to bring up the **Advanced** dialog.

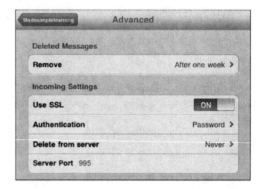

Removing Email Messages from the iPad After Deletion

You can select how frequently you want email removed completely from your iPad once it is deleted.

Touch the **Remove** tab and select the option that is best for you; the default setting is **Never**.

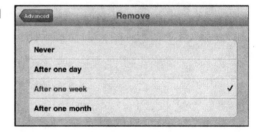

Using SSL/Authentication

SSL/Authentication features were discussed previously, but the **Advanced** email options screen supplies another location to access these features for a particular email account.

Deleting Messages from the Server

You can configure your iPad to handle the deletion of messages from your email server. Usually, this setting is left at **Never**, and this function is handled on your main computer. If you use your iPad as your main email device, however, you might want to handle that feature from the phone itself. Follow these steps to use your iPad to remove deleted emails on the server:

1. Touch the **Delete from Server** tab to select the feature that best suits your needs: **Never, Seven Days,** or **When removed from Inbox**.

2. The default setting is **Never**. If you want to choose **Seven Days**, that option should give you enough time to check email on your computer, as well as your iPad, and then decide what to keep and what to get rid of.

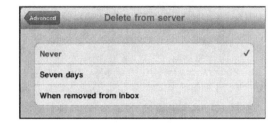

Changing the Incoming Server Port

As you did with the **Outgoing Server Port** earlier, you can change the **Incoming Server Port** if you are having trouble receiving email. It is very rare that your troubles will be related to the port you receive mail on, which means that you will rarely need to change this number. If your email service provider gives you a different number, just touch the numbers and input a new port. The value for an **Incoming Server Port** is usually 995, 993, or 110; however, the port value could also be another number.

Troubleshooting Email Problems

Usually, your email works flawlessly on your iPad. Sometimes—whether it is a server issue, a network connectivity issue, or an email service provider requirement—email may not work as flawlessly as you would hope.

More often than not, there is a simple setting that needs to be adjusted or a password that needs to be re-entered.

If you try out some of the troubleshooting tips that follow and your email is still not working, then your email server may just be down temporarily. Check with your email service provider to make sure your mail server is up and running; you might also check whether your provider has made any recent changes that would affect your settings.

TIP: If these tips that follow do not solve the problem, please check out Chapter 28: "Troubleshooting" for more helpful tips and resources.

Email Isn't Being Received or Sent

If you can't send or receive email, your first step should be to verify you are connected to the Internet. Look for Wi-Fi or 3G connectivity in the upper-left corner of your **Home** screen (see the "How Do I Know When I'm Connected?" section of "Quick Start Guide" for details.

Sometimes, you need to adjust the outgoing port for email to be sent properly. Do so by following these steps.

1. Tap **Settings**.

2. Touch **Mail, Contacts, and Calendars**.

3. Touch your email account that is having trouble sending messages under **Accounts**.

4. Touch **SMTP** and verify that your outgoing mail server is set correctly; also check that it is set to **ON**.

5. Touch **Outgoing Mail Server** at the top and verify all the settings, such as **Host Name**, **User Name**, **Password**, **SSL**, **Authentication**, and **Server Port**. You might also try 587, 995, or 110 for the **Server Port** value; sometimes that helps.

6. Click **Done** and the email account name in the upper-left corner to return to the **Email** settings screen for this account.

7. Scroll down to the bottom and touch **Advanced**.

8. You can also try a different port setting for the server port on this screen, such as 587, 995, or 110. If those values don't work, contact your email service provider to get a different port number and verify your settings.

Verifying Your Mail Account Settings

Follow these steps to verify your account settings:

1. Tap the **Settings** icon.

2. Tap **Mail, Contacts, Calendars**.

3. If you received an error message from a particular email account, touch that that account.

4. Verify that the **Account** is set to **ON**.

5. Verify that your email **Address** is correct in the **POP Account Information** section.

6. Verify that all the information in the **Host Name**, **User Name**, and **Password** fields is correct.

7. If you received an error message while trying to send an email, the issue will be most likely in the **SMTP** settings in your **Outgoing Mail Server** area.

8. Tap **SMTP** to adjust more settings.

9. Touch the **Primary Server** tab and make sure that it is set to **ON**.

10. Underneath the **Primary Server** tab, you will see other SMTP servers that are used for your other email accounts. One option is to use one of the other SMTP servers that you know is working. In that case, just touch the tab for that server and turn that switch to **ON**.

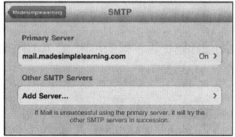

11. Tap the **Primary Server** address to view and adjust more settings.

12. Verify that the **Primary Server** is **ON**.

13. Contact your email service provider to verify other settings, such as **Host Name**, **User Name**, **Password**, **SSL**, **Authentication**, and **Server Port**. We will share more details and some tips about these settings in the sections that follow.

14. Tap the **Done** button when finished and then tap the button with your email account listed in the upper-left corner to return to previous screens. Or, you can tap the **Home** button to exit to your **Home** screen.

Using SSL

Some SMTP servers require the use of Secure Socket Layer ("SSL") security. If you are having trouble sending email and the **Use SSL** switch is set to **OFF**, try setting it to **ON** to see if that helps.

Changing the Method of Authentication

Under the SSL switch is an **Authentication** tab. Usually, **Password** is the correct setting for this switch. We don't recommend that you change this setting unless you have specific directions from your email service provider to make a change.

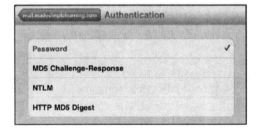

Changing the Server Port

Most often, when you configure your email account, the server port is set for you. Sometimes, there are tweaks that need to be made that are specific to your ISP.

If you have been given specific settings from your ISP, you can change the server port to try to alleviate any errors you might be seeing. Follow these steps to change the **Server Port** settings:

1. Go back to the specific **SMTP** settings for your account.

2. Touch the tab for the **Primary Server**, as you did in the "Verify Mail Account Settings" section.

3. Scroll down to **Server Port** and touch the screen on the number indicated.

4. This causes a keyboard to pop up that you can use to input a new port number (the one given you by your ISP). Most often, the number provided by your ISP will be 995, 993, 587, or 110; however, if you're given a different number, just input it.

5. When you are done, touch the **SMTP** tab in the upper-left corner to return to the previous screen.

Chapter 14

Working with Contacts

Your iPad gives you immediate access to all your important information. Just like your computer or your smartphone, your iPad can store thousands of contacts for easy retrieval. In this chapter, we'll show you how to add new contacts (including how to do so from an email address), customize your contacts by adding new fields, organize your contacts with groups, quickly search or scroll through contacts, and even display a contact's location with the **Maps** app on the iPad. We will also show you how to customize your **Contacts** view, so it is sorted and displayed just the way you like it. Finally, you will learn a few troubleshooting tips that will save you some time when you run into difficulties.

The beauty of the iPad is how it integrates all of your apps, so you can email and map your contacts right from the **Contact** entry screen.

Loading Your Contacts onto the iPad

In Chapter 3: "Sync Your iPad with iTunes," we show you how to load your contacts onto the iPad using the **iTunes** app on your Mac or Windows computer. You can also use the Exchange (Active Sync) or MobileMe services described in the Chapter 4: "Other Sync Methods."

When Is Your Contact List Most Useful?

The **Contacts** app is most useful when two things are true:

1. You have many names and addresses in it.

2. You can easily find what you need.

Two Simple Rules to Improve Your Contact List

We have a couple of basic rules to help make your **Contacts** list on your iPad more useful.

Rule 1: Add anything and everything in to your Contacts app.

> You never know when you might need that obscure restaurant name, that plumber's number, or other business or professional contact's information.

Rule 2: As you add entries, make sure you think about how to find them in the future (First Name, Last Name, Company).

> We have many tips and tricks in this chapter to help you enter names, so that they can be instantly located when you need them.

TIP: Here's a good way to find restaurants: Whenever you enter a restaurant into your **Contacts** list, make sure to put the word "restaurant" into the company name field, even if it's not part of the name. Then, when you type the letters "rest," you should instantly find all your restaurants!

Adding a New Contact Right on Your iPad

You can always add your contacts right on your iPad. This is handy when you're away from your computer—but have your iPad—and need to add someone to your **Contacts** list. It's very easy to do; we'll show you how in the next section.

Contacts

Tap the Plus Sign to Add a Contact

From your **Home** screen, touch the **Contacts** icon and you'll see the **All Contacts** list (see Figure 14–1). Tap the **Plus Sign (+)** in the lower-right corner of the **Contacts** list to add a new contact.

Tap the **plus sign (+)** to add a new contact.

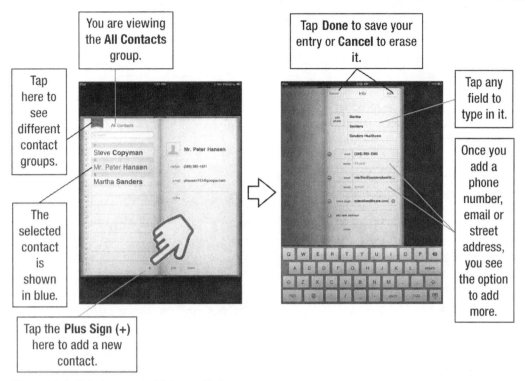

You are viewing the **All Contacts** group.

Tap **Done** to save your entry or **Cancel** to erase it.

Tap here to see different contact groups.

Tap any field to type in it.

The selected contact is shown in blue.

Once you add a phone number, email or street address, you see the option to add more.

Tap the **Plus Sign (+)** here to add a new contact.

Figure 14–1. *Entering a contact into your iPad*

Tap any of the fields (First, Last, Company, and so on) to type in information.

> **TIP:** Keep in mind that the search feature of the **Contacts** list uses the First, Last, and Company fields. When you add or edit contacts, adding a special word to the Company field can help you find a particular contact later. For example, adding the words "Cece friend" to the Company field can help you find all of Cece's friends quickly using the search feature.

Adding New Fields and Changing Labels

You will notice that the initial screen for adding a contact shows only a few fields for entering information: mobile (phone numbers), email (email addresses), home page (web page address), add new address (street address), notes, and add field.

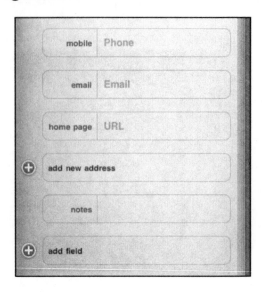

Apple has purposely done this to make the screen less cluttered. You will notice that, as you start typing a phone number, email address, or street address, a new field appears immediately under the one you are typing. This allows you to add multiple items easily. If you want, you may tap the name of the field (e.g., mobile) and change it to something else like (e.g., home or work).

Adding a Contact Photo

It's easier to identify people with pictures, so you may want to add pictures for your contacts, where available. To add a photo to a contact, tap the **add photo** button next to the First and Last fields.

If you are changing a photo, you'll see **edit** at the bottom of the existing photo when you are in "edit contact" mode.

After you touch the **add photo** button, you'll see that you can do the following:

- **Take a Photo** (for iPad 2 with its camera)

- **Choose a Photo**

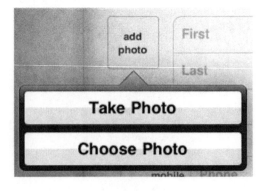

If there's a photo already in place, you will also see these options:

- **Edit a Photo**

- **Delete a Photo**

If you select **Choose Photo**, then you will be able to navigate to one of your photo albums and select a photo by tapping it.

You'll notice that the top and bottom of the photo become grayed out and that you can manipulate the picture by dragging it around with your finger. You can also pinch to zoom in or out.

Once the picture is sitting where you want it, just touch the **Use** button in the upper-right corner and that picture will be set for the contact.

Adding a New Phone Number

Tap in the Phone field and use the number keys to type the phone number.

> **TIP:** Don't worry about parentheses, dashes, or dots; the iPad will put the number into the correct format. Just type the digits of the area code and number. If you know the country code, it's a good idea to put that in, as well.

Let's say that this the phone number you just typed is not a mobile phone, but some other type of phone. The good news is that you can change it. Tap the label of the field—**mobile**, in this case—and change the label to **home, work**, or some other type (see Figure 14–2).

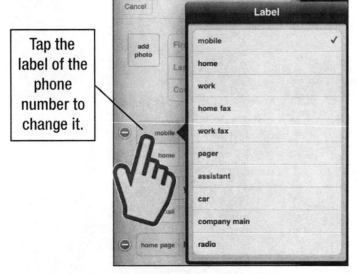

Figure 14–2. *Changing the field label of the phone number*

> **TIP:** Sometimes you need to add a pause to a phone number. For example, you might need to do so when the phone number is for someone at an organization where you have to dial the main number and then an extension. This is easy to do on the iPad. You just add a comma between the main number and the extension, like this:
>
> 386-555-1234 , 19323
>
> If you dialed this number (from your iPhone, for example), the phone would dial the main number, pause for two seconds, and then dial the extension. If you need more of a pause, you would simply add more commas.

Adding Email Addresses and a Web Site Address

Tap the **Email** tab and enter the email address for your contact. You may also be able to tap the label to the left of the email address and select whether this is a home, work, or other email address (sometimes you cannot change this label, depending on what type of contact system you are synchronizing with).

Under the Email field, you'll also find a home page field in which you can enter the address of your contact's web site.

Adding New Contact Fields

If you need to add more fields to the contact entry, just tap the **add field** button at the bottom of the **Contact** entry screen.

Next, select any of the available fields to add to that particular contact.

For example, to add a Birthday field to this contact, just touch **Birthday**.

When you touch **Birthday**, you're presented with a wheel. You can turn the wheel to the corresponding date to add the birthday to the contact information.

> **TIP:** Suppose you've met someone at the bus stop—someone you want to remember. Of course you should enter your new friend's first and last name (if you know it). But you should also enter the words "bus stop" in the Company field. Then, when you type the letters "bus" or "stop," you should instantly find everyone you've met at the bus stop, even if you can't remember their names!

Adding the Street Address

To add a street or physical address, tap the add new address field. You will see all the required fields appear on the screen (Street, City, State, Zip Code, and Country). As you did with the phone number, you can change the label to show whether this is a home, work, or other address.

When you are done, just touch the **Done** button in the upper-right corner of the **New Contact** form.

> **TIP:** If you've just moved into a new neighborhood, it can be quite daunting to remember everyone's name. A good practice to follow is to add the word "neighbor" into the Company field for every neighbor you meet. Then, to instantly call up all your neighbors, simply type the letters "neigh" to find everyone you've met!

Linking Contact Cards (Unified Contacts)

NOTE: The Link (**Unified Contacts** view) feature only appears on your iPad if you have at least two separate contact accounts set up, and you have a duplicate first and last name (but not different prefix, suffix, or middle names) across more than one contact account. For example, if you have a Gmail account and an Exchange or iTunes synced contact account, both with the name "John Smith," your **Contacts** app on the iPad will give you the **Link** option at the bottom of the **Edit** screen, as shown in this section.

As your **Contacts** list grows over time, it is common to end up with several duplicate contact entries, each with partial information. For example, you may have added a new contact from someone's email address or mobile phone number, but you already had his contact filed under a slightly different name (e.g., **Peter** vs. **Pete**).

On your iPad, you can merge or *Link* two or more contact cards together to see all the information in what the iPad calls the *Unified Contact*. Follow these steps to link contact cards together:

1. Select one of the duplicate contact entries and tap the **Edit** button under the **Contact** details screen.

2. Once you're editing the contact, tap the **Link Cards** button (a **Person** icon with a plus sign) at the bottom of the screen.

3. Next, locate and tap the correct contact. You can do this by tapping the **Groups** button at the top to select another Group, using the **Search** window at the top, or swiping up or down to find contacts.

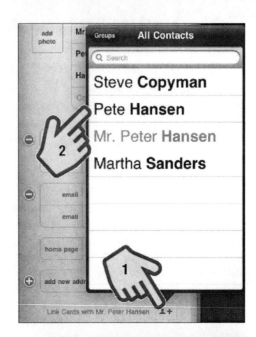

4. Now you can see the selected contact details and confirm that you want to connect the contacts by tapping **Link** in the upper-right corner. If this is not the contact you wish to link, then press the **All Contacts** button in the upper-right corner and select a different contact.

5. To link additional contacts or unlink contacts, tap the **Link and Unlink Contacts** button (a **Person** icon with number next to it) in the bottom of the **Contact** screen.

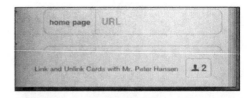

6. You know you have linked contacts because, instead of seeing **Info** at the top, it now says **Unified Info.** Tap the **Done** button in the upper-right corner to save the linking of contacts.

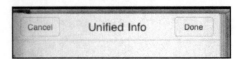

When you're done, you will now see only a single contact entry for all the contacts you have linked together. You know these are linked or *Unified* contacts because there is a **Unified Info** link at the bottom and a **Person** icon with a number showing the number of linked contacts (see Figure 14–3).

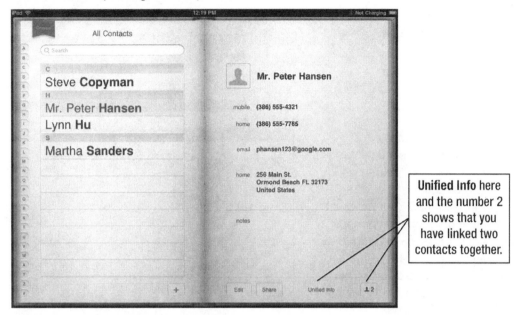

Figure 14–3. *Viewing linked contacts on your iPad*

> **TIP:** Learning the names of the parents of your school-age children's friends can be fairly challenging. In the First field, however, you can add not just the name of your child's friend, but the names of the child's parents, as well (e.g., **First: Samantha (Mom: Susan, Dad: Ron)**). Then, in the Company field, add the name of your child and "school friend" (e.g., **Cece school friend**). Now just typing your child's name in your **All Contacts** search box instantly finds every person you've ever met at your child's school. Now you can say, "Hello, Susan, great to see you again!" without missing a beat. *Try your best to covertly look up the name!*

Sharing Contacts

If someone asks you for contact information from your iPad, there is no need to copy and paste it or read it out loud. Instead, you can click the **Share** button and email it to this person as an email attachment. The attachment is sent in a vCard (.vcf) format, which is a standard format for electronic business cards. Follow these steps to share contact information:

1. Open your **Contacts** list and locate the contact you wish to send.

2. Tap the **Share** button under the contact details.

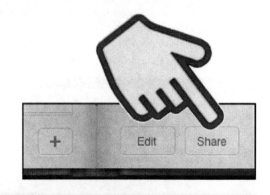

3. Next, address the email message and send it. You have now sent all the contact details in vCard (.vcf) format. Your recipient should be able to open the email message and tap (or save) the contact information to add it to her own contact list—all without retyping anything!

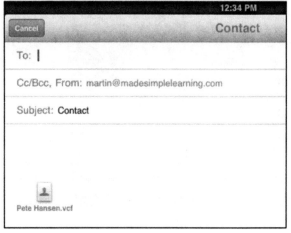

Start a FaceTime Video Call with a Contact

If you like to use **FaceTime** to make video calls, you can do that right from your **Contacts** list. Open up your **Contacts** list and locate the contact. Next, tap the **FaceTime** button at the bottom of the **Contact** details screen.

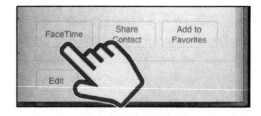

To learn all about **FaceTime** calls, please see Chapter 18: "FaceTime Video Messaging and Skype."

Making a Contact a FaceTime Favorite

If you use **FaceTime** video chat a lot with someone, you may want to make her a *Favorite*. To do this, open up your **Contacts** list and locate the contact. Next, tap the **Add to Favorites** button at the bottom of the **Contact** details screen.

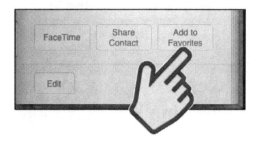

Deleting Contacts

Sometimes, you want to get rid of contacts on your iPad. Follow these steps to do so:

CAUTION: Remember that, if you sync your contacts to your computer or online **Contacts** list, then deleting a contact from your iPad will also delete that contact from your computer or online contact list (e.g., Google or Hotmail).

1. Locate the contact you wish to delete and tap the **Edit** button under the **Contact** details screen.

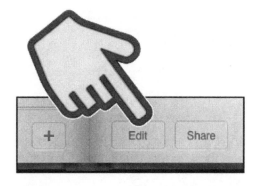

2. Scroll all the way to the bottom of the **Edit Contact** screen to see the **Delete Contact** button. Tap **Delete Contact**.

3. You may then see a pop-up confirmation. Tap **Delete** to remove this contact.

Searching Your Contacts

Let's say you need to find a specific phone number or email address. Just touch your **Contacts** icon as described previously, and you'll see a **Search** box at the top of your **All Contacts** list (see Figure 14–4).

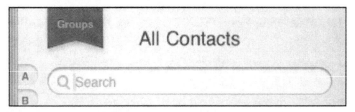

Figure 14–4. *The Search box for All Contacts*

Enter the first few letters of any of these three searchable fields:

- First Name
- Last Name
- Company Name

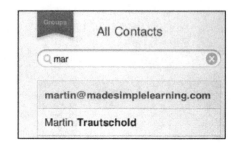

The iPad begins to filter immediately and displays only those contacts that match the letters typed.

> **TIP:** To further narrow the search, hit the space key and type a few more letters.

When you see the correct name, just touch it and that individual's contact information will appear.

Quickly Jump to a Letter by Tapping and Sliding on the Alphabet

If you hold your finger on the alphabet on the left edge of the screen and drag it up or down, you can jump to that letter.

Search by Flicking

If you don't want to manually input letters, you can just move your finger and flick from the bottom up to see your contacts move quickly on the screen. Just continue to flick or scroll until you see the name you want. Tap a name and the contact information will appear.

Search Using Groups

If you have your contacts sorted by groups on your PC or Mac and you sync your iPad with the computer, those groups will be synced to your iPad. Just touch the **Groups** tab at the top left of the **All Contacts** window and select which group you'd like to search within.

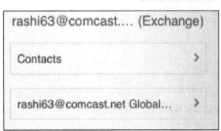

This example shows two groups—one is from a Microsoft Exchange account (i.e., a company email account), and one is from regular contacts.

If you have an Exchange ActiveSync account and your company has enabled it, your Exchange Global Address List shows up under the **Groups** tab, as well. You can search to find anyone in your company there.

> **NOTE:** You can't create groups on the iPad. Instead, they must be created on your computer or on another contact list (e.g., a MobileMe web site or **Outlook**) and synced to your iPad.

Adding Contacts from Emails

Often you'll receive an email and realize that the contact is not in your address book. Adding a new contact from an email is easy.

Open the email from the contact you'd like to add to your **Contacts** list. Then, in the email's From field, touch the name of the sender next to the **From:** tag.

If the sender is not in your address book, you'll be taken to a screen that lets you choose whether to add that email address to an existing contact or to create a new one.

If you select **Create a New Contact**, you'll be taken to the same **New Contact** screen we saw earlier (see Figure 14–1).

But suppose this is someone's personal email address, and you already have an entry for that person with the work email. In that case, you would select **Add to Existing Contact** and choose the correct person. Next, you'd give this email address a tag—*personal*, in this case.

Sending a Picture to a Contact

If you want to send a picture to a contact, you will need to do that from the **Photos** app (see Chapter 16: "iPad Photography").

Sending an Email Message from Contacts

Since many of the core apps (**Contacts**, **Mail**, and **Messages**) are fully integrated, one app can easily launch another. So, if you want to send an email to one of your contacts, open the contact and tap the email address. The **Mail** app will launch, and you can compose and send an email message to this person.

Start your **Contacts** by touching the **Contacts** icon. Either search or flick through your contacts until you find the contact you need.

In the contact information, touch the email address of the contact you'd like to use.

You'll see that the **Mail** program launches automatically with the contact's name in the To: field of the email. Type and send the message.

Showing Your Contacts Addresses on the Map

One of the great things about the iPad is its integration with the **Google Maps** app. This is very evident in the **Contacts** app. Let's say you want to map the home or work address of any contact in your address book. In the old days (pre-iPad), you'd have to use Google or MapQuest or some other service and laboriously retype or copy and paste the address information. It was very time-consuming; fortunately, you don't have to do this on the iPad.

Simply open the contact as you did earlier. This time, touch the address at the bottom of the contact information.

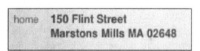

Your **Maps** app (which is powered by **Google Maps**) immediately loads and drops a **Pushpin** icon at the exact location of the contact. The contact name will appear above the **Pushpin**.

Touch the tab on the top of the **Pushpin** to get to the **Info** screen.

Now you can select **Directions To Here** or **Directions From Here**.

Next, type the correct start or end address and touch the **Route** button in the lower-right corner. If you decide you don't want the directions, just tap the **Clear** button in the top left.

What if you have just typed the address in your **Maps** app, but have not clicked away from your **Contacts** list? In that case, you might want to touch **Add to Contacts** to add this address.

TIP: To return to your contact information, tap the **Home** button and then tap **Contacts**.

Changing Your Contact Sort Order and Display Order

Like other settings, the options for the **Contacts** are accessible via the **Settings** icon.

Touch the **Settings** icon, scroll down to **Mail, Contacts, Calendars**, and touch the tab.

Scroll down and you'll see **Contacts** with two options underneath. To change the sort order, touch the **Sort Order** tab and select whether you want your contacts sorted first by first name or last name.

You may want to change how your contacts are displayed. Here's where you get it done; you can choose **First, Last** or **Last, First**. Tap the **Display Order** tab and choose whether you want your contact displayed in first-name or last-name order. Tap the **Mail, Contacts...** button in the upper-left corner to save your settings changes.

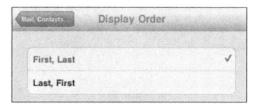

Searching for Global Address List Contacts

Sometimes you will want to search your Global Address List (GAL) contacts. Open your **Contacts** app as you normally would and touch the **Groups** button in the top-left corner. Look for the group that has **Global** next to it in your **Group** list and touch it. This gives you access to your Global Address List if you are connected to your organization's server.

Contact Troubleshooting

Sometimes, your **Contacts** app might not work the way you expect. If you don't see all your contacts, review the steps in the Chapter 3: "Sync Your iPad with iTunes" or Chapter 4: "Other Sync Methods" to learn how to sync with your **Address Book** application. Make sure you have selected **All Groups** in the settings in **iTunes**.

> **TIP:** If you are syncing with another contact application, such as **Contacts** in Gmail, make sure you select the option closest to **All Contacts**, rather than a subset like a particular group.

When Global Address List Contacts Don't Show Up

This next section is for Microsoft Exchange users. Sometimes you may encounter a problem where your GAL contacts don't show up. If this happens, begin by making sure you are connected to a Wi-Fi or 3G cellular data network.

Next, check your Exchange settings and verify you have the correct server and login information. To do so, tap the **Settings** button, then scroll to and touch **Mail, Contacts, and Calendar**. Find your Exchange account on the list and touch it to look at the settings. You may need to contact technical support at your organization to make sure your Exchange settings are correct.

Chapter 15

Your Calendar

The iPad makes the old calendar that used to hang on the fridge obsolete. In this chapter, we will show you how to utilize the **Calendar** app on the iPad to its full potential. We will show you how to schedule appointments, how to manage multiple calendars, how to change views on your calendar, and even how to deal with meeting invitations.

> **NOTE:** Throughout most of this chapter, we talk about syncing your iPad calendar with another calendar because it is nice to have your calendar accessible on your iPad and in other places. If you choose, you can also use your iPad in a *standalone* mode, where you do not sync to any other calendar. In this case, all the steps we describe for adding, viewing, and managing events apply equally to you. It is critical, however, that you use the iTunes automatic backup feature (or sync wirelessly to a Google, MobileMe, or Exchange calendar) to save a copy of your calendar, just in case something happens to your iPad.

Manage Your Busy Life on Your iPad

The **Calendar** app is a powerful and easy-to-use application that helps you manage your appointments, keep track of what you have to do, set reminder alarms, and even create and respond to meeting invitations (for Exchange users).

Today's Day and Date Shown on the Calendar Icon

The **Calendar** icon is usually right on your iPad **Home** screen. You will quickly notice that your **Calendar** icon changes to show today's date and day of the week. The icon to the right shows that it is a Friday and the 16th of the month.

TIP: If you use your iPad's **Calendar** app often, you might want to think about pinning or moving it to the Bottom Dock—you learned how to do this in the section on docking icons in Chapter 6.

Syncing or Sharing Your Calendar(s) with Your iPad

If you maintain a calendar on your computer or on a web site such as Google Calendar, you can synchronize or share that calendar with your iPad either using iTunes and your sync cable or by setting up a wireless synchronization (see Chapters 3 and 4 for more information on syncing).

After you set up the calendar sync, all of your computer calendar appointments will be synced with your iPad calendar automatically, based on your sync settings (see Figure 15–1).

If you use iTunes to sync with your calendar (e.g., **Microsoft Outlook**, **Entourage**, or Apple's **iCal**), your appointments will be transferred or synced every time you connect your iPad to your computer.

If you use another method to sync (e.g., Mobile Me, Exchange, or similar), this sync is wireless and automatic, and it will most likely happen without you having to do anything after the initial setup process.

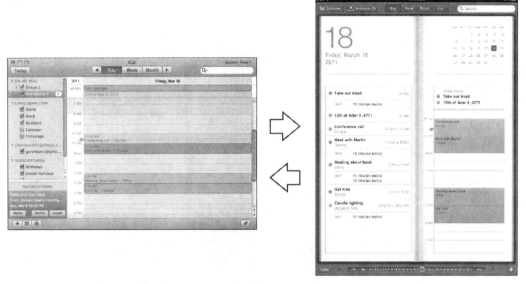

Figure 15–1. *Synching a PC or Mac calendar to the iPad*

Viewing Your Schedule and Getting Around

The default view for the calendar is your **Day** view. It will show you at a glance any upcoming appointments for your day. Appointments are shown in your calendar (see Figure 15–2). If you happen to have several different calendars that you have set up on your computer, such as **Work** and **Home**, then you will see these as separate colors on your iPad's calendar.

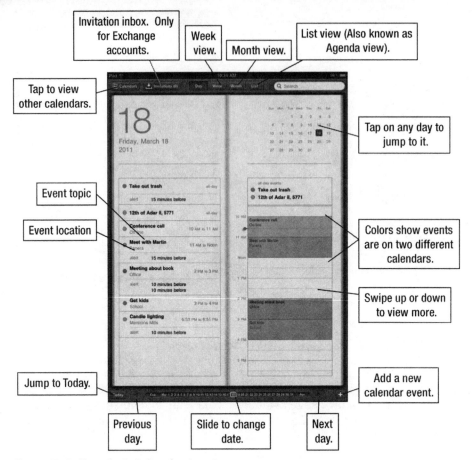

Figure 15–2. *The calendar's Day view layout*

You can manipulate the calendar in various ways:

- **Move a day at a time:** If you tap the **Triangle** icons next to the **Slider** control at the bottom, you move forward or backward a day.

- **Change views:** Use the **Day**, **Week**, **Month**, and **List** buttons at the top to change the view.

> **TIP:** Drag the **Slider** control at the bottom by moving left or right to advance quickly through days.

- **Jump to today:** Use the **Today** button at the bottom-left corner.

The Calendar's Four Views

Your iPad's **Calendar** app comes with four views: **Day**, **Week**, **Month**, and **List**. You can switch views by tapping the name of the view at the bottom of the screen. Here's a quick overview of the four views:

Day view: When you start the **Calendar** app, the default view is usually the **Day** view. This allows you to quickly see everything you have scheduled for the day. At the top of the **Calendar** app are buttons to change the view.

List (or Agenda) view: Touch the **List** view button at the top, and you can see a list of your appointments along the left-hand side.

Depending on how much you have scheduled, you might see the next day's or even the next week's worth of scheduled events.

Week view: Touch the **Week** view button at the top and you can see all your appointments for the week.

Similarly, tap any appointment to see details about that appointment.

Once you see the details, you can tap the **Edit** button to change them.

Month view: Touch the **Month** view and you can see a layout of the full month. Days with appointments have a small dot in them. The current day will show up highlighted in blue.

> **Tip**: Double-tap any day to jump to the **Day** view for that date. To return to the **Today** view, just touch the **Today** tab at the bottom left.
>
>

Navigating between months is easy:

- **Go to the next month:** Tap the **Triangle** icon to the right of the **Month** slider at the bottom.

- **Go to the previous month:** Tap the **Triangle** icon to the left of the **Month** slider.

To advance days in **Day** view, just touch the **Arrow** icons to either side of the **Date** slider at the bottom.

NOTE: While you can scroll in the **Calendar** app, you cannot swipe through your days, which runs counter to what you might expect.

Working with Several Calendars

Your iPad's **Calendar** app can track various calendars. The number of calendars you see depends on how you set up your synchronization using iTunes or other sync methods. In the example that follows, we have categorized personal appointments in our **Home** calendar and categorized work appointments in a separate **Work** calendar.

In the appointments in our **Calendar** app, we have our **Home** calendar appointments showing up in red and our **Work** calendar appointments in orange or green.

When you set up your **Sync** settings, you were able to specify which calendars you wanted to sync with your iPad. You can customize your calendar further by following these instructions:

Changing the colors: You will need to change the color of the calendar in the program on your computer that is synced to your iPad; this will change the colors on your iPad.

Adding a new calendar: It's a two-step process to add a new calendar to sync with your iPad:

1. Set up that new calendar on your computer's **Calendar** program.

2. Adjust your **Sync** settings to make sure this new calendar syncs to your iPad.

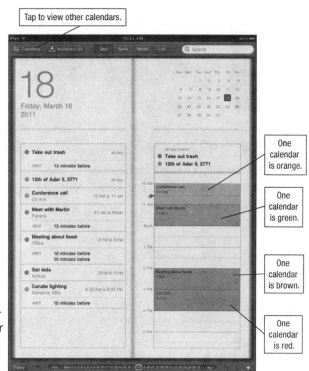

Tap to view other calendars.

One calendar is orange.

One calendar is green.

One calendar is brown.

One calendar is red.

Viewing only one calendar: To view just one calendar at a time, tap the **Calendars** button at the top and select only the calendar you wish to see.

Adding New Calendar Appointments/Events

You can easily add new appointments right on your iPad, and they will be synced (or shared with) your computer the next time the sync takes place.

Adding a New Appointment

Your instinct will most likely be to try to touch the screen at a particular time to set an appointment; unfortunately, this is not how setting appointments work.

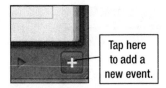

Tap here to add a new event.

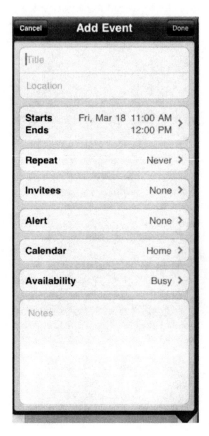

To add a new calendar event from any calendar view, follow these steps.

1. Tap the + icon at the bottom-right corner of the screen. The **Add Event** screen will now show.

2. Next, touch the box marked **Title** and **Location**.

3. Type in a title for the event and the location (optional). For example, you might type "Meet with Martin" as the title and input the location as "Office." Or, you might choose to type "Lunch with Martin" and then choose a very expensive restaurant in New York City.

4. Touch the **Blue Done** button in the upper-right corner to return to the **Add Event** screen.

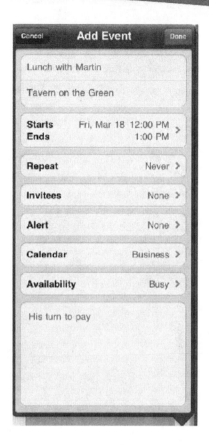

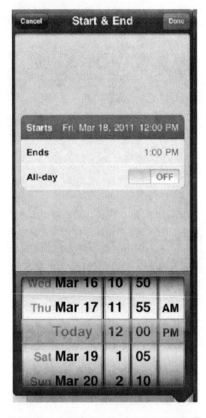

5. Touch the **Starts** or **Ends** tab to adjust the event timing. To change the start time, touch the **Starts** field to highlight it in blue. Next, move the rotating dials at the bottom to reflect the correct date and start time of the appointment.

6. To change the end time, touch the **Ends** field and use the rotating dials.

   Alternatively, you can set an all-day event by touching the switch next to **All-day** to set it to **ON**.

NOTE: You will see a tab labeled **Invitees** before the **Repeat** tab only if you sync to an Exchange calendar. We show you how to use the **Invitees** tab to invite people to calendar events in Chapter 24: "Other Sync Methods."

Recurring Events and Alerts (Alarms)

Some of your appointments happen every day, week, or month at the same time. If the appointment you are scheduling is a repeating or recurring appointment, just touch the **Repeat** tab and then select the correct option from the list.

Touch **Done** to get back to the main **Event** screen.

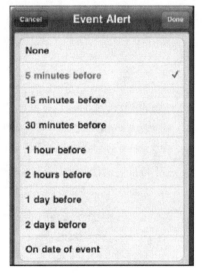

An audible reminder of an upcoming appointment— an *alert*—can help keep you from forgetting an important event. Follow these steps to create an alert:

1. Touch the **Alert** tab and then select the option for a reminder alarm. You can have no alarm at all or set a time anytime from five minutes before the event all the way to two days before—whatever works best for you.

2. Touch **Done** to get back to the main **Event** screen.

3. After you add an alert, you are given the option to add a second (optional) alert.

This can be really useful if you need a second reminder to ensure you do not miss the event.

For example, if you need to pick up your kids at the bus stop, you might want one alert 15 minutes ahead of time, then a final alert 5 minutes ahead of time, so you can be absolutely certain that you don't miss the pickup.

TIP: Another good example of creating two alerts occurs when you have to take your child out of school for a doctor or dentist appointment.

Set the first alert for the night before to write a note to the school and give it to your child.

Set the second alert for 30 minutes prior to the appointment, so you can leave enough time to pick up your child and get her to the appointment.

Choosing Which Calendar to Use

If you use more than one calendar in **Outlook**, **Entourage**, **iCal**, or some other program and you sync your iPad with that program, you will have various calendars available to you.

> **NOTE:** If you create an event and choose an Exchange calendar, you'll have an option to invite other users to the event.

Touch the **Calendar** button in the upper-left corner to see all your calendars.

Tap the calendar you want to use for this particular event. Usually, the calendar selected is the last one you selected for the previous event you scheduled on your iPad.

Switching an Event to a Different Calendar

You will notice that when you edit the calendar event on your iPad, you will not have the option to switch calendars.

If you wish to change the scheduled calendar on your iPad, you will need to delete the original event and schedule a new event on the preferred calendar.

> **TIP:** To delete the calendar event, tap the event, and then select the **Edit** button. Swipe to the bottom of the **Edit** screen and select **Delete Event**. Next, you will need to confirm that you want to delete the event.

Availability

You can choose your availability from the following options: **Busy** (default) or **Free**. Depending on your Exchange settings, you might also see **Tentative** or **Out of Office**.

> **NOTE:** You will only see the **Availability** field if the calendar you are using for this event is synced with the MobileMe, Exchange, or Exchange/Google settings.

Using Copy-and-Paste Text in the Calendar

The iPad's **App Switcher** program means you can now easily jump between any two apps. There may be times when you want to jump between your **Email** and your **Calendar** apps to copy and paste information. The information to copy and paste could be anything, such as driving directions or critical notes you need at your fingertips for a meeting. Follow these steps to copy and paste information between your **Email** and **Calendar** programs:

1. Create a new calendar event or edit an existing one, as explained previously in this chapter.

2. Scroll down to the **Notes** field and tap it to open it.

3. Double-tap the **Home** button to bring up the **App Switcher.**

4. If you see the **Mail** icon, tap it. If you don't see the **Mail** icon, swipe left or right to look for it. Once you find it, tap it to open the **Mail** app.

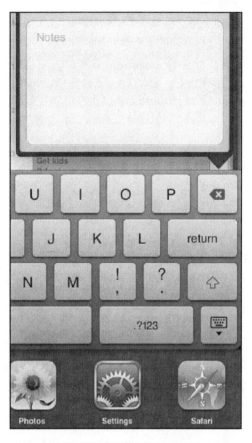

5. Double-tap a word, then use your fingers to drag the blue handles to select the text you want to copy.

6. Tap the **Copy** button.

7. Double-tap the **Home** button to bring up the **App Switcher.**

8. Tap the **Calendar** icon. It should be the first icon on the left, since you just jumped out of it.

9. Now tap and hold in the **Notes** field. When you let go, you should see the **Paste** pop-up field. If you don't see it, then hold your finger down a bit longer until you do see it.

10. Tap **Paste**.

11. Now you should see the text you copied pasted into the **Notes** field. Tap **Done** to save your changes.

Adding Notes to Calendar Events

If you want to add some notes to this calendar event, tap **Notes** and type a few notes.

> **TIP:** If this is a meeting somewhere new, you could type or copy/paste some driving directions. Close and then open the appointment again, and then tap the location you just added. Your **Maps** app will load to guide you.

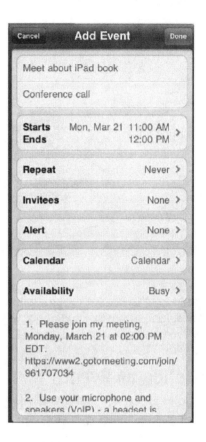

Editing Appointments

Sometimes, the details of an appointment may change and need to be adjusted (see Figure 15–3). Fortunately, this is an easy task on your iPad.

First, locate the appointment that needs to change and touch it. In the upper-right corner, you will see the **Edit** button. Touch **Edit** and you will return to the **Edit Event** screen showing the appointment details.

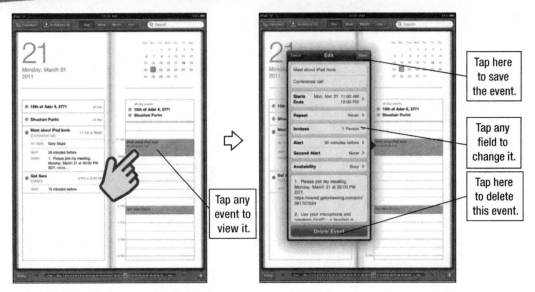

Figure 15–3. *Editing an appointment*

Just touch the tab in the field you need to adjust. For example, you can change the time of this appointment by touching the **Starts** or **Ends** tab, and then adjusting the time for the event's starting or ending time.

Deleting an Event

Notice that, at the bottom of the **Edit** screen, you also have the option to delete this event. Simply touch **Delete Event** at the bottom of the screen to do so.

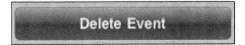

Meeting Invitations

For those who use Microsoft Exchange or Microsoft Outlook regularly, meeting invitations become a way of life. You receive a meeting invitation in your email, you accept the invitation, and then the appointment gets automatically placed in your calendar.

On your iPad, you will see that invitations you accept get put right into your calendar. In the example to the right, if we touch the **Meeting Invitation** icon at the bottom of the email, the event will get put right into our calendar.

> **NOTE:** If you use an Exchange or Google calendar, you can invite people and reply to meeting invitations on your iPad. See the "Working with the Google or Exchange Calendar" section of Chapter 4 "Other Sync Methods" to learn more.

If you touch the meeting invitation in your calendar, you can see all the details that you need: the dial in number, the meeting ID, and any other details that might be included in the invitation.

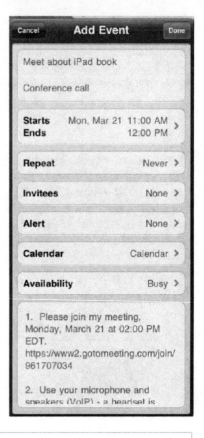

NOTE: At the time of writing, you can accept meeting invitations on your iPad from your Exchange account, and you can create them as long as you choose the Exchange calendar or MobileMe calendar. Invitations will also transfer automatically from **Entourage**, **iCal**, or **Outlook** if you have iTunes set to sync with those programs.

Calendar Options

There are just a few options to adjust in your **Calendar** app; you can find these in the **Settings** app. Just touch **Settings** from your **Home** screen.

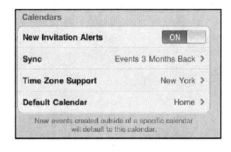

Scroll down to the **Mail, Contacts, Calendars** tab and touch it. Scroll down to **Calendars**, and you will see three options. The first option is a simple switch to be notified of **New Invitation** alerts—if you receive any meeting invites, it is good to keep this set in the default **ON** position.

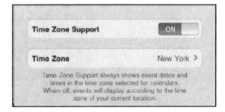

Next, you can choose your time zone. This setting should reflect your **Home** settings from when you set up your iPad. If you are traveling, however, and want to adjust your appointments for a different time zone, you can change this to any other city you would like.

Changing the Default Calendar

We mentioned earlier that you can have multiple calendars displayed on your iPad. This option allows you to choose which calendar will be your default calendar.

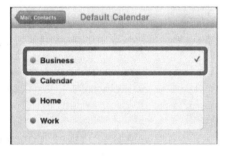

That means that when you go to schedule any new appointment, this calendar will be selected by default.

If you wish to use a different calendar—say, your **Work** calendar—you can change that when you actually set the appointment, as shown earlier in this chapter.

iPad Photography

Previous versions of the iPad did not include a camera; the iPad 2 rectifies that shortcoming with not one, but two cameras: a 0.7-megapixel camera on the back and a 0.3-megapixel VGA camera on the front for video chats and self-portraits (you will learn more about using the front-facing camera in the new **FaceTime** app in Chapter 18: "FaceTime Video Messaging and Skype").

Also new is the **Photo Booth** app which allows you to take self-portraits and really be creative – we show you how at the end of the chapter.

> **NOTE:** The resolution on the iPad makes pictures look beautiful. However, it's nowhere near the quality of the camera on the new iPhone 4, so pictures will lose some quality when you sync them and view them on your computer. Think of the iPad camera as a video camera that takes stills, not a still camera that captures video.

Viewing and sharing your pictures on the iPad is truly a joy, due in large part to the beautiful, large high-resolution screen. In this chapter, we discuss the many ways to get pictures onto your iPad . We also show you how you to use the touch screen to navigate through your pictures, zoom in and out, pinch open albums, and manipulate your photos.

> **TIP:** Did you know that you could take a picture of the entire screen of your iPad by pressing two keys simultaneously? Now you can prove that you got the high score on Tetris!
>
> Here's how to get it done: press both the **Home** button and the **On/Off/Sleep** key on the top-right edge (you can also press one, hold it, and then press the other). If you have done this correctly, the screen should flash and you'll hear a camera sound. The screen capture you have taken will be in your **Camera Roll** album in the **Photos** app.

Using the Camera App

The **Camera** app (see Figure 16–1) should be on your **Home** page—usually on the first screen at the top. If you don't see it, then swipe left or right until you find it.

Touch the **Camera** icon and the shutter of the camera opens with an animation on your screen.

Switch between the front and rear cameras

Touch screen to see **Zoom** control slider.

Thumbnail of previous picture taken. Touch to launch **Photo** app.

Toggle between **Camera** and **Video Camera**

Touch to take picture

Figure 16–1. *The layout of the Camera app*

Geo-Tagging

Geo-tagging is a feature that puts your GPS (geographic positioning system) coordinates into the picture file. If you upload your pictures to services like Flickr, the coordinates of your picture can help your friends locate where the picture was taken. The iPad supports geo-tagging, not only on the 3G version, but also over Wi-Fi. The latter approach requires that you be connected to a Wi-Fi network, and it uses Wi-Fi triangulation to embed GPS coordinates into the image.

Geo-tagging also shows up in the **Places** album of your iPad. Touch the **Places** tab and you will see pushpins for all the geo-tagged photos.

Touch one of the pushpins and a small thumbnail of the geo-tagged photo will show up next to the location.

In this example, I touched the pushpin near Boston, and I found a picture I took of my son when I was visiting him at school.

CAUTION: The downside of geo-tagging is that, if you share them online, people will know where you live, work, and so on. You may want to be selective about using it and what you share when using it.

NOTE: If you use a Mac, be aware that the **iPhoto** app uses geo-tagging to put photos into the **Places** category of **iPhoto**.

If you have Location Services turned on (see Chapter 1: "Getting Started") when you start the camera, you will be asked if it is OK to use your current location.

To double-check whether it is on, do the following:

1. Start your **Settings**.

2. Go to **General**.

3. Then touch **Location Services**. You will see a screen like the one here.

4. Make sure the switch next to **Camera** is toggled to **ON**.

Taking a Picture

Taking a picture is as simple as pointing and shooting, yet there are some adjustments that you can make if you choose to.

Once your camera is on, center your subject in the screen of your iPad.

When you are ready to take a picture, just touch the **Camera** button along the bottom. You will hear a shutter sound, and the screen will show an animation indicating that the picture is being taken.

Once the picture is taken, it will drop down into the window in the lower-left corner. Touch that small thumbnail, and the **Camera Roll** album of your **Photos** app will load.

Using the iPad's Zoom

The iPad camera includes a 5x digital zoom.

> NOTE: A digital zoom is never as clear as an analog zoom, so be aware that picture quality is usually degraded slightly when using the iPad's zoom feature.

To use the zoom feature, just touch the screen and move the **Zoom** control slider, as shown in Figure 16–1.

Switching Cameras

As mentioned previously, the iPad comes with two cameras: a .7-megapixel camera for most photography and a VGA camera for self-portraits or for use in **FaceTime** video calls (see Chapter 18: "FaceTime Video Messaging and Skype").

To switch between the cameras, do the following:

1. Touch the **Switch Camera** icon in the **Camera** app.

2. Wait for the camera to switch to the front-facing camera and line up the shot.

3. Touch the **Switch Camera** icon again to switch back to the standard camera.

TIP: Because of the placement of the front-facing camera, faces can look somewhat distorted. Try moving your face back a bit and adjusting the camera angle to get a better image.

Viewing Pictures You Have Taken

Your iPad stores pictures you take in what is called your **Camera Roll**. You can access the **Camera Roll** from inside both the **Camera** and **Photos** apps. In the **Camera** app, touch the **Pictures** icon in the bottom-left corner of the **Camera** screen.

Once you touch a picture to view, you can swipe through your pictures to see all the pictures in the **Camera Roll**.

To get back to the **Camera Roll**, press the **Camera Roll** button in the upper-left corner.

To take another picture, touch the **Done** button in the upper-right corner.

Note that the picture to the right was taken using the **Photo Booth** app. Read about it at the end of this chapter.

Getting Photos onto Your iPad

You have many options for loading photos onto your device:

- *Sync using iTunes:* Probably the simplest way is to use iTunes to sync photos from your computer. This is described this in detail in Chapter 3: "Sync Your IPad with iTunes."

- *Receive as email attachments*: While this is not useful for large numbers of pictures, it works well for one or a few photos. Check out Chapter 13: "Email on your iPad" for more details about how to save attachments. (Once saved, these images show up in the **Camera Roll** album.)

- *Save images from the Web*: Sometimes you'll see a great image on a web site. Press and hold it to see the pop-up menu and then select **Save Image**. (Like other saved images, these end up in the **Camera Roll** album.)

- *Download images from within an app*: A good example of this is the wallpaper image shown in Chapter 7: "Personalize and Secure your iPad."

- *Sync with iPhoto (for Mac users)*: If you use a Mac computer, your iPad will most likely sync automatically with **iPhoto** or **Aperture**.

Here are a few steps to get iPhoto sync up and running:

1. Connect your iPad and start **iTunes**.

2. Go to the **Photo** tab along the top row of **Sync Options**.

3. Choose the **Albums**, **Events**, **Faces**, or **Places** you want to keep in sync with the iPad (see Figure 16–2).

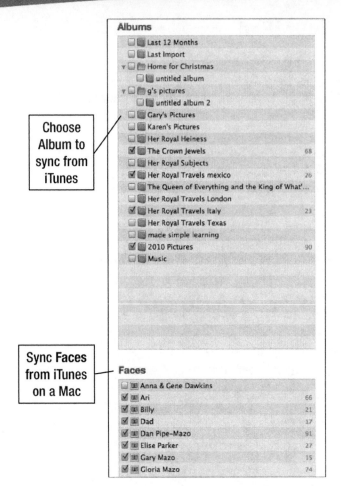

Figure 16–2. *Choosing albums, faces, or events from iTunes to sync with the iPad*

Drag and drop (for Windows users): Once you connect your iPad to your Windows computer, it will appear in Windows Explorer as a portable device, as shown in Figure 16–3. Here are the steps required to drag and drop photos between your iPad and computer:

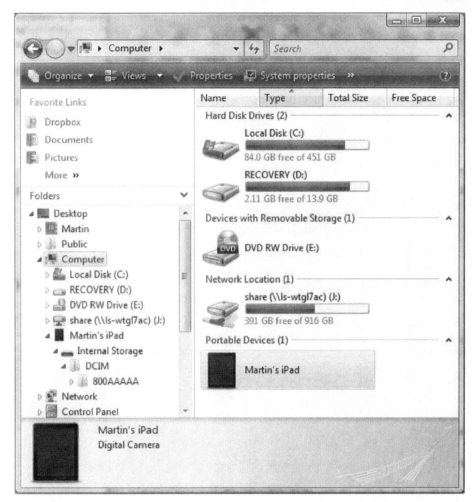

Figure 16–3. *Windows Explorer showing the iPad as a portable device (connected with a USB cable)*

1. Double-click the iPad image under **Portable Devices** to open it.

2. Double-click **Internal Storage** to open it.

3. Double-click **DCIM** to open it.

4. Double-click **800AAAAA** to open it. (This will have a unique name on your PC.)

5. You will see all the images in the **Saved Photos** album on your iPad.

6. To copy images from your iPad, select and then drag and drop images out of this folder onto your computer.

> **TIP:** Here's how to select multiple images in Windows.
>
> Draw a box around the images, or click one image and then press **Ctrl+A** to select them all. Hold down the **Ctrl** key and click individual pictures to select them. Right-click one of the selected pictures and choose **Cut** (to move) or **Copy** (to copy) all of the selected images. To paste the images, press and click any other disk or folder, such as **My Documents**, and then navigate to where you want to move or copy the files. Finally, right-click again and select **Paste**.

Viewing Your Photos

Now that your photos are on your iPad, you have several cool ways to look through them and show them to others.

Launching from the Photos Icon

If you like using your **Photos** app, you might want to place it in your Bottom Dock for easy access if it's not already there (see Chapter 6: "Organize your Icons and Folders.")

To get started with photos, touch the **Photos** icon.

The first screen shows your photo albums, which were created when you set up your iPad and synced it with iTunes. Chapter 3: "Sync Your iPad with iTunes" showed you how to choose which photos to sync with your iPad. Any changes to the library on your computer will be automatically updated on your iPad.

Along the top, there are buttons for five categories of photos (depending on the photo software on the PC or Mac with which the iPad is synced). In the image to the right, you see **Photos**, **Albums**, **Events**, **Faces**, and **Places**.

> **NOTE**: This iPad was synced to **iPhoto** on a Mac; PC users will see different options.

Choosing a Library

From the **Photo Albums** page, touch one of the library buttons to show the photos in that album. The screen will immediately change to show you thumbnails of the pictures in this library.

Tap and drag your finger up and down to view all the pictures. You can flick up or down to quickly move throughout the album.

Preview an Album by Pinching Open

When you're trying to locate a particular image, one of the cool things you can do on your iPad is to preview a particular album by pinching it open.

Place two fingers on the album and slowly *pinch open* your fingers. Notice that all the images spread out across the screen.

If you see the photo you want, continue pinching open to fully open the album. End your pinch with a flick to open the album.

If you don't see the image you want, simply close your fingers again to close the album and then try another one.

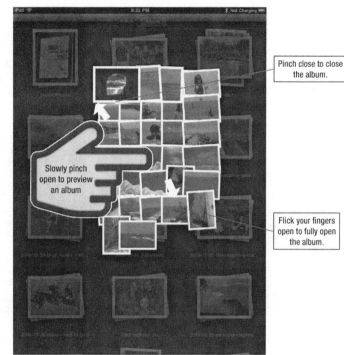

Pinch close to close the album.

Slowly pinch open to preview an album

Flick your fingers open to fully open the album.

> **TIP**: You can close an album that is fully open by *pinching closed* across the entire screen of thumbnails.

Working with Individual Pictures

Once you locate the picture you want to view, just tap it. The picture then loads onto the screen.

> **NOTE:** If your photos were shot in **Landscape** mode, they will not take up the full screen on your iPad.

> **TIP:** The picture here was shot in **Landscape** mode. To see it in a full screen, you have to turn your iPad on its side or just double-tap it to fill the screen.

Moving Between Pictures

The swipe gesture is used to move from one picture to the next. Just swipe your finger left or right across the screen, and you can move through your pictures.

> **TIP:** Drag your finger slowly to move more gradually through the picture library.

When you reach the end of an album, tap the screen once and you'll see a tab in the upper-left corner that has the name of the photo album. Touch that tab and you'll return to the thumbnail page of that particular album.

To get back to your main photo album page, touch the button that says **Albums** at the top of the screen.

Use the Thumbnail Bar to Move Between Pictures

Instead of swiping left and right to move between your pictures, you can bring up the soft-key controls on the screen. To do this, simply tap the screen once. Tap it again to make the soft keys disappear.

Along the very bottom of the screen, you'll see a small **Thumbnail** bar over which you can gently slide your finger (see Figure 16–4). You can quickly slide through the whole album using this bar. You can also just tap a thumbnail to see that particular picture.

Just drag your finger across this **Thumbnail** bar to quickly move through the photos.

Figure 16–4. *Use the **Thumbnail** bar to advance through pictures.*

Zooming In and Out of Pictures

There are two ways to zoom in and out of pictures on your iPad: double-tapping and pinching.

Double-Tapping

As the name suggests, *double-tapping* is a quick double-tap on the screen to zoom in on the picture, as shown in Figure 16–5. You will be zoomed in to the spot where you double-tap. To zoom out, just double-tap once more.

See Chapter 1: "Getting Started" for more help on double-tapping.

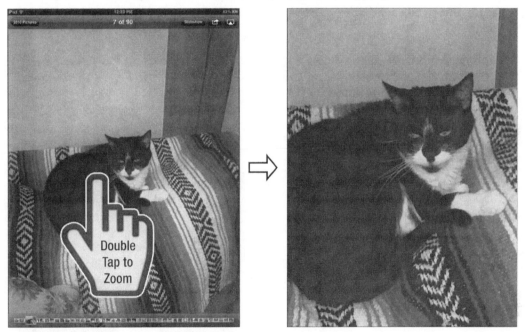

Figure 16–5. *Double-tapping on a picture to zoom*

Pinching

Also described in Chapter 1: "Getting Started," *pinching* is a much more precise form of zooming in. While double-tapping zooms in or out only to one set level, pinching allows you to zoom in or out just a little bit or quite a lot.

To pinch, hold your thumb and forefinger close together and then slowly (while touching the screen) separate them, making the picture larger. To zoom out, start with your thumb and forefinger apart and move them together.

> **NOTE:** Once you have activated the zoom feature using either method, you will not be able to easily swipe through your pictures until you return the picture to its standard size.

Viewing a Slide Show

You can view the pictures in your photo album as a slide show if you'd like. Just tap the screen once to bring up the on-screen soft keys. In the upper-right corner is a **Slideshow** button—just touch it once to start the slide show. You can start the slide show from either the **Photo Library** screen of from any picture you are viewing.

Slideshow Options let you adjust how long each picture remains on the screen. It also lets you choose music, transitions, and other settings, as shown in Figure 16–6. To end the slide show, just tap the screen.

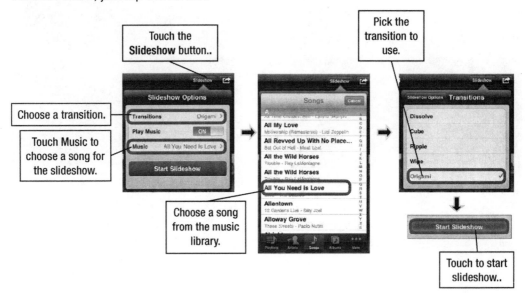

Figure 16–6. *Configuring your slide show*

Adjusting Slideshow Options

To configure a slide show, you will need to change your settings. To do so, touch the **Settings** icon on the **Home** screen.

Scroll down to the **Photos** tab and touch the screen. You will then see the various options you can use, including four options you can adjust for slide shows.

To specify how long to play each slide, touch the **Play Each Slide For** tab. You can choose a range between 2 and 20 seconds.

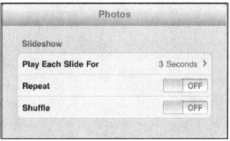

If you want pictures to repeat in a slide show, just move the **Repeat** switch to **ON**.

If you want the pictures to move in an order different from the way they are listed, choose **Shuffle**. Like the **Shuffle** command on the music player, this option will cause the pictures to play in a random order.

Using a Picture as Your iPad Wallpaper

For information on how to select and use a picture as your iPad wallpaper (and more wallpaper options), please go to Chapter 7: "Personalize and Secure your iPad."

> **NOTE:** You can have different pictures for your **Home** screen and **Lock** screen or use the same picture for both.

Emailing a Picture

As long as you have an active Internet connection (see Chapter 5: "Wi-Fi and 3G Connectivity"), you can send any picture in your photo collection via email. Tap the **Options** button on the **Top** icon bar—usually the one furthest to the right (or second from the right if you have **AirPlay** enabled). If you don't see the icons, tap the screen once.

Choose the **Email Photo** option and the **Mail** app will automatically launch (see Figure 16–7).

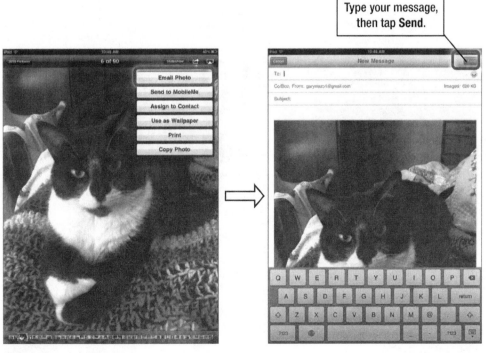

Figure 16–7. *Emailing a photo*

Touch the **To** field as you did in Chapter 13: "Email on your iPad" and select the contact to receive the picture. Tap the **Blue +** button to add a contact.

Type in a subject and a message, and then touch **Send** in the upper-right corner. That's all there is to it.

Email, Copy, or Delete Several Pictures At Once

If you have several pictures you want to email, copy, or delete at the same time, you can do it from the **Thumbnail** view, as shown in Figure 16–8.

> **NOTE:** The **copy** function allows you to copy and paste multiple pictures into an email message or other app. **Share** renames the image to photo.png; **copy**-and-**paste** leaves it with the DCIM folder file name, .png. When you select **Share**, a pop-up window will ask you if you want to send them in small, medium, large, or original size with the size of attachment in MB.
>
> At publishing time, you could share or email a maximum of five pictures. This may change with future software.

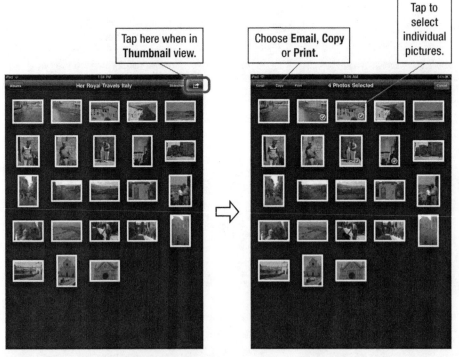

Figure 16–8. *Selecting multiple images to email*

AirPlay

Just as with music and videos, you can use Apple's proprietary **AirPlay** feature to "send" your pictures to your Apple TV (or another **AirPlay**-compatible device).

The **AirPlay** icon is on the Top Icon Bar, furthest to the right. From any picture or album, touch the **AirPlay** icon. Next, choose the **AirPlay** device to "move" your pictures from your iPad to the larger screen of your TV.

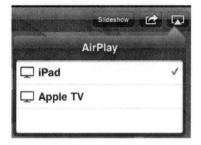

Printing a Picture

New to iOS 4.3 is **AirPrint**. **AirPrint** is Apple's proprietary built-in printing function. **AirPrint** works with pictures, documents, and other apps. The cool part: You don't need to install printer drivers as you must on your PC or Mac.

Follow these steps to print a picture:

1. Select any picture from your album, as you did previously.

2. Touch the **Envelope** icon.

3. Choose **Print** from the options.

4. **AirPrint** will search for a compatible **AirPrint** printer when you touch the **Printer Options** button.

5. Choose how many copies you want to print.

6. Touch the **Print** button and your picture will print out.

Assigning a Picture to a Contact

Chapter 14: "Working with Contacts" covers how to add a picture when editing a contact. You can also find a picture you like and assign it to a contact. Begin by finding the photo you want to use.

As you did when selecting wallpaper and emailing a photo, tap the **Options** button—the one furthest to the right of the upper row of soft keys. If you don't see the icons, tap the screen once.

When you touch the **Options** button, you'll see a drop-down list of choices: **Email Photo**, **Assign to Contact**, **Use as Wallpaper**, and **Copy Photo**.

Touch the **Assign to Contact** button.

Select a Picture, then choose Assign to Contact.

You will see your contacts on the screen. You can either perform a search using the **Search** bar at the top or just scroll through your contacts.

Once you find the contact to which you would like to add the picture, touch the name.

... then tap to select the contact.

Type a few letters of the first, last or company name ...

You will then see the **Move and Scale** screen. Tap and drag the picture to move it; use pinch to zoom in or out.

When you have it just as you want it, touch the **Use** button to assign the picture to that contact.

Tap here when you are ready to use the photo.

NOTE: You will return to your **Photo** library, not to the contact. If you want to double-check that the picture was set to your contact, exit the **Photo** app, start the **Contact** app, and then search for that contact.

Deleting a Picture

You might wonder why can't you delete certain pictures from your iPad (i.e., the **Trash Can** icon is missing).

You'll notice that the **Trash Can** icon is not visible for any photo that is synced from iTunes. You can delete such pictures only from your computer library. Then, the next time you sync your iPad, they will be deleted.

When you are looking through pictures in your **Camera Roll** (which is not synced with iTunes, but is comprised of pictures you save from email messages or download from the Web), you'll see the **Trash Can** icon in the **Top** icon bar to the right. This **Trash Can** icon does not appear when you are viewing pictures from your **Photos** library or other synced albums.

If you don't see the bottom row of icons, tap the photo once to activate them. Then tap the **Trash Can** icon; you will be prompted with the option to delete the picture.

Touch **Delete Photo** and the picture will be deleted from your iPad.

Downloading Pictures from Web Sites

You now know how to transfer pictures from your computer to your iPad and save them from email messages. You can also download and save pictures right from the Web onto your iPad.

> **CAUTION:** We strongly encourage you to respect image copyright laws as you download and save images from the Web. Unless the web site indicates an image is free, you should check with the web site owner before downloading and saving any pictures.

Finding a Picture to Download

The iPad makes it easy to copy and save images from web sites. This can be handy when you are looking for a new image to use as wallpaper on your iPad.

First, tap the **Safari** web browser icon and search for iPad wallpaper to locate a few sites that might have some interesting possibilities (see Chapter 11: "Surf the Web with Safari" for help).

Once you find a picture you want to download and save, tap and hold it to bring up a new menu of options that includes **Save Image** (among others), as shown in Figure 16–9. Choose this option to save the picture in your **Camera Roll** album.

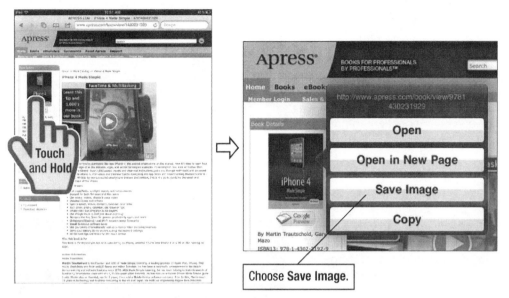

Figure 16–9. *Saving an image from a web site*

Now touch your **Photo** icon and you should see the picture in the **Camera Roll** album.

Photo Booth

New to the iPad is a very fun piece of software that will be familiar to Mac users: **Photo Booth**. **Photo Booth** uses the front camera of the iPad and allows the user to create some very cool and different visual effects.

Start by touching the **Photo Booth** icon and you will see nine squares, each with a different visual image: **Thermal Camera**, **Mirror**, **X-Ray**, **Kaleidoscope**, **Normal**, **Light Tunnel**, **Squeeze**, **Twirl**, and **Stretch**.

Just touch one of the image choices and it will fill the screen.

To capture one of the images, touch the **Camera** icon, just as if you were taking a picture. As you capture images, they will appear in a row towards the bottom of the screen.

To return and choose a different image type, touch the icon in the lower-left corner.

To use the back camera with the associated image type, just touch the **Switch Camera** button.

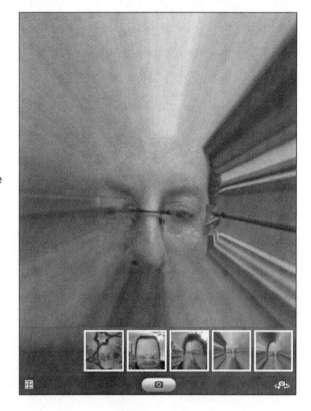

You can have a lot of fun with **Photo Booth**. The pictures you capture will be stored in your **Camera Roll**, so you can email them, post them to Facebook, and share them with the world!

Chapter 17

Recording and Editing Videos

Your iPad is a very capable video recorder. You can record and export HD video up to 720p. You can then publish that video straight to YouTube or MobileMe or even send it to an email recipient. In this chapter, we will also show you how to shoot and quickly *trim* your videos, as well as upload them.

Video Recording and Editing

New to the iPad this year is the capability to record videos using the **Camera** app and to edit videos with the **iMovie** app that Mac users have been using for some time. With **iMovie**, you can actually create movies by joining movie clips, adding pictures and transitions, and then adding your own audio track. When you're finished, you can upload the movie to the Web.

In the next section, you will learn how to add video clips, audio, pictures, and transitions. You will also learn how to produce a high quality, high definition video right on your iPad.

Starting the Video Recorder

The software for the video recorder is actually part of the **Camera** app (see Figure 17–1). Follow these steps to use the built-in video recorder:

1. Start the **Camera** app (see Chapter 16: "iPad Photography" for more information on how to do this).

2. Move the slider in the lower-right corner from the **Camera** icon to the **Video Recorder** icon.

3. Try to keep the iPad steady as you record your scene.

4. Touch the **Stop** button when you are done recording.

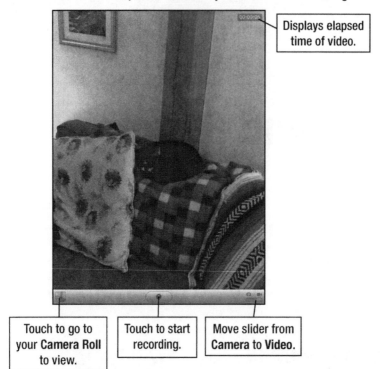

Displays elapsed time of video.

Touch to go to your **Camera Roll** to view.

Touch to start recording.

Move slider from **Camera** to **Video**.

Figure 17–1. *The layout and controls of the video recorder*

Adjust Point of White Balance

The iPad video camera is fixed focus. You can adjust the point of white balance of the video based on the subject. Follow these steps to take advantage of this feature:

1. To focus on something in the foreground of the video, touch the screen in the foreground. This brings up a small box that shows the area of white balance.

2. To switch the white balance to a subject in the background, touch another part of the screen. The box will temporarily display the new area of white balance.

Trimming the Video

The iPad allows you to perform edits on your video right on the phone. Once the video has been recorded and you press the **Stop** button, the video immediately goes into your **Camera Roll**.

Touch the small image of the video in the lower-left corner to bring up the video. At the top of the screen, you will see a timeline with all the frames of your video at the top of the screen (see Figure 17–2). Follow these steps to edit your just recorded video:

1. Drag either end of the timeline and you will see that the video goes into **Trim** mode.

2. Drag the ends of the video on either end until it is the length you desire.

3. When the video is the correct length, touch the **Trim** button in the upper-right corner.

4. Next, select either **Trim Original** or **Save as New Clip**. The latter option saves another version of the newly trimmed video.

Trim video by moving the trim handles on either end of the video.

Touch the **Trim** button and choose to **Trim Original** or **Save as New Clip**. Touch **Trim** again once you have made the adjustments.

Progress bar is shown once **Trim** button is touched.

Figure 17-2. *Trimming a video*

NOTE: Videos are much larger than pictures; make sure you keep an eye on your storage space if you save many videos to the **Camera Roll**.

Sending the Video

As with photos, you have several options for using your iPad to send recorded video to others. Follow these steps to send a video from your iPad:

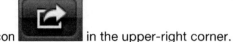

1. Touch the **Send** icon in the upper-right corner.

2. Choose your preferred option for sending the video: **Email**, **MMS**, **MobileMe**, **YouTube**, or **Copy**.

3. The next screen you see will depend on the choice you made in Step 2. If you selected **Email**, your **Email** app will launch.

Uploading to YouTube

The iPad allows you to upload an HD (720p) video right to your **YouTube** account. You just need to be connected to a Wi-Fi network. Follow these steps to upload a video to YouTube:

1. Locate the video you wish to upload in your **Camera Roll**.

2. Touch the **Send** icon.

3. Choose **Send to YouTube**.

4. Enter a title, description, and *tags* for the video.

5. Choose Standard Definition or HD.

6. Choose a category for the video.

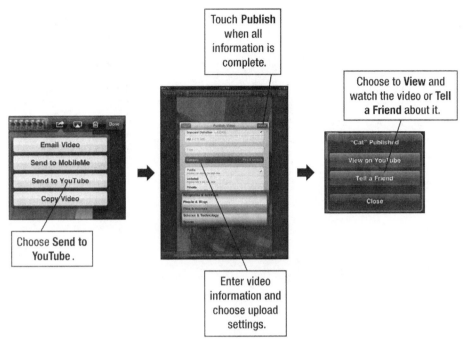

Figure 17–3. *Uploading a video to YouTube*

NOTE: To upload a video to MobileMe or YouTube, you need to have an account with the site you want to upload to (see Chapter 4: "Other Sync Methods" to learn more about MobileMe).

Using iMovie

Mac users have been enjoying the **iMovie** app for years. This app lets you combine movie clips with pictures and music, enabling you to add fancy transitions between scenes to make a professional-looking movie.

One great feature of the new iPad is that users can enjoy the power of **iMovie** right on their iPad. The **iMovie** app is a US $4.99 download from the App Store. It is usually listed under either the **Featured** apps or the **Enhanced for iPad 2** apps sections. You can also just search the App Store for "iMovie" to go straight to the download page (see Chapter 21: "The Amazing App Store" for more information on searching the App Store for content).

Getting Started with iMovie

The **iMovie** app works with projects. If you have stored projects, they appear on the **Projects** page. This will most likely be your first time using the app, so you won't have any projects. Follow these steps to start an **iMovie** project:

1. Tap the **Plus sign** icon ![plus icon] to start a new project.

2. Touch the **Settings** icon and select a theme for the project. Glide through the available themes. Current themes include **Modern**, **Bright**, **Travel**, **Playful**, **Neon**, **Travel**, **Simple**, **News**, and **CNN Report**.

3. Select **Theme Music ON** if you want to use specific music designed for that theme.

4. Tap one of the **Insert Media** icons to choose media for your movie. To choose a video, touch the **Video** soft key at the left. To choose photos, touch the **Photos** soft key next to it. Finally, to choose a sound track from your own music files, touch the **Audio** soft key and navigate to the song desired (see Figure 17–4).

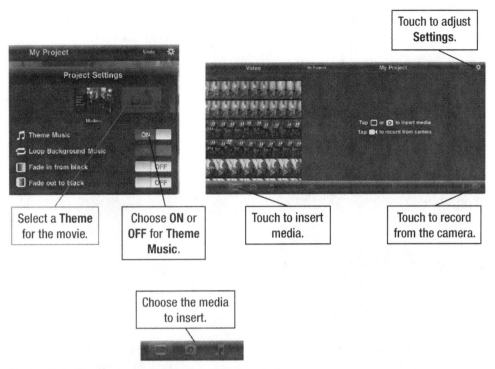

Figure 17–4. *Choosing media to add to your **iMovie** project*

Constructing Your Movie

Creating a movie in **iMovie** is as simple as adding new content, transitions, and audio. Follow these steps to build your movie:

1. Tap the **Insert Media** button again and choose a movie clip or photo from your **Photos** app.

2. Adjust the length of the clip by moving the **Yellow Dots** at either end towards the center. Notice the time of the clip changes as it is adjusted.

3. Tap the **Blue Arrow** when you are ready to add the clip to the Project timeline.

4. Add another video clip or photo to the timeline, repeating the steps described previously.

5. There is now a small **Double Arrow** icon between the different media in the project. This is the **Transition** icon. Double-tap the **Transition** icon to bring up the **Transitions Settings** menu (see Figure 17–5).

6. Choose a transition (currently there are only three choices: **None**, **Cross Dissolve**, and **Theme**).

7. Choose a transition length. These can range from .5 seconds to 2.0 seconds.

8. Next, touch either the **Up Arrow** or **Down Arrow** below the **Transition** icon to adjust the overlap and transition from one clip or photo into another.

9. Touch the **Transition** icon to exit the menu.

10. Add music by touching the **Audio** button and choosing a soundtrack from your **Music** library.

11. Touch the **Waveform** button to see the actual audio waveforms and where they will be in the video.

12. Touch the **Record** button to add a voice over recording to the video.

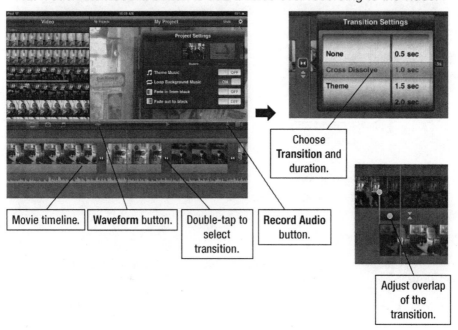

Figure 17–5. *Adding transitions to the* ***iMovie*** *project*

Follow these steps to preview the movie:

1. Slide the **Timeline** control at the bottom to the beginning, and then touch the **Play**

    button.

2. When you are done, touch the **My Projects** button in the top center of your screen. This will return you to the **Projects** screen.

Sharing Your Movie

Touch the **Share** button and **iMovie** gives you the option to share your movie to **YouTube**, **Facebook**, **Vimeo**, or **CNNiReport**. It also gives you the option to send the project to **iTunes**.

Choose the site to which you wish to share the project. An options screen will appear that lets you choose the export size of the movie. You can choose to export your movie as an HD (720p), large (540p), or medium (360p) movie file.

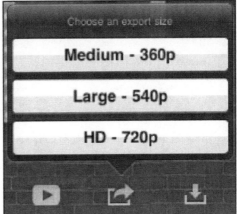

NOTE: HD 720p movies have the best quality; however, these can be quite large, depending on the length of the movie. Obviously, it will take longer to email or upload an HD movie than an equivalent-length large- or medium-sized movie.

The **Export** screen marks the progress of the movie export. Follow these steps to share a project from your **Camera Roll**:

1. Choose **Camera Roll** from the options in the **Share** menu.

2. Go to your **Camera Roll** (see Chapter 16: "iPad Photography" for more information on how to do this).

3. Find the new movie in the **Camera Roll**. You will see a **Video** icon at the bottom of the picture; the image will also show the length of the video.

4. Touch the video from the **Camera Roll**.

5. Choose **Share** from the soft keys at the bottom.

6. Choose to send your project through one of the following methods: **Email**, **MobileMe**, **YouTube**, or **Copy**.

> **NOTE**: To maintain your high quality 720p video, you should sync it back to your computer. Manual uploads over Wi-Fi will possibly let you share your movie at the highest quality. Syncing your movies to iTunes will ensure that the original quality is preserved.

Uploading to YouTube

The iPad allows you to upload an HD (720p) **iMovie** project right to your YouTube account. You just need to be connected to a Wi-Fi network. Follow these steps to upload a video to YouTube:

1. Locate the project you wish to upload in your **iMovie** projects.

2. Touch the **Share** icon.

3. Choose **YouTube**.

4. Enter a **Title**, **Description**, and **Tags** for the video.

5. Choose **Medium**, **Large**, or **HD** for the **Size**.

6. Choose a **Category** for the video.

7. Touch the **Share** button when done.

8. Finally, choose to either **View on YouTube** or to **Tell a Friend** (via email) that the video has been published (see Figure 17–6).

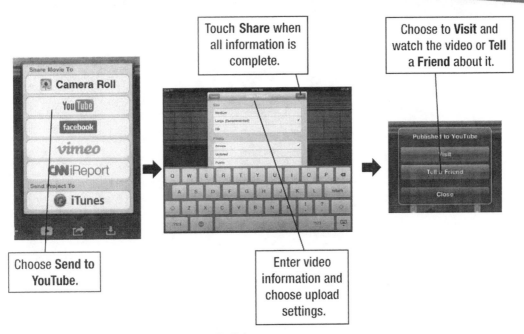

Figure 17–6. *Uploading an* ***iMovie*** *project to YouTube*

Chapter 18

FaceTime Video Messaging and Skype

Your iPad brings many new capabilities to your life, some of which seemed like science fiction just a few years ago. For example, video calling is now not only possible, but also extremely easy to use with the new **FaceTime** app.

FaceTime

As long as you and your caller are on iOS device and you're both on a Wi-Fi network, you can have unlimited video calls. In this chapter, we will show you how to enable and use the **FaceTime** program, as well as how to start having fun with this great new feature.

Making calls over Wi-Fi is also possible with **Skype**, the popular video calling and chat program that many of us use on our computers. We will show you how you can also use the **Skype** app on your iPad.

Video Calling

For many years, we have watched TV episodes and movies debut future technology like this. For example, many of these episodes and movies have shown people talking on small, portable phones and having video conversations. Even *The Jetsons* cartoon in the 1970s had this as a future concept.

The iPad makes that future thinking a reality today.

Setting up FaceTime

FaceTime needs to be set up the first time you use it on your iPad. The process is usually pretty painless. Because the iPad is not a phone, **FaceTime** needs to be associated with an email address to work. Follow these steps to associate **FaceTime** with an email address:

1. Touch the **FaceTime** icon (it's usually located on the first **Home** screen of the iPad).

2. Sign into your Apple account using either your **Apple ID** or your **MobileMe** user name and password. If you don't have an account (or if you want to create new one specifically for **FaceTime** purposes), just touch the **Create New Account** button (see Figure 18–1).

3. Once the account is set up, you can choose the email address you want to use for placing **FaceTime** calls. You can also add other email addresses to use with your **FaceTime** account.

> **NOTE:** Once **FaceTime** is set up, you can always make adjustments or add additional email addresses by going to **Settings** and then to the **FaceTime** tab. From this tab, you can choose to add more email addresses or change your caller ID for **FaceTime** calls.

Figure 18–1. *Setting up a FaceTime account on your iPad*

Video Calling with FaceTime

FaceTime is the featured app highlighted in many of Apple's iPhone and iPad commercials. Essentially, **FaceTime** is free over Wi-Fi calling that allows you to see the caller on the other end of the conversation through the phone's front-facing camera.

> **NOTE**: For now **FaceTime** is only available on the Mac, the new iPhone 4, iPod touch, and the newest iPad 2 devices running iOS 4.3 and higher; also, it's only available over a Wi-Fi network.

Enabling FaceTime Calling on Your iPad

When you first use your iPad, **FaceTime** is not yet enabled. To enable the iPad to receive and make **FaceTime** calls, follow these steps:

1. Go to your **Settings** icon and touch it.

2. Scroll down to the **FaceTime** option tab.

3. Toggle the **FaceTime** switch to the **ON** position.

Using FaceTime

Once **FaceTime** is enabled, you can place a **FaceTime** call from the **FaceTime** app or from the **FaceTime** button at the bottom of a contact page. **FaceTime** will only work, however, if the other caller is on an iPad 2, iPod touch or iPhone 4, and the **FaceTime** feature is enabled on both devices.

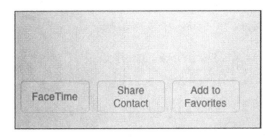

To initiate a **FaceTime** call, follow these steps:

1. Touch the **FaceTime** icon (initially on the first **Home** screen) on your iPad.

2. Choose a **Favorite**, a **Recent**, or a **Contact** who is capable of receiving a **FaceTime** call. The app will ask the caller on the other end to **Accept** the **FaceTime** call.

Accepting a call from someone else is also easy. Simply **Accept** the **FaceTime** call from the other caller by touching **Accept** button or by **Sliding to Answer** if the iPod is in **Sleep** mode (see Figure 18–2).

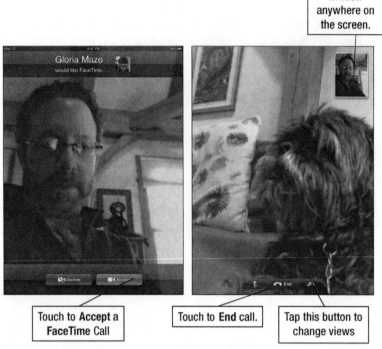

Drag the small window anywhere on the screen.

Touch to **Accept** a FaceTime Call

Touch to **End** call.

Tap this button to change views

Figure 18–2. *Accepting a FaceTime call*

Once a **FaceTime** call is initiated, follow these steps to conduct a video conference:

1. Hold the phone away from you a bit.

2. Make sure you are *framed* properly in the window.

3. You can move the small image of yourself around the screen to a convenient spot.

4. Touch the **Switch Camera** button to show the **FaceTime** caller you are looking at. The **Switch Camera** button will now use the standard camera on the back of the iPad. In Figure 18–3, I get to see what my friend's daughter is doing and she gets to see her mom and me in the lower-right corner.

5. Touch the **End** button to end the **FaceTime** call.

6. Touch the **Mute** button to temporarily mute the call.

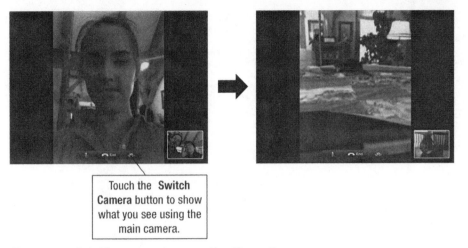

Touch the **Switch Camera** button to show what you see using the main camera.

Figure 18–3. *Switching camera views on a FaceTime call*

NOTE: You can use **FaceTime** in both **Portrait** and **Landscape** modes on the iPad 2. Just remember that, when you are in **Landscape** mode, the camera will be off to the side of the device.

Setting Favorites in FaceTime

Just as when using an iPhone, you can set **Favorites** for **FaceTime** calling on your iPad. The favorites that you set need to be individuals who have an iPad 2, an iPod touch, or an iPhone 4. These people also need to set up their device for **FaceTime** calls. Follow these steps to add people to your **Favorites**:

1. Start the **FaceTime** app as you did previously.

2. Touch the **Favorites** soft key at the bottom (see Figure 18–4).

3. Touch the **Plus** (**+**) sign and then choose a contact to add to your **Favorites**.

NOTE: When choosing a contact, choose either the person's iPhone number or the email address associated with the person's **FaceTime** account.

Figure 18–4. *Adding a favorite in FaceTime*

Multitasking Using FaceTime

One of the great features of your new iPad is that it uses the latest iOS software from Apple, which allows you to multitask (see Chapter 8: "Multitasking and Voice Control" to learn more about how to switch between apps).

When you are in a **FaceTime** call, just double-click the **Home** button to see other apps that are running. Go to another app and you will see a bar at the top of the screen that says, "Touch to resume FaceTime." Some users have reported difficulty getting back to the **FaceTime** call after this method.

Simply touch that bar to go back to the call.

Making Phone Calls and More with Skype

Social networking is all about keeping in touch with our friends, colleagues, and family. Passive communication through sites such as www.facebook.com and www.myspace.com is nice; however, sometimes there is just no substitute for hearing someone's voice.

Amazingly, you can make phone calls using the **Skype** app from any iPad. Calls to other Skype users anywhere in the world are free. A nice thing about Skype is that it works on computers and many mobile devices, including iPhone 4s, iPod touches, some BlackBerry smartphones, and other mobile devices. You will be charged for calls to mobile phones and landlines, but the rates are reasonable.

NOTE: You can only make a video call with the **Skype** app if you have a front-facing camera like the ones on the iPad 2, iPhone 4, or iPod touch.

Downloading Skype to Your iPad

You can download the free **Skype** app from the App Store by searching for "Skype" and installing it. If you need help getting this done, please check out Chapter 21: "The Amazing App Store." You should be aware, however, that like **Facebook** and other apps, there is no native iPad version of **Skype**, so you will be using an iPhone app.

Creating Your Skype Account on Your iPad

If you need to set up your Skype account and have not already done so from your computer (see the "Using Skype on Your Computer" section later in this chapter), then follow these steps to set up **Skype** on your iPad:

1. Tap the **Skype** icon from your **Home** screen.

2. Tap the **Create Account** button.

3. Tap **Accept** if you accept the **No Emergency Calls** pop-up warning window.

4. Enter your **Full Name**, **Skype Name**, **Password**, and **Email**, and then decide whether you want to **Get News and Offers** by setting the switch at the bottom.

5. Tap the **Done** button to create your account.

Log into the Skype App

After you create your account, you're ready to log into **Skype** on your iPad. To do so, follow these steps:

1. If you are not already in **Skype**, tap the **Skype** icon from your **Home** screen.

2. Type your **Skype Name** and **Password**.

3. Tap the **Sign In** button in the upper-right corner.

4. You should not have to enter this login information again; it is saved in **Skype**. The next time you tap **Skype**, it will automatically log you in.

Finding and Adding Skype Contacts

Once you have logged into the **Skype** app, you will want to start communicating with people. To do so, you will have to find them and add them to your **Skype** contacts list:

1. If you are not already in **Skype**, tap the **Skype** icon from your **Home** screen and log in, if asked.

2. Tap the **Contacts** soft key at the bottom.

3. Tap the **Search** window at the top, and then type someone's first and last name or **Skype Name**. Tap **Search** to locate that person.

4. Once you see the person you want to add, tap his name.

Tap here and type a name to search.

Then, tap the name to select it.

5. If you are not sure whether this is the correct person, tap the **View Full Profile** button.

6. Tap **Add Contact** at the bottom.

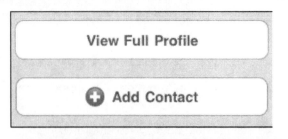

7. Adjust the invitation message appropriately.

8. Tap the **Send** button to send this person an invitation to become one of your **Skype** contacts.

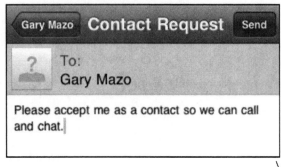

9. Repeat the procedure to add more contacts.

10. When you are done, tap the **Contacts** soft key at the bottom.

11. Tap **All Contacts** from the **Groups** screen to see all new contacts you have added.

12. Once this person accepts you as a contact, you will see him listed as a contact in your **All Contacts** screen.

TIP: Sometimes you want to get rid of a **Skype** contact. You can remove or block a contact by tapping her name from the contact list. Tap the **Settings** icon (upper-right corner) and select either **Remove from Contacts** or **Block**.

Tap the Settings icon.

Then, tap to Remove or Block this contact.

Making Calls with Skype on Your iPad

So far you have created your account and added your contacts. Now you are ready to finally make that first call with **Skype** on your iPad:

1. If you are not already in **Skype**, tap the **Skype** icon from your **Home** screen and log in, if asked.

2. Tap the **Contacts** soft key at the bottom.

3. Tap **All Contacts** to see your contacts.

4. Tap the contact name you wish to call (see Figure 18–5).

5. Tap the **Call** button.

6. You may see a **Skype** button and a **Mobile** or other phone button. Press the **Skype** button to make the free call. Making any other kind of call requires that you pay for it with *Skype Credits*.

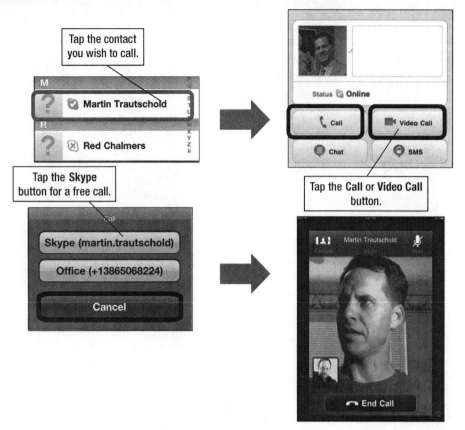

Figure 18–5. *Placing calls from **Skype** on your iPad*

> **NOTE:** You can call toll free numbers for free using **Skype Out** on your iPad. The following notice comes from the Skype web site at www.skype.com:
>
> "The following countries and number ranges are supported and are free of charge to all users. We're working on the rest of the world. France: +33 800, +33 805, +33 809 Poland: +48 800 UK: +44 500, +44 800, +44 808 USA: +1 800, +1 866, +1 877, +1 888 Taiwan: +886 80."

Switching Cameras with Skype

Just as you can in the **FaceTime** app, you can show the individual with whom you are talking on **Skype** your surroundings by "switching" to the back camera of the iPad.

Simply touch the **Camera** soft key in the top-left corner and choose whether you wish to display the **Front Camera**, **Back Camera**, or **No Camera** on the screen.

If you choose **No Camera**, **Skype** will still work, but you will have only a voice call—and no video image.

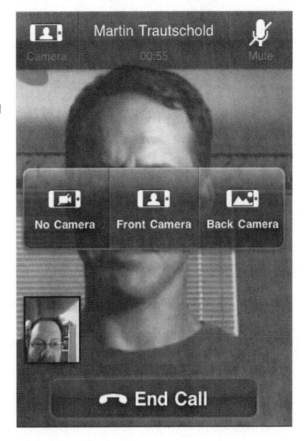

Receiving Calls with Skype on Your iPad

Apple's iOS innately supports background *voice over Internet protocol* (VoIP) calls. With the latest version of **Skype**, you can have **Skype** running in the background and still be able to receive a **Skype** call when it comes in. You can even (theoretically) be on a voice call and then answer your **Skype** call!

> **TIP: Skype** is a huge battery drain. If you want to call someone you know who uses **Skype** on her iPad, just send her a quick email or give her a quick call to alert her to the fact you would like to talk to her using the **Skype** app.

Buying Skype Credits or a Monthly Subscription

Skype-to-**Skype** calls are free. However, if you want to call people on their landlines or mobile phones from **Skype**, then you will need to purchase Skype Credits or purchase a monthly subscription plan. If you try to purchase the credits or a subscription from within the **Skype** app, it will take you to the Skype web site. For this reason, we recommend using **Safari** on your iPad or using your computer's web browser to purchase these credits.

> **TIP:** You may want to start with a limited amount of Skype Credits to try out the service before you sign up for a subscription plan. Subscription plans are the way to go if you plan on using the **Skype** app to talk to a lot for non-Skype callers (e.g., regular landlines and mobile phones).

Follow these steps to use **Safari** to buy Skype Credits:

1. Tap the **Safari** icon.

2. Type www.skype.com in the top address bar and tap **Go**.

3. Tap the **Sign In** link at the top of the page.

4. Enter your **Skype Name** and **Password**, and then tap **Sign me in**.

5. If you are not already on your **Account** screen, tap the **Account** tab in the right side of the Top Nav Bar.

6. At this point, you can choose to buy credits or a subscription:

   - Tap the **Buy pre-pay credit** button to purchase a fixed amount of credits.

   - Tap the **Get a subscription** button to buy a monthly subscription account.

7. Finally, complete the payment instructions for either type of purchase.

Chatting with Skype

In addition to making phone calls, you can also chat via text with other **Skype** users from your iPad. Starting a chat is very similar to starting a call; follow these steps to do so:

1. If you are not already in **Skype**, tap the **Skype** icon from your **Home** screen and log in, if asked.

2. Tap the **Contacts** soft key at the bottom.

3. Tap **All Contacts** to see your contacts.

4. Tap the name of the contact you wish to chat with (see Figure 18–6).

5. Tap the **Chat** button.

6. Type your chat text and press the **Send** button. Your chat will appear in the top of the screen.

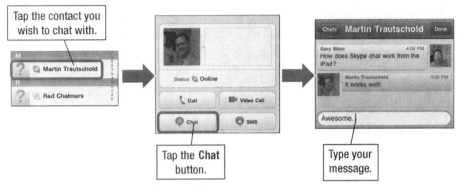

Figure 18–6. *Chatting with* **Skype** *on your iPad*

Adding Skype to Your Computer

You can use the **Skype** app on your computer, as well. We will show you how this works next. You can also use **Skype** to make video calls on your computer if you also have a web cam hooked up.

To create a Skype account and download **Skype** software for your computer, follow these steps:

1. Open a web browser on your computer.

2. Go to www.skype.com.

3. Click the **Join** link at the top of the page.

4. Create your account by completing all required information and clicking the **Continue** button. Notice that you only have to enter information in the required fields, which are noted with an asterisk. For example, you do not need to enter your gender, birthdate, and mobile phone number.

5. You are now done with the account setup process. Next, you are presented with the option of buying Skype Credits; however, this is not required for free **Skype**-to-**Skype** phone calls, video calls, or chats.

TIP: You only need to pay for **Skype** if you want to call someone who is not using **Skype**. For example, calls to phones on landlines or mobile phones (not using **Skype**) will cost you. At publishing time, pay-as-you-go rates were about US 2.1 cents per minute; monthly subscriptions ranged from about US $3 – $14 for various calling plans.

6. Next, click the Get Skype link in the Top Nav Bar of the site to download **Skype** to your computer.

7. Click the **Get Skype for Windows** button or the **Get Skype for Mac** button.

8. Follow the instructions to install the software.

9. Once the software is installed, launch it and log in using your Skype account.

10. You are ready to initiate (or receive) phone calls, video calls, and chats to anyone else using **Skype**, including all your friends with **Skype** on their iPads.

Chapter 19

Productivity and File Transfer

You already know that your iPad is great for consuming or enjoying content. It is your music player, your video player, and your gaming console; and it brings you news, weather, sports, and more. The iPad isn't just for fun and games, though. In this chapter, we take a look at Apple's three productivity powerhouse apps: **Pages** (compatible with **Microsoft Word**), **Keynote** (compatible with **Microsoft PowerPoint**), and **Numbers** (compatible with **Microsoft Excel**).

If you are a Mac user, you may already be familiar with **Pages**, **Keynote**, and **Numbers**, which are part of the **iWork for Mac** suite. With these three apps on your iPad, you can create content—not just consume it.

Each has wonderfully creative tools built in, and each can produce professional **Microsoft Office**–compatible documents that you can then email, upload to an online account, or present on your iPad.

File Transfer Options

As soon as you start working with files on your iPad, you will want to know how to transfer files you create on your iPad or how to move files from your computer or elsewhere to your iPad. In this chapter, we summarize file transfer options (see Table 19–1). Some options are described in detail elsewhere in this book, while other apps will be described in this chapter.

Table 19–1. *File Transfer Options*

Mode of Transfer	Name	Cost	Where to Learn More
USB cable	**iTunes**	Free	"File Sharing (File Transfer) Between Your iPad and Your Computer" in Chapter 3.
WiFi network	**GoodReader**	Free	"Transferring Files to Your iPad" in Chapter 26.
USB cable	**DiskAid**	US $9.90	The "DiskAid File Transfer" section in this chapter.
WiFi / 3G networks	**Dropbox**	Free	The "Dropbox File Transfer" section in this chapter.
WiFi / 3G networks	**MobileMe iDisk**	US $99/year individual or US $149/family	The "Wireless Sync using the MobileMe Service" section of Chapter 4.
WiFi / 3G networks	**SugarSync**	Starts at US $4.99/mo. for 30GB	Company web site: www.sugarsync.com
WiFi / 3G networks	**Box.net**	Free for personal, US $15/user/mo. for business	Company web site: www.box.net
WiFi / 3G networks	**Google Docs**	Free	Company web site: http://docs.google.com

Of course, you can always email files to get them on or off your iPad, but usually this only works well for a limited number of files or small-sized files. Sometimes, files are just too big to send as email attachments. That's when you need a file transfer solution such as **DiskAid** or **Dropbox**.

Next, we'll cover two file transfer options: **DiskAid**, which that works by connecting your iPad to your computer with the USB cable; and **Dropbox**, which provides wireless file transfer.

DiskAid File Transfer

If you prefer to use a USB cable and really gain access to all the files on your iPad, including spreadsheets, word processing documents, presentation files, pictures, videos, and even things like **FaceTime** call history, voice memos, and notes—then **DiskAid** is a good choice.

DiskAid works on both a PC and a Mac. At publishing time, you can download a free 14-day trial. This trial lets you give the software a test run before you pay the US $9.90 purchase price.

You can obtain the software directly from the DiskAid web site at www.digidna.net/products/diskaid/download.

After you run **DiskAid** on your computer and connect your iPad using the USB cable to your computer, you should see the main screen showing you the apps installed on your iPad (see Figure 19–1).

To copy files, you need to do the following:

1. Select an iPad app in the left column of **DiskAid**. In this example, we chose **GoodReader**.

2. Open a window to browse files from your computer and drag and drop selected files onto the main window on the right side of **DiskAid**.

3. Next, disconnect your iPad and check the app (in this case, **GoodReader**). You should see the files you just dragged and dropped.

> **TIP:** To copy files from your iPad to your computer, follow the reverse procedure drag and drop the file from your iPad to your computer folder. You can also delete files from your iPad by highlighting them in **DiskAid** and pressing the **Delete** key on your computer keyboard.

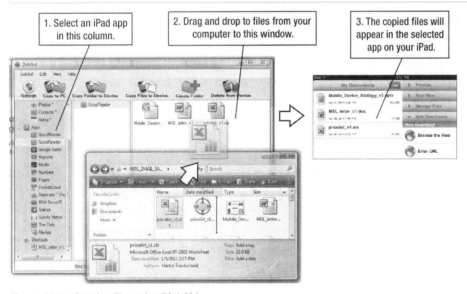

Figure 19–1. *Copying files using DiskAid*

Dropbox File Transfer

Dropbox is different from **DiskAid** in a few ways. First, it is wireless; no USB cable connection to your computer is required. Second, **Dropbox** allows you to sync files between, not just your iPad and computer, but to multiple computers (e.g., Windows, Mac, and Linux) and the Dropbox web site. Third, you need to install an app on your iPad and your computer. The nice thing is that you can store and transfer up to 2 GB (gigabytes) of files for free. If you want to store up to 50 GB, then the price is US $9.99/month or US $99.00/year. Larger plans are available.

> **TIP:** With **Dropbox**, you can also secure your files with pin codes to further protect them. This means you could securely store and access personal information, tax information, and personal photos on your mobile device.

Follow these steps to use **Dropbox** on your iPad:

1. Sign up for your free account and download the computer (PC or Mac) app from www.dropbox.com.

2. Next, go to the App Store on your iPad and locate and download the free **Dropbox** app.

3. Log into **Dropbox** on your iPad using the same username and password you created when you first set up your account.

4. Any files or folders you drag into the **Dropbox** folder on your computer will be wirelessly synchronized to the **Dropbox** app on your iPad (see Figure 19–2).

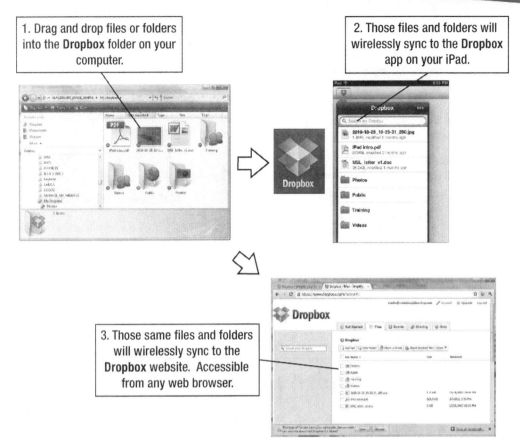

Figure 19–2. *Copying files using* **Dropbox**

Files placed in the **Dropbox** app on your iPad will also appear in the Dropbox folder on your computer, as well as on the www.dropbox.com web site. In other words, important files are backed up automatically at www.dropbox.com.

You can even share specific folders on your Dropbox account with others, such as colleagues, friends, or family members. This is a great way to share files both small and large since you don't have to worry about the size limitations sometimes encountered when sending email attachments.

Now that you know the basics of how to transfer small and large files to and from your iPad, you're ready to dig into some good productivity apps.

Productivity Apps

As we mentioned previously, using **Pages** as your word processor, **Numbers** as your spreadsheet, and **Keynote** for presentations can really boost your mobile productivity with your iPad.

Downloading Pages, Keynote, and Numbers

Pages, **Keynote**, and **Numbers** are all available to be purchased and downloaded from the App Store. At publishing time, each app costs US $9.99.

It is probably easiest to search for **Pages** by typing it into the **Search** window in the upper-right corner.

Next, from the **Pages** download page, get to **Keynote** and **Numbers** by looking in the **More iPad Apps by Apple** section in the lower-left corner.

Using Pages

Pages is Apple's word processing program. If you use a Mac, you will be familiar with the layout and functionality of the Pages program. While not meant to be a full substitute for a desktop word processor, Pages is quite capable and can allow you to edit and create very professional-looking documents.

With **Pages** you can do much more than create documents; you can also then send them via email or upload them to an online account for easy viewing, sharing, and printing.

Using Pages for the First Time

When you first start **Pages**, you will see that there is one sample document entitled "Getting Started." This is a great tutorial for many of the features found within **Pages**. We recommend going through this document and reading about the various styles, objects, and toolbars associated with **Pages**.

To start a new document, touch the **New Document** button at the bottom. When you touch the **New Document** button, you have the option of either starting a new document from scratch or duplicating the document that is showing.

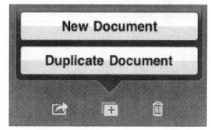

TIP: If you want to use an existing document as a template, it is useful to choose **Duplicate Document**. Otherwise, choose **New Document** to create a new document.

Choosing a New Document Template

When you choose **New Document**, you have 16 available templates from which to choose. The templates are general, like **Poster, Proposal,** or **Term Paper**. You can choose to start with a template (which might make the formatting easier) or simply choose **Blank** (at the top left) to start with a blank page (see Figure 19–3).

Everything within the template can be changed or adjusted, so don't be afraid to experiment.

> **NOTE:** Templates are very helpful for documents that require a certain format and presentation, such as resumes and letters.

Once you make your selection, you are ready to start writing and editing to turn the template into the perfect document.

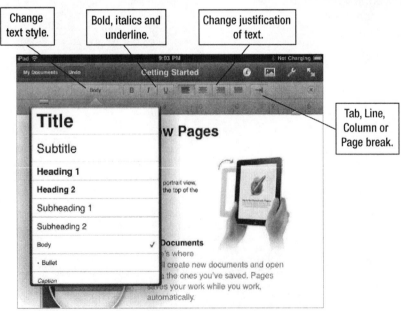

Figure 19–3. *The page layout in* **Pages**

Change text style.

Bold, italics and underline.

Change justification of text.

Tab, Line, Column or Page break.

Working With Tools and Styles

Like most word processors, **Pages** gives you many options for adding various styles to the document. The built-in toolbars give you easy access to most of the features for customizing your document.

There are four specific buttons on the toolbar in the upper-right corner that will prove to be quite useful in your writing: **Information**, **Picture/Object**, **Tools**, and **Full Screen**.

Information Button

The **Information** button only works after you select text or another item, such as a graphic.

This button enables you to accomplish the following:

- Set a particular style, such as Heading, Subheading, or Caption
- Change the font, font size, or color
- Change the settings for lists with bullets and numbers
- Change the alignment/justification and line spacing

Follow these steps to adjust a style in a document:

1. Select text in the document.

2. Tap the **Information** button.

3. Tap the **Style** button.

4. Scroll through the list to choose the appropriate style and then touch it. A **Checkmark** icon will then appear next to the style you have chosen.

You can also add **Bold**, *Italics*, <u>Underline</u>, or ~~Strikethrough~~ by touching the appropriate button.

Selecting Text to Apply a Style to or Cut/Copy

The style you select can be applied to the next text you type, or it can be applied to selected text already in the document.

Do this to select text you have typed:

1. Double-tap to select a word.

2. Triple-tap to select a paragraph.

Do this to select text in a **Pages** template:

1. Press and hold a word to select it.

2. Double-tap to select a paragraph.

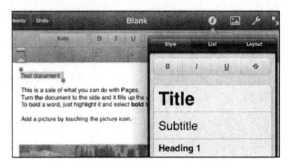

Once the text is selected, choose the style to apply to the text you have selected by using the tool bar or the **Information** (i) button, as shown.

Picture/Object Button

Next to the **Information** button, you will
find the **Picture/Object** button. Touch this
button to insert media, tables, charts, or
shapes into the document.

When you first touch this button, you will
see the **Media** tab highlighted, and all your
photo albums will be visible.

To choose a photo, navigate through the
available albums and select the desired
photo to use.

To add a table to the document, touch the
Table tab and choose from the various
table formats shown.

NOTE: There are six screens of tables; swipe from right to left to advance through the screens.

Follow these steps to insert a chart:

1. Touch the **Chart** tab and swipe
   through the screens.

2. Tap the chart you want to insert.

Follow these steps to edit the data behind
the chart (see Figure 19–4):

1. Double-tap the chart so that it flips
   around, showing you a data table.

2. Type the data needed to create the
   chart.

3. Press **Done** in the upper-right
   corner when finished to see the
   updated chart.

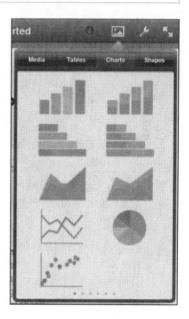

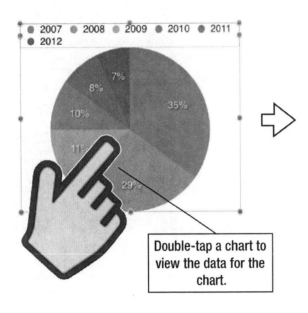

Double-tap a chart to view the data for the chart.

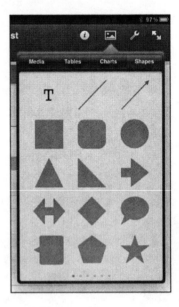

Now you can edit the data for the chart.

Figure 19–4. *How to edit chart data in* **Pages**

Do this to insert a shape:

1. Touch the **Shape** tab and swipe through the screens.

2. Tap the shape you want to insert.

Do this to move or resize the shape:

1. Press and hold the shape to drag it around the page.

2. Touch the two corners and pinch open or closed to make it smaller or larger.

3. Put two fingers inside the shape and spin it around to rotate the shape.

To move or resize the picture, chart, or object, simply tap once to bring up the blue dots. Touch and hold the object and move it anywhere you wish on the page. You will notice that text will move around the object as you move it.

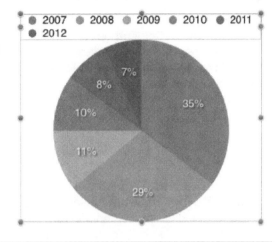

TIP: To change or adjust the text wrapping, simply touch the **Information** button while the picture or object is highlighted and choose **Arrange**. Touch the **Wrap** button and choose a style for the word wrap.

The Tools Button (Print, Find, Settings, and Help)

Next to the **Pictures/Objects** button is the **Tools** button. Touch this to access the **Find**, **Print**, **Document Setup**, **Settings**, and **Go to Help** tools.

The **Settings** option allows you to turn **ON** or **OFF** the **Check Spelling** option and choose whether to display various features: **Word Count**, **Center Guides**, and **Edge Guides**.

Touch the **Document Setup** tool and you will see what looks like a blueprint. To add or edit a header or footer, touch the **Tap to Edit Header/Footer** buttons.

To adjust the margins, just drag the triangles in from the sides or from the top and bottom of the page.

When you are done with your adjustments, simply touch the **Done** button in the upper-left corner.

To hide all tool bars and just focus on a blank screen for writing, touch the **Full Screen** icon in the upper-right corner. To enable the tool bar again, just tap the screen.

The Style Buttons and Ruler

The **Style** buttons and ruler are visible only when you are in a field with editable text. Simply touch the screen anywhere text can be input or edited and you will see the ruler at the top (see Figure 19–5).

> **NOTE:** If you turn your iPad to **Landscape** orientation, the menus and style bar disappear. To get the menus and style bar back, turn your iPad back to **Portrait** orientation.

At both edges of the ruler, there are sliding guides for tabs and indentations. Simply slide to adjust the margins and tabs for your document.

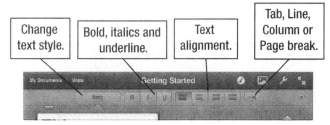

Figure 19–5. *The Style buttons*

On top of the ruler, you will find many of the same buttons that you saw when you touched the **Information** button. You can adjust the paragraph and character styles; align or justify text; and set tabs, page breaks, and column breaks by touching the appropriate button.

Navigator

Navigator is a very cool tool built into **Pages**. Follow these steps to use it:

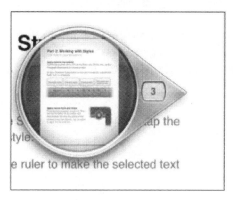

1. Hold your finger along the right-hand edge of the page and slowly drag down or up.

2. A small **Magnifying Glass** icon appears with a little "snapshot" of the pages in the document.

3. Each little bit you move downwards shows the next page.

4. When you find the page you wish to read or edit, remove your finger from the screen and you will jump to that page.

Numbers Spreadsheet

Numbers is a powerful spreadsheet program, much like **Numbers** for the Mac or **Microsoft Excel** for Windows.

Numbers

Numbers allows you to create, edit, and read complex spreadsheets; input and calculate formulas; and set up multiple worksheets within a spreadsheet. These worksheets are displayed across the top of each file as file folder tabs known as *sheet tabs*.

Using Numbers for the First Time

Just like **Pages**, **Numbers** comes with a "Getting Started" file to help you with some of the various features of the program. It is a very good idea to thumb through this guide before you start creating your own spreadsheets.

Choosing a Template

As in **Pages**, the **New Document** button for **Numbers** gives you the option of starting a new spreadsheet or using a duplicate spreadsheet.

NOTE: To use **Duplicate Spreadsheet**, you need to have the spreadsheet you wish to duplicate in the main window.

Follow these steps to create a new document in **Numbers**:

1. Touch the **New Document** button and you will be asked to choose a template.

2. Choose **Blank** to start from scratch or choose one of the templates provided to get started.

In the following example, we chose the **Budget** template to work with.

Using the Toolbar in Numbers

In the upper-right corner, just like in **Pages**, you will find the **Numbers** toolbar. The icons are identical to those in **Pages**, but the functions are a bit different (see Figure 19–6).

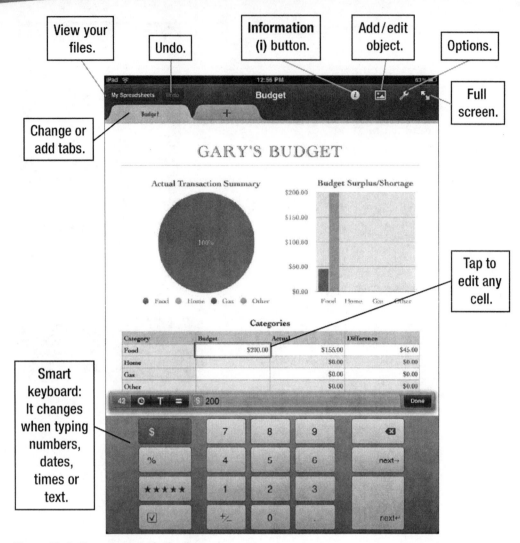

Figure 19–6. *The page layout in* **Numbers**

Information Button

The **Information** button 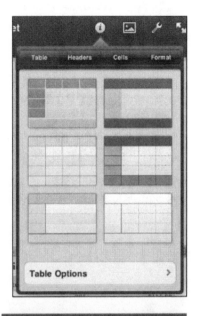 in **Numbers** looks identical and sits in the same place that it does in **Pages**. In order to use the **Information** button, you need to have text, a chart, graph, or object selected.

If you have a chart selected, the chart options are displayed. If you have a table selected, the table options are displayed.

In this example, we touched a chart and then touched the **Information** button. We touched **Chart Options** and can now choose everything from text size to font to the type of chart. The options are truly staggering.

Take some time to walk through the **Numbers** "Getting Started" guide to see all the options available.

> **TIP:** We could write a full book on each of these programs. Take some time to just touch icons and options to see for yourself how things change as you make individual selections. Have fun—this is very powerful and creative software to work and play with!

Picture/Object Button

Next to the **Information** button, you will find the **Picture/Object** button. Touch this button to insert media, tables, charts, or shapes into the document. In **Numbers**, this button functions exactly the same as it does in **Pages**.

Tools Button

Next to the **Pictures/Objects** button is the **Tools** button. Touch this to access the **Find**, **Print**, **Settings**, and **Go to Help** tools.

Use the **Find** button to search for any word or phrase in a **Numbers** document—just like **Pages**.

When the word is located, the text will be highlighted..

Use **Go to Help** to jump to the Apple web site for support with **Numbers**.

Editing Cells, Charts, and Graphs

Numbers is a very powerful spreadsheet program. Just like a traditional spreadsheet program on your computer, it can be used to edit each cell, input formulas, and customize charts and graphs.

Working with Charts and Graphs

The first time you work with **Numbers**, we suggest you open one of the templates. In this example, we are using the **Budget** template. Notice the pie chart, which is based on four criteria:

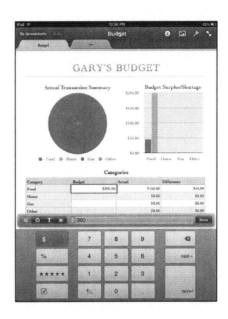

1. Double-tap the chart to select it, and the cells used to create the chart are highlighted.

2. Double-tap an individual cell, and the formula calculator pops up.

Numbers senses what type of field you are trying to enter. In the **Budget** template, **Numbers** knows we need to enter dollar amounts. We can simply type in a new amount and press the **Done** button; the changes are reflected in the chart shown previously.

Working with Tables

If you have spent any time at all working with spreadsheets, you know that tables are a mainstay of spreadsheet construction.

Tap any table in your spreadsheet to highlight it.

You add columns to the table by holding and dragging the column handle left or right (see Figure 19–7).

Similarly, you add or remove rows by holding and dragging the row handle up or down.

To move the table entirely, just touch and hold the top bar and reposition the table where you desire.

Categories			
	Actual	Difference	
$500.00	285	$215.00	
$1,000.00	$800.00	$200.00	
$800.00	$0.00	$800.00	
	$0.00	$0.00	
$2,300.00	$1,085.00	$1,215.00	

Figure 19–7. *Adding and removing rows and columns in tables*

> **TIP:** It is easy to make mistakes when using **Numbers**. If something doesn't look right, just touch the **Undo** button to undo the last edit or addition. Touch **Undo** a couple of times to keep undoing things you might not have wanted to do.

There really is so much more to do with **Numbers**—again, we encourage you to read the "Getting Started" guide to see additional features!

Keynote Presentations

Keynote is the third jewel in the triple crown of **iWork**. **Keynote** is comparable to **Keynote** on your Mac or **Microsoft PowerPoint** on your PC. Like **Pages** and **Numbers**, **Keynote** is a very powerful and capable piece of presentation software. We won't be able to cover every aspect of this software, but we can get you started and working with presentations using **Keynote**.

Keynote

Using Keynote for the First Time

Just like **Pages** and **Numbers**, **Keynote** comes with a "Getting Started" file to help you with some of the various features of the program. It is a very good idea to thumb through this guide before you start creating your own spreadsheets.

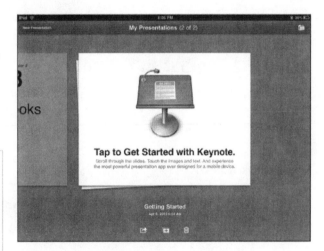

NOTE: Unlike **Pages** and **Numbers**, **Keynote** works only in **Landscape** mode since this is presentation software.

Choosing a Template

As with **Pages**, the **New Presentation** button gives you the option of starting a new presentation or using a duplicate presentation.

NOTE: You need to have the presentation you wish to "duplicate" visible in the main window.

Touch the **New Presentation** button and you will be asked to choose a template.

You can select from several blank presentations ("White," "Black," or "Gradient") to start from scratch, or you can choose one of the templates or themes provided to get started.

In the following example, we chose the **Parchment** template to work with.

Using the Toolbar in Keynote

In the upper-right corner, just like in **Pages** and **Numbers**, you will find the **Keynote** toolbar. The icons are similar to those in **Pages** and **Numbers**, but the functions are a bit different, as shown in Figure 19–8.

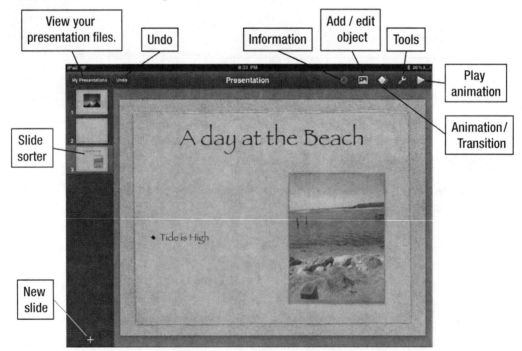

Figure 19–8. *The page layout in* **Keynote**

The Information Button

The **Information** button looks identical and sits in the same place as it does in **Pages**. In order to use the **Information** button, you need to have a text box, picture, graph, or object highlighted. Simply touch anywhere to activate the object and then tap the **Information** button.

Touch a text box and the text options are displayed. Touch a picture and the picture options are displayed.

In this example, we touched a text box and then touched the **Information** button.

We touched **Text Options**, and now we can choose everything from the text size to the font to the style of text.

The options are truly staggering. Take some time to walk through the "Getting Started" guide to see all the options available.

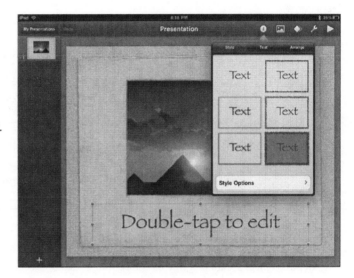

TIP: We could write a full book on each of these apps. Take some time to just touch icons and options to see for yourself how things change as you make individual selections. Have fun—this is very powerful and creative software to work and play with!

Picture/Object Button

Next to the **Information** button in **Keynote**, you will find the **Picture/Object** button. Touch this button to insert media, tables, charts, or shapes into the document. This button functions exactly the same as it does in **Pages** and **Numbers**.

> **TIP:** In all three programs, pictures can be rotated just by touching and holding two fingers on the picture and rotating your fingers—very cool!

Tools Button

Next to the **Pictures/Objects** button is the **Tools** button. Touch this to access the **Find**, **Go to Help**, **Edge Guides**, **Slide Numbers**, and **Check Spelling** tools.

Use the **Find** button to search for any word or phrase in the document—just like **Pages** and **Numbers**. When the word is located, the text will be highlighted in yellow. Just touch to edit.

Use **Go to Help** to jump to the Apple web site for support with this app.

The **Edge Guides**, **Slide Numbers**, and **Check Spelling** toggles are exactly the same as in **Pages**.

Add a Slide

Follow these steps to add a slide:

1. Touch the **Plus** button in the lower-left corner.

2. Choose the style of slide you wish to add.

3. Double-tap to edit the text and use the tool buttons to add images or objects as you did before.

Animation Button

In **Keynote**, you can customize the transition animation from one slide to the next:

4. Touch the **Animation** button to see an **Animation** tab next to each slide in the presentation.

> **NOTE:** You can also add **Magic Moves**, which copies the slide and then lets you change aspects and animate those changes.

5. Touch the tab to see the **Transitions** menu.

6. Choose an effect and then tap the **Options** button at the bottom to adjust the timing of the transition and whether it occurs when tapping the screen or after the previous transition.

7. Tap **Done** in the upper-right corner when you are finished working with transitions.

The Play Button

To play the slideshow, just touch the **Play** button in the top-right corner. Based on the transition settings you set, the presentation will begin to play.

Sharing Your Work

The Share function in **iWork** is the same in each of the three programs. Touch the **Share** button and five options are presented to you: **Email Presentation**, **Share via iWork.com**, **Send to iTunes**, **Copy to iDisk**, and **Copy to WebDAV**.

Email Presentation

Sending a document, spreadsheet, or presentation via email is easy. Close the document, spreadsheet, or presentation, and then tap the **Share** command underneath.

Choose **Email Presentation** and your **Mail** app will load with the file shown as an attachment. Add a recipient as we showed you in Chapter 13: "Email on your iPad," type in your message, and then tap **Send**.

Share via iWork

When you touch **Share via iWork.com**, a window pops up, asking you to input your Apple ID or your MobileMe ID and password. Input the correct information and your file is now stored online for easy retrieval from any computer. This is a great way to share and collaborate on work.

Once you try to use the iWork.com service for the first time, you will be asked to send a verification email.

Check the verification email and follow the instructions to begin sharing your work online.

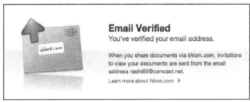

Log in to www.iwork.com, sign in with your
Apple ID and password, and your "Shared
Documents" will now be available.

> **TIP:** This is a great way to collaborate on
> work and also to send something from
> your iPad that might be too large to email
> to someone to view and print.

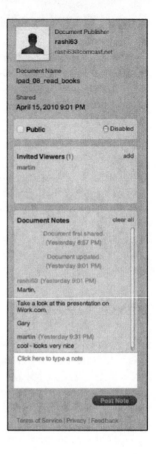

Printing a File

To print any presentation, tap the **Tools** icon (the **Wrench** icon) and select **Print**. Then
you can select any **AirPrint**-compatible printer and adjust number of copies and specific
pages to print.

> **TIP:** We show you details about how to use **AirPrint** and compatible printers in the "Print
> Messages" section of Chapter 13: "Email on Your iPad."

Faxing a File via E-Fax Service

Faxing a file via an e-fax service is a great trick if you are away from your home or office,
and you want to get a quick print-out or send a quick fax.

NOTE: In order to do this, you have to first sign up for an electronic fax service such as www.efax.com, so you can send faxes as email attachments.

Once you have your e-fax account, you can send the document to a fax machine as an email attachment by following these steps:

1. Choose the **Share ➤ Email Presentation** in any of the apps.

2. Choose **PDF format**.

3. Address the email message with the fax number in the format required by your e-fax service. Some of the services have the following format: (fax number)@faxsend.com or 3865551212@faxsend.com

4. Once the email is sent, it is converted to a fax by your fax service and sent to the appropriate fax machine.

Export a File

Follow these steps to export an **iWork** file:

1. Choose **Share ➤ Export** in any of the **iWork** apps.

2. Choose the file type in which you would like the document to be transferred to the computer.

3. Transfers are handled through iTunes the next time you connect your iPad to the computer. The usual formats are the default for the particular application. You also have a PDF option for export.

NOTE: Pages can export to **Word** for Mac or PC, but **Keynote** and **Numbers** cannot yet export to their Microsoft PC equivalents (**PowerPoint** and **Excel**). You can always choose to export to a PDF file from **Pages**, **Numbers**, and **Keynote**.

In the next section, we will cover how to import these documents into your iPad using file sharing.

File Sharing

File sharing is the ability to take a document that you create in **iWork** and share it via iTunes. File sharing takes place in iTunes through the **Apps** tab at the top of the screen. Click **Apps** and scroll down to the **File Sharing** section at the bottom of the screen.

> **TIP:** We also show you how to use file sharing in the "File Sharing" section of Chapter 3: "Sync with iTunes."

Each program that is installed on your iPad and capable of file sharing is shown at the bottom. Follow these steps to retrieve a shared file to your iPad:

1. Click the app from which you have shared the file (in this case, **Keynote**). All the documents that you have shared on your iPad are shown.

2. Highlight the document to save and then touch the **Save To** button in the lower-right corner.

    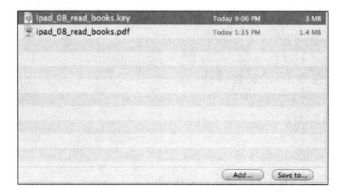

3. From there, you simply navigate to the folder in which you want to save the document.

4. Now the file is on your computer for easy viewing, editing, and printing.

TIP: Good alternatives to **Pages**, **Keynote**, and **Numbers** are **Documents to Go** and **QuickOffice**. Both of these alternatives are combined into a single app, rather than being available as three separate apps.

iTunes on Your iPad

In this chapter, you will learn how to locate, buy, and download media using the **iTunes** app right on your iPad. With the **iTunes** app, you will be able to download music, movies, TV shows, podcasts, and audiobooks. You will also be able to download free educational content from leading universities with the **iTunes U** service. You will also learn how to redeem iTunes gift cards.

Some of us still remember going to the record store when that new single or album came out. It was an exciting feeling, browsing through all the vinyl albums (or later, through tapes and CDs), and looking at all the music we wanted.

Those days are pretty much gone with the iPad. All the music, movies, TV shows, and more are available right from the iPad itself.

iTunes is a music, video, TV, podcast, and more store—virtually every type of media you can consume on your iPad is available for purchase or rent (and often for free) right from the iTunes store.

Just released for iTunes is a new sort of music social networking aspect called Ping. You can use this service to follow artists, see what your friends are listening to, and more.

Getting Started with iTunes on the iPad

Earlier in this book, we showed you how to get your music from iTunes on your computer into your iPad (see Chapter 3: "Sync Your iPad with iTunes"). You will also learn more about using iTunes on your computer in Chapter 26: "New Media: Reading Newspapers, Magazines, and More." One of the great things about iTunes is that it is very easy to buy or obtain music, videos, podcasts, and audiobooks, and then use them within minutes right on your iPad.

The iPad allows you to access the mobile version of iTunes right on your device. After you purchase or request free items, they will be downloaded to your iPad's **iPod** app or **Videos** app. They will also be automatically transferred to your iTunes library on your computer the next time you perform a sync, so you can also enjoy the same content on your computer.

A Network Connection Is Required

You do need an active Internet connection (either Wi-Fi or 3G/cellular) in order to access the iTunes store. Check out Chapter 4: "Other Sync Methods" to learn more about network connectivity.

Starting iTunes

When you first received your iPad, **iTunes** was one of the icons on the first **Home** screen page. Touch the **iTunes** icon and you will be taken to the mobile iTunes Store.

> **NOTE:** The **iTunes** app changes frequently. Since the **iTunes** app is really a web site, it is likely to change somewhat between the time we wrote this book and when you are looking at it on your iPad. Some of the screen images or buttons may look slightly different than the ones shown in this book.

Navigating iTunes

The **iTunes** app uses icons similar to other programs on the iPad, so getting around the app is quite easy. There are three buttons at the top and seven icons (*soft keys*) at the bottom to help you navigate the app. Look at Figure 20–1 to see the soft keys and features. Scrolling works just like scrolling in any other program; move your finger up or down to look at the selections available.

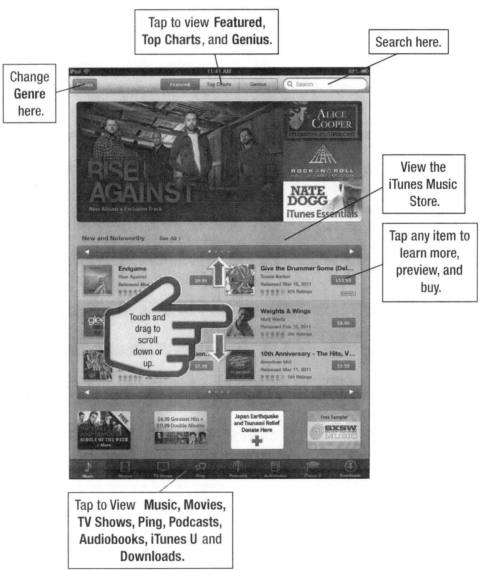

Figure 20–1. *The iTunes layout*

Finding Music with Featured, Top Charts, and Genius

Along the top of the iTunes music store screen are three buttons: **Featured**, **Top Charts**, and **Genius**. By default, you are shown the **Featured** selections when you start the **iTunes** app.

Top Charts—the Popular Stuff

If you like to see what is popular in a particular category, you will want to browse the **Top Charts** category. Tap **Top Charts** at the top, and then tap a category or genre to see what is popular for that category.

> **CAUTION:** These songs or videos are selling well, but that doesn't mean that they will appeal to you. Always give an item a preview and check out the reviews before you pay for it.

Tap to view Top Charts.

...then, choose **Top Songs** or **Top Albums** and browse the top of the charts

Tap the **Genre** button in the upper-left corner to select a particular genre. For example, if you touch **Singer Songwriter**, you will see the top ten songs or albums in that category only.

The initial view shows you the **Top Songs** on the left and **Top Albums** on the right.

You simply scroll through the lists as you would in any other program on the iPad.

Genres—Types of Music

Touch the **Genres** button to browse music based on a genre. This is particularly helpful if you have a favorite type of music and would like to browse just that category.

There is an extensive list of genres to browse; again, just scroll down the list as you would in any other iPad program.

Go ahead and browse through the music until you see something that you would like to preview or buy.

Browsing for Videos (Movies)

Touch the **Movies** or **TV Shows** buttons on the bottom to browse all the video-related items (see Figure 20–2).

Figure 20–2. *Browsing the* **Movies** *category in iTunes on your iPad*

You can also use your finger to scroll all the way to the bottom of the page to check out the links there, including these links in particular:

- **New to Rent or Own**
- **Highlights by Genre**
- **All HD Movies**

Tap any movie or video to see more details or preview the selection. You have the option to rent or buy some movies and TV shows.

Rentals: Some movies are available for rent for a set number of days.

> **NOTE:** The rental period in the US is 24 hours, while the rental period in Canada is 48 hours. Other countries may vary slightly; many have no rentals at all.

Buy: This option allows you to purchase and own the movie or TV show forever.

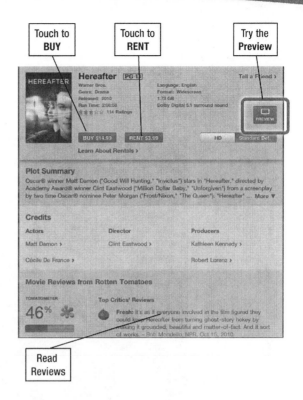

Finding TV Shows

When you're done checking out the movies, tap the **TV Shows** button at the bottom to see what is available for your favorite shows (see Figure 20–3).

When you tap a TV series, you will see the individual episodes available. Tap any episode to check out the 30-second preview. See Chapter 10: "Viewing Videos, TV Shows, and More" for more information on watching videos. When you're finished with the preview, tap the **Done** button.

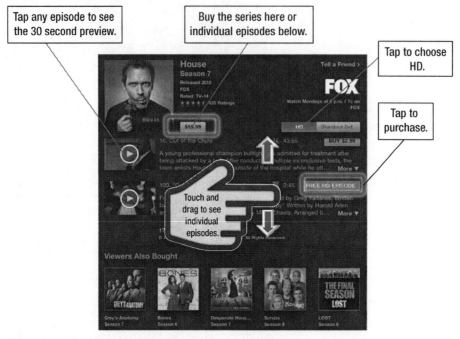

Figure 20–3. *Buying and browsing TV episodes or seasons*

When you are ready to buy, you can choose to buy an individual episode or the entire TV series. Many, but not all TV Series, allow you to purchase individual episodes.

For example, maybe you want to get your fix of *House* and see the pilot episode that you missed. You can do this quickly and easily on your iPad.

> **NOTE:** There is also a **Free TV Episode** category, where you can get samples and bonus content.

Audiobooks in iTunes

Audiobooks are a great way to enjoy books without having to read them. Some of the narrators are quite entertaining; it is almost like watching a movie. For example, the narrator of the Harry Potter series can do dozens of truly amazing voices. We recommend that you try out an audiobook on your iPad; audiobooks are especially great when you are on an airplane and want to escape from the rest of the passengers, but don't want to have the light on.

TIP: If you're a big audiobook listener, getting an Audible.com subscription can get you the same content at cheaper prices.

If you are an audiobook aficionado, be sure to check out the audiobooks in iTunes.

You can use the top three buttons to browse the audiobooks in iTunes:

- **Featured**
- **Top Charts**
- **Categories**

iTunes U—Great Educational Content

If you like educational content, then check out **iTunes U**. You will be able to browse whether your university, college, or school has its own section.

For example, we looked up Harvard University (see Figure 20–4). In just a few minutes of browsing, we discovered a campus-wide discussion of Harvard's most renowned faculty in a series called *Harvard Thinks Big 2*.

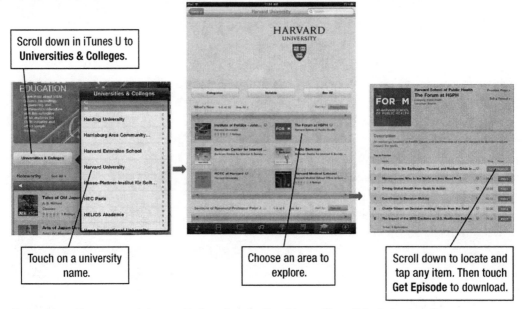

Scroll down in iTunes U to **Universities & Colleges.**

Touch on a university name.

Choose an area to explore.

Scroll down to locate and tap any item. Then touch **Get Episode** to download.

Figure 20–4. *You can search for a particular university, then browse iTunes U by that university.*

If you are in a location with a good wireless signal, you can tap the title of the audio or video item, and then listen to or watch it as a stream. If your signal gets interrupted, however, you will lose your place in the video. There are many advantages to actually downloading the file (if possible) for later viewing, not least of which is that you get more control of the video-watching experience.

Download for Offline Viewing

If you know you are going to be out of wireless coverage for a while, such as on an airplane or in the subway, you will want to download the content for later offline viewing or listening. Tap the **Free** button to change it to a **Download** button, and then tap it again. You can then monitor the download progress (some larger videos may take ten minutes or more to complete) by tapping the **Downloads** button at the bottom right of the screen. When the download is complete, the item will show up in the correct area in your **iPad** icon.

> **NOTE:** Any file larger than 20MB cannot be downloaded over the 3G network; you must use Wi-Fi for larger files.

Searching iTunes

Sometimes you have a good idea of what you want, but you are unsure where it is located or perhaps you don't feel like browsing or navigating all the menus. The **Search** tool is for you.

In the top-right corner of the **iTunes** app, as in virtually every other iPad app, you have a **Search** window.

Touch **Search**, and the **Search** window and the on device keyboard will pop up. Once you start typing, the iPad will begin to try to match your entry with possibilities.

Tap here, then type the Artist, Song, Movie or Show you are looking for.

Touch the correct Artist, Album, etc.

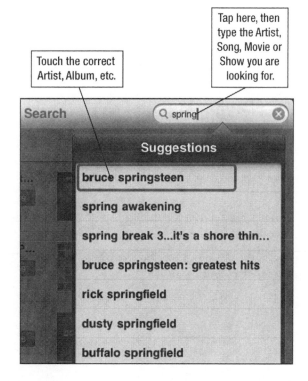

Search

Q spring

Suggestions

bruce springsteen

spring awakening

spring break 3...it's a shore thin...

bruce springsteen: greatest hits

rick springfield

dusty springfield

buffalo springfield

Type in the artist, song name, video name, podcast name, or album you are searching for, and the iPad will display detailed matches. Be as general or as specific as you like. If you are just looking to browse all particular songs by an artist, type the artist's name. If you want a specific song or album, enter the full name of the song or album.

When you locate the song or album name, simply touch it and you will be taken to the purchase page.

Purchasing or Renting Music, Videos, Podcasts, and More

Once you locate a song, video, TV show, or album, you can touch the **Buy** or (if you see it) **Rent** button. This will cause your media to start downloading. (If the content is free, then you will see **Free** button that you tap turn into a **Download** button.)

We suggest you view or listen to the preview, as well as check out the customer reviews first, unless you are absolutely sure you want to purchase the item.

Previewing Music

Touch either the title of the song or its track number to the left of the song title; the album cover will flip over and launch the **Preview** window.

You will hear a representative clip of 30 seconds of the song.

Touch the **Stop** button and the track number will be displayed again.

Touch here to **Preview** or stop.

Touch any other song track number to preview it.

Check out Customer Reviews

Many items in iTunes offer customer reviews. The reviews range from a low of one star to a high of five stars.

> **CAUTION:** You need to be aware that, while many reviews are clean, some can have explicit language. that may not be caught by the iTunes store right away.

Reading the reviews might give you a fairly good idea of whether you would like to buy the item.

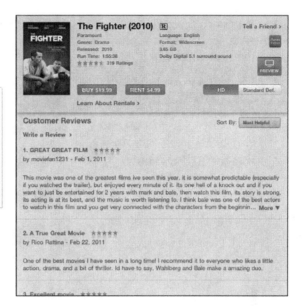

Previewing a Video, TV Show, or Music Video

Pretty much everything on iTunes offers a preview. Sometimes you will see a **Preview** button, as with music videos and movies. TV shows are a little different; you tap the episode title to see the 30-second preview.

Most movies and TV shows also give you an **HD** or **Standard Def.** button. Remember that HD movies and episodes are usually a bit more expensive.

We highly recommend checking out the reviews, as well as trying the preview before purchasing items on iTunes.

Typical movie previews or trailers will be longer than 30 seconds—some are 2 minutes 30 seconds or longer.

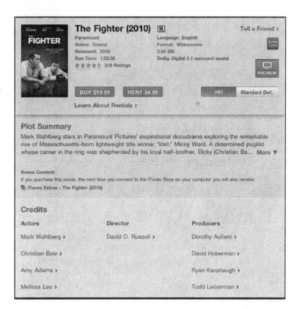

Purchasing a Song, Video, or Other Item

Once you are sure you want to purchase a song, video, or other item, follow these steps to buy it:

1. Touch the **Price** button of the song or the **Buy** button.

2. The button will change and turn into a green **Buy Now**, **Buy Song**, **Buy Single**, or **Buy Album** button.

3. Tap the **Buy** button.

4. You will see an animated icon jump into the shopping cart. Type in your iTunes password and touch **OK** to complete the sale.

You can check the progress of the download by touching the **Downloads** button in the lower-right corner.

The song will then become part of your music library, and it will be synced with your computer the next time you connect your iPad to iTunes on your computer.

After the download is complete, you will see the new song, audiobook, podcast, or iTunes U podcast inside the correct category within your **iPod** app.

> **NOTE:** Purchased videos and iTunes U videos go into the **Videos** app, not the **iPod** app on your iPad.

Podcasts in iTunes

Podcasts are usually a series of audio segments; these may be updated frequently (such as hourly news reports from National Public Radio) or not updated at all (such as a recording of a one-time lecture on a particular topic).

You can use the top three buttons to browse the podcasts in iTunes:

- Featured
- Top Charts
- Categories

Downloading a Podcast

Podcasts are available in **Video** and **Audio** varieties. When you locate a podcast, just touch the title of the podcast (see Figure 20–5). Luckily, most podcasts are free. If it is free, you will see a **Free** button instead of the typical **Buy** button.

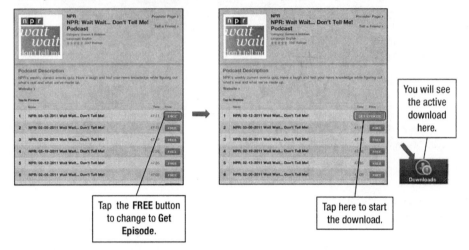

Tap the **FREE** button to change to **Get Episode**.

You will see the active download here.

Tap here to start the download.

Figure 20–5. *Downloading a podcast*

When you touch the button, it turns into a green button that says **Download**. Touch **Download** and an animated icon jumps into your **Downloads** icon at the bottom bar of soft keys. A small number displayed in red reflects the number of files downloading.

The Downloads Icon—Stopping and Deleting Downloads

As you download items, they appear in your **Downloads** screen. This behavior is just like the behavior of iTunes on your computer.

You can touch the **Downloads** icon along the bottom row to see the progress of all your downloads.

Where the Downloads Go

All of your downloads will be visible in either your **iPod** app or your **Videos** app, organized by category. In other words, if you download a

podcast, you will need to go into your **iPod** app
and touch the **Podcasts** icon on the sidebar to
see the downloaded podcast.

> **NOTE**: If you don't finish a download on your iPad, and you can't find it in the download queue,
> you can try going to a desktop **iTunes** app and hitting **Check for Available Downloads**.

Sometimes, you may decide that you do not want the all downloads you selected. If you
want to stop a download and delete it, swipe your finger over the download to bring up
the **Delete** button, and then tap **Delete** (see Figure 20–6).

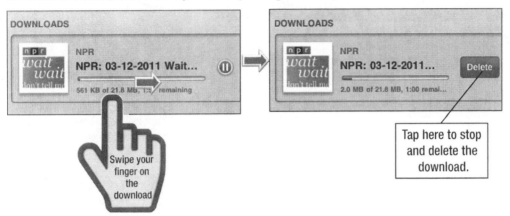

Figure 20–6. *Deleting a file while downloading it*

Redeeming an iTunes Gift Card

One of the cool things about iTunes on your iPad is that, just as with iTunes on your
computer, you can redeem a gift card and receive credit in your iTunes account for your
purchases.

At the bottom of the **iTunes** screen, you should see the **Redeem** button (see Figure 20–7).

Tap the **Redeem** button to start the process of entering your Gift Card Number for an
iTunes store credit.

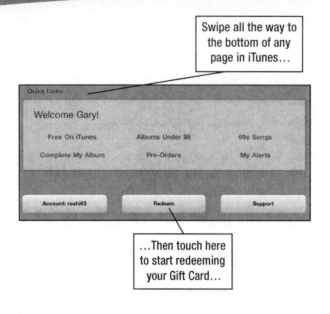
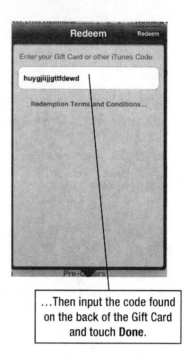

Swipe all the way to the bottom of any page in iTunes...

...Then touch here to start redeeming your Gift Card...

...Then input the code found on the back of the Gift Card and touch **Done**.

Figure 20–7. *Redeem an iTunes gift card*

You will then be prompted to enter your iTunes gift card info or gift certificate info in the box. Once you do this, you will have credit for downloads in the iTunes store—it is that easy!

NOTE: If you have more than one iTunes account, you can log in or out right in the **iTunes** app, as well.

Ping: Apple's Music Social Networking App

Recently, Apple introduced the Ping service as part of **iTunes 10**. You can read more about the desktop version in Chapter 30: "Your iTunes User Guide." Ping is also built into the **iTunes** app on the iPad.

Ping gives you the opportunity to follow your favorite music artists and view videos, pictures, or content the artist might choose to post. Ping also allows you to follow friends, see what they are listening to, and make comments to their posts.

> **CAUTION**: If your Ping account is public, everyone who follows you will see what you buy. If you also have Twitter set up, it can spam your timeline if you buy a lot of music.

Using Ping on the iPad

Ping is located along the bottom soft keys of the **iTunes** app. If you set up Ping from your desktop **iTunes** app (see Chapter 30 for more information), then you will find that it is already set up on your iPad (or any other iOS device you have).

> **NOTE**: If Ping doesn't show up on your iPad after you've enabled it on a desktop version of **iTunes**, you might need to sync your iPad once before it appears on the **iTunes** app.

You will notice three soft keys across the top: **Activity**, **People**, and **My Profile**. When Ping launches, it displays the **Activity** screen, which shows the artists and friends you are following, as well as their recent activity.

Touching the **People** soft key at the top will show you the people you are following, as well as those who are following you.

Touch the **My Profile** soft key, and you can also see who you are following and add comments to be seen by those who are following you.

Touch the **My Info** button at the bottom, and you can see your picture and the music that you like, which you chose when you set up your Ping account in **iTunes 10**.

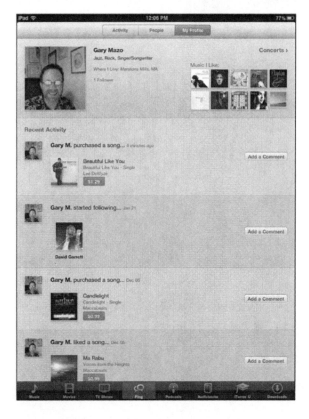

Ping is in its infancy now, but it promises to become a more full-featured social networking site devoted exclusively to music in the not-too-distant future.

Chapter 21

The Amazing App Store

You have just seen how easy it is download music, videos, and podcasts from iTunes right onto your iPad. You have also learned how to download iBooks from the iBooks store.

It is just as easy to download new applications from Apple's amazing App Store. Apps are available for just about any function you can think of—games, productivity tools, and social networking—whatever you can imagine. As the advertising says: "There's an app for that."

In this chapter, you will learn how to navigate the App Store, how to search for apps, and how to download them. You will also learn how to maintain and update your apps once they are downloaded onto your iPad.

> **NOTE:** If you purchase a new iPad Wi-Fi or unlocked iPad 3G while travelling and bring it home to a country where it's not yet sold, there's a good chance your iTunes ID won't work to buy apps. The work-around is to buy iPad apps on a desktop version of iTunes (which does work) and sync them over.

Learning More About Apps and the App Store

In a very short amount of time, the App Store has exploded in volume. There are apps for just about anything you can imagine. Apps come in all prices; in many cases, they are even free.

A Few Cool Apps

With more than 350,000 apps in the store and 70,000 iPad-specific apps, it is impossible to give you a top-ten list of apps. Instead, we've listed a number of apps that we like or have heard are really cool. Table 20-1 lists of a number of fun, cool, useful, or simply entertaining apps. The table also shows whether an app is free; however, it does not otherwise include pricing because prices change frequently in the App Store.

Table 20-1. *Cool iPad Apps*

App Name	Type	What it does	Free / Paid
Pandora Radio	Music	Create your own customized radio station to listen to your favorite artists for free (learn more about this in Chapter 9).	Free
Slacker Radio	Music	Create your own customized radio station to listen to your favorite artists for free (learn more about this in Chapter 9).	Free
Google Earth	Mapping	Zoom around the world with a birds-eye view. Swipe, rotate, and zoom to see the world at an amazing level of detail.	Free
Skype	Phone & Chat	Turn your iPad into a speakerphone. Call anyone else in the world who also has a Skype account—for free (learn more about this in Chapter 18)!	Free
IM+	Instant Messaging	Connect to a variety of instant messaging networks, including the following: **Google Talk**, **Windows Live Messenger**, **Yahoo! Jabber**, **MySpaceIM**, **ICQ**, **MSN**, **iChat**, and **AIM**.	Free
Text+ 4	Text Messaging	Send free text and multimedia messages to anyone with a mobile phone.	Free
Flashlight	Lighting	Turn your iPad into a flashlight or strobe light to help you when it's dark.	Free
Words with Friends	Games	Lets you play a Scrabble-like game with your friends (or anyone else).	Free

App Name	Type	What it does	Free / Paid
Angry Birds	Games	Shoot birds across the screen to knock down buildings.	Paid
ESPN Fantasy Football	Games	Manage your favorite teams and leagues. Follow games in real time to see how you're doing.	Paid
Evernote	Note	Take notes, store pictures, and create voice notes. Categorize and sort your notes (learn more about this in Chapter 24).	Free
Facebook or **Flipboard**	Social Networking	Stay up-to-date with all your friends on Facebook (learn more about this in Chapter 23).	Free
Kindle	E-Book Reader	An alternative to the **iBooks** reader, this app allows you to read Kindle books from `www.amazon.com` (learn more about the **Kindle** reader in Chapter 12).	Free
GoodReader	E-Book Reader	Lets you read PDFs and E-Books, as well as unzip compressed `.zip` files and more (learn more about **GoodReader** in Chapter 26).	Free
iMovie	Video Editor	Edit movies you take with your iPad right on the device (learn more about this in Chapter 17)!	Paid
Weather Bug	Weather	See forecasts for the weather anywhere. This app lets you see radar maps, 10-day and hourly forecasts, and more.	Free
Remote	Remote Control	Control music on your computer (iTunes) or your Apple TV (learn more about this in Chapter 29).	Free

Where to Find Apps News and Reviews

You can find reviews in the App Store itself, and we recommend you check out the App Store reviews. However, sometimes you will probably want more information from some experts. The blogs are a great place to find news and reviews.

Here is a list of Apple iPad/iPhone/iPod touch-related blogs with reviews of apps:

- The iPhone Blog: www.tipb.co
- Touch Reviews: www.touchreviews.net
- Touch My Apps: www.touchmyapps.com
- The Unofficial Apple Weblog: www.tuaw.com
- Cult of Mac: www.cultofmac.com
- App Smile: www.appsmile.com

App Store Basics

After only a short time on the site, you should find the App Store to be quite intuitive to navigate. However, there are some basics to familiarize yourself with that will make the App Store experience much more enjoyable.

A Network Connection Is Required

After you set up your App Store (iTunes) account, you still need to have the right network connectivity (either Wi-Fi or 3G/cellular) to access the App Store and download apps. Check out Chapter 4: "Wi-Fi and 3G Connectivity" to learn how to tell if you are connected.

Starting the App Store

The **App Store** icon should be on your first page of icons on the **Home** screen. Tap the icon to launch the **App Store**.

The App Store Home Page

Like iTunes, the **App Store** app has buttons on top and soft keys at the bottom that help direct you in your purchases (see Figure 21–1).

Along the top, there are buttons for **New** apps and **What's Hot,** as well as a **Release Date** app listing. Along the bottom are icons for **Featured, Genius, Top Charts, Categories,** and **Update**.

Scrolling is handled the same way as in iTunes and in other programs—just move your finger up and down to scroll through the page.

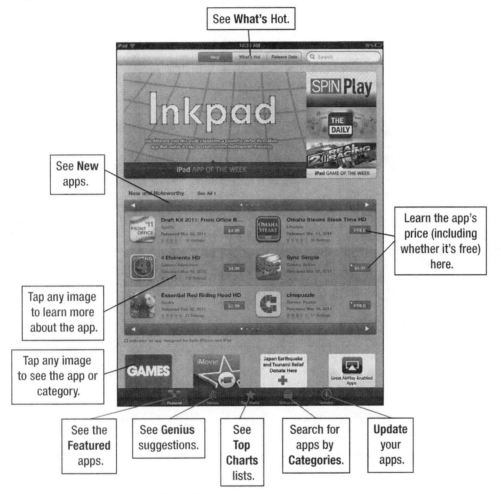

Figure 21-1. *Layout of the App Store's **Home** page*

You will notice that there are two main sections on the App Store's **Home** page: **New and Noteworthy** and **Staff Favorites**. Each section has several pages. Touch the arrows to advance through the pages or touch the **See All** tab.

> **NOTE:** Since the App Store is essentially a web site, it will change frequently. Some of the details and nuances of the App Store might be a bit different after this book goes to print.

Viewing App Details

Once you find an app that interests you, you can explore many options to help you decide whether a particular app is for you. Figure 21–2 shows you some of the options available.

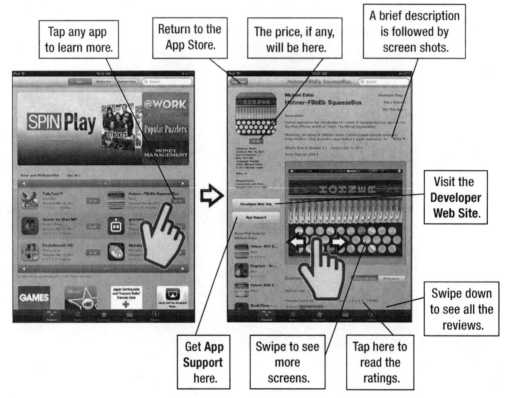

Figure 21–2. *Viewing details about an app*

Finding an App to Download

Begin by looking around the default view, which shows the **Featured** apps. The App Store loads with the **New and Noteworthy** apps in the middle of the page for browsing. Touch the arrows in the title bar to advance through the screens of apps.

You can also see highlighted new apps at the top in a "graphic" view. Just touch one of the images at the top of the page to see information about that app.

> **NOTE:** As with iTunes, you can download only apps under 21MB while on 3G. Bigger apps require a Wi-Fi connection.

View What's Hot

Touch the **What's Hot** button on the top and the hottest apps in the store will now be visible on the screen. Again, just scroll through the "hot" apps to see if something catches your eye.

> **NOTE:** The fact that an app is in the **What's Hot** category does not necessarily mean you will also believe it is useful or fun. Check out the app descriptions and reviews carefully before you purchase anything.

Using Categories

Sometimes all the choices can be a bit overwhelming. If you have a sense of what type of app you are looking for, touch the **Categories** button along the bottom row of icons.

The apps are now in **Category** tabs, ranging from **Games** to **Finance** to **Medical** to **Photography**—and all sorts of other possibilities.

> **NOTE:** It is possible that more categories will be added at the time you read this; this section changes frequently in the App Store.

Find the category of what you are searching for and touch the tab. For example, if you are looking for a weather-related app, you can just touch the **Weather** tab.

You can then browse the featured **Weather** apps in the category or touch the **Sort by** button to see all the weather apps sorted by **Name**, **Most Popular**, or **Release Date**.

Looking at the Top Charts

Touch the **Top Charts** icon along the bottom row and the **App Store** program will change the view again. This time it will show you the top ten paid and top ten free apps. The left-hand column will show the **Top Paid** apps, and the right-hand column will show the **Top Free** apps.

Scroll down to the bottom of the **Top Charts** page and you will see a second category: **Top Grossing**. For some, seeing how much an app grosses is important. To see a more complete list of either category of top apps, touch the **Show More**

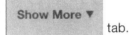 tab.

Chapter 22

Games and Fun

Your iPad excels at many things. It is a multimedia workhorse, and it can keep track of your busy life, as well. Two areas where the iPad really excels are as a gaming device and for hosting iPad-specific apps that really take advantage of its large, high resolution touch screen. You can even find versions of popular games you might only expect to find on dedicated gaming consoles.

The iPad brings many advantages to portable gaming: the high definition screen makes for realistic visuals, the high quality audio provides great sound effects, and the accelerometer allows you to really interact with your games. For example, in racing games, you can "steer" your car by turning the iPad as you hold it.

> **NOTE:** We have written more than a dozen books about BlackBerry devices and other smartphones, and we have many BlackBerry, WebOS, iOS, and Android devices lying around the house. The smartphones don't disappear into our children's rooms; rather, it is the iPad that our children (and our spouses) have decided is fun enough to grab. We regularly discover that the iPad has disappeared from its charger and have to yell out, "Where is my iPad? I need to finish this book!"

The iPad as a Gaming Device

Thanks to the built-in accelerometer—essentially a device that detects movement (acceleration) and includes a built-in gyroscope that detects tilt—the iPad is capable of doing things that most portable game systems can't.

With literally thousands of gaming titles to choose from, you can play virtually any type of game you wish on your iPad.

> **NOTE:** Some of these games do require that you have an active network connection, either Wi-Fi or 3G, to engage in multiplayer games.

With the iPad, you can play a driving game and use the iPad itself to steer—just by turning the device. You can also touch the iPad to brake or tilt it forward to accelerate.

This game is so realistic that it might make someone car sick!

Tap to brake.

Tilt the iPad left / right to steer the car.

Real Racing HD

Or, you can try a first-person battle game. With the new graphics engine of the iPad, games like Chair's *Infinity Blade* look amazing and play very smoothly.

The graphics, battle scenes, and 3D environment on *Infinity Blade* are unlike anything else available for the iPad and rival more expensive console games in quality.

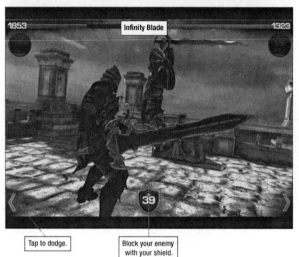

Infinity Blade

Tap to dodge.

Block your enemy with your shield.

Where to Get Games and Fun Apps

Games are found, like all iPad apps, at the App Store (see Figure 22–1). You can get them either through iTunes on your computer or by using the device's **App Store** program.

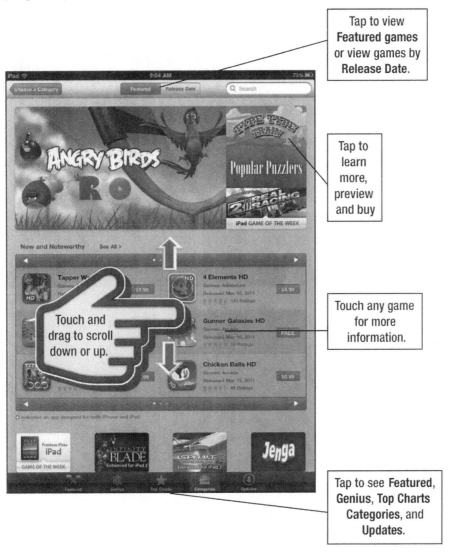

Tap to view
Featured games
or view games by
Release Date.

Tap to
learn
more,
preview
and buy

Touch any game
for more
information.

Tap to see **Featured,
Genius, Top Charts
Categories,** and
Updates.

Figure 22–1. *Layout of the App Store's **Game** section*

To get a game, start the **App Store** program as you did in the last chapter, and then use the **Categories** icon to take you to the **Games** tab. You will also find many games in the **Featured** section of the App Store, as well as in the **New and Noteworthy** section. Figure 22–2 shows the app-purchase page for a game available for the iPad.

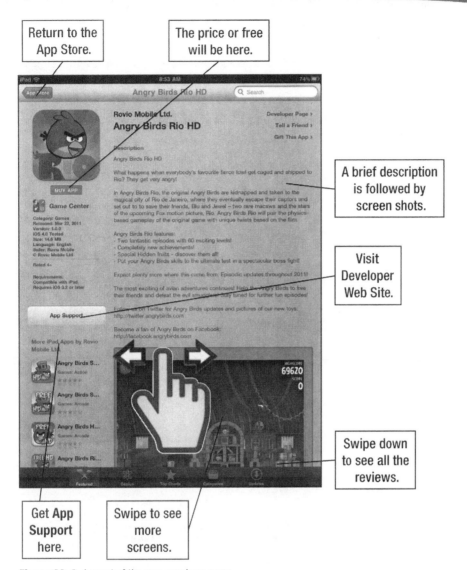

Return to the App Store.

The price or free will be here.

A brief description is followed by screen shots.

Visit Developer Web Site.

Swipe down to see all the reviews.

Get **App Support** here.

Swipe to see more screens.

Figure 22–2. *Layout of the app-purchase page*

Read Reviews Before You Buy

Many of the games have user reviews
that are worth perusing. Sometimes,
you can get a good sense of the
game before you buy it. If you find a
game that looks interesting, don't be
afraid to do a simple **Google** search
on your computer to see if any
mainstream media outlets have done
a full review.

> **CAUTION:** Beware that some
> reviews may contain explicit
> language.

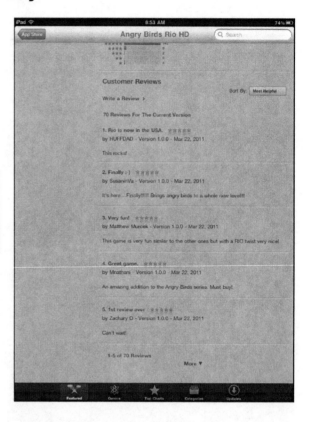

Look for Free Trials or Lite Versions

More and more frequently, game
developers are giving users free
trials of their games to see if they
like them before they buy. You will
find many games have both a
Lite/Free version and a Full version
in the App Store.

Some games are "free," supported
by the inclusion of ads within the
app. Other apps are free to start, but
require in-app purchases for
continued play or additional
features.

Be Careful When You Play

Given the size of the iPad, some games have been modified from their iPhone/iPod touch versions. You don't use the iPad to "cast" your line in a fishing game, as you would in the iPhone version; however, you can move around a bit in driving and first person shooter games—so be mindful of your surroundings! For example, make sure you have a good grip on your device, so it doesn't slip out of your hand—we recommend a good silicone case to help with this.

> **CAUTION:** Games like **Angry Birds** can be quite addictive and hamper productivity!

Two Player Games

The iPad really opens up the possibility for two-player gaming. In this example, we are playing checkers against one another—using the iPad as a game board.

Similar two-person apps can also be found for other board games, such as chess, Scrabble, and more.

> **TIP:** When playing a two-person game such as checkers, make sure you *lock* the screen orientation, just as you do when you read a book. Do this by moving the **Rotation Lock** switch to the **locked** position (see Chapter 8).

Online and Wireless Games

The iPad also allows online and wireless peer-to-peer play if the game supports it. Many new games are incorporating this technology. In **Scrabble**, for example, you can have multiple players on their own devices. You can even have the iPad as your game board and up to four individual iPhones as wireless "racks" to hold your letters. Just flick the letters off the rack, and they go onto the board—very cool!

You can also play Scrabble online against Facebook Friends. You can do this over a local network or as a multiplayer *pass-n-play* game.

> **NOTE:** If you just want to play against a friend who is nearby, select Wi-Fi mode for multiplayer games. If you just want to play against new people, try going online or against Facebook Friends!

Playing Music with Your iPad

There are many music games and apps for the iPad. The size of the screen and the technology of the device make it possible to play just about any instrument using the iPad.

For years, Mac users have had the ability to learn music using the **GarageBand** app on their computers. Recently, Apple introduced the first **GarageBand** app for the iPad, and it is spectacular.

GarageBand allows you to choose whether you want to play drums, keyboard, guitar, or bass—all using the touch screen on the iPad (see Figure 22–3).

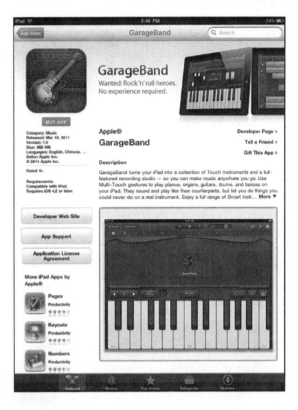

GarageBand also contains an audio recorder that allows you to create and record soundtracks on the iPad. You can even plug in your electric guitar (using a third-party adapter) and use the built-in guitar amp to adjust the sound, volume, and tone of your instrument.

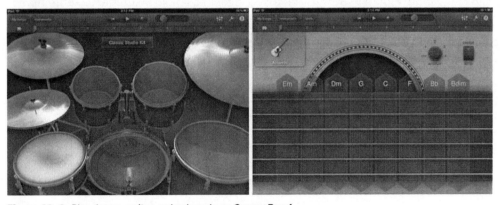

Figure 22–3. *Play drums, guitar, or keyboards on* **GarageBand**.

The new crop of music apps allows you to really use the iPad as an instrument.

One amazing new app is called **Magic Fiddle**. Made by Smule, this app actually lets you play the strings of a violin.

Magic Fiddle is just US $2.99.

Download the app and just have fun with it!

If you have children, they might enjoy it, as well.

> **NOTE:** This app is not meant to replace your priceless Stradivarius; however, it does provide a fun introduction to the violin.

Playing Magic Fiddle

You can play **Magic Fiddle** in **StoryBook** mode, either as a solo instrument in **Solo** mode or by using the built-in **Songbook** feature to play popular pieces (see Figure 22–4).

To change a string color or key, tap the **Settings** icon on the **Main** screen.

To play in **Solo** mode, hold the iPad like a violin, resting it on your shoulder to play.

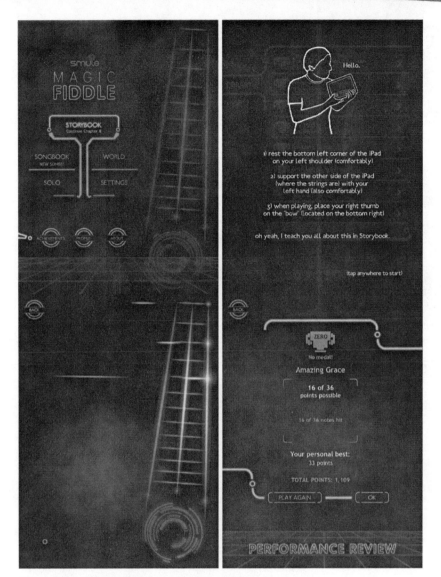

Figure 22–4. *Magic Fiddle's screens and controls*

The World View

Tap the **Back** button and select **World** (see Figure 22–5). This shows you a globe with people happily playing the violin in various places around the world. Sometimes you will see a duet.

If you like the way someone is playing, then hit the **Love** icon.

If you do not like the music you are hearing, then hit the **Next** icon (the two right arrows).

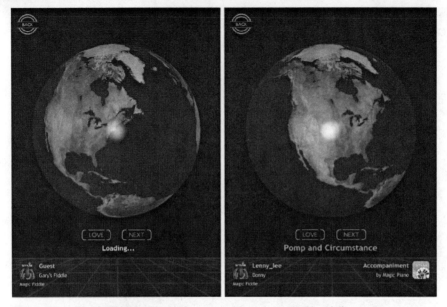

Figure 22–5. *Magic Fiddle's* **World** *view—watching others play the violin*

Game Center

Last year, Apple introduced a new concept to portable gaming: **Game Center**. **Game Center** is a place for you to meet up with friends, invite friends to play a game, or to share accomplishments from games you and your friends both play.

Setting up Game Center

The first time you start **Game Center** from your iPad, you will be asked to either sign in using your **Apple ID** and password or your **MobileMe ID** and password. Input your biographical information and then input an email address (or several email addresses) to authenticate **Game Center** use.

TIP: If you register and verify several email addresses, it will be easier for your friends to find you on **Game Center** and invite you to become part of their **Game Center** network.

Make sure that the **Allow Game Invites** and **Find me By Email** buttons are turned **ON**, so that your friends can ask you to play.

Using Game Center

Once you have set up **Game Center**, the fun begins. Start **Game Center** and you will see how many friends you have, how many **Game Center** games you have, and how many achievements you have earned. All this is visible from the **Me** tab [Me] at the bottom.

Touch the **Friends** tab [Friends] and you will see how many **Game Center** friends you have. It appears that this maxes out at 500 friends.

Touch the **Games** tab [Games] and you will see how many **Game Center** games are on your device.

> **NOTE**: Once you have a **Game Center** account, you can log in from any iOS device to see your games, friends, and achievements.

Touch the **Requests** tab [Requests] to either see pending requests or touch the **+** sign to invite contacts (through email addresses) to become your **Game Center** friends.

Playing a Multiplayer Game

Some **Game Center** games allow you to play (and invite) a **Game Center** friend to a one-on-one game. Some games will match you up with other players online, while others only allow you to share your achievements with your friends.

The screenshot to the right shows the **Game Center** with several games enabled: Some games only allow the user to share achievements, whereas others allow the user to play against friends or to get matched up online.

In a multiplayer game (like **Adrenaline Golf**), you can start the game either from within **Game Center** or from the game's icon on the iPad.

The screenshot to the right displays your options when a user chooses **Play Multiplayer** in **Adrenaline Golf**. Doing so brings up options for **Automatic Match Making** or **GameCenter Invite**.

Choosing **Automatic Match Making** prompts the iPad to find opponents for the user to play against.

Other Fun Stuff: Sports on the iPad

There are so many great apps that can provide users with endless hours of entertainment on the iPad. Since the iPad 2 was released just before Spring of 2011, **March Madness, NBA Basketball, MLB Spring Training**, and many more apps were underway.

At Bat 2011 for iPad is a US $14.99 application that is well worth the entry fee for any baseball fan. It also highlights the iPad's capabilities.

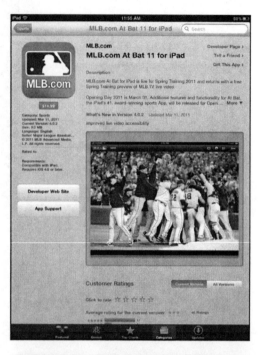

The **NCAA March Madness On Demand** app allowed users to keep track of every game of this year's college basketball tournament.

The **March Madness** app actually had a live TV feed, so that every game broadcast could be played on the iPad.

This seems to be the direction that other apps are moving in, providing not only game-time stats and news, but also allowing users to watch live sports on the iPad. This is very cool!

The **NBA Game Time Courtside** app allows me to follow my Celtics on their march through the regular season and into the playoffs.

During each regular season game, I can see who is on the court and follow the scoring in real time right on my iPad!

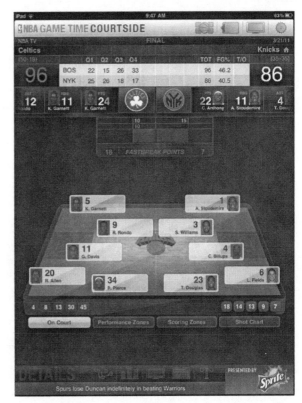

Chapter 23

Social Networking

Your iPad can help keep you in touch with others in lots of innovative ways that go far beyond what e-mail and the Web traditionally enable.

Some of the most popular places to "connect" these days are those sites that are often called *social networking sites* — places that allow you to create your own page and connect with friends and family to see what is going in their lives. Some of the most popular web sites for social networking include Facebook, Twitter, and LinkedIn.

In this chapter, we will show you how to access these various sites. You will learn how to update your status, *tweet*, and keep track of those who are both important or simply of interest to you.

We will also introduce you to some great third-party apps that give you access to some of the social networking features in a new, innovative manner.

Facebook

Facebook was founded in February of 2004. Since that time, it has served as the premier site for users to connect, reconnect, and share information with friends, co-workers, and family. Today, more than 400 million people use Facebook as their primary means of "catching up" with the people who matter most to them.

> **NOTE:** You cannot play Facebook Games on your iPad. This may disappoint you if you are a big Facebook Game player. You can, however, play against Facebook Friends in games like Scrabble (see Chapter 22: "Games and Fun").

On your iPad, you have three primary ways of accessing your
Facebook page at the time of publishing:

- Use **Safari** to go to the standard (full) web site:
  www.facebook.com.

- Use a third-party app like **Flipboard** (shown later in
  chapter).

- Use the official iPhone/iPad touch **Facebook** app.

NOTE: The authors recommend either **FlipBoard** or **Friendly Facebook for iPad** as the best iPad
solutions for accessing Facebook at the moment. The iPhone/iPad touch app is more limited than
the full site version, but it is easier to navigate. Remember that this app was originally created for
the iPhone/iPod touch, so it will not fill up the screen. You can always touch the **2x** button to
make it bigger—but an enlarged screen will not look as sharp or clear as the desktop-based
Facebook web page.

Logging into facebook.com from Safari

To log in on the web-based app, start
up the **Safari** browser and go to
www.facebook.com. Log in in just as you
do on your computer.

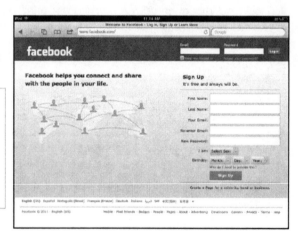

TIP: If the full web site seems
overwhelming, log in to
touch.facebook.com or
m.facebook.com to access the
mobile site.

Getting Around facebook.com

The nice thing about facebook.com is that you already know how to get around the site
if you have ever used Facebook on your computer. It works essentially the same way.

Tap any of the links in the **Left Nav Bar** to get to your **News Feed**, **Messages**, **Events**,
Photos, **Friends**, and so on (see Figure 23–1).

Navigate with these links.

Tell everyone "What's on your mind."

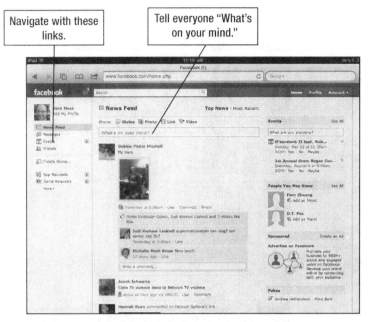

Figure 23–1. *The facebook.com web page in the **Safari** browser*

Status Update/News Feed

Once you log onto the Facebook web site with **Safari**, you will have the option to write "What's on your mind" and see your **News Feed** from your friends.

Finding Facebook Friends

In the web-based Facebook page, you can find friends by touching the **Search** field and starting to type in the name of the friend you are looking for.

You can also touch the **Account** dropdown box from your **Home** page and then touch **All Connections** on the left side to see your friends.

Your friends are also listed under **Lists** along the left-hand sidebar.

> **NOTE:** If you are using either touch.facebook.com or m.facebook.com, you will have a **Friends** tab at the top; simply touch this to see your list of friends.

Uploading a Photo to facebook.com

Unfortunately, there was an issue with uploading a photo to Facebook at the time of publishing: the simple **Upload Photo** that you use from your desktop computer did not work with the **Safari** browser. Instead, you were asked to send an e-mail to a uniquely generated e-mail address that appears in Facebook after you tap **Upload Photo**. The subject of your e-mail becomes the text for the uploaded photo. One nice thing about uploading photos to Facebook by e-mail is that you can send a bunch of photos at one time and have them upload in the background. This differs from the **Facebook** app, which requires that you wait for each photo to upload before you do the next.

We won't show you the detailed steps for uploading photos to Facebook via e-mail; instead, we recommend that you install the **Facebook** app and use it to upload photos. It is much easier to use this approach. See the "Uploading Pictures with the Facebook App" section later in this chapter for the upload steps.

Downloading and Installing the Facebook App

In order to find the app, use the **Search** feature in the App Store and type in **Facebook**.

You can also go to the Social Networking category in the App Store and find the official **Facebook** app, as well as many other Facebook-related apps.

> **NOTE:** Some of the apps may look like official Facebook apps, and they do cost money. However, the only official app is the iPhone/iPod touch app mentioned previously.

In order to connect to your account on Facebook, you will need to locate the icon you just installed and click it. We use the example of the **Facebook** app here, but the process is very similar for the rest of the apps, as well.

Once the **Facebook** app is successfully downloaded, you should see the icon shown here.

Facebook App Basics

Once the **Facebook** app is downloaded
and installed, the first thing you will see
is the **Login** screen. Input your account
information—your email address and
password.

After you log in the first time, you will see
a **Push Notifications** warning message.

Click **OK** if you want to allow these
messages, which can be pokes from
other Facebook friends, notes, status
update notifications, and so on.

Once you log in, you will see the
Facebook screen shown in Figure 23–2.
Tap the **Facebook** logo to navigate
around the app.

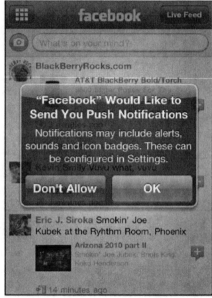

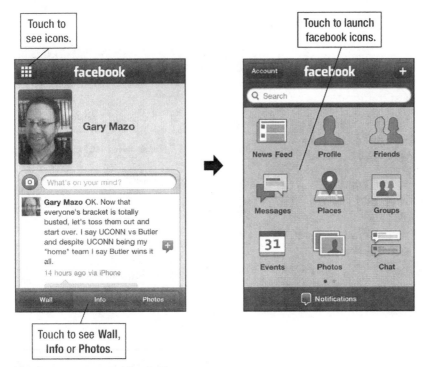

Figure 23–2. *Using the Facebook app*

Navigating Around Facebook

Toggle between the **Navigation** icons and your current location by tapping the word **Facebook** at the top of the page.

For example, if you are in the **News Feed** and tap **Facebook**, you will see all the icons. Tap **Facebook** again and you will return to the **News Feed**.

From the icons page, you can access your **News Feed**, **Profile**, **Friends, Notifications**, **Places**, **Requests**, **Events**, **Photos**, or **Chat**.

Communicating with Your Friends

Follow these steps to communicate with your Facebook Friends:

1. Tap **Facebook** at the top to see all the icons.

2. Tap the **Friends** icon to see your list of friends displayed.

3. Touch the friend you want to communicate with, and you will go to her Facebook page. From here, you can write on the **Wall** and see your friend's **Info** and **Photos**.

Uploading Pictures with the Facebook App

An easy and fun thing to do with Facebook is to upload pictures. Follow these steps to upload pictures in the **Facebook** app:

1. From the **Facebook** main icons, tap **Photos**.

2. Choose an album, such as **Mobile Uploads**.

3. Tap the **Camera** next to the **What's on your mind?** box. Next, tap the **Take Photo or Video** to snap a picture or make a video to upload. Or, you can tap **Choose From Library** to navigate through the pictures on your iPad until you find the picture you wish to upload.

4.   Next, tap **Write a caption...** to write a caption, if so desired.

5.   To finish the upload, tap the blue **Upload** button. The photo will go into your **Mobile Uploads** folder.

> **NOTE**: When you upload a photo, the image quality won't be the same as it was originally on your iPad.

Gary Mazo Went to get the mail and a huge hawk was having lunch.

9 minutes ago

Facebook Notifications

Depending on your settings for Facebook push notifications, you can be inundated by updates, wall posts, and invitations. If you don't have too many Facebook friends, and you want to know when someone is writing something on your wall or commenting on a post or picture, just set your push notification to **On**.

When a notification comes in, it will appear on your screen—even if your iPad is locked.

In this example, Gary's friend posted on his wall, and he has a message waiting in his inbox.

The **Facebook** icon tells him he has a waiting notification to respond to or view.

Tapping the icon launched the **Facebook** app, and Gary could see and respond to the message.

He was able to see a notification icon in the **Messages** section, which was indicated by the **Red (1)** circle. He was also able to see that he had a new **Wall Post** notification at the bottom of the screen.

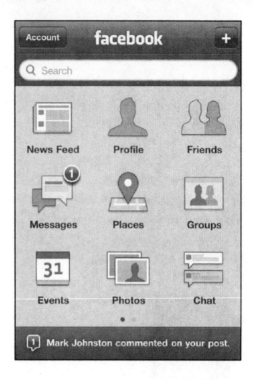

Expanding or Reducing the Size of the App

Since this **Facebook** app was designed for the smaller screen of the iPhone or iPod touch, you will notice it opens up as a smaller app in the center of the screen. To see a larger size app, tap the **2x** in the bottom-right portion of the screen, as shown in Figure 23–3.

Text and images will look
slightly grainy at 2X size.

Tap the **2X** button to expand
the app to full screen.

Tap the **1X** button to return to
smaller size.

Figure 23–3. *Expand the app to full screen with the 2x button.*

Settings to Customize Your Facebook App

Follow these steps to adjust settings for the
Facebook app:

1. Tap the **Settings** icon.

2. Tap **Facebook** in the left column.

3. You can now adjust various options:

   ■ **Shake to Reload:** This feature
     reloads or updates the page
     when you shake your iPad.

   ■ **Vibrate**: This feature lets you
     specify your desired vibration
     settings when you receive
     notifications.

   ■ **Push Notifications:** These
     features have simple **ON/OFF**
     toggle switches. Touch **Push
     Notifications** to see the detailed
     switches on the next screen.

Facebook	
General	
Shake to Reload	ON
Alerts	
Vibrate	ON
Play Sound	ON
Push Notifications	>
Version	3.1.2
About	>

You can see the **Push Notifications** settings screen for the **Facebook** app on the right.

Touch each switch to turn it **ON** or **OFF**.

For each switch that is in the **ON** position, you will receive push notifications when something changes. For example, your iPad will notify you when you receive a message that somebody has confirmed you as a friend, tagged you in a photo, or commented on your wall.

> **TIP:** The latest version of the **Facebook** app will allow you to use **Facebook Places** to see nearby friends. It also features **New Style** messages and **Groups**.

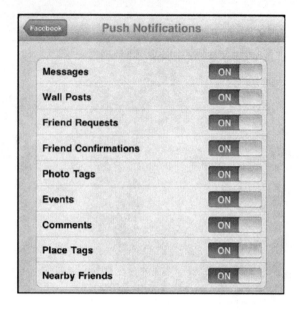

Using the Flipboard and Friendly Facebook Apps

While it is frustrating that there is no "official" iPad Facebook app, there are two very good alternatives (both free) in the App Store. Both can make the Facebook experience more enjoyable on the iPad's big screen.

Friendly Facebook for iPad has a free version available in the App Store. Just search for "Facebook" in the App Store and you should find the app.

Once the app is installed, you can see your **Live Feed**, **Events**, and **Places** marked as buttons across the top of the app (see Figure 23–4). Just touch one of the buttons to jump to that particular section.

At the very top, you can find buttons for your **Profile** or **Friends**, as well as a **Home** button to go to the live **News Feed**.

There are also smaller icons at the top for **Messages**, **Notifications**, **Requests**, and a handy link to your **Facebook Games** page.

Figure 23–4. *Friendly Facebook for iPad* screens

Flipboard for iPad

One of the authors' favorite apps is **Flipboard**, which is billed as a personal social magazine for the iPad.

Essentially, you can add sections to the **Flipboard** app from any of numerous content providers. From there, you can "browse" in a magazine style (flipping the pages) to any web site or content provider.

You can use **Flipboard** to set up accounts for Facebook, Twitter, and Flickr (among other accounts

This feature works great with regards to Facebook. Begin by downloading **Flipboard** from the App Store.

When you start **Flipboard** for the first time, you can set up accounts as you add sections. Setting up Facebook is as easy as touching **Add a Section** and then entering your Facebook login information.

You will then see your Facebook page as a magazine. You can touch an item to bring it to full screen, or you can "flip" the pages to go through all the Facebook posts.

Touch the **Facebook** button at the top of the page and you can jump to **Your Wall, Photos of You, Mews Feed Photos, News Feed Links, Groups, Pages, Friends Lists,** or **Friends** (see Figure 23–5).

Touch a friend's button to jump to his page.

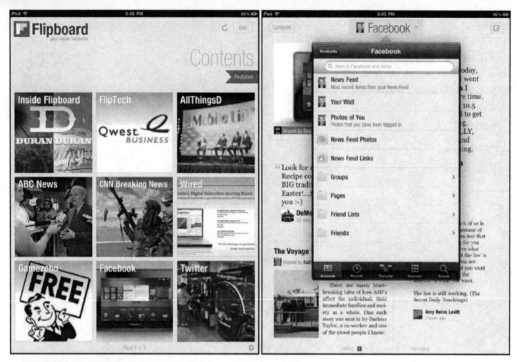

Figure 23–5. *Flipboard's* Facebook screens

LinkedIn

LinkedIn has very similar core functionality to Facebook, but it tends to be more business and career focused. Facebook, on the other hand, is focused more on personal friends and games. With LinkedIn, you can connect and reconnect with current and past business associates. The service lets you send messages, see what people are up to, have discussions, and more.

As the time of publishing, the status of LinkedIn was very similar to Facebook. You can go to the regular LinkedIn site on the **Safari** browser or download the **LinkedIn** app for the iPhone.

Which is better? We liked the **LinkedIn** app for the iPhone slightly better than the full LinkedIn.com site in **Safari**. The service was easier to navigate using the **LinkedIn** app with the large buttons, but you could see more on the screen in the **Safari** version. We recommend giving both options a try and seeing which you like better—it is really a matter of personal preference.

LinkedIn.com on the Safari Browser

To get to LinkedIn on your browser, follow these steps:

1. Tap the **Safari** icon.

2. Tap the **Address** bar at the top of the browser.

3. Type in this address: www.linkedin.com. If you see www.linkedin.com appear in the dropdown box as you are typing it, then just touch the link to jump to it.

4. Enter your LinkedIn username and password to log in and see the LinkedIn **Home** page, as shown in Figure 23–6.

Figure 23–6. *The LinkedIn **Home** page on your **Safari** web browser*

> **TIP:** Remember to zoom by double-tapping or pinching open/closed to see more of the web page.

You navigate around and interact with LinkedIn.com just as you would on your computer. The only difference is that you use your finger instead of the mouse to click links.

Downloading the LinkedIn App

It's easy to acquire the **LinkedIn** app. Start the **App Store** app on your iPad, type "LinkedIn" into the **Search** window, and locate the app. It's free, so tap the **FREE** button to install it.

Logging In to LinkedIn App

Once the **LinkedIn** app is installed, click the **LinkedIn** icon and enter your login information.

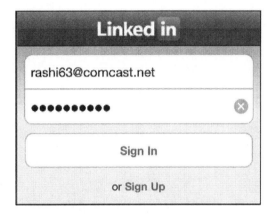

Navigating the LinkedIn App

The **LinkedIn** app has an icon-based navigation style similar to Facebook. Tap any icon to move to that function, and then tap the **Home** icon in the upper-left corner to return to the **Home** screen (see Figure 23–7).

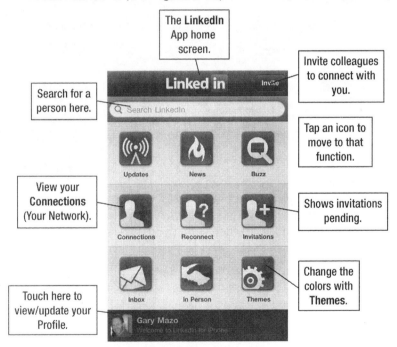

Figure 23–7. *The LinkedIn app's Home screen*

Communicating with LinkedIn Connections

One of the things you will likely do the most with the **LinkedIn** app is communicate with your connections. Here's the easy way to do so:

1. Touch the **Connections** icon.

2. Scroll through your connections or type in a connection name in the **Search** box.

3. Touch the contact you are looking for.

4. Touch the **Send** icon  in the upper-right corner and then choose **Send Message**.

Twitter

Twitter was started in 2006. Twitter is essentially an SMS (text message)-based social networking site. It is often referred to as a *micro-blogging site* where the famous and not-so-famous share what's on their mind. The catch is that you have only 140 characters to get your point across.

With Twitter, you subscribe to *follow* someone who *tweets* messages. You might also find that people will start to follow you. If you want to follow us, we are @mtrautschold on Twitter.

Making a Twitter Account

Making a Twitter account is very easy. We do recommend that you first establish your Twitter account on the Twitter web site at www.twitter.com. When you establish your account, you will be asked to choose a unique user name—we use @garymadesimple—and a password.

You will then be sent an e-mail confirmation. Click the link in your e-mail and you will be taken back to the Twitter web site. You can make tweets or choose people to follow on the web site; you can also read tweets from your friends.

Twitter Options for the iPad

There are many options for using Twitter on the iPad. The easiest way to follow others and to tweet is to use one of the Twitter apps from the App Store.

There are many Twitter apps from which to choose. We will highlight two Twitter apps in this book: **TweetDeck** and the official **Twitter** app. Both are very well designed and easy to use.

NOTE: Both of these apps allow you to perform essentially the same tasks on Twitter—it really is a matter of personal preference!

Download Twitter Apps

Go to the App Store, touch
Categories, and choose **Social
Networking**. You should see both
TweetDeck and **Twitter** in the
Social Networking section. If not,
simply touch the **Search** window and
type in either app name.

Download the apps as you would any
other app to the iPad.

Starting the Twitter App for the First Time

Touch either app icon and the program
will start. The first time using either app
will require you to sign in to Twitter. Your
user name is the one you picked when
you first signed up for Twitter.

Using TweetDeck

The **TweetDeck** app gives you a very clean **Home** screen. You see the tweets from those you are following along the bottom-left section of the screen under the **All Friends** label.

To the right, you usually see the **Mentions**, which are responses to your tweets. These work almost like a text message conversation.

The controls for **TweetDeck** are in the upper-right corner. There are five icons available to you (see Figure 23–8).

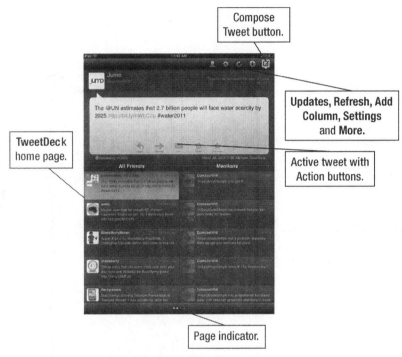

Figure 23–8. *The layout of* **TweetDeck***'s* **Home** *page*

People

Tap the **Profile** icon (person) to see the **Search** box and type in the name or username of the individual you are looking to follow.

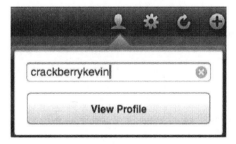

In this example, I looked for my friend Kevin who goes by "CrackBerryKevin." When you find desired the user, touch the **View Profile** button to see his Twitter profile.

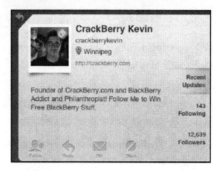

Accounts and Settings

There are several adjustable fields in the **Accounts and Settings** section of the app. Touch the **Manage Accounts** tab to add or edit a Twitter account.

Touch **Sign into an Account** to sign in to another Twitter account you may have. To do this, touch the tab and input your username and password.

Touch the **Settings** tab to adjust auto correction, auto capitalization, and sound options. You can also choose your picture service if you have a specific service for uploading pictures to Twitter.

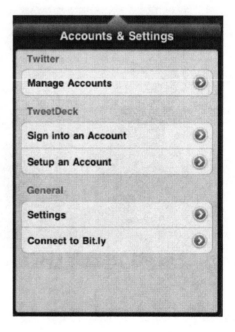

Refresh

Touching the **Refresh** button simply refreshes your tweets.

Add Column

The **Add Column** button adds another column to your Twitter **Home** screen. Just slide from right to left to advance from one column to the next. The dots at the bottom indicate how many screens you have to move through. You can add a column for **Search**, **Direct Messages**, **Mentions**, **Favorites**, **Twitter Trends**, **Twitter Lists**, **Twitter Search**, and **All Friends**.

Compose Tweet

Touch the **Compose Tweet** icon

and the **Tweet composition** screen is displayed. Your Twitter ID is in the **From:** line, and you have 140 characters to express what is on your mind.

When you are done, touch the **Send** button in the upper-right corner.

Reading and Replying

Touch a tweet to bring it to the **Main** screen. This makes the tweet nice and large, and you can touch a link within the tweet to launch the **Web** view. If you want to view the link in **Safari**, touch the **View in Safari**

button.

> **NOTE:** After you view the link in **Safari**, you need to close **Safari** and restart **TweetDeck**.

At the bottom of the **Tweet** window, you will see five icons: **Reply, Forward, DM, Email,** and **Favorite**.

Each icon will bring up an additional window and the onscreen keyboard for you to type your **Reply**, **Forward** the tweet, send a **Direct Message** to the author, **Email** the tweet, or set it as a **Favorite**.

Using Twitter

The official **Twitter** app takes a streamlined approach to using Twitter. The **Home** screen shows you the tweets from those you are following. Touch the full message and a new column appears on the right. This column shows the full tweet and information about the author, as well as icons for **Reply**, **Favorite**, **Retweet**, and **Send**.

You can see five icons along the left-hand side. The first icon is the main **Twitter Timeline** feed. The other icons are **Mentions**, **Direct Messages**, **Links**, **Profile**, and **Search**.

The **Compose Tweet** icon is in the lower-left corner (see Figure 23–9).

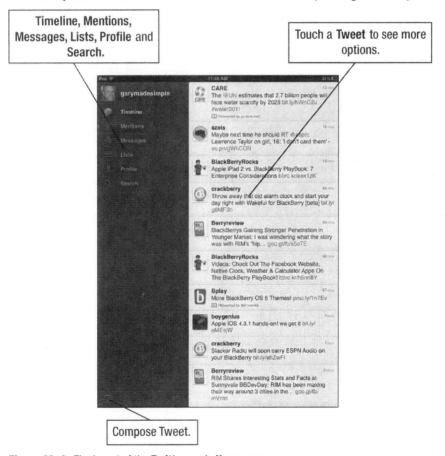

Timeline, Mentions, Messages, Lists, Profile and Search.

Touch a **Tweet** to see more options.

Compose Tweet.

Figure 23–9. *The layout of the **Twitter** app's **Home** page*

Refreshing Your List of Tweets

To refresh your list of tweets, pull down the **Main** page and you will see the **Pull down to refresh** notification at the top. Once the page is pulled down, you will see a **Release to refresh** note. Release the page and it will refresh the tweets.

Your Twitter Profile

You touch **Profile** to display your Twitter profile.

To see your tweets, just touch **Tweets**.

To see those tweets you have labeled as favorites, touch the **Favorites** button.

To see those individuals who you are following, touch the **Following** button.

NOTE: Numbers corresponding to your followers, those you are following, your favorites, and your tweets are displayed below the title of the appropriate button.

Compose Button

Touch the **Compose** button  and the **New Tweet** screen pops up. The character counter will count down from 140 as you type your message.

At the bottom of the **Compose Tweet** screen, you will see icons for **Direct Mentions**, **Hash Tags (#)**, **Picture Uploads**, and **GeoTagging** the tweet.

As you touch an icon, suggestions will pop up in a separate window.

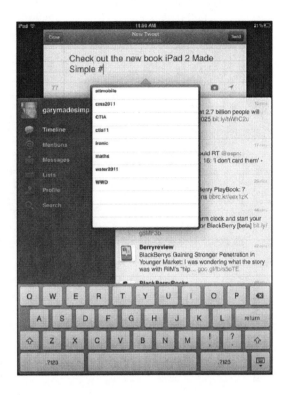

Options Within Tweet

From the **Twitter** app's **Home** screen, touch one of your tweets to bring up a list of options. You can **Reply**, **Set as Favorite**, **Retweet**, and **Translate/Send/Email** the Tweet. Just touch the corresponding button to initiate the action.

You can see the details for the **Link** and **Mail** options shown in Figure 23–10.

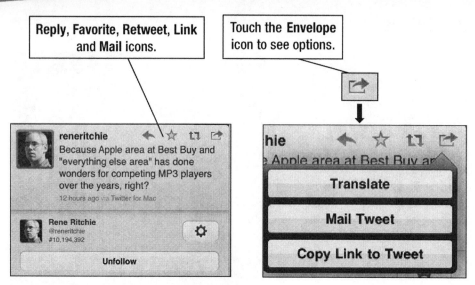

Figure 23–10. *Options within a tweet in the **Twitter** app*

Chapter 24

Eliminate Your Paper Notes

In this chapter, we will give you an overview of the **Notes** app and a popular alternative app called **Evernote**, which you can use to write notes, make grocery lists, and make lists of movies you'd like to watch or books you'd like to read. We will also show you how to organize and even email notes to yourself or others. Ideally, we hope that **Notes** will become so easy to use on the iPad that you can eventually get rid of most, if not all, of your paper sticky notes!

Exploring Additional Notes Apps

Later in this chapter, we will give you an in-depth view of an excellent—and free—alternative to the **Notes** app called **Evernote**. There are various other free or low-cost notes apps in the App Store, but **Evernote** stands apart at this time. With **Evernote**, you can tag and organize your notes, add pictures to notes, add voice notes, and show the location where you originally wrote your note. Another nice thing about **Evernote** is that it will auto-synchronize your notes with the Evernote web site (so you can manage notes from your computer) and many other mobile devices you might own.

> **TIP:** The **Notes** app that comes with the iPad is pretty basic and utilitarian. If you need a more robust notes application that can sort, categorize, import items into an app (PDF, Word, and so on), have folders, search, and more; then you should check out the App Store on your iPad. Do a search for "notes" and you will find at least a dozen notes-related apps ranging from $0.99 and up.

The Notes App

If you are like many people, your desk or wall is filled with little yellow sticky notes—notes to do with everything imaginable. Even with our computers, we still tend to leave these little notes as reminders. One of the great things about the iPad is that you can write your notes on familiar yellow notepaper, and then keep them neatly organized and sorted. You can even email them to yourself or someone else to make sure that the information is not forgotten.

The **Notes** app on the iPad gives you a convenient place to keep your notes and simple "to do" lists. You can also keep simple lists, such as a grocery list, or a list for other stores, such as a hardware or pet store. If you have your iPad with you, you can add items to these lists as soon as they occur to you, and they can be accessed and edited at any time.

Sync Notes

You can sync notes with your computer or other web site using the methods we show you in Chapter 3: "Sync Your iPad with iTunes" and Chapter 4: "Other Sync Methods." Figure 24–1 shows an example of using **iTunes** to sync notes from **Microsoft Outlook** to the **Notes** app on an iPad. The nice thing about syncing notes is that you can add a note on your computer and have it just "appear" on your iPad. Then, when you are out and about, you can edit that note and have it synced back to your computer. You no longer need to retype or remember things. You always have your iPad with you, so taking notes anywhere at anytime can be a great way to never forget anything important.

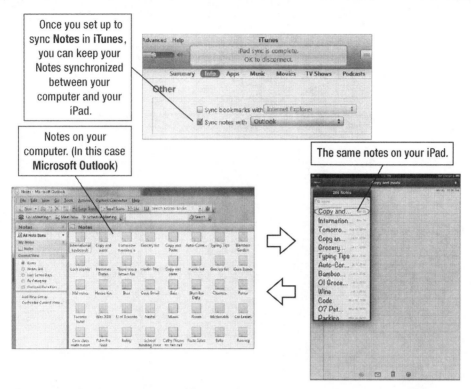

Once you set up to sync **Notes** in **iTunes**, you can keep your Notes synchronized between your computer and your iPad.

Notes on your computer. (In this case **Microsoft Outlook**)

The same notes on your iPad.

Figure 24–1. *Syncing notes between **Microsoft Outlook** and the iPad **Notes** app using **iTunes***

Getting Started with Notes

As with any other application, simply tap the **Notes** icon to start it.

After starting the **Notes** app, you see what looks like a typical yellow note pad.

Your **Notes** appear in the list as tabs to touch. Touch the name of the note you wish to view or edit (see Figure 24–2). The contents of the note are then displayed.

You can scroll in **Notes** as you do in any program. You will notice that the date and time the note was last edited appears in the upper-left corner.

When you are done reading the note, just touch the **Notes** button in the top-left corner to return to the main **Notes** screen.

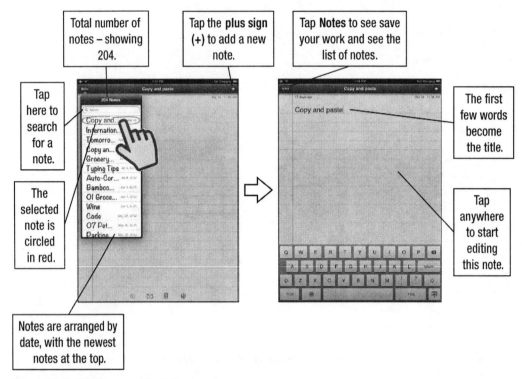

Total number of notes – showing 204.

Tap the **plus sign** (+) to add a new note.

Tap **Notes** to see save your work and see the list of notes.

Tap here to search for a note.

The first few words become the title.

The selected note is circled in red.

Tap anywhere to start editing this note.

Notes are arranged by date, with the newest notes at the top.

Figure 24–2. *Getting around the **Notes** app*

Multiple Notes Accounts

If you happen to be syncing at least one IMAP email account and your computer using **iTunes**, then you will see that your notes from each of these accounts are kept separate. This is very similar to how your contacts are kept in separate groups by your email account and how your calendars are kept separate by your email account.

In order to see multiple notes accounts, you have to set a switch in the **Account Setup** screen.

When you set up your IMAP email account in **Settings ➤ Mail, Contacts, Calendars**, you will see options to turn **Notes** syncing **ON** or **OFF**. In order to see these notes accounts, you have to set the **Notes** switch to **ON**, as shown for this Gmail account.

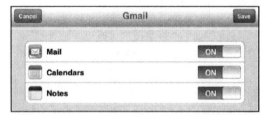

To view the various Notes accounts, tap the **Accounts** button in the upper-left corner of the **Notes** app.

Then, on the next screen, you can tap selections to view **All Notes** or your notes for each account. In this image, the options are **Gmail** or **From My PC** (notes synced in this case from **Microsoft Outlook** using **iTunes**).

Notes you add to an individual account will be kept with that account. For example, if you add notes to **Gmail**, then those notes would show up only on your **Gmail** account.

How Are My Notes Sorted?

You see that all notes are listed in reverse chronological order, with the most recently edited notes at the top and the oldest at the bottom.

The date that is shown is the last time and date that the particular note was edited, not when it was first created. Thus you will notice the order of your notes moving around on the screen.

This sorting can be a good thing because your most recent (or frequently edited) notes will be right at the top.

> **TIP:** If you want a nice app to keep track of your to-do lists, you should check out the **Appigo Todo.** It is currently US $4.99 in the App Store.

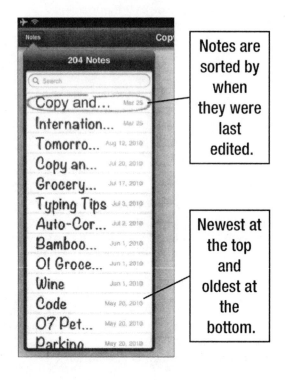

Notes are sorted by when they were last edited.

Newest at the top and oldest at the bottom.

Adding a New Note

To start a new note, touch the **Plus Sign (+)** in the upper-right corner.

The notepad is blank, and the keyboard pops up for you to begin typing. You can hide the keyboard if you wish by tapping the **Hide Keyboard** key in the bottom-right corner.

> **TIP:** You can change the font for **Notes** in your **Settings** app. Apple has changed the choices once already, but at publishing time the three choices were Noteworthy, Helvetica, and the original Marker Felt.

Adding a Title to the Note

The first few words you type before you hit the **Return** key will become the title of the note. So think about what you want as the title and type that first. In the image shown to the right, "**Grocery list**" becomes the title of the note.

Put a new item on each line and tap the **Return** key to go to the next line.

> **NOTE: ABOUT SAVING NOTES**
>
> The nice thing is that you never have to click a **"Save"** button because your note is saved automatically as soon as you are done typing it.

When you are done editing your note, you can do any of the following:

- To exit the app, press the **Home** button to exit the **Notes** app.

- If you are in **Portrait** mode, tap the **Notes** button in the top-left corner to see the list of notes.

- If you are in **Landscape** mode, tap any other note to view it.

Searching for Notes

After you end up with more than a few notes, you'll want to know how to quickly find a note. Tap in the **Search** bar at the top of the list of notes and type one or more words.

All the notes where those words exist in the note's title or body will be instantly listed.

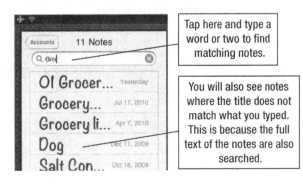

Tap here and type a word or two to find matching notes.

You will also see notes where the title does not match what you typed. This is because the full text of the notes are also searched.

Editing Your Notes

You can easily edit or change the contents of a note. For example, you might keep a "Things to Do" note and quickly edit it when you think of something else to add to the list (or when your family reminds you to get something from the store!).

Tap the "Things to Do" note from the list of notes or tap the **Search** window and type "things" to quickly find it.

To start editing, touch the screen anywhere; the cursor moves to that spot for editing.

If you double-tap a word, the blue handles used in copy and paste appear. (See Chapter 2: "Typing Tips, Copy/Paste, and Search" to learn more about copy and paste.)

> **TIP:** Using the blue selection handles is the best way to select a large amount of text; it is both faster and more precise.

Remember: You can touch and hold your finger on a word to make the **Magnifying Glass** icon appear, so you can insert the cursor on the exact spot you are looking for.

When you release your finger, you will see a pop-up menu that has **Select**, **Select All**, and—if you've recently copied text— **Paste**.

When done editing, tap the **Home** button to exit or, if you are in the **Portrait** view, touch the **Notes** button to bring up the list of notes. If you are in **Landscape** mode, you can tap any other note to view it.

Sending a Note via Email

One convenient feature of the **Notes** app is the ability to email a note (see Figure 24–3). Let's say we wrote a grocery note and wanted to email it to someone to pick up the groceries on the way home. While editing or viewing the note, we could touch the **Envelope** icon at the bottom of the screen.

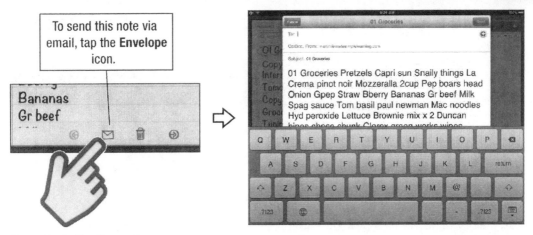

Figure 24–3. *Emailing a note*

See the Next or Previous Notes

To move through multiple notes, just touch the **Arrow** icons at the bottom of the

screen. If you touch the **Forward** arrow, the page turns, and you can see the next note. To go back, just hit the **Back** arrow.

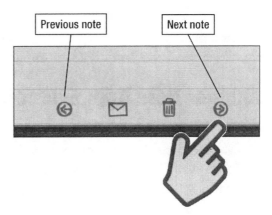

Deleting Notes

To delete a note, tap it to open it from the main **Notes** screen and then touch the **Trash Can** icon at the bottom.

The iPad then prompts you to **Delete Note.** Click this button to do so.

To cancel, tap your finger anywhere else on the screen besides the **Delete Note** button.

Creating a New Calendar Event from an Underlined Day and Time

Try typing in the words "tomorrow morning" or "at 9:30pm tomorrow" in a note, and then save it.

The next time you open that note, you will see that the words have been underlined. If you touch and hold the underlined words, you will see a button asking if you want to **Create Event**.

Tap the button to create a new **Calendar** event for the underlined date and time.

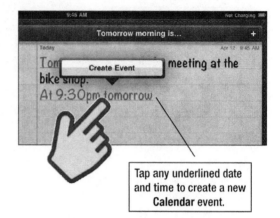

Tap any underlined date and time to create a new **Calendar** event.

TIP: Whenever date and time words are underlined, the iPad recognizes them as potential **Calendar** events. This works in notes, email messages, and other places on your iPad.

Another Note App: Evernote (Free for Basic Use)

A visit to the App Store will show you many note-taking apps designed for the iPad.

To learn about some of the most popular notes-related apps, check out this list of the top five such apps from TiPb.com:

www.tipb.com/2010/03/05/tipb-top-5-iphone-note-apps-2/

Evernote is one of the more popular notes apps that is free for basic use. If you need to have more storage space, you can pay a monthly or annual service plan. Check on the App Store or www.evernote.com for the latest prices and features.

Evernote is great because, when you enter a note in **Evernote**, you can *auto-synchronize* it with your Mac, iPhone, BlackBerry, or PC. All text is searchable, and you can even use **Evernote** to *geo-locate* (have your iPad track your location and tie it to a particular note).

TIP: You can even record voice notes with **Evernote**.

Getting Started with Evernote

Start by going to the App Store and downloading **Evernote**.

Once **Evernote** is downloaded and installed, you need to touch the **Evernote** icon to start the application.

The first time you use **Evernote**, you will be prompted to sign up for a free account. Type in your email address and set a password, and you are ready to start.

Adding and Tagging Notes

The **Home** screen shows you your notes. To add a new note, just touch the **New note** button in the lower-left corner and type your note.

Tap **New note** to start writing a new note.

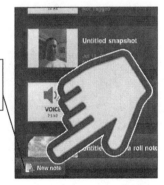

Give your note a unique title and then add some tags to the note. These tags are used to help organize your notes, and they can be useful when searching through your notes. In this example, we have set several tags, including "book," "todo," and "work." If we add those tags to appropriate notes, then the notes can be sorted by those individual tags.

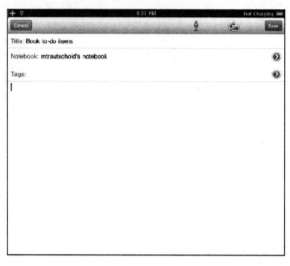

Once you type a few tags separated by commas, these are added to a pulldown list, so they are easier to select in the future. This also helps you avoid mistyping any of your tags (see Figure 24–4).

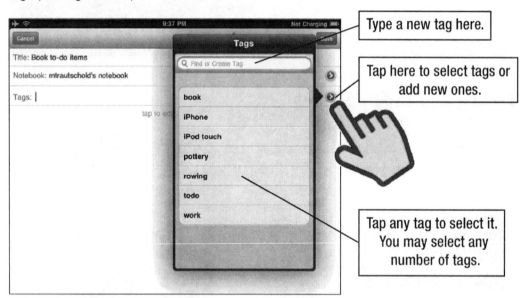

Figure 24–4. *Tagging a note in* **Evernote**

Adding a Voice Recording a Note in Evernote

By tapping the **Microphone** icon in the Upper Bar when you are adding or editing a note, you can record your voice (or anything else around you) to add to your current note (see Figure 24–5).

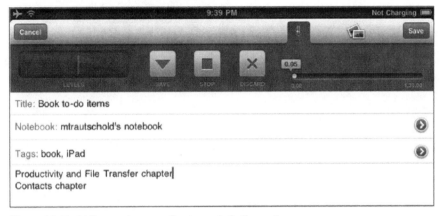

Figure 24–5. *Adding a voice recording to a note in* ***Evernote***

Adding a Picture from Your Library to Your Note

You can easily add any picture from your Photo library to a note in **Evernote** by touching the **Photos** icon in the top of the **Edit Note** window (next to the **Save** button (see Figure 24–6). **Evernote** will even identify the text in the picture and make that text searchable.

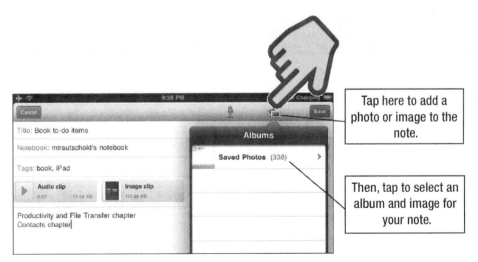

Tap here to add a photo or image to the note.

Then, tap to select an album and image for your note.

Figure 24–6. *Adding a photo from your library to a note in* ***Evernote***

Emailing, Printing, Deleting, or Editing a Note

You may email or print your notes by touching the **Send** icon at the bottom of the screen, and then select it just as you would in the **Notes** app.

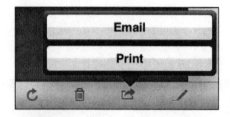

To delete a note, tap the **Trash Can** icon on the Bottom Bar.

Sometimes, you want to be sure you are seeing the latest information on your note, or you want to make sure the information you just added is synced to the Evernote server. To do this, tap the **Refresh** icon.

To edit a note, just touch the **Pencil** icon at the bottom of the screen. This brings up the **Editing** screen.

Various Views of Notes in Evernote

You have various options for customizing the way you view your notes in **Evernote**. Select any of the views listed across the top of the main screen: **All notes**, **Notebooks**, **Tags**, **Places**, or **Searches**.

Touch **All notes** to view all your notes.

Touch **Notebooks** to see all your notebooks (see Figure 24–7).

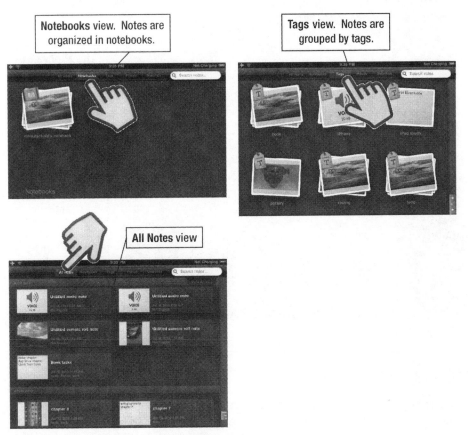

Figure 24–7. *Evernote's **Notebooks**, **Tags**, and **All Notes** views*

The Evernote Places View

One cool **Evernote** view is the **Places** view. You can have **Evernote** tag your notes by the place where you created them. For example, if you traveled to another state, province, or country, **Evernote** would track that you took notes in that particular region.

Figure 24–8 shows a note taken in California and several taken in Florida.

The **Places** view of your notes.

Notes are shown on a map where they were created.

Adjust views between **Map**, **Satellite** and **Hybrid**.

Figure 24–8. *The Evernote Places view*

Evernote Viewing Options

You have various options to customize the views of your notes in **Evernote**. Tap the **View options** tab under the **Search** box in the upper-right corner to customize your current view. In Figure 24–9, we have customized the view by selecting **Title** for **Sort By** and **Thumbnails** for **View by**.

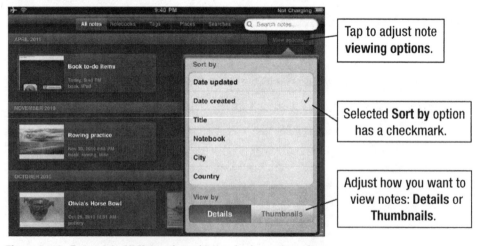

Tap to adjust note **viewing options**.

Selected **Sort by** option has a checkmark.

Adjust how you want to view notes: **Details** or **Thumbnails**.

Figure 24–9. *Evernote's All Notes view with the viewing options shown*

Evernote Synchronization and Settings

To synchronize your notes with the **Evernote** server for retrieval on your Mac, PC, or other Evernote-connected device (such as a BlackBerry or iPhone), you would touch the **Radar Dish** icon in the lower-right portion of the screen to make the **Settings** screen appear (see Figure 24–10).

If you scroll down the **Settings** screen, you can check out the total usage of your Free (or paid) account.

The Free account gives you 40 MB of data, which is more than 100,000 text notes. Tap the **Approximate notes remaining** option to get a feel for how many picture or voice notes this might include.

If you are running out of space, then you might want to upgrade by touching **Go Premium** option in the top of the **Synchronization** window.

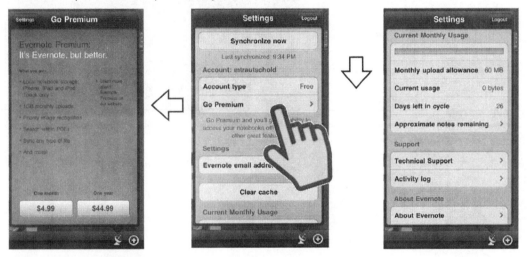

Figure 24–10. *Evernote's Settings screens*

Viewing or Updating Notes in Evernote on Your Computer or Other Mobile Device

One of the cool things about **Evernote** is that it wirelessly synchronizes or shares notes with your account on the Evernote server. You can then log in to your account from your PC, Mac, iPhone, or BlackBerry to check out or update your notes. This is a great feature if you have multiple devices, and you would like to stay up-to-date or add notes from any of them. In Figure 24–11, we logged into the www.evernote.com site and saw the same notes that we were creating and viewing on our iPad.

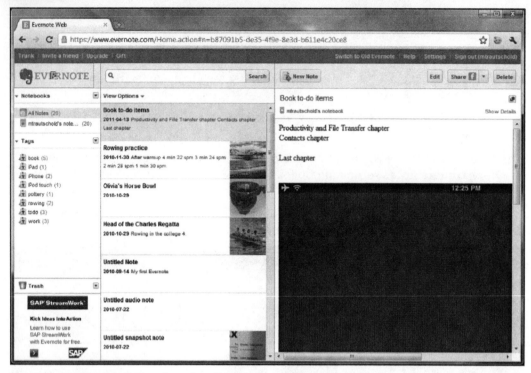

Figure 24–11. *Evernote* *syncs notes automatically to your account on the web.*

Chapter 25

Bluetooth on the iPad

In this chapter, we will show you how to pair your iPad with any Bluetooth device, whether it be another computer, stereo speakers, or a wireless keyboard accessory. Many iPad users are surprised to find out that the iPad actually ships with Bluetooth 2.1 and its enhanced data rate (EDR) technology. Thanks to the technology known as A2DP (Stereo Bluetooth), you can also stream your music to a capable Bluetooth stereo.

> **NOTE:** You must have a capable third-party Bluetooth adapter or Bluetooth stereo to stream your music via Bluetooth technology. Also, there is now AVRCP profile support, so many music controls on a Bluetooth device (including **Play**, **Pause**, or **Skip**) will work fine.

You can think of Bluetooth as a short-range, wireless technology that allows your iPad to connect to various peripheral devices without wires. Popular devices are headsets, computers, and vehicle sound systems.

Bluetooth is believed to be named after a Danish Viking and king, Harald Blåtand, whose name has been translated as *Bluetooth*. King Blåtand lived in the tenth century and is famous for uniting Denmark and Norway. Similarly, Bluetooth technology unites computers and telecom. According to legend, his name derives from his very dark hair, which was unusual for Vikings. Blåtand means dark complexion. There does exist a more popular story that the king loved to eat blueberries, so much so that his teeth became stained the color blue.

We used the following links as our sources for this information; they also serve as good places to learn more about King Blåtand:

- http://cp.literature.agilent.com/litweb/pdf/5980-3032EN.pdf
- http://www.cs.utk.edu/~dasgupta/bluetooth/history.htm
- http://www.britannica.com/eb/topic-254809/Harald-I

Understanding Bluetooth

Bluetooth allows your iPad to communicate with things wirelessly. Bluetooth is a small radio that transmits from each device. Before you can use a peripheral with the iPad, you have to *pair* it with that device to connect it to the peripheral. Many Bluetooth devices can be used up to 30 feet away from the iPad.

Bluetooth Devices that Work with the iPad

Among other things, the iPad works with Bluetooth headphones, Bluetooth stereo systems and adapters, Bluetooth car stereo systems, and Bluetooth wireless keyboards. The iPad supports A2DP, which is known as *Stereo Bluetooth*.

> **NOTE**: With iOS 4.3, the iPad 2, can also pair with an iPhone 3GS or iPhone 4 for BT tethering.

Pairing with a Bluetooth Device

Your primary uses for Bluetooth might be with Bluetooth headphones, Bluetooth stereo adapters, or a Bluetooth keyboard. Any Bluetooth headphones should work well with your iPad. To start using any Bluetooth device, you need to first pair (connect) it with your iPad.

Turn on Bluetooth

The first step to using Bluetooth is to turn the Bluetooth radio **ON**. Follow these steps to do so:

1. Tap your **Settings** icon.

2. Next, touch the **General** tab in the left column.

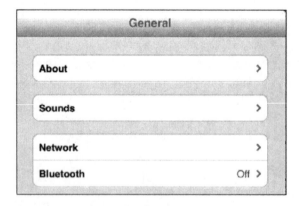

3. You will see the **Bluetooth** tab in the right-hand column. By default, Bluetooth is initially **OFF** on the iPad. Tap the switch to move it to the **ON** position.

> **TIP:** Bluetooth is an added drain on your battery. If you don't plan on using Bluetooth for a period of time, think about setting the switch back to **OFF**.

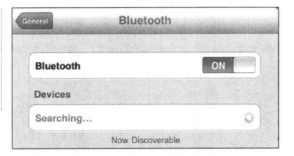

Pairing an iPad with Headphones or Any Bluetooth Device

As soon as you set Bluetooth to **ON**, the iPad will begin to search for any nearby Bluetooth devices—like a Bluetooth headset or keyboard (see Figure 25–1). For the iPad to find your Bluetooth device, you need to put that device into *pairing mode*. Read the instructions carefully that came with your headset—usually there is a combination of buttons to push to achieve this.

> **TIP:** Some headsets require you to press and hold a button for five seconds until you see a series of flashing blue or red/blue lights. Some accessories, such as the Apple wireless Bluetooth keyboard, automatically start up in pairing mode.

Once the iPad detects the Bluetooth device, it will attempt to automatically pair with it. If pairing takes place automatically, there is nothing more for you to do.

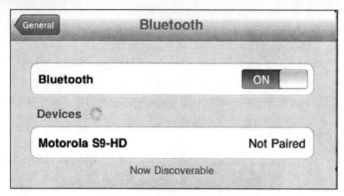

Figure 25–1. *A Bluetooth device discovered, but not yet paired*

If the image in Figure 25–2 stays unchanged, then tap the device (e.g., the Motorola Stereo Bluetooth Headphones) to bring up a pop-up window that asks for a pairing ID.

NOTE: In the case of a Bluetooth device such as a keyboard, you may be asked to enter a randomly-generated series of numbers (passkey) on the keyboard itself. Other devices may not ask for a PIN at all just touch the device name and the status will change to **Connected** (see Figure 25–2.)

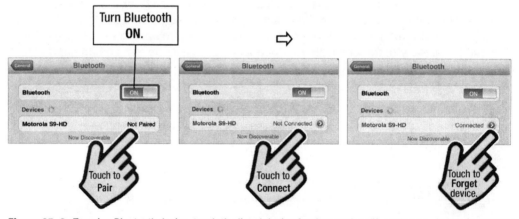

Figure 25–2. *To pair a Bluetooth device, touch the listed device for the passkey (if needed) or simply connect the device to the iPad.*

If the iPad asks for a PIN or pass code to be entered, the keyboard will be displayed, and you will need to enter the four-digit pass code supplied by the headset manufacturer. Most devices use 0000 or 1234, which is why the iPad can try to automatically pair with most devices. Check your headset documentation to learn the correct pass code or PIN for your device.

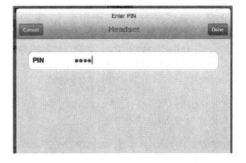

Bluetooth Stereo (A2DP)

 One of the great features of today's advanced Bluetooth technology is the ability to stream your music without wires via Bluetooth. The fancy name for this technology is A2DP, but it is usually referred to as *Stereo Bluetooth*.

Connect to a Stereo Bluetooth Device

The first step to using Stereo Bluetooth is to connect to a capable Stereo Bluetooth device. This can be a car stereo with this technology built in, or a pair of Bluetooth headphones or speakers.

Put the Bluetooth device into pairing mode per the manufacturer's instructions, and then go to the Bluetooth settings page from the **Settings** icon, as demonstrated earlier in the chapter.

Once connected, you will see the new Stereo Bluetooth device listed under your Bluetooth devices. Sometimes it will simply be listed as "Headset." Just touch the device and you will see the name of the actual device next to the **Bluetooth** tab in the next screen, as shown here.

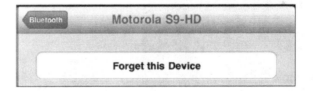

Next, tap your **iPod** icon and start any song, playlist, podcast, or video music library. You will notice the **AirPlay** icon in the upper-left corner of the screen (see Chapters 9 and 10 for more information on **AirPlay**).

The **AirPlay** icon also controls sending your music to a Bluetooth device.

Tap the **AirPlay** icon to see the available Bluetooth devices for streaming your music (see Figure 25–3).

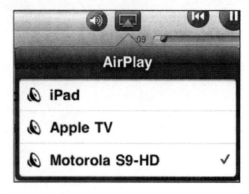

> **NOTE**: In both the **Now Playing** view and the **Current** song view, the **Bluetooth** icon will be up at the top, towards the right-hand side of the **Volume** bar.

First, tap here to see Bluetooth Audio Devices…

...Then, tap to select your Stereo Bluetooth Device.

This **Check Mark** icon shows the connected device.

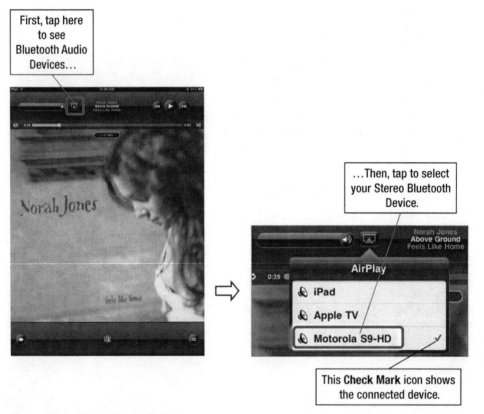

Figure 25–3. *Select a Bluetooth device.*

In the previous screens, you learned how to select the **Motorola Bluetooth Headset** by tapping it. Your music will now start to play from the selected Bluetooth device. You can verify this by touching the **Bluetooth** icon on the screen once more. You should see the **Speaker** icon next to the new Stereo Bluetooth device, and you should hear your music coming from that sound source, as well.

Disconnect or Forget a Bluetooth Device

Sometimes, you might want to disconnect a Bluetooth device from your iPad.

It is easy to do this. Get into the Bluetooth settings as described earlier in this chapter. Touch the device you want to disconnect from in order to bring up the next screen, then tap the **Forget this Device** button and confirm your choice.

> **NOTE:** Bluetooth has a range of only about 30 feet; if you are not nearby or using a Bluetooth device, you should turn off **Bluetooth**. You can always turn it back on when you are actually going to be using it.

Doing this will delete the Bluetooth profile from the iPad (see Figure 25–4.)

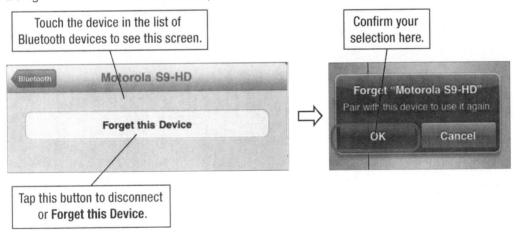

Figure 25–4. *Forget or disconnect a Bluetooth device.*

Chapter 26

New Media: Reading Newspapers, Magazines, and More

In Chapter 12, we spoke about how the iPad has revolutionized the world of reading. The iPad is not only unparalleled in the realm of reading E-Books, but it is also unparalleled in dealing with new media such as online newspapers and magazines, PDF files, and more.

In this chapter, we will explore how to enjoy new media with your iPad and its vivid screen and terrific touch interface. The iPad is even set to revitalize the comic book industry with comic books that look beautiful and are amazingly interactive.

Newspapers on the iPad

Remember the days when newspapers were delivered to the house? Invariably, if there was one puddle in the sidewalk, that was where the newspaper landed! You took it out of that plastic bag, shook it off, and tried to make out what was in section two—the section that got soaked.

Enter the iPad Interactive Newspaper

Well, those days may be gone forever. Users now have the opportunity to interact with their news and even get their paper delivered every day—but to their iPad instead of their driveway.

New this year is an iPad-only newspaper from News Corps.: **The Daily**. **The Daily** is a highly interactive news app that is delivered new each morning (currently US only) right to your iPad.

Many newspapers are developing apps for the iPad, with new apps seeming to appear every day. We will also take a quick look at several apps for the iPad from the largest newspapers in the United States and examine how they revolutionize reading the news (see Figure 26–1).

Figure 26–1. *The front pages of various newspaper apps*

The Daily

The Daily deserves special mention because it is the first (of most likely many) iPad-specific daily newspapers. The app is free to download in the App Store, and it comes with a free trial of two weeks to a month or so.

After the free trial, **The Daily** reverts to a subscription model—not unlike a traditional newspaper. However, the rates are more favorable than a traditional newspaper at this time—just $.99 a week or $39.99 for an entire year.

When you touch the icon for **The Daily** app, you will first see that the days' news is being retrieved and delivered to the iPad.

Once the news is delivered, navigating **The Daily** is quite intuitive. The experience starts with a typical **Front Page** section that displays the main story of the day.

At the top, however, you can quickly jump sections to **News**, **Gossip**, **Opinion**, **Arts and Life**, **Apps and Games,** or **Sports**. Just touch the desired section at the top of the **Front Page** to jump there.

At the top is a **Visual Browser**. Touch the very top of any article and you can see small thumbnails of all the pages of **The Daily**. Just scroll through and find the page that interests you.

Tapping the button in the upper-right corner opens up **The Carousel** view, which allows you to browse **The Daily** in large **page-by-page** images.

The lower-right corner has a button for the **Control Panel**. This allows you to watch a daily video, listen to stories read aloud, or autoplay through **The Carousel** to find a story that interest you.

Tap the **Share** icon  and you can easily share a web-friendly version of the story with e-mail contacts, Facebook Friends, or on Twitter.

Popular Choices: The New York Times, The Wall Street Journal, and USA Today

Each of these three papers has a circulation of millions of readers, and each has taken a different approach to bringing you the news on the iPad.

> **NOTE:** You can always go and visit the dedicated web site for any news source. Some are optimized for the iPad, while others offer you a full web experience. Others will require registration and/or a paid subscription to view the paper's full content.

You must first follow several steps in the App Store to find, download, and install a news app on the iPad:

1. The first step is to locate your desired news app in the App Store. You may find one or more news apps in the **Featured** section.

2. Next, touch the **Categories** button at the bottom of the page and then touch the **News** icon. This takes you to all the news apps in the App Store. Browse or search for your desired news app, just as you would for any other app.

3. Once you locate the desired news app, download it as you would any other app.

NOTE: Many news apps are free. Others are free to try, but require you to buy them to continue receiving them. Still others offer limited free content, but you need to subscribe to gain access to the full content.

4. Once the app is downloaded, touch its icon to start it.

The New York Times App

The New York Times offers a slimmed-down version of the paper in its free iPad app.

At the bottom-left corner is a button labeled **Sections**. Touch the **Sections** button and all the available sections are displayed.

The caveat is that most sections have a blue dot next to them, which signifies that registration (subscription) is required to view them.

The **Top News** and **Most E-Mailed** sections are always available.

> **NOTE**: The New York Times have very recently moved to a subscription model. Touch any section with a blue dot and you will be taken to the latest pricing.

Navigating **The New York Times** app is as simple as sliding screens from right to left. You can touch a section, and then slide the screen to the left to see additional pages in that section. Touch an article again, and then slide the screen to the left again to continue reading additional pages in that article.

To go back to the **Home** page, touch the **Top News** button in the lower-left corner.

To e-mail an article, just touch the **E-mail Article** button

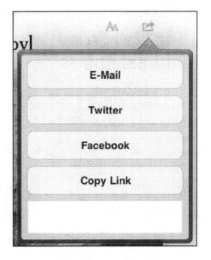

in the upper-right corner. This button is only available when you are inside an article, not on the **Home** page.

Moving Through and Enjoying Content

After you play for a while with all these various **News** apps—you will begin to realize that there is no real standard for navigating around them. This means you'll need to become familiar with each app and its own way of navigating articles, as well as how to return to the **Main** screen. Here's a short guide for generally navigating these types of apps:

Showing or Hiding Control Buttons or Captions: Tapping the screen once will usually show hidden controls or picture captions. You can tap them again to re-hide them.

Getting to the Details of an Article: Usually you tap the article or its headline to see the next screen.

Getting to the Next Page of an Article: Usually you swipe right to read more. Sometimes you swipe up.

Viewing a Video: Tap a video to start playing it. Usually, this plays the video in the same portion of the screen without expanding it.

Expanding a Video or Image Size: You can try pinching open in the video or image, and then double-tapping the video or image. Look for an **Expand** button; you may also try rotating to **Landscape** mode.

Reducing a Video or Image Size: You can try pinching closed inside the video or image. Look for a **Close** or **Minimize** button; you may also try rotating back to **Portrait** mode.

The Wall Street Journal App

The Wall Street Journal app, however, takes a different approach to delivering the news. Once the app is launched, you will be prompted to create an online account.

Once the account is created, you have access to a subset of content from *The Wall Street Journal*.

Material that is unavailable to free account users is marked with a small **Key** icon, indicating that material is locked.

If you fully subscribe to **The Wall Street Journal** app, all articles and tools become available.

Touch the **Sections** button at the bottom to see all the sections of current issue of the paper.

The **Home** page of the app shows this week's newspapers along the top; it shows **Saved Articles**, **Saved Selections**, and **My Watchlists** below this week's newspapers.

In the free version of the app, only the **Now** section of the news along the top row is viewable. All other papers from the week have the **Key** icon next to them; as mentioned earlier, this indicates they are locked and viewable only by paying subscribers.

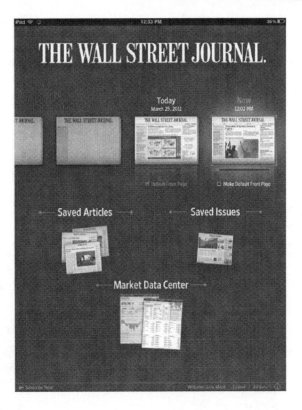

The articles that do not have a small **Key** icon next to them are available for you to read. Touch an article and it loads onto the iPad.

Similar to **The New York Times** app, **The Wall Street Journal** app lets you slide the screen to the left to continue reading the article.

You will notice that some articles have a video clip embedded where you would normally find a photograph. Touch the video and it will start playing right inside the paper—a very cool and interactive feature.

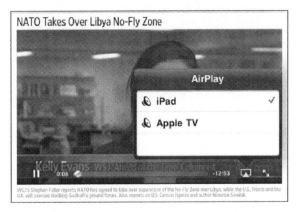

> **NOTE**: Some apps—like the **Wall Street Journal** app—are **AirPlay** compatible, so you can send your video right to your TV (see Chapter 10: "Viewing Videos, TV Shows, and More").

Adjusting Options: Font Sizes and Share, E-mail, or Save an Article

In the various apps for reading newspapers and other content, you will usually find a button or icon to change font sizes. That same button or a button near it may also allow you to share, save, or e-mail an article to a friend. Some apps allow you to share the article with a social networking site, such as Facebook or Twitter.

> **TIP:** Almost all newspaper or magazine apps will allow you to change font sizes and e-mail or otherwise share an article. Look for a button or icon that says **Tools**, **Options**, **Settings**, or something similar. In some apps, the font-size adjustment option will show **Small A** and **Large A** icons.

In the **Wall Street Journal** app, touch the **Share** button in the lower-right corner to share an article. This app gives you options to save or e-mail an article:

Email Article: This option sends this article in an e-mail.

Facebook: Share the article on your **Facebook** page.

Twitter: Post a link to the article on your **Twitter** account.

The **Wall Street Journal** app also gives you three choices for text sizes:

- **Small Text Size**
- **Standard Text Size**
- **Large Text Size**

In the **USA Today** app, the **Font Sizes** and **Share** icons are separated, as shown to the right.

Touch the **Share** icon to e-mail an article or share it with a social networking site.

Similarly, you can touch the **Small A/Large A** icons to adjust font sizes.

Doing so brings up a **Slider** control that lets you slide from smaller to larger font sizes.

Tap the screen anywhere off the **Slider** control to hide the control.

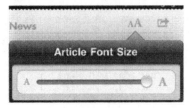

In the **New York Times** app, you have one button in the lower-right corner of the article screen that allows you to adjust **Settings**.

In this app and others, you will often see an option for **Breaking News** alerts. These will send you an **Alert** notice as soon as something important happens and gets posted to the site.

USA Today App

The **USA Today** app has a very similar look and feel to the print version of its daily newspaper. Touch the **USA Today** icon and you will be taken to the **Home** section of the paper. One of the first things you will notice is a group of rotating stories along the top of the screen.

USA TODAY

The main stories are listed along the right-hand side. You can scroll through these stories; when you find a story you wish to view, just touch the headline.

When you are in the **Article View** mode, you can adjust the font size by touching the **Font Size** icon in the upper-right corner. You can also e-mail the article by touching the **Share** icon and touching **E-mail** from the dropdown-box list.

If an article is more than one page long, you can scroll upwards to continue reading the article. Sliding the screen from right to left will advance you to the next article.

> **TIP:** If you touch the **Weather** box, you can customize it for your local weather by entering a city name or zip code.

To go to back to the **Home** screen, touch the **Newspaper** icon in the upper-left corner.

To go to another section of the paper, touch the **USA Today** icon at the top-left corner of the **Home** page, and then choose either **Money**, **Sports**, **Life**, **Tech**, or **Travel** to advance to that section of the paper. To go back, touch the same icon in the upper-left corner.

There are currently no locked articles or subscriptions required to use the **USA Today** app, but this may change at some point in the future.

Magazines on the iPad

It is no secret that both newspapers and magazines have suffered declines in readership over the last few years. The iPad offers a totally new way of reading magazines that might just give the industry the boost it needs.

> **NOTE**: Soon, all current magazine apps will be required to switch to the new (iOS 4.3) subscription model. As a consequence, in-app purchase of individual issues may remain, but subscription offers will likely be added (and some publishers may pull their apps and leave the store instead).

Pictures are incredibly clear and brilliant on magazines for the iPad. Navigation is usually easy, and stories seem to come to life—much more so than in their print counterparts. Imagine adding video and sound integration right into the magazine, and you can see how the iPad truly enhances the magazine-reading experience.

Some magazines, such as *Time Magazine*, also include links to live or frequently updated content. These might be called **Newsfeeds**, **Live Edition**, or **Updates**. Check for them in the magazine you purchase—these will give you the most up-to-date information.

> **TIP:** Make sure to check the user ratings for a magazine or other app before you purchase it. Doing so may save you some grief and/or some money!

The App Store is filled with both individual magazines that can be purchased (or limited content that can be viewed for free) and magazine readers that provide a sampling of many magazines, allowing you to subscribe to weekly or monthly delivery of a given magazine from your iPad.

More and more magazines are offering digital editions in the App Store. *Time*, *Newsweek*, *Wired*, *Outside*, *GQ* have such editions, and many more seem to be popping up each day.

One magazine with strong reviews is **Time Magazine for the iPad**, which is free to download. It includes sample content as well as in-app purchases that can be made on a per-issue basis. Most issues retailed for US $4.99 at the time of writing.

Unlike when using other media, you don't touch an article to read the magazine; instead, you simply slide from screen to screen paging through the magazine.

To make the text more viewable, **Pinch** and **Zoom** both work in many of the magazine apps.

Many magazines are for sale in the App Store, including *Popular Science*, *Men's Health*, *WIRED*, *Outside*, *GQ*, *Time*, and others. Most are priced from $2.99 to $4.99 per issue.

Navigating Around Magazines

As Figure 26–2 shows, there are various types of home pages, depending on the magazine. This example shows the **Time Magazine** app and the **Newsweek** app side-by-side.

The **Newsweek** app gives you some free content to browse, whereas the **Time Magazine** app lets you *preview* issues and then buy content.

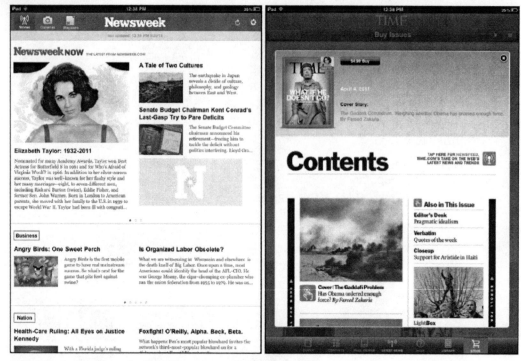

Figure 26–2. *Pages from the Time Magazine and Newsweek apps*

The Zinio Magazine App—a Sampler

One app, **Zinio**, takes a unique approach. The **Zinio** app is free in the App Store, giving you a sampling of more than 20 magazines. Each sample has a few full articles to read. Reading an article in **Zinio** requires following a few simple steps:

1. Begin by touching the cover of the magazine you wish to read.

2. Next, touch the screen and you will see a sliding bar across the bottom that shows screen shots of the articles available for free.

3. To advance pages, slide the screen from right to left or touch the image along the bottom bar to jump to that page.

4. Some magazines will be giving away full, free issues. Just touch the **Featured** button at the bottom to see what is available for the week. Touch the magazine cover to download the issue.

5. Touch the **Library** button to see those issues stored in your library for viewing.

This image is from a free issue of *Car and Driver*; it was available for download in the week we composed this chapter.

To subscribe to any of the magazines featured in **Zinio**, touch the **Shop** button at the bottom right of the screen.

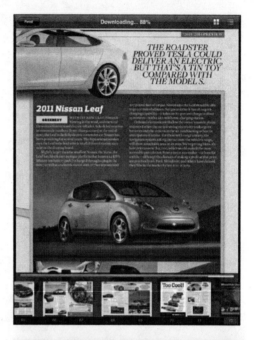

You can navigate magazines by category along the left-hand side, or you can slide the icons at the bottom to see available magazines.

There are many popular magazines from which you can choose. The categories cover everything from art to sports and much more. Prices vary, but you will often find a price for a single issue and a price for a yearly subscription.

For example, at the time of writing the newest issue of *Popular Mechanics* was $1.99 on **Zinio**, with a yearly subscription of $7.99.

Some of the subscriptions make great sense. A single issue of *Bike Magazine* (one of my favorites) was $5.99 at the time of writing, but a yearly subscription was only $9.00.

A closer look showed me that there were more than 16 cycling magazines that one could subscribe to.

Comic Books on the iPad

One genre of *new media* poised for a comeback with the advent of the iPad is the comic book. The iPad, with its relatively large high-definition screen and powerful processor, makes the pages of comic books come alive.

There were already a few different comic book apps available when we wrote this book, but none from a company more famous than Marvel Comics.

Locate the **Marvel Comics** app in the App Store. Go to **Categories** and then go to **Books**. The app is free, and comic books can be purchased from inside the app.

At the bottom of the **Home** screen are three buttons: **My Comics**, **Store**, and **Settings**. Purchases you make will be under the **My Comics** heading.

The App Store gives you the opportunity to download both free comics and individual issues for sale. Most sell for $1.99 per issue.

You can see four tabs along the top:

- **Featured**
- **New**
- **Popular**
- **Free**

Each tab takes you to a new list of comics to browse, much like the iTunes store.

Touch the **Browse** button to browse by **Genre**, **Creator**, **Storylines/Arcs**, or **Series**. Or you can type in a search to find a particular comic.

You can read a comic book in one of two ways. First, you can swipe through the pages and read one after the other. Second, you can double-tap a frame to **Zoom** in and then tap the screen to advance to the next frame in the comic strip. From there, you can just swipe from right to left to advance a frame; or, if you want to go back, swipe from left to right.

To return to the **Home** screen or see the on-screen options, just touch and hold anywhere on the screen for about a second and then release. You will see a **Settings** button in the top-right corner, a page **Thumbnail** view (just like **Photos**) at the bottom, and a **Close** button in the upper-left corner that will take you to the **Home** screen.

NOTE: The makers of this app, **ComiXology**, also make the **Comics** app that contains the Marvel comics, as well as a bunch of others, including Archie, Image, and Top Cow. You will also see DC Comics and other vendors in the App Store.

The iPad As a PDF Reader

In Chapter 12, we showed you how to open attachments in your e-mail, including PDF files. While you can read just about any type of attached file, you don't have the option of saving PDF files on the iPad for future viewing.

Fortunately, there are a few programs available that turn the iPad into a very capable PDF viewing program. One such program with multiple uses is **GoodReader**.

The **GoodReader** app is in the App Store in the **Productivity** section. At the time of publishing, this app was only US $4.99.

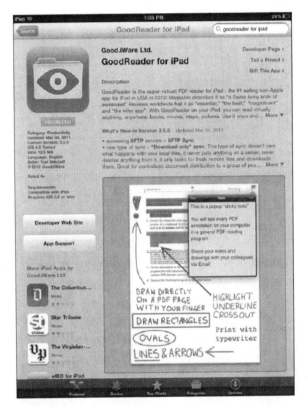

Transferring Files to Your iPad

One of the great things about the **GoodReader** app is that you can use it to wirelessly transfer large files from your Mac or PC to the iPad for viewing in the **GoodReader** app. You can also use **GoodReader** for document sharing in iTunes, as we discussed in Chapter 3: "Sync Your iPad with iTunes." Follow these steps to transfer a file with **GoodReader**:

1. Touch the small **Wi-Fi** icon at the bottom to bring up the **Wi-Fi Transfer Utility**. You are then prompted to type in either an IP address into your browser or a Bonjour address if you use the **Bonjour** service.

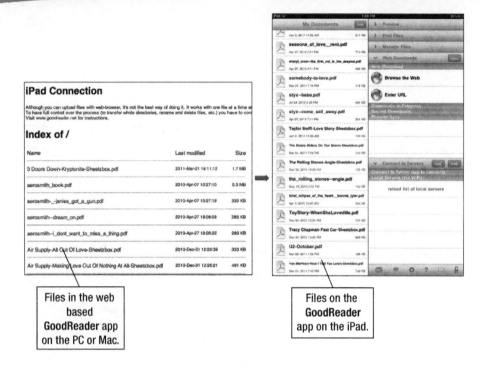

Figure 26–3. *Linking iPad and a computer to upload files*

2. Type the address shown in the pop-up window from the **GoodReader** into a web browser on your computer. Now, you can make your computer act as a server. You will see that your computer and iPad are now connected (see Figure 26–3).

3. Click the **Choose File** button inside your web browser on your computer to locate files to upload to your iPad.

4. Once you have selected the file, click **Upload Selected File** and the file will be automatically transferred to your iPad inside **GoodReader** (see Figure 26–4).

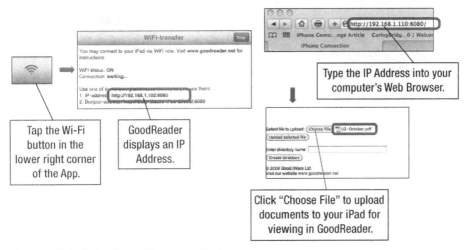

Tap the Wi-Fi button in the lower right corner of the App.

GoodReader displays an IP Address.

Type the IP Address into your computer's Web Browser.

Click "Choose File" to upload documents to your iPad for viewing in GoodReader.

Figure 26–4. *Uploading a file to your iPad*

Why is this useful? Well, for one of the authors (Gary), the iPad has become a repository for more than 300 pieces of piano sheet music. This means no more downloading PDF files, printing them out, putting them into binders, and then trying to remember which song is in which binder. Now, all his music is catalogued on the iPad. All he has to do is put the iPad on the piano, and he has access to all his music in one place.

> **NOTE:** You can also transfer **Word**, **Excel**, and **PowerPoint** files in the same manner. We believe that using the document transfer utility in iTunes might make this a bit easier (see Chapter 19: "Productivity and File Transfer" for more information).

Navigating the **GoodReader** app's PDF viewer is quite easy. Tap the center of the screen quickly to bring up the onscreen controls. You can then go to your library or touch the **Turn Page** icon to turn the page.

The easiest way to move through pages is simply to swipe from right to left on the screen.

You can also flick up or down to turn pages.

To go to another PDF file or another piece of sheet music, just touch the center of the iPad quickly and touch the **My Documents** button in the upper-left corner.

Connecting to Google Docs and Other Servers with GoodReader

You can also connect to **Google Docs** and other servers with **GoodReader**. Follow these steps to do so:

1. In the **Connect to Servers** tab on the right-hand side of the **GoodReader** screen, click the **Add** button (see Figure 26–5).

2. Select **Google Docs**. You can select from a number of different servers, including mail servers, MobileMe iDisk, Public iDisk, Dropbox, box.net, FilesAnywhere.com, MyDisk.se, WebDAV Server, and FTP Servers.

3. Enter your **Google Docs** username and password to log in.

4. Once you have made the connection, a new **Google Docs Server** icon will appear under the **Connect to Server** tab on the right-hand side of the page.

5. Tap the new **Google** tab to connect to the server. (An Internet connection is required to connect.)

6. Now you will see a list of all the documents you have stored on **Google Docs**. Tap any document and select the file type to download it. Usually PDF works well for this.

7. Once the file is downloaded, it will appear on the left-hand side of **GoodReader**. Simply touch the file to open it.

Figure 26–5. *Connecting **GoodReader** to other document servers*

Chapter 27

Maps

Mapping on your iPad, whether you have a 3G+Wi-Fi or a Wi-Fi-only model, is pretty amazing. As we explore the power of the **Maps** app in this chapter, you'll see how to find your location on the map—even if you're just using Wi-Fi. You'll learn how to change views between **Classic**, **Satellite**, **Hybrid**, and **Terrain**. You'll also see how, if you need to find out the best route, you can check out the traffic and construction view using **Maps**. If you want to find the closest pizza restaurant, golf course, or hotel to your destination, that's easy, too. And you can use Google's **Street View** right from your iPad to help you get to your destination. It is easy to add an address you have mapped to your contacts. There's also a digital compass feature that can be quite handy and is fun to play with.

Getting Started with Maps

The beauty of the iPad is that the apps are designed to work with one another. You've already seen how your **Contacts** are linked to the **Maps** app.

The **Maps** app is powered by Google Maps—the leader in mobile mapping technology. With **Maps** you can locate your position, get directions, search for things nearby, see traffic, and much more.

Simply touch the **Maps** icon to get started.

Determining Your Location (the Blue Dot)

When you start the **Maps** program, you can follow these steps to have it start at your current location:

1. Tap the **Arrow** icon at the center of the Top Nav Bar.

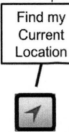

Find my Current Location

The **Blue dot** = your location

2. Maps will ask to use your current location—touch **OK** or **Don't Allow**.

   We suggest choosing **OK**, which makes it much easier to find directions from or to your current location.

NOTE: Even if you only have the Wi-Fi-equipped iPad, it will still be able to find your approximate location. The Wi-Fi iPad uses router-based locations. This is usually accurate, but if someone moved to a new state with an old router, the iPad might think you are still in that old location.

If you see a circle around the dot, then your location is approximate.

Various Map Views

The default view for **Maps** is **Classic,** a basic map with a generic background and streets shown with their names. **Maps** can also show you a **Satellite** view, or a combination of **Satellite** and **Classic** views called **Hybrid**. There's also the new **Terrain** view, which looks like a relief map. Finally, another view called **List** view appears only when you perform a search that generates a list of turn-by-turn directions. You can switch among all the views using the steps described in the next section.

Changing Your Map Views

Follow these steps to change from one map view to another:

1. Touch the turned-up edge of the map in the lower-right corner.

2. The corner of the map turns up to reveal buttons for views, **Traffic**, **Drop Pins**, and more (see Figure 27–1). Tap the view you'd like to switch to:

    ■ **Classic:** a regular map with street names (see Figure 27–2).

    ■ **Satellite**: a satellite picture with no street names (see Figure 27–1).

    ■ **Hybrid**: a combination of **Satellite** and **Classic** views; that is, a **Satellite** view with street names (Figure 27–2).

    ■ **Terrain:** a relief map showing the terrain such as mountains (see Figure 27–3).

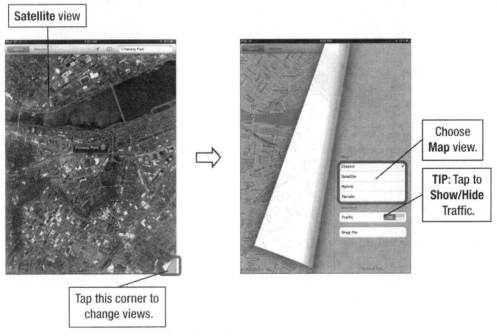

Satellite view

Tap this corner to change views.

Choose **Map** view.

TIP: Tap to **Show/Hide** Traffic.

Figure 27–1. *Satellite* *view and how to change to another map view*

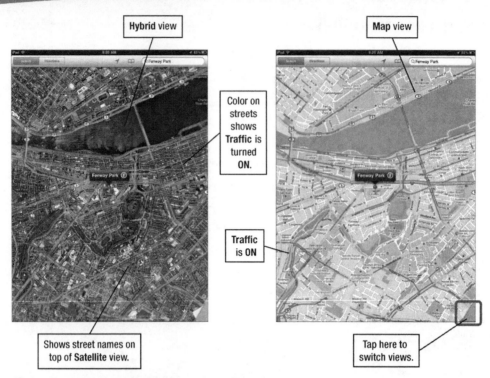

Hybrid view

Map view

Color on streets shows **Traffic** is turned **ON**.

Traffic is ON

Shows street names on top of **Satellite** view.

Tap here to switch views.

Figure 27–2. *Hybrid* and *Classic* views with traffic enabled

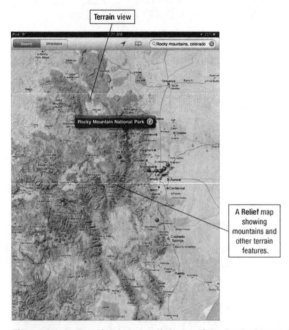

Terrain view

Rocky Mountain National Park

A **Relief** map showing mountains and other terrain features.

Figure 27–3. *Terrain* view—a relief map of the Rocky Mountains west of Denver, Colorado

As noted, **List** view is only available when your search produces multiple results (like "pizza 32174") or you've asked for directions, as shown in Figure 27–4.

List view
For **Search** results.

List view
For turn-by-turn
directions.

Tap for more details
on this item

Figure 27–4. *List views for directions and search results*

Checking Traffic

Your **Maps** program can do much more than tell you how to get somewhere; it can also check traffic along the way. This feature is supported only in the US for now. Follow these steps to check local traffic:

1. Tap the lower-right corner of the map to see the options.

2. Turn **Traffic** to **ON**.

TIP: You can also "turn" the page like a book to get to this view. The animation is just like the one in the **iBooks** app.

Tap here to show **Traffic.**

If there is a traffic situation on a highway, you usually see yellow lights instead of green ones; and sometimes, the yellow lights might be flashing to alert you to traffic delays.

You may even see **Construction Worker** icons to indicate construction zones.

Maps uses the following colors on major streets and highways to indicate the speed that traffic is moving:

Green = 50 MPH or more

Yellow = 25 – 50 MPH

Red = Less than 25 MPH

Gray (or no color) = No traffic data is currently available

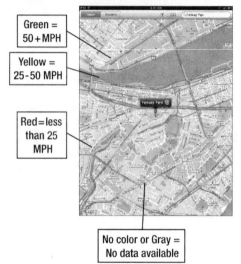

Green = 50+MPH

Yellow = 25-50 MPH

Red=less than 25 MPH

No color or Gray = No data available

Search for Anything

Because **Maps** is tied to Google Maps, you can search for and find just about anything: a specific address, a type of business, a city, or other point of interest, as shown in Figure 27–5. Follow these steps to find a location:

1. Touch the **Search** bar in the top-right corner of the screen.

2. Type in your address, a point of interest, or a town and state you would like to map on your iPad.

Google Maps Search Tips

You cam enter just about anything in the search:

- First Name, Last Name, or Company Name (to match your Contacts)
- 123 Main Street, City (some or all of a street address)
- Orlando Airport (find an airport)
- Plumber, painter, or roofer (any part of a business name or trade)
- Golf courses + city (find local golf courses)
- Movies + city or ZIP/postal code (find local movie theaters)
- Pizza 32174 (search for local pizza restaurants in ZIP Code 32174)
- 95014 (ZIP Code for Apple Computer headquarters in California, USA)
- Apress Publishing

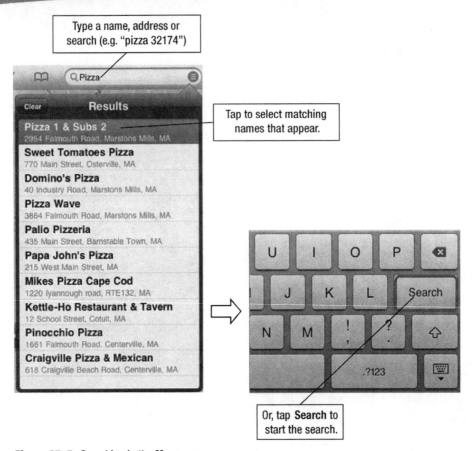

Figure 27–5. *Searching in the Maps app*

To use numbers, tap the **123** key on the keyboard. For letters, touch the **ABC** key to switch back to a letter-based keyboard.

Mapping Options

Now that your address is on the **Maps** screen, there are a number of options available to you.

Touch the **Blue Information** icon next to the address to see some of these options.

If you have mapped a particular place or one of your contacts, you'll see the details as shown in Figure 27–6. You can also get directions, share a location, or add as a bookmark.

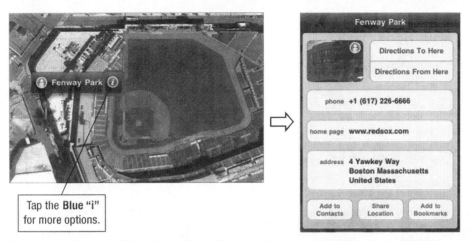

Tap the **Blue "i"** for more options.

Figure 27–6. *Touch the **Blue Information** button to see the mapped location or contact details.*

If you have mapped an address or point of interest, you'll see a different screen when you tap the **Blue Information** button. You'll find a small street view image and buttons to get **Directions**, **Add to Contacts**, **Share Location,** or **Add to Bookmarks,** as shown to the right.

Working with Bookmarks

Bookmarks work in **Maps** very much as they do in the **Safari** web browser app. A bookmark simply sets a record of places you've visited or mapped and want to remember in the future. It is always easier to look at a bookmark than to perform a new search.

Adding a New Bookmark

Bookmarking a location is a great way to make it easy to find that place again. Follow these steps to do so:

1. Map a location, as shown in Figure 27–7.

2. Touch the **Blue Information** icon next to the address.

3. Touch **Add to Bookmarks**.

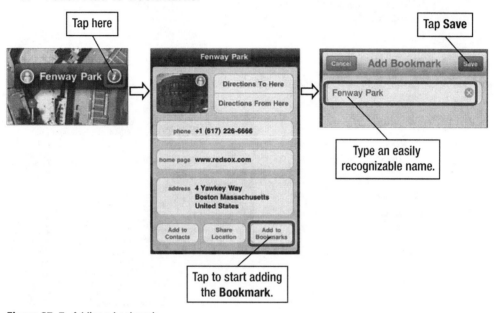

Figure 27–7. *Adding a bookmark*

4. Edit the bookmark name to make it short and recognizable—in this case, we edited the address to simply say *Fenway Park*.

5. When you are done, touch **Save** in the top-right corner.

TIP: You can search for bookmark names just as you search for names in your Contacts.

Accessing and Editing Your Bookmarks

To view your bookmarks, follow these steps:

1. Tap the **Bookmarks** icon next to the **Search** window in the top row.

2. Tap any bookmark to immediately jump to it.

3. Tap the **Edit** button at the top of the bookmarks to edit or delete bookmarks:

    a. To reorder the bookmarks, touch and drag the right edge of each bookmark up or down.

    b. To edit the name of a bookmark, touch it and retype the name. After editing the name, touch the **Bookmarks** button in the top left to get back to your list of bookmarks.

    c. To delete a bookmark, swipe to the left or right on the bookmark and tap the **Delete** button.

4. Tap the **Done** button when you are finished editing your bookmarks.

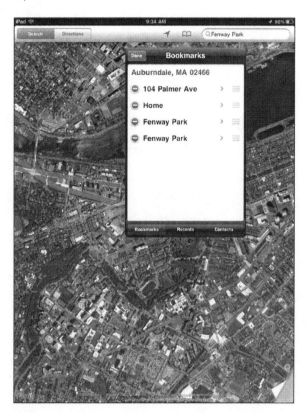

Add a Mapped Location to Contacts

It is easy to add a location you mapped to your contact list:

1. Map an address.

2. Tap the **Blue Information** button.

3. Tap **Add to Contacts**.

4. Tap either **Create a New Contact** or **Add to Existing Contact**.

5. If you choose **Add to Existing Contact**, you then scroll through or search your contacts and select a name. The address will automatically be added to that contact.

Searching for Things (Stores, Restaurants, Hotels, Movies, Anything) Around Your Location

Follow these steps to search for things near your current location:

1. Map a location on the map or use the **Blue Dot** icon for your current location.

2. Tap the **Search** window. Let's say we want to search for the closest pizza restaurants. Typing "pizza" maps all the local pizza restaurants.

3. Notice that each mapped location may have a **Street View** icon on the left and the **Blue Information** icon on the right.

Tap for Street View

Tap for more info.

Tap for **Search** List.

Tap to see more information.

4. If you want to zoom in or out, you can pinch the screen open or closed, or you can double-tap the screen.

5. Just as with any mapped location, when you touch the **Blue Information** icon, you can see all the details, such as the pizza restaurant's phone number, address, and web site.

6. If you want directions to the restaurant, just touch **Directions to Here** and a route is instantly calculated.

Tap for **Directions**.

Tap to visit **Home** page.

NOTE: If you touch the **Home Page** link, you will exit **Maps** and **Safari** will start. You will then need to restart **Maps** again when you're done.

Zooming In and Out

You can zoom in and out in the familiar way by double-tapping and pinching. To zoom in by double-tapping, just double-tap on the screen as you would on a web page or picture.

Dropping a Pin

Let's say you're looking at the map, and you find something you'd like to set either as a bookmark or as a destination.

In this example, we are zooming in and looking around greater Boston. We stumble upon Fenway Park and decide it would be great to add it to our bookmarks, so we drop a pin on it, as shown in Figure 27–8:

1. Map a location or move the map to a location where you'd like to drop the pin.

2. Tap the lower-right corner of the map.

3. Tap **Drop Pin**.

4. Now, drag the pin around the map by touching and holding it. In this example, we move it right onto Fenway Park.

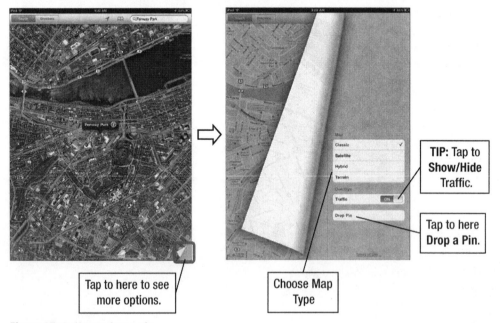

Figure 27–8. *How to drop a pin*

TIP: How can you find the street address of any location on the map?

When you **Drop a Pin**, Google Maps will show you the actual street address. This is very handy if you find a location by looking at **Satellite**, **Hybrid** or **Terrain** view, but need to get the actual street address.

Dropping a pin is also a great way to keep track of where you parked—very helpful in an unfamiliar location (especially with the iPad 3G).

Using Street View

Google's **Street View** (Figure 27–9) is really fun in **Maps** on the iPad. Google has been hard at work photographing just about every address across the United States and elsewhere. The pictures are then fed into its database and that's what shows up when you want to see a picture of your destination or waypoint.

NOTE: Google's **Street View** is just making its way beyond the US borders. Several major cities in various parts of the world are now mapped.

If there is a street view available, you will see a small icon to the left of the address or bookmark on the map—a small **Orange Person** icon.

In this example, Gary wants to check the street view of his Red Sox' shrine—Fenway Park:

1. In this case, to map the address, we tapped the work address under Fenway Park on our **Contacts** list. We could have mapped it by typing an address in the search window, by searching for a type of business, or by touching the address in the **Contacts** app.

2. To the left of the name is the **Street View** icon.

3. We tap the icon to immediately shift to a street view of the address.

4. What is very cool is that we can navigate around the screen in a 360-degree rotation by swiping left, right, or even up or down—this lets us look at the places next to and across the street from our destination.

To return to the map, we just touch the lower-right corner of the screen.

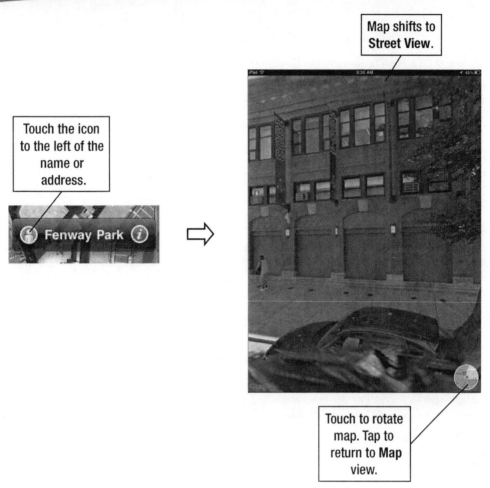

Touch the icon to the left of the name or address.

Map shifts to Street View.

Touch to rotate map. Tap to return to **Map** view.

Figure 27–9. *Using Google's Street View*

Getting Directions

One of the most useful functions of the **Maps** program is that we can easily find directions to or from any location. Let's say we want to use our current location and get directions from Gloria's store to Fenway Park in Boston.

Tap the Current Location Button First

To find directions to or from your current location, you don't have to waste time typing your current address—just locate yourself by tapping the current location button in the center of the Top Information Bar. You may need to repeat this step a few times until you see the **Blue Dot** icon on the screen.

Now you can do one of two things:

- Tap the **Directions** button at the left end of the top information bar.

- Or, you can touch the **Blue Information** icon as discussed previously, and then select **Directions to Here** (see Figure 27–10). Unless you specify otherwise, **Maps** will then calculate directions from your current location to the destination.

Figure 27–10. *Choose **Directions to Here** and **Maps** will route your trip.*

Choose Start or End location

We can follow these steps to choose a start or end location for a given route:

1. If the destination is in our **Bookmarks**, we can touch the **Bookmarks** icon.

2. Next, we choose the location that is bookmarked.

3. We could tap **Bookmarks**, **Recents**, or **Contacts** to find our destination.

4. In this case, we tap **Bookmarks**.

5. Finally, we tap **Fenway Park**.

> **NOTE:** As soon as you touch the **Directions From Here** button, your recent searches will be automatically displayed, as shown in Figure 27–10. You can also touch the **Destination** box
>
>
>
> and type in a destination.

6. After we select Fenway Park from **Bookmarks**, the routing screen takes us to an overview screen.

7. A **Green Pushpin** icon is dropped at the start location, and a **Red Pushpin** icon is dropped at the end location— in this case, Fenway Park.

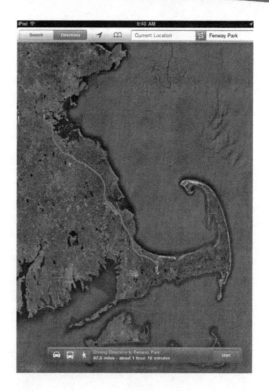

Looking at the Route

Before you start the trip, you will see a **Start** button in the lower-right corner of the screen. Tap the **Start** button and the routing directions begin. The **Start** button changes to **Arrow** buttons that allow you to move between the steps in the trip.

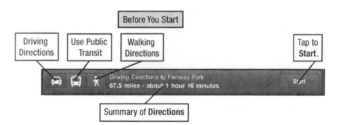

As Figure 27–11 shows, you can look at the route as either a path on the map or as a list.

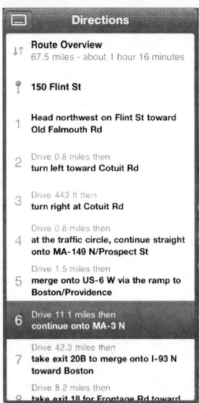

Figure 27–11. *Two ways of viewing directions*

You can move the screen with your finger to look at the route, or just touch the **Arrow**

icons ⬛ at the bottom to show the route in step-by-step snapshots.

You can also touch the **List** ⬛ button, which will show detailed step-by-step directions.

Switching between Driving, Transit, and Walking Directions

Before you start your directions, you can choose whether you are driving, using public transportation, or walking by tapping the icons on the left side of the blue bar at the bottom of the directions screen, as shown in Figure 27–12.

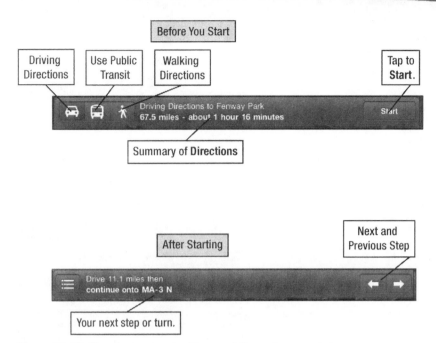

Figure 27–12. *Choosing your mode of transportation and your next steps*

Reversing the Route

To reverse the route, touch the **Reverse** [S] button, which is at the top between the **Start** and **End** fields. This can be useful if you're not great at reversing directions on your own or if your route uses lots of one-way streets.

Maps Options

Currently, the only setting that affects your **Maps** app is Location Services, which is critical for determining your current location. Follow these steps to adjust these settings:

1. Touch the **Settings** icon.

2. Now find the **Location Services** tab and touch it. Move the **Location Services** switch to the **ON** position.

3. Make sure the switch next to **Maps** is also set to the **ON** position, so **Maps** can approximate your location.

> **NOTE:** Keeping the **Location Services** switch set to **ON** will reduce battery life by a small amount. If you never use the **Maps** app or don't care about your location, set it to **OFF** to save your battery life.

Using the Digital Compass

The iPad has a very cool *digital compass* feature built in. This can be helpful when you need to literally get your bearings and figure out which way is north.

Calibrating and Using the Digital Compass

Before you can use the digital compass, you need to calibrate it. You should only need to calibrate the compass the first time you use it. Follow these steps to do so:

1. Start **Maps** as you normally would.

2. Tap the **Current Location** arrow twice—it changes from to .

3. You'll see a small digital compass appear on the screen, as shown in Figure 27–13.

4. The first time you use digital compass, the calibration symbol appears on the screen. ∞

5. Move your iPad in a "figure 8" pattern, as shown on the screen.

> **NOTE:** The iPad may ask you to move away from any source of interference while you go through the calibration process.

6. Hold your iPad level to the ground. If you calibrated it successfully, the compass will rotate and point north.

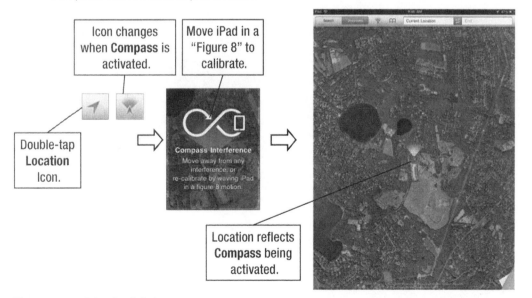

Figure 27–13. *Using the digital compass*

Chapter 28

Troubleshooting

The iPad is usually highly reliable. Occasionally, like your computer or any complicated electronic device, you might have to reset the device or troubleshoot a problem. In this chapter, we give you some useful tools to help get your iPad back up and running as quickly as possible. We start with some basic quick troubleshooting and move into more in-depth problems and resolutions later in the "Advanced Troubleshooting" section.

We also cover some other odds and ends related to your iPad and give you a list of resources where you can find more help with your iPad.

Basic Troubleshooting

We will begin by covering a few basic tips and tricks to get your iPad back up and running.

What to Do If the iPad Stops Responding

Sometimes, your iPad won't respond to your touch—it freezes in the middle of a program. If this happens, try these steps in order to see if the iPad will start responding (see Figure 28–1).

1. Press the **Home** button to see if that exits to the **Home** screen.

2. If one particular app is causing trouble, try double-clicking the **Home** button to open the **App Switcher** bar. Then press and hold *any* icon

in the **App Switcher** bar until they all shake and a red circle with a minus sign appears in the upper-left corner of the icon. Tap the **Red Circle** icon to close the app.

3. If the iPad continues to be unresponsive, try pressing the **Sleep/Power** key until you see **Slide to Power Off**. Then press and hold the **Home** button until you return to the **Home** screen—this should quit the program.

4. Make sure your iPad isn't running out of power. Try plugging it in or attaching it to your computer (if it's plugged in) and see if it will start to respond.

5. If holding the **Home** button doesn't work, you will need to try to turn off your iPad by pressing and holding the **Power/Sleep** button for three to four seconds. Next, slide the **Slide to Power Off** slider at the top of the screen. If you cannot power off the iPad, then see the following instructions about how to reset the iPad.

6. After you power off the iPad, wait a minute or so, and then turn on the iPad by holding the same **Power** button for a few seconds.

7. You should see the Apple logo appear on the screen. Wait until the iPad starts up, and you should be able to access your programs and data.

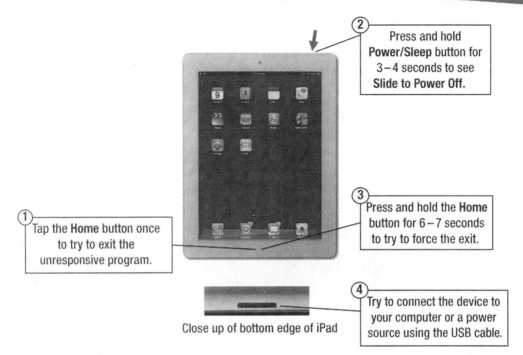

② Press and hold
Power/Sleep button for
3 – 4 seconds to see
Slide to Power Off.

③ Press and hold the **Home**
button for 6 – 7 seconds
to try to force the exit.

① Tap the **Home** button once
to try to exit the
unresponsive program.

④ Try to connect the device to
your computer or a power
source using the USB cable.

Close up of bottom edge of iPad

Figure 28–1. *Basic troubleshooting steps*

If these steps don't work, you will need to reset your iPad.

How to Hard-Reset Your iPad

Resetting your iPad is your last option for dealing with an unresponsive iPad. It is
perfectly safe, and it usually fixes many types of problems (see Figure 28–2).

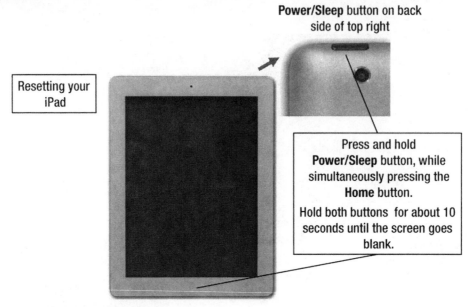

Power/Sleep button on back side of top right

Resetting your iPad

Press and hold **Power/Sleep** button, while simultaneously pressing the **Home** button.

Hold both buttons for about 10 seconds until the screen goes blank.

Figure 28–2. *Resetting your iPad*

Follow these steps to hard-reset your iPad:

1. Using two hands, press and hold the **Home** button and the **Power/Sleep** button at the same time.

2. Keep both buttons held down for about eight to ten seconds. You will see the **Slide to Power Off** slider. Ignore that and keep holding both buttons until the screen goes blank.

3. After a few more seconds, you should see the Apple logo appear. When you see the logo, just release the buttons, and your iPad will be reset.

How to Soft-Reset Your iPad

There are various things you can reset in the **Settings** app, from the **Home** screen layout, to the network settings, to all data on your device. Follow these steps to perform a soft-reset:

1. Tap the **Settings** icon.

2. Tap **General** in the left column.

3. Tap **Reset** at the bottom of the right column.

4. Tap **Reset All Settings** to reset network, keyboard, home screen layout, and location warnings. Tap **Reset** to confirm from the pop-up window.

5. Tap **Erase All Content and Settings** to erase absolutely everything from your iPad. Then tap **Erase** to confirm this action in the pop-up window.

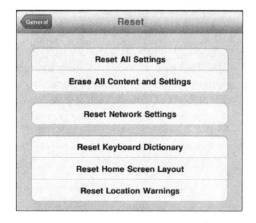

6. Tap **Reset Network Settings** to clear out all your Wi-Fi (and 3G) network settings.

7. Tap **Reset Keyboard Dictionary** to reset the spelling dictionary.

8. Tap **Reset Home Screen Layout** to return to the factory layout; this is the state of the device when you first received your iPad.

9. Tap **Reset Location Warnings** to reset the warning messages you receive about allowing apps to use your current location.

> **NOTE:** If you still cannot get your iPad working, try using the steps described in the "Device Firmware Update (DFU) Mode" section later in this chapter.

No Sound in Music or Video

There are few things more frustrating than hoping to listen to music or watch a video, only to find that no sound comes out of the iPad. Usually, there is an easy fix for this problem:

1. Check the volume by using the **Volume Up** key in the upper-right edge of your iPad. You might have accidentally lowered the volume all the way or muted it.

2. If you are using wired headphones from the headphone jack, unplug your headphones and then put them back in. Sometimes, the headset jack isn't connected well.

3. If you are using wireless Bluetooth headphones or a Bluetooth stereo setup, try these steps:

    a. Check the volume setting (if available on the headphones or stereo).

    b. Check to make sure the Bluetooth device is connected. Go into the **Settings** icon. Tap **General** in the left column and **Bluetooth** in the right column. Make sure you see your device listed and that its status is **Connected**. If it is not connected, then touch it and follow the directions to pair it with the iPad.

> **NOTE:** Sometimes you may actually be connected to a Bluetooth device and not know it. If you are connected to a Bluetooth Stereo device, no sound will come out of the actual iPad.

4. Make sure the song or video is not in **Pause** mode.

5. Bring up the music or video controls by double-clicking the **Home** button, then swipe to the right to see the music or video controls at the bottom (as shown in the image to the right). Once you bring up the controls, verify that the song is not paused and that the volume is not turned down all the way, as shown here.

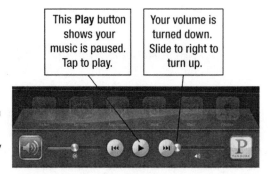

This **Play** button shows your music is paused. Tap to play.

Your volume is turned down. Slide to right to turn up.

6. Check the **Settings** icon to see if you (or someone else) has set the **Volume Limit** on the iPad:

    a. Touch the **Settings** icon.

    b. Tap **iPod** in the left column.

    c. See if the **Volume Limit** is **ON**. Touch **Volume Limit** to check the setting level. If the limit is unlocked, simply slide the volume to a higher level. If it is locked, you need to unlock it first by tapping the **Unlock Volume Limit** button and entering the four-digit code (see Figure 28–3).

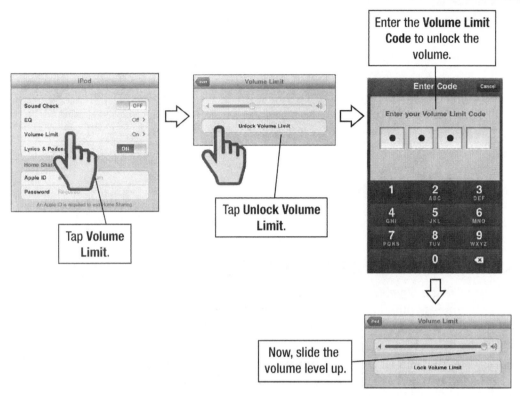

Enter the **Volume Limit Code** to unlock the volume.

Tap **Unlock Volume Limit**.

Tap **Volume Limit**.

Now, slide the volume level up.

Figure 28–3. *Checking the volume limit in* ***Settings***

If none of these steps help, check out the "Additional Troubleshooting and Help Resources" section later in this chapter. If that doesn't help, then try to restore your iPad from a backup file using the steps described in the "Restore Your iPad from a Backup" section in this chapter. Finally, if that does not help, then contact the store or business that sold you your iPad for assistance.

If You Can't Make Purchases from iTunes or the App Store

You have this new, cool device. So you go to the iTunes Store or the App Store, but you receive an error message or you find you are not allowed to make a purchase. Follow these steps to try to fix the problem:

1. Both stores require an active internet connection. Make sure you have either a Wi-Fi connection or a cellular data connection. Check out Chapter 4: "Wi-Fi and 3G Connections" for assistance.

2. Verify that you have an active iTunes account. We show you how to set up a new iTunes account in the "Create an iTunes Account" section of Chapter 26: "Bonus iTunes User Guide."

NOTE: If you are traveling to a country where iPads are not yet sold, then you may not have an on-device App Store or **iTunes** app. If this is the case, you will need to purchase items using **iTunes** on your computer and sync them to your iPad.

Advanced Troubleshooting

Now we will delve into some more advanced troubleshooting steps.

Device Firmware Update (DFU) Mode

When none of the other steps described previously get your iPad working again, as a last resort you can put the iPad into **Device Firmware Update** (**DFU**) mode and restore your data using iTunes. These steps are courtesy of the iPhone, iPad, and iPod touch Blog (www.tipb.com).

Getting your iPad into **DFU** mode can take a few tries; it's quite tricky. After you do this, you will need to use **iTunes** to restore your data from a recent backup of your iPad:

1. Plug your iPad into your Mac or Windows PC and make sure **iTunes** is running.

2. Hold down both the **Power/Sleep** button (on top of your device) and the **Home** button (on the front underneath the screen).

3. Keep them both held down from about 10 seconds. (If you see the Apple logo, you've held them too long, and you will need to start again.)

4. Let go of the **Power/Sleep** button but keep holding the **Home** button for about five seconds. (If you see the **Plus into iTunes** screen, then you held it too long and will need to start again.)

5. If the screen stays black, that's it! Your iPad should now be in **DFU** mode.

6. Now, **iTunes** should say that it has detected your device in **Recovery** mode and that it needs to be restored.

7. Follow the instructions to restore your device. We show you more details about this in the "Restore your iPad Operating System" section later in this chapter.

Physical iPad Damage (Apple Care vs. Alternatives)

If you accidentally damage your iPad—perhaps you get it wet, drop it, break the screen, dent the back, or otherwise damage it—you may think that the Apple Care Extended Warranty will cover the damage. This is not the case.

> **CAUTION:** The Apple Care Extended Warranty does not cover accidental damage (e.g., water, broken screen, drop, dent, and so on).

There are several alternative warranties available. If you purchase your iPad from a major retailer such as Best Buy, you can buy an extended warranty that does cover accidental damage. However, these retailer warranties can be quite expensive. We found one warranty that was more affordable and still covers accidental damage. This warranty is from SquareTrade (www.squaretrade.com); at the time of publishing, it cost about $95 USD for two years of coverage.

If you don't want to buy an extended warranty, then you can do a web search to try to find an iPad repair store. There are several options online, and they change frequently. Do some research on the web and find one that looks reputable and has some solid customer reviews.

> **TIP:** Call the iPad repair store and ask in detail about their policies regarding your specific damage and who pays for the shipping charges. Also ask what happens if they cannot repair the iPad.

Re-register with Your iTunes Account

Every iPad is associated with or tied to an iTunes account. That association allows you to purchase iTunes music and videos, as well as apps from your iPad. It is also that association that allows you to play music from your **iTunes** account on your computer on your iPad.

Sometimes, your iPad might "lose" its registration and connection with the **iTunes** service. Usually, this is a very simple fix. Just connect your iPad to the computer via the USB cable, and the **iTunes** app will walk you through the process of re-associating your iPad with your **iTunes** account. We show the detailed steps of how to do this in Chapter 1: "Getting Started."

If you have trouble registering your iPad through iTunes, then Apple provides an online resource that you can get to from your computer or iPad web browser.

You can access the site at this URL:

https://register.apple.com/cgi-bin/WebObjects/GlobaliReg.woa

You should see a screen similar to the one shown in Figure 28–4.

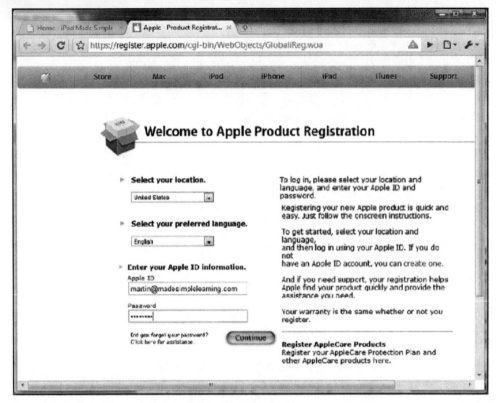

Figure 28–4. *The online registration site from Apple's login page*

Follow these steps once you access Apple's online registration site:

1. Complete the information, enter your Apple ID and password, and click **Continue**.

2. Select whether you are registering **One product** or **More than one product**. In this case, we chose **One product** (see Figure 28–5).

Figure 28–5. *Step 1 on Apple's online registration site*

3. Now, choose the category, product line, and product. In this case, we chose **iPad** category, **iPad** product line, and **iPad Wi-Fi**. This moved us through Steps 2–4 at once (see Figure 28–6).

Figure 28–6. *Steps 2–4 on Apple's online registration site*

4. Now you need to enter your iPad serial number and other information about how you will use the iPad.

TIP: To locate the serial number, connect your iPad to your computer and load the **iTunes** app. Click your iPad in the Left Nav Bar and click **Summary** in the Top Nav Bar. The serial number is at the top of the **Summary** screen (see Figure 28–7).

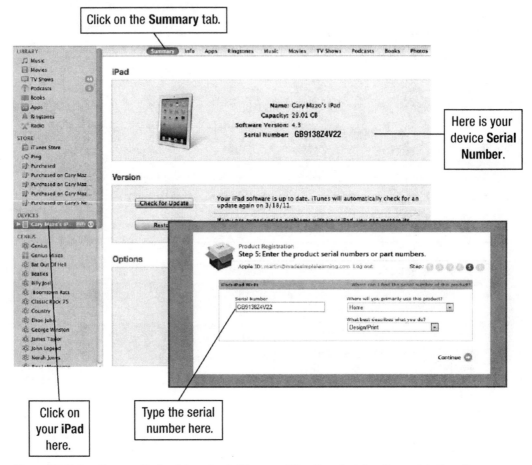

Click on the **Summary** tab.

Here is your device **Serial Number**.

Click on your **iPad** here.

Type the serial number here.

Figure 28–7. *Locating your iPad serial number in* **iTunes** *and Step 5 on Apple's online registration site*

5. Now click **Continue** and you should have successfully registered your iPad.

iPad Does Not Show Up in iTunes

Occasionally, when you connect your iPad to your PC or Mac, your iPad may not be recognized in the **iTunes** screen.

In the first screen—and this is what you should see—your iPad will be listed under DEVICES (see Figure 28–8). In the second screenshot, you will notice that there is no device shown, even though your iPad is connected to the computer.

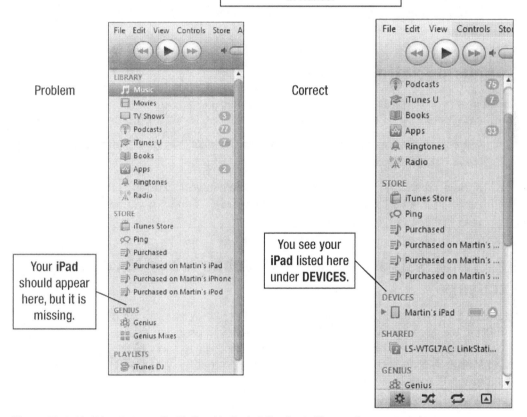

After connecting your iPad to your computer, you should see it listed in iTunes.

Problem

Correct

Your **iPad** should appear here, but it is missing.

You see your **iPad** listed here under **DEVICES**.

Figure 28–8. *Verifying that your iPad is listed in the Left Nav Bar in **iTunes** when connected to your computer*

Follow these steps if you don't see your device listed:

1. Check the battery charge of the iPad by looking at the battery level in the top right of the **Home** screen. If you have let the battery run too far down, **iTunes** won't see it until the level of the battery rises a bit.

2. If the battery is charged, try connecting the iPad to a different USB port on the computer. Sometimes, if you have always used one USB port for the iPad and switch it to another port, the computer won't see it.

3. If this still does not fix the problem, try disconnecting the iPad and restarting the computer. Then, reconnect the iPad to the USB port.

4. If this still does not work, download the latest update to **iTunes** or completely uninstall and re-install **iTunes** on the computer again. If you choose this option, just make sure that you back up all the information in **iTunes**.

5. We have included detailed steps showing you how to upgrade to the latest version of **iTunes** in the "Upgrade iTunes" section of Chapter 26: "Bonus iTunes User Guide."

Synchronization Problems

Sometimes, you might be having errors when synchronizing your iPad with your computer (PC or Mac). Follow these steps to try to resolve such problems:

1. Begin by following all the steps we outlined in the "iPad Does Not Show Up in iTunes" section.

2. If the iPad still will not sync, but you can see it in your **iTunes** Left Nav Bar, go back to Chapter 3: "Sync Your iPad with iTunes" and check your sync settings very carefully.

Resolving Issues with Apple's Mobile Me or Microsoft Exchange

Microsoft Exchange is a push email and content server usually set up by an enterprise administrator. **Mobile Me** is Apple's own wireless sync program that you can set up (for a fee). This program will keep your information wirelessly in sync. However, if you are using **Mobile Me** or Exchange to sync personal information, you won't be able to sync this through **iTunes**.

On your iPad, go to your **Settings** icon and tap **Mail, Contacts, and Calendars** in the left column.

If **Mobile Me** or Exchange is set up, it will show up in your list of **Accounts** at the top of the right column. If you don't see one of these on the list, then you are not using them to sync to your iPad.

If you do see one of these items listed, touch the account and then uncheck any categories or items that you would prefer to sync through **iTunes**.

Now, when you go back into **iTunes**, those categories should show up as Microsoft sync options.

> **NOTE:** If you do uncheck or deselect **Calendars** or **Contacts** in the Mobile Me or Exchange accounts, you won't be able to see that information anymore on the iPad until you set up the synchronization from the computer via **iTunes** (see Chapter 3: "Sync Your iPad with iTunes").

Reinstalling the iPad Operating System (With or Without a Restore)

Sometimes, you might have to do a clean install of your iPad operating system to get your iPad back up and running smoothly.

> **Tip**: This process is virtually identical to the process to update your iPad with a new version of the operating system.

During this process you will have three choices:

1. If you want to get the iPad back to its normal state with all your data, you will have to use the **iTunes** Restore function.

2. If you plan on getting a clean start and tying the iPad to an **iTunes** account, you would use the Setup a new iPad function at the end of this process.

3. If you plan on giving away or selling your iPad, then you would simply eject the iPad from **iTunes** at the end of this process (before doing a restore or new setup).

> **CAUTION:** This "restore process" will wipe your iPad totally clean. You will need to resynchronize and re-install all of your apps and re-enter your account information, such as the details of your email accounts. This process could take 30 minutes or longer, depending on how much information you have synced to your iPad.

Follow these steps to re-install the iPad operating system software with the option of restoring data to your iPad from a previous backup:

1. Connect your iPad to your computer and load up **iTunes**.

2. Click your **iPad** in the DEVICES category in the Left Nav Bar.

3. Click **Summary** in the Top Nav Bar.

4. Now you will see the iPad's **Information** screen. Click the **Restore** button in the middle screen (see Figure 28–9).

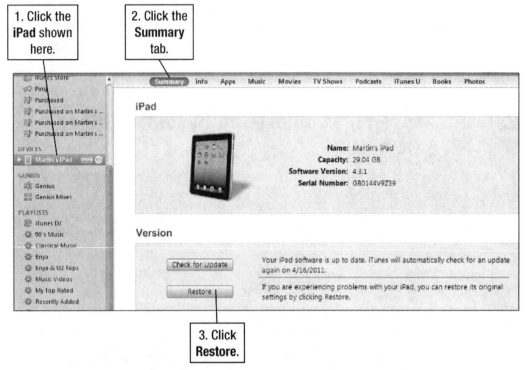

Figure 28–9. *Connecting your iPad and clicking the* **Restore** *button in* **iTunes** *in the* **Summary** *screen*

5. Now you may be asked if you want to back up your iPad. Click **Backup** just to be safe.

6. You may then be are warned that all data will be erased. Click **Restore** to continue (see Figure 28–10).

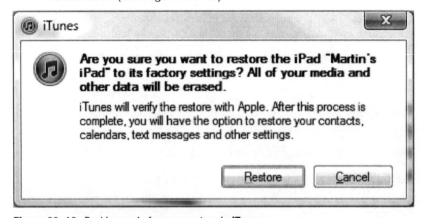

Figure 28–10. *Backing-up before you restore in* **iTunes**

7. You will now see an **iPad Software Update** screen. Click **Next ▶** to continue.

8. Next, you will see the **Software License Agreement** screen. Click **Agree** to continue and start the process.

9. Now, **iTunes** will download the latest iPad software, back up and sync your iPad, and then re-install the iPad software completely. This process will erase all data and restore your iPad to its original "clean" state. You will see status messages at the top of **iTunes** similar to the one shown in Figure 28–11).

Figure 28–11. *The software update/restore process: the status window at top of **iTunes***

10. After your iPad is backed up and synced, its screen will go black. The Apple logo will appear, and you will see a status bar under the logo. Finally, a small pop-up window will appear in **iTunes** to tell you the update process is complete. Click **OK** to be brought to the **Set Up your iPad** screen (see Figure 28–13):

    a. If you want to keep your iPad clean (i.e., without any of your personal data), then select the top option, **Setup as a new iPad**. You might want to use this option if you are setting up this iPad for someone else (you will need the person's Apple ID and password).

    b. If you are giving away or selling your iPad, simply click the **Eject** icon next to the iPad and you're done (see Figure 28–12).

Figure 28–12. *Ejecting the iPad if you are giving it away or selling it*

    c. Select **Restore from the backup of:** and verify the pulldown option is set to the correct device.

11. Finally, click **Continue** (see Figure 28–13).

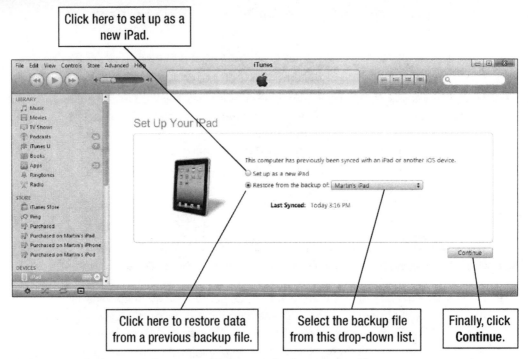

Click here to set up as a new iPad.

Click here to restore data from a previous backup file.

Select the backup file from this drop-down list.

Finally, click **Continue**.

Figure 28–13. *Setting up a device as a new iPad or restoring from a backup file*

12. If you chose to restore, then after a little while you will see a **Restore in Progress** screen on your iPad and a status window in **iTunes** that says, "Restoring iPad from backup..." This screen also shows a time estimate.

13. Next, you will see a little pop-up window saying, "The settings for your iPad have been restored." In a few seconds, you will see your iPad appear in the Left Nav Bar under DEVICES in **iTunes**:

   a. If you sync your information with **iTunes**, all data will be synced now.

   b. If you use **MobileMe**, Exchange, or another sync process, you will probably have to re-enter passwords on your iPad to get those sync processes back up and running.

Additional Troubleshooting and Help Resources

Sometimes you may encounter a particular issue or question that you cannot find an answer to in this book. In the sections that follow, we provide some good resources that you can access from the iPad itself and from your computer's web browser. The iPad on-device user guide is easy to navigate and may provide some quick information that you seek. The Apple Knowledgebase is helpful if you are facing a troubleshooting problem that is proving especially difficult to resolve. The iPhone/iPad-related web blogs and forums are also good places to locate answers and even ask unique questions you might be facing.

The On-Device iPad User Guide

Open up your **Safari** web browser to view the online user guide for your iPad:

1. Tap the **Bookmarks** button next to where you enter a web site address.

2. Select **iPad User Guide**.

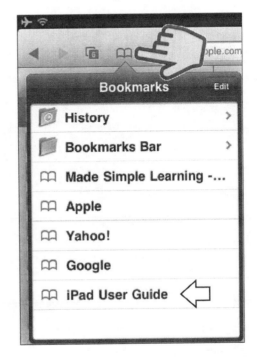

If you don't see that bookmark, then type this into the **Safari** address bar on your iPad:

`help.apple.com/ipad`

> **TIP:** To view the manual in PDF format from your computer, go to
> `http://help.apple.com/ipad/4/interface/`.

Once you get to the guide on your iPad, you should see a screen similar to the one shown in Figure 28–14.

The nice thing is that you already know how to navigate around the guide. Tap any topic in the left column to reveal that topic in the right column.

Read the topic or touch another link from the right column to learn more.

Tap the button at the top of the right column to back out one level.

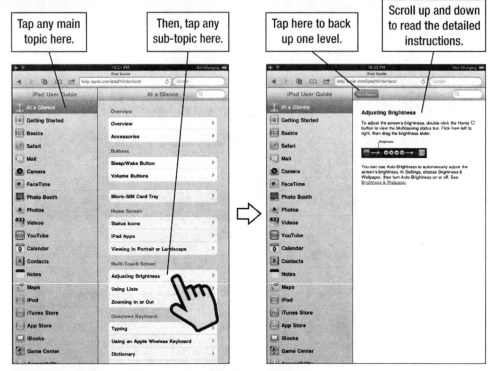

Figure 28–14. *Using the iPad manual from* **Safari** *on your iPad*

Check out the Apple Knowledgebase for Helpful Articles

On your iPad or computer's web browser, go to this web page:

http://www.apple.com/support/ipad/

Next, click a topic in the Left Nav Bar (see Figure 25–15).

Figure 28-15. *The Apple Knowledgebase web site for the iPad*

iPad-Related Blogs

One of the great things about owning an iPad is that you immediately become a part of a worldwide camaraderie of iPad owners.

Many iPad owners would be classified as "enthusiasts" and are part of any number of iPad user groups. These user groups, along with various forums and web sites, serve as a great resource for iPad users.

Many of these resources are available right from your iPad, and others are web sites that you might want to visit on your computer.

Sometimes you might want to connect with other iPad enthusiasts, ask a technical question, or keep up with the latest and greatest rumors. The blogs are a great place to do that.

Here are a few popular iPad (and iPhone or iPod touch) blogs:

- www.tipb.com
- www.iphonefreak.com
- www.gizmodo.com (iPad section)

> **TIP:** Before you post a new question on any of these blogs, please do a search on the blog to make sure your question has not already been asked and answered. Also, make sure you are posting your question on the right section (e.g., iPad) of the blog. Otherwise, you may incur the wrath of the community for not doing your homework first!

Also, do a web search for "iPad blogs" or "iPad news and reviews" to locate more blogs.

iPad 2's Soul Mate: iTunes...

Your iPad 2 is inextricably tied to **iTunes**—the e-commerce center of Apple. **iTunes** is not only where you buy music, videos, and apps, but it's also where you organize all of the great content you can use on your iPad 2. Use the new Ping social networking feature in **iTunes** to keep up to date with your favorite artists' and friends' taste in music. You can even use Ping to meet up with friends and buy tickets for upcoming concerts. Learn how to purchase exciting new content—and even how to find it for free. Learn something new with iTunes U or find give your music library a fresh new feel using the Genius mix. We even help you learn how to save money with the **iTunes** Home Sharing feature, which now works on your iPad, too!

Your iTunes User Guide

In this chapter, we will show you how to do virtually everything you might want to do with **iTunes**. We cover **iTunes** version 10 with the cool social networking feature called Ping (see Figure 29–1). We will help you get **iTunes** installed and updated, then take you on a guided tour. We will also describe all the great ways to organize and view your music and videos, as well as how to prepare for putting them on your iPad.

At the time of publishing, the latest version of the **iTunes** app was 10.2.1.1. When you read this, your version may be slightly higher, but the vast majority of the content will be similar.

Besides Ping, we will cover iTunes DJ, the Genius feature, and the money-saving Home Sharing feature. We will also show you how to import music CDs, DVDs, PDFs, and E-Book files, as well as how to get album artwork for all your music. We will even teach you about authorizing computers to share content using **iTunes**. Finally, we will provide some useful troubleshooting tips for **iTunes**.

> **NOTE:** If you are looking to set up your iPad for the first time, please check out Chapter 1: "Getting Started." If you are trying to sync your computer to your iPad using **iTunes**, please check out Chapter 3: "Sync Your iPad with iTunes."

If you need to install the **iTunes** software on your computer, please jump to the "Downloading and Installing iTunes Software" section later in this chapter. If you already have the **iTunes** software installed, then go to the "Updating iTunes Software" section to make sure you have the latest version.

Figure 29–1. *The* ***iTunes*** *screen showing the Ping feature, which is new in version 10.0*

Seeing If iTunes Is Already Installed

If you are a Windows PC user, then begin by looking for the **iTunes** icon on your desktop and double-clicking it. If you don't find it, then click the **Windows** logo or the **Start** button in the lower-left corner and type "iTunes." If you don't see the **iTunes** app appear in the search results, then you might not have **iTunes** installed. If that's the case, then follow the steps in the next section, "Downloading and Installing iTunes Software." If **iTunes** is installed, you will see it appear—just click its icon to start it and skip to the "iTunes Guided Tour" section.

If you are a Mac user, **iTunes** is installed by default on your computer. Check to see if the **iTunes** icon is on your desktop or Desktop Dock. If you see it, then double-click it and skip to the "iTunes Guided Tour" section. If you do not see the **iTunes** icon, then start the **Finder**, click **Applications**, and look for **iTunes** in the alphabetical list of apps.

Downloading and Installing iTunes Software

If you have never installed **iTunes** before on your computer, you can download the software directly from the Apple web site by following these steps:

1. Open a web browser on your computer, such as Apple's **Safari**, Microsoft's **Internet Explorer**, Google's **Chrome**, or Mozilla's **Firefox**.

2. Type the web address `www.itunes.com/download` into the top of your browser, and then press **Enter**. This web address works for both Windows PC and Mac users.

3. Next, select the software that matches your computer's operating system, assuming that you're given a choice.

4. If you are given a choice to run or save the software, choose **Run** so that the installation will start automatically once the download is complete.

5. If the installation does not start right away, then locate the file you downloaded (Windows users should look for a file with a name like `iTunes.exe`, and Mac users should look for something like `iTunes_Install.dmg`). Double-click the install file to start the installation.

6. Follow the on-screen instructions to install **iTunes**.

Updating iTunes Software

It's easy to update your **iTunes** software because the program checks its version status by default and will automatically let you know if a newer version is available for download. After you start **iTunes**, if a newer version of **iTunes** is available, you will see a pop-up window. As noted previously, the version number will be higher than the 10.0 shown in Figure 29–2.

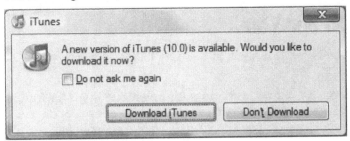

Figure 29–2. *The Apple **Software Update** screen*

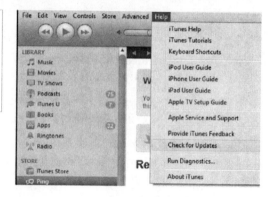

TIP: If you want to be sure you are using the latest version, then select **Help ➤ Check for Updates** from the **iTunes** menu.

After you click **Download iTunes**, you will be taken to the **iTunes** web site. Select the appropriate software for your computer and click the **Download Now** button.

You can also get to this download page by going to **www.iTunes.com** and clicking the **Download iTunes** button.

Follow the on-screen instructions to install the updated **iTunes** on your computer.

TIP: To determine your computer operating system on Windows, click the **Start** button or **Windows** logo in the lower-left corner. Next, right-click **Computer** and select **Properties**. On the Mac, click the **Apple** logo in the upper-left corner and select **About This Mac** from the menu.

What iTunes Can Do For You

The **iTunes** software on your computer allows you to do many things, including the following:

- **Buy apps, music, videos, TV shows, and more (or download them for free):** You can purchase or download free apps, music, movies, TV shows, podcasts, iBooks, PDF files, and audiobooks. You can even download educational content from iTunes U, a special area in iTunes devoted to educational content from universities and other institutions of learning. The best part: Much of this content is free!

- **Organize your media:** You can use the various views and automatic playlists, and set up your own custom playlists.

- **Participate in Social Networking:** Using the new Ping feature in **iTunes**, you can follow your favorite artists and learn what music they are talking about. You can also share your favorite music with your friends, and you can even see who is going to the concert next weekend.

- **Sync your music, videos, contacts, and more to your iPad:** You want to be able to take all your great music and videos with you on your iPod—use **iTunes** to sync your content and go (see Chapter 3: "Sync Your iPad with iTunes").

- **Play your music, videos, and audio content:** The **iTunes** app serves as a great media player for your computer, enabling you to play all your media, including music, videos, TV shows, and podcasts.

- **Back up and restore your iPad:** This option lets you back up and restore your iPad data.

Common Questions About iTunes

What follows is a list of frequently asked questions about **iTunes** for the iPad, followed by short answers that address the core concern or issue raised by the question.

*Is the **iTunes** software on my computer the same as the **iTunes** app on my iPad?*

The **iTunes** software on your computer does the same job as a number of apps on your iPad. You need the following apps on your iPad to do all that **iTunes** can do on your computer: **iPod**, **Videos**, **iTunes**, **iBooks**, and the **App Store**.

I have an iPhone or another iPod; can I share music and videos with my new iPad?

Yes! You can definitely keep listening to all your music and sharing all your videos on all of your Apple devices, including your new iPad.

*Can I use my existing **iTunes** software and account?*

Yes! You can use the same **iTunes** software already installed on your computer, as well as your existing iTunes account, to set up your iPad.

Can I use my purchased apps from my iPhone or iPod touch?

Yes, but with limitations. iPhone and iPod touch apps will work; however, iPhone/iPod touch-specific apps will show up in a small window in the middle of the screen and typically will not rotate as you tilt your iPad on its side (**Landscape** mode). You can press a small **2X** button to expand the app to fill the screen, but it will look a little grainy.

iTunes Guided Tour

After you have the latest version of **iTunes** installed (which was version 10 at the time of writing this book), you're ready to take a quick guided tour of the **iTunes** interface on your computer. The nice thing is that the interface looks very much the same on PCs and Macs.

When you first start **iTunes**, you will see the main window with controls at the top to play your music or videos (see Figure 29–3). You will also see the Left Navigation (Nav) Bar, which lets you select from your library, the iTunes Store, your iPad (when connected), shared media, Genius playlists, and your own playlists. The Top Nav Bar adjusts, depending on what you have selected in the Left Nav Bar. Also, the center main window adjusts, depending on selections from the Left and Top Nav Bars, as well as what is inside the main window itself.

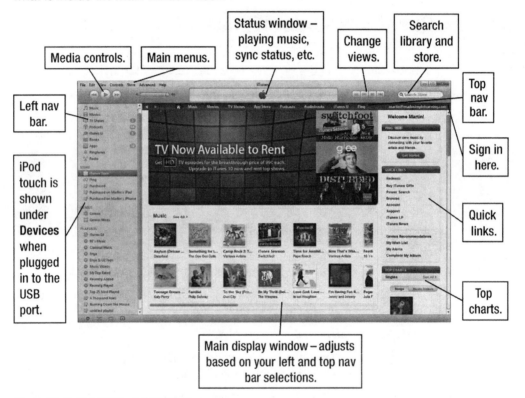

Figure 29–3. *The **iTunes** main window*

Starting from the top left of the main window, you can see the following menus, controls, windows, and other visual elements:

- **Main menus:** These are located just above the media controls, and they provide access to all the actions **iTunes** can perform through a logical and convenient set of menus. While a lot of the functionality in these menus is available in buttons and toolbars, these menus are where you'll find what you're looking for in a logical list.

- **Media controls:** These buttons let you play, pause, or skip to the next song or video, as well as adjust the volume.

- **Status window:** Located in the top-middle section of **iTunes**, this window shows you the status of what is currently going on (sync status, whether you're playing a song/video, or any other related messages).

- **View adjustment buttons:** These buttons allow you to adjust views between **List**, **Grid**, or **Cover Flow** views. (These are only active when you are in your own media libraries.)

- **Search box:** This box allows you to search your library or the iTunes Store for a particular song, video, TV show, or anything else based on the text you enter.

- **Sign-in link:** Located just below the **Search** box in the upper-right corner, this button allows you to sign into the iTunes Store or create a new Apple ID. Notice that the figure to the right shows **martin@madesimplelearning. com** instead of **Sign in**. This is because Martin has already signed in with his **Apple ID**.

- **Top Nav Bar:** This set of buttons under the status window will vary, depending what you have selected in the Left Nav Bar. Sometimes there are very few buttons; other times, they will stretch across the screen. Click any of these buttons to change the content shown in the main window.

- **Left Nav Bar:** This bar allows you to view your library (e.g., music, videos, TV shows, and podcasts), the iTunes Store and Ping, your purchased content, any currently connected devices (your iPad, iPod, iPhone, and so on), shared libraries, Genius mixes, and your own playlists.

- **Main window:** This is where you can see all the content based on your selections in the Left and Top Nav Bars. For example, if you selected your iPad in the Left Nav Bar and **Apps** in the Top Nav Bar, you would see a screen similar to the one shown in Figure 29–3.

Apple Video Tutorials for iTunes

In addition to all the information provided in this book, you can find some good video tutorials from Apple to help you start using the **iTunes** app. You can check these tutorials out from within the **iTunes** app by clicking the **Help** menu and selecting **iTunes Tutorials**.

Using Ping in iTunes

As we mentioned, Ping is the new social networking feature focused on music; it is available in **iTunes** version 10 and higher. It allows you to follow your favorite artists, as well as those of your friends. The feature also lets you share your likes and dislikes with people, find out about local concerts, and more.

Getting Started and Creating Your Profile

To get started, click **Ping** in the **Store** section in the Left Nav Bar of **iTunes**.

> **NOTE:** If you have already registered and enabled Ping, but are not signed into your iTunes account with your Apple ID, then you will see a message to **Turn On Ping** in the main window. Just click the link and log in to see your Ping account.

Now click the **Turn On Ping** button ⬤ Turn On Ping ⬤ in the main window. You will need to sign into the iTunes service again to get started with Ping. Next, you will need to create your profile for Ping. Enter your first and last name, enter your gender, add an optional picture, indicate where you live, give a brief bio, and finally select up to three music genres you like.

Click **Continue** to select how music is displayed on your profile. The default is **Automatically display all music I like, rate, review, or purchase**. However, you can adjust this to meet your preferences. Click **Continue**.

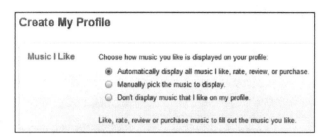

Finally, you can choose to allow people to follow you with or without approval (the default) or not allow them to follow you at all. Select your choice, and then click **Done** to finish setting up your Ping profile.

After you complete your setup, you will see a page similar to this one, with recommendations based on music you have purchased in the iTunes Store. To start following artists, click the **Follow** buttons at the bottom or type a search to follow a friend or artist.

You can also click the **Invite** button to invite your friends to join Ping.

If you want, you can invite your friends by email by clicking the **Invite** button and entering their email addresses.

Following Your Favorite Artists

To find artists to follow, type their names in the **Search** window of the **Ping** screen. When you see the artists appear, click the **Follow** button. We searched for and found The Rolling Stones, but note that this is not the rock group—this is a person who has taken the band's name.

CAUTION: Make sure this says **Artist**, not **People**, if you want to follow an artist.

CAUTION: Some people have (or have used) the same name as artists, so make sure to click the **Show Artists** link to the right of the search window. Otherwise, you might end up following Peter Gabriel the beer-drinking German who enjoys alternative, electronic, and rock, instead of the artist Peter Gabriel.

Following Your Friends and Other People

Use the same Find feature to locate and follow your friends and others. In the next example, Martin has decided to follow Gary Mazo, so Martin searches for Gary's name. After clicking **Follow**, a pop-up window is displayed, telling Martin that Ping will have to send a name, photo, and email address to Gary, so he can approve the request. Notice what Gary will see on his iPad when Martin requests to follow him (see Figure 29–4).

Click **Request** here.

The person you want to Follow sees this request on his or her iPod touch, iPad, or iPhone.

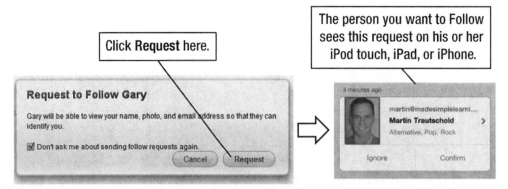

Figure 29–4. *A Follow request from the Ping feature in **iTunes** as it appears on a mobile device*

Recent Activity Feed

The heart of Ping is all the updates you receive from the artists and people you are following. The default view when you start Ping is shown to the right; however, if you are in some other view, then you need to click the **Recent Activity** link in the **PING** box in the upper-right corner.

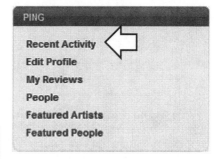

> **NOTE:** Everything you or your family purchases on the same Home Share account will show up as purchased on your Ping account. Hey, at least you can blame that lame ballad on your spouse or the gangsta rap on your teenage child.

The **Recent Activity** view will show all the recent activity for you and your followed friends and artists (see Figure 29–5). It's very similar to your Wall in Facebook. It allows you to provide comments, *like* what you see posted, and read comments from other followers. Have fun, let your opinions be heard, and get in on the conversation!

If the friends that you follow allow you to see their purchases, you can comment on those as well. Of course, the **iTunes** app makes it easy for you to purchase albums or songs that your friends purchase with the handy **Buy** button next to the listed item.

Figure 29–5. *Ping's* **Recent Activity** *page gives you the ability to add a comment or say that you like something.*

Navigating Back and Forth in iTunes

Sometimes you want to simply get back to the page you just left when you clicked a link. It might not be obvious, but there are little **Triangle** icons in the upper-left corner of the main **iTunes** window that allow you to navigate back and forth through pages in Ping and other parts of the **iTunes** app.

Concerts: Find Out and Share with Friends

When you click an artist's page in **Ping**, you can see if they have any upcoming concerts scheduled by looking for the **Concerts** box in the lower-right corner of the page. The accompanying image shows upcoming concerts for U2. Click the **See All** link in the Title Bar of the box to see all details and tell people whether you're going to any of these concerts.

After clicking the **See All** link, you will see details of all concerts. You can click the **I'm Going** button to show others that you're attending and the **Tickets** button to try purchasing tickets. If you click **I'm Going**, you can add a comment about your post for your friends to see—for example, maybe you'll tell them what seat you have, so they can find you.

Seeing What Artists Like in Ping

If you go to some artists' pages in Ping, you can see what music they like in the upper-right corner. In this image, we can see that U2 likes Elbow, TV on the Radio, The National, and more. Click any of the album covers to listen to and even purchase songs from the album.

Using the Ping Dropdown Menu for a Song

Next to all your songs in most of the **iTunes** views, you will see a little **Ping** dropdown menu. Click the **Ping** menu to **Like**, **Post**, or **Show Artist Profile**. You can also view the iTunes store to see more songs by that artist, album, or even other songs in the same genre, as shown to the right.

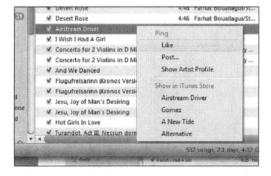

Viewing Ping in the Right Column

As you move between items in your music library, you will soon notice that Ping will show up at the top of the right column. You can say if you **Like** the song or **Post** a comment on the song from this column.

Ping Mobile

You can access Ping right from the **iTunes** app on your iPad. To see Ping, start your **iTunes** app on your iPad, and then tap the **Ping** soft key in the bottom row.

Notice that you can switch between **Activity**, **People**, and **My Profile** by tapping those buttons along the top.

The image to the right shows the **Activity** tab.

Changing Views in iTunes

There are many ways to view your music, videos, and other media in **iTunes** on your computer. Getting familiar with these views on your computer will also help you understand your iPad because your iPad has many of the same views. There are four customizable views in **iTunes**: **Song List**, **Album List**, **Grid**, and **Cover Flow**.

> **NOTE:** Album List view is new in **iTunes** version 10.0. It is a nice view because it groups your songs by album and shows you the album art in the **Album** column.

Song List View

Click the leftmost of the view icons to see the **Song List** view (see Figure 29–6). You can re-sort the list by any column by clicking that column's heading. For example, to sort by name, you would click the **Name** column heading. To reverse the sort order, just click the same column heading again. **Song List** view can be especially helpful for finding all the songs by a particular artist or on a particular album.

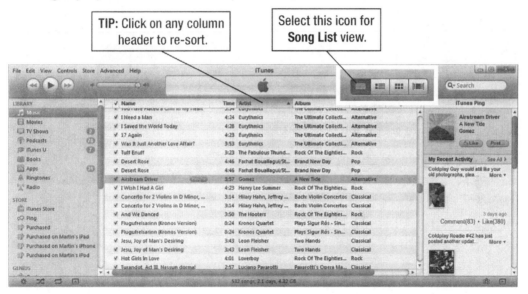

Figure 29–6. *Song List* view

Album List View

As we mentioned earlier, this is a new view in **iTunes** version 10.0. Click the second view icon to see **Album List** view (see Figure 29–7). You can re-sort the list by any column by clicking that column's heading. For example, you can sort by name by clicking the **Name** column heading. To reverse the sort order, just click the same column heading again. The **Album List** view can be especially helpful for finding all the songs by a particular artist or on a particular album.

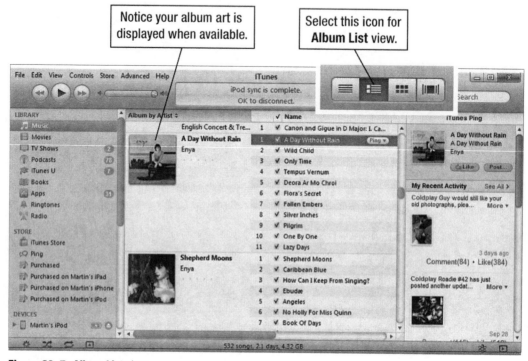

Figure 29–7. **Album List** view

Grid View

Click the third icon to show **Grid** view (see Figure 29–8). This is a very graphical view, and it is helpful if you want to quickly find album or poster art.

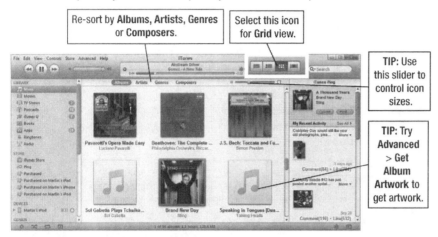

Figure 29–8. *Grid view*

Cover Flow View

Click the rightmost icon to see **Cover Flow** view (see Figure 29–9). This is a fun view because it is visual, and you can quickly flip through the images using the slider bar to browse through the album covers. Like **Grid** and **Album List** views, this view provides an easy way to find an album when you know what the cover looks like.

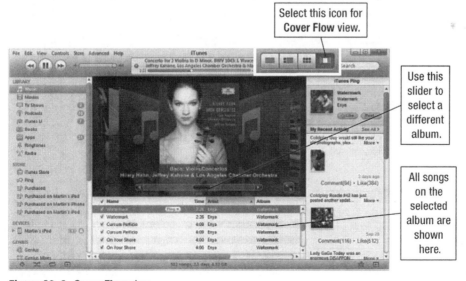

Figure 29–9. *Cover Flow view*

Playing Songs, Videos, and More

If you are new to **iTunes**, these basic pointers can help you get around the app (see Figure 29–10):

- **Playing a song, video, or podcast:** Double-click an item to start playing it.

- **Controlling the song or video:** Use the **Rewind**, **Pause**, and **Fast Forward** buttons, in addition to the **Volume** slider in the upper-left corner, to control the playback.

- **Moving to a different part of the song or video:** Just click the **Diamond** icon in the slider bar under the song name at the top of the window and drag it left or right as desired.

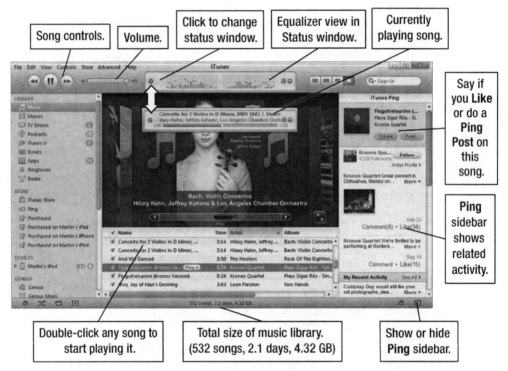

Figure 29–10. *Playing your songs, videos, and more in* ***iTunes***

The iTunes Visualizer

There is a very interesting visual feature in **iTunes** that is quite entertaining. It looks like a screen saver that reacts to the music you are playing. There are two versions: the iTunes Classic Visualizer and the new iTunes Visualizer. To see a visualizer, from the menu select **View ➤ Show Visualizer** (alternatively, on Windows you can press **Ctrl+T**, and on the Mac you can press **Command+T**). To change between the Classic and New

Visualizer versions, from the menu select **View ➤ iTunes Visualizer** or **iTunes Classic Visualizer**. Figure 29–11 shows examples of the two visualizers.

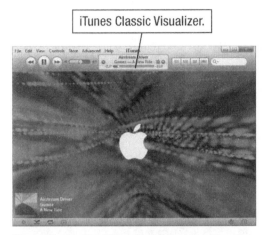
iTunes Classic Visualizer.

New iTunes Visualizer.

Figure 29–11. *The iTunes Classic and New Visualizers*

Using the iTunes Equalizer

You can enhance the sound of your music by matching the built-in equalizer to the type of music you are listening to. To view the iTunes Equalizer, from the menu select **View ➤ Show Equalizer** (alternatively, on Windows you can press **Ctrl+Shift+2**, and on the Mac you can press **Command+J** and check **Equalizer**). You can choose from over 20 preset settings, including **Classical**, **Rock**, **Pop**, and **R&B**, and you can modify the settings to fit your individual tastes.

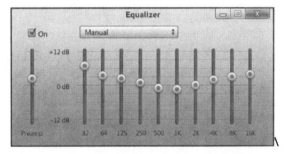

iTunes Mini Player

Sometimes you want to keep **iTunes** playing on your computer, but you don't want it taking so much screen real estate. Luckily, **iTunes** has a built-in miniature version called the Mini Player.

To show the Mini Player, from the menu,

select **View ➤ Switch to Mini Player**
(alternatively, on Windows you can press
Ctrl+M, and on the Mac you can press
Shift+Command+M). To switch back to
regular view, press the same shortcut
key.

Drag the lower-right corner to see the
Status window.

iTunes DJ

If you want to listen to your music in a new
order without running out of songs, you
should try out the iTunes DJ feature. To
start it, click **iTunes DJ** at the top of your
Playlists section in the Left Nav Bar.

iTunes DJ will play a continuous mix of
music based on your entire music library
or a single playlist. To adjust the source,
click the dropdown menu next to **Source**
at the bottom of the screen.

You can see the list of songs that the DJ is about to play in the **iTunes DJ** main window.
To change the order in which the songs will be played, you can simply drag and drop a
song higher or lower in the list (see Figure 29–12).

Figure 29–12. *iTunes DJ and changing the order of songs to be played*

You can also add songs to the iTunes DJ list or play them next by right-clicking the song in your library and selecting **Add to iTunes DJ** or **Play Next in iTunes DJ**.

Apple Remote App

One fun thing to do is to use the **Remote** app on your iPad or other Apple device. To get started, open the App Store on your iPad and do a search for "Remote." The **Remote** app from Apple is free, so be careful not to purchase one of the paid apps that appear. Make sure you are downloading the **Remote** app made by Apple.

After you get the app installed on your iPad, tap it to start it. Next, you need to connect the app to **iTunes** on your computer by entering a four-digit passcode:

1. On your iPad, tap the **Remote** app to start it (see Figure 29–13).

2. If you are starting the **Remote** app for the first time, then tap **Add an iTunes Library**. If you have already added Home Sharing or another library, then you will need to tap the **Settings** (**Gear** icon) in the upper-right corner of the **Remote** app. Next, tap **Add an iTunes Library** and you should see a four-digit passcode.

3. On your computer, start **iTunes**. In the **Devices** section, your iPad should now be displayed with the **Remote** icon next to it. Click it to get started.

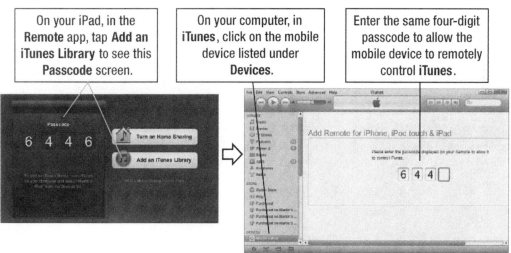

Figure 29–13. *Connecting your mobile device (iPad, iPhone, or iPod touch) to* **iTunes** *using Apple's* **Remote** *app*

With your iPad (or other Apple device) connected, you can now remotely control **iTunes**. For example, you can play, pause, skip a song, or even change playlists—virtually anything you can do related to playing music when sitting at your computer!

AirPlay: Wirelessly Stream Your iTunes Music Around Your House

Apple has had the **AirTunes** app for a while. This app allows you to stream your iTunes music to specially designed wireless speakers throughout your house. Recently, Apple changed the app's name to **AirPlay**, and it has expanded the number of manufacturers that build this new standard into their speaker, dock, and stereo systems. **AirPlay** even transmits information from **iTunes** about the currently playing song, including the song name, artist name, time played, and time remaining. **AirPlay** will work audio-only with **Airport Express** and also stream video with **Apple TV**.

To make sure the next speakers, dock, or stereo you purchase is compatible, look for language such as "Apple AirPlay Compatible" in the product description or packaging. Many manufacturers have products with this new standard already, including iHome, Sony, Denon, Marantz, B&W, and JBL.

TIP: You can use the **Apple Remote** app (described in the "Apple Remote App" section of this chapter) to control **iTunes** when you have music streaming through your wireless speakers—even when you are nowhere near your computer! This is a great feature to help you enjoy and control your music throughout your house with your iPad.

Using iTunes Search

If your library does not already contain hundreds or thousands of songs and other media, it will soon! How do you quickly find that special song you are in the mood for right now? The quickest way to locate an individual song or video is to use the search field in the upper-right corner of the **iTunes** app.

First, in the Left Nav Bar, click the type of content you wish to find. For example, click **Music** to find songs, **Podcasts** to find podcasts, **Apps** to find apps, and so on.

After selecting the category of media in the Left Nav Bar, click in the **Search** field and start typing any part of the name of a song, artist, composer, album, podcast, TV show, app, or audiobook.

You will notice that, as soon as you type the first letter, **iTunes** will narrow your search results (shown in the main window) by that letter. In this case, **iTunes** is finding all matching songs/videos that have the letter (or series of letters) that match any part of the artist, album, composer, or song/video name.

In the example shown in Figure 29–14, we clicked **Podcasts** and typed "Marketplace" into the **Search** window to find the podcasts of the NPR radio show, *Marketplace* (see Figure 29–14).

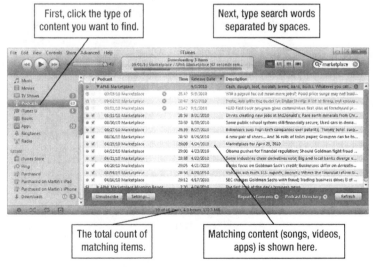

Figure 29–14. *Searching for media in **iTunes***

TIP: If you want to narrow your search by a specific category such as artist, composer, song name, or title, then click the little **Magnifying Glass** icon in the **Search** field to see a dropdown list. Click any item in the dropdown list to narrow the search using that item.

Tap the magnifying glass to select a specific search category.

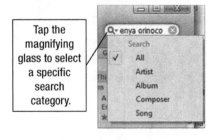

Ways to Search iTunes

You can type any combination of words to match the item you are trying to find. For example, assume you know that the song you want has the word "love" in the title, and the song is by U2. You could just type in those two words, separated by a space—"Love U2"—and you will immediately be shown all matching items (see Figure 29–15). In this case, only two songs match, so you can quickly double-click the song you want to listen to. Search is also contextual. This means that if you are in your music library, the search function will search for music; if you are in your apps library, the search will look only for apps. In every search, both your own library and the **App Store** (if you have a live Internet connection) will be searched.

Mix and match artist names and song names.

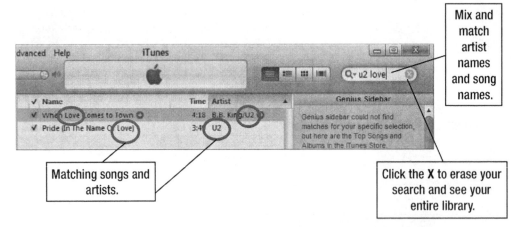

Matching songs and artists.

Click the X to erase your search and see your entire library.

Figure 29–15. *Use two or more words separated by spaces to quickly narrow the search results.*

When you are done searching, click the little **X** in the circle next to the search words to clear out the search and see all your songs and videos again.

Creating a New Playlist

You may be used to listening to all the music on a particular album, but you will soon find the benefits of creating your own custom playlists. These are lists of particular songs that you group together. You can create a normal playlist or a smart playlist.

You can group playlists however you like, as in this example:

- Workout music
- Favorite U2 songs
- Traveling music

> **TIP:** You can create playlists in your iTunes library or directly on your iPad. To create a playlist for your computer, click any existing playlist under the **Playlists** heading in the Left Nav Bar. To create a new playlist directly on your iPad, click your iPad, listed under **Devices** in the Left Nav Bar. Depending on what you have highlighted in the Left Nav Bar, your new playlist will be created either on the computer or on the iPad.

Creating a Normal Playlist

A normal playlist is one in which you can drag and drop songs manually onto your new playlist.

Once you have decided whether to create your playlist on your iPad or on your computer, you are ready to get started. Follow these steps to create a new normal playlist:

First, click the plus sign (+) to start creating a new play list.

Then, type your playlist name.

1. Press **Ctrl+N** (or **Command+N** on the Mac) to select a new playlist from the **File** menu. Or, you can simply click the **New Playlist** button in the lower-left corner of **iTunes**, as shown to the right.

2. Type the name of your playlist in the entry that appears in the Left Nav Bar.

> **TIP:** If you want to create a new playlist with songs very similar to another playlist, then right-click the playlist and select **Duplicate**.

After creating and naming your playlist, you are ready to add songs to your new playlist (see Figure 29–16). To select from your entire library, click **Music** on the **Library** tab.

To select songs from an existing playlist, click that playlist.

Scroll up to view your music library.

Or, click down here to view songs from a specific playlist.

Figure 29–16. *Locating songs to add to a playlist*

Adding Individual Songs

You can easily add individual songs to your new playlist:

1. Click any individual song to select it, and then keep holding down the mouse button as you drag the song over to your new playlist.

2. To put the song into the playlist, drop it by letting go of the mouse button when the song name you are dragging is over the name of the playlist.

Click and drag any song over to your playlist.

Drop the song on your playlist.

Adding Multiple Songs or Videos (Not in a List)

You can add multiple items in two simple steps:

1. To add selected songs that are not listed sequentially, press and hold the **Ctrl** key (Windows) or the **Command** key (Mac), and then click the individual songs/videos. Once you are done selecting songs/videos, release the **Ctrl/Command** key.

2. After all the songs/videos are selected (highlighted), click one of the selected songs, and then drag and drop the entire selected group onto your playlist.

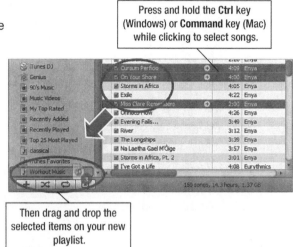

Press and hold the **Ctrl** key (Windows) or **Command** key (Mac) while clicking to select songs.

Then drag and drop the selected items on your new playlist.

Adding a List of Songs or Videos

You can also add a list of songs/videos using this pair of steps:

1. To add a list of songs/videos to a playlist all at once, press and hold the **Shift** key. While pressing the **Shift** key, click the top item in the list and then click the bottom item. Both items clicked, as well as all the items between them, will be selected.

2. After all the songs/videos are selected (highlighted), click one of the selected songs, and drag and drop the entire selected group onto your simple playlist.

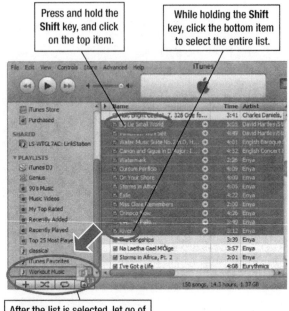

Press and hold the **Shift** key, and click on the top item.

While holding the **Shift** key, click the bottom item to select the entire list.

After the list is selected, let go of **Shift** key, then click to drag and drop the list onto your Playlist.

Creating a New Smart Playlist

A smart playlist is one that **iTunes** creates for you based on your selections. For example, you can create a smart playlist for your ten most-played songs, specific artists, or a specific genre, and you can even limit the playlist to a certain size based on the number of songs or their size (in MB or GB).

To start creating a smart playlist, select **File ➤ New Smart Playlist** (alternatively, on Windows you can press **Ctrl+Alt+N** and then select **New Smart Playlist** from the **File** menu; and on the Mac you can press **Command+Option+N** and just input the search parameters).

Figure 29–17 illustrates that you have many options for creating a smart playlist. All of the default playlists you see in **iTunes** are smart playlists. Default categories include **90's Music, Classical Music, Music Videos, My Top Rated, Recently Added, Recently Played,** and **Top 25 Most Played**.

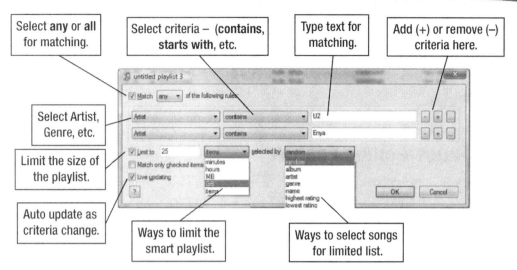

Select **any** or **all** for matching.

Select criteria – (**contains**, **starts with**, etc.

Type text for matching.

Add (+) or remove (–) criteria here.

Select Artist, Genre, etc.

Limit the size of the playlist.

Auto update as criteria change.

Ways to limit the smart playlist.

Ways to select songs for limited list.

Figure 29–17. *The Smart Playlist settings screen*

Editing a Smart Playlist

The best way to get a feel for how the smart playlist function works is probably to check out some of the preset smart playlists. To edit a smart playlist, select **Edit Smart Playlist** from the **File** menu. In Figure 29–18, you can see the smart playlist for **90's Music**; you can also see that it will pull all music and music videos from 1990 to 1999. Check out a few other default smart playlists to begin learning how the myriad options interact to create a very powerful playlist function.

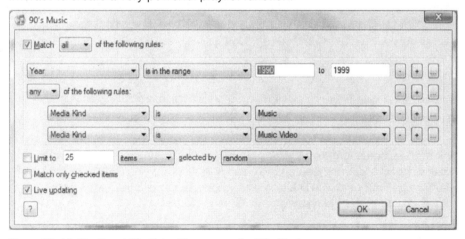

Figure 29–18. *The Smart Playlist settings screen for* ***90's Music***

> **NOTE:** The **Live Updating** feature of smart playlists allows them to scan whenever you play a song or add any new media (e.g., songs and videos) to your library; it then includes any new songs that it deems may fit the criteria of the smart playlist. This makes the playlists really dynamic.

The iTunes Genius Feature

The iTunes Genius feature can do all sorts of fun things to help enhance your music and video library in **iTunes**. You can take advantage of it by following these steps:

1. Click **Genius** in the Left Nav Bar, and then click the **Turn On Genius** button. If you don't see the **Genius** item, then click **Store** and **Turn On Genius** from the **iTunes** menu.

2. If you are not already logged into the iTunes Store, you will be asked to log in. If you do not yet have an Apple ID, then please jump to the "Creating an iTunes Account" section later in this chapter to learn how to create one.

3. Read and agree to the Genius license agreement to continue.

4. Next, you will see a window on your screen for some time (longer if your library is large) that says the Genius feature is starting.

5. In order for the Genius feature to work correctly, **iTunes** needs to understand the types of music and videos you have in your library. It will use this information to help make suggestions on similar music or videos that you don't yet own, but might want to purchase. When this step is done, you will see a final success screen telling you Genius is now set up. Now you are ready to start using the Genius feature!

> **TIP:** You can use the Genius feature on your iPad, but only after you have enabled it on your computer (as just described).

You can think of the Genius feature as your personal shopper, one who knows your tastes and makes good recommendations (Genius suggestions). You can also think of the Genius feature as your personal DJ, one who knows the music that goes well together and will create a great playlist for you (Genius playlists).

Creating Genius Mixes and Playlists

Follow these steps to create a Genius mix and playlist:

1. Right-click a song in your library that you would like for your Genius playlist and select **Start Genius**.

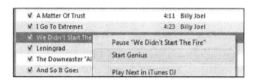

2. After you click the **Start Genius** dropdown item, the screen will immediately change to show you the **Genius** mix of all songs that **iTunes** thinks match the type of song you selected (see Figure 29–19); these suggestions are based on computer algorithms and feedback from other **iTunes** users. You may be surprised at the list of music or even artists that you would not normally put together into a playlist.

> **TIP:** Genius mixes and playlists provide a great way to keep your music library fresh, helping you to put together songs that go well together—often in combinations that you might not have thought about yourself.

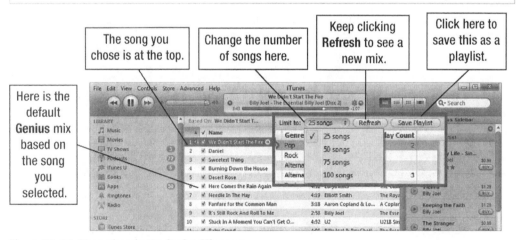

Figure 29–19. *The options for the **Genius Mix** screen*

3. On the **Genius Mix** screen, you have options to choose between 25, 50, 75, or 100 songs. Click the **Refresh** button to see a new (usually slightly different) mix/playlist.

4. If you like the mix and want to save it as a playlist, click the **Save Playlist** button in the upper-right corner. Notice that the playlist is saved under the **Genius** section in the left column. The default name of the playlist is the name of the song you first clicked. You can change this name by double-clicking the playlist name. You will see it turn into editable text; from here, you can type a new name.

Turning Off Genius

To turn off the Genius feature and remove all your Genius mixes and playlists, select **Store** from the **iTunes** menu, and then choose **Turn Off Genius**.

Updating Genius

If you have added a lot of music, videos, or other content to your iTunes library, periodically you will want to send an update to the Genius function in **iTunes**. To send this update, select **Store** from the **iTunes** menu, and then choose **Update Genius**.

How to Back Up and Restore Your iTunes Library

In order to protect the sizable investment in your iTunes music, videos, and more, you should periodically back up your library. You can use the built-in CD or DVD burner in your computer to back up your library, but this process becomes cumbersome if you have a large media library. When you have a larger iTunes library, you should backup your library to an external hard disk.

Back up with CDs or DVDs (for Smaller Libraries)

For smaller iTunes libraries, you can use CDs or DVDs to backup your media. To do this, select **File ➤ Library ➤ Backup to Disc** from the **iTunes** menu. You will see a window with several options (see Figure 29–20). We recommend selecting the default and backing up everything; however, you could also choose to back up just purchases from the iTunes Store. After you insert all the disks required for the backup, you will see a backup complete message. If you have recently backed up to disk, then you can save time and space by checking the **Only back up items added or changed since last backup** box.

TIP: If you need to back up to DVD or CDs, we highly recommend opting for the DVD method to do the backup, since it can hold four to eight times the content of a CD.

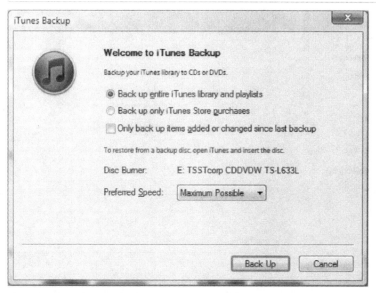

Figure 29–20. *The options for **iTunes** backup*

To Restore from CDs or DVDs

All you need to do to start restoring your library is to insert the first backup CD or DVD, and **iTunes** will ask you if you would like to restore from the backup disk.

TIP: You can also restore individual files by clicking the backup disk under the **Devices** section listed in the Left Nav Bar, and then dragging-and-dropping files from the backup to your library. However, a few items are lost from restored files, such as bookmarks of the last played content.

Back up to an External Hard Disk (for Larger Libraries)

As your iTunes library grows larger, it could take you dozens or even a hundred or more DVDs or CDs to complete the backup, so you should use an external hard disk instead. This method works best only when your iTunes library is located in a single folder.

Step 1: Make Sure All Media Is in a Single Folder

You can use **iTunes** to move all your media to a single folder by following these steps:

1. From the **iTunes** menu, select **Edit ➤ Preferences** (Windows) or **iTunes ➤ Preferences** (Mac).

2. Click the **Advanced** tab and check the box next to **Copy files to iTunes Media folder when adding to library** in the middle of the page.

3. Click **OK**.

4. From the **iTunes** menu, select **File ➤Library ➤ Organize Library** to see the window to the right.

5. Check both checkboxes as shown and click **OK.**

6. This will cause all your media to be copied to a single iTunes media folder.

Step 2: Drag and Drop Your Library to an External Hard Disk

This assumes you have purchased and connected an external hard disk. If you don't have one, you can find one by visiting your local computer store or doing a web search for "external hard disk" for your computer operating system type, whether it's a Windows or Mac. Follow these steps to copy your library to an external hard disk:

1. Open a window on your computer and locate your iTunes library. The default media location for your iTunes library is:

   - **Windows XP:** \Documents and Settings\username\My Documents\My Music\

   - **Windows Vista or Windows 7:** \Users\username\music\iTunes\iTunes music\

   - **Mac OX X:** /Users/username/Music/

2. Open another window on your computer for your external hard disk.

3. Drag and drop the iTunes library onto the external hard disk window to copy all the files. This will take quite a while if your library is very large, but at least you won't be swapping disks every few minutes!

Restoring from an External Hard Disk Backup

Restoring from an external hard disk backup is a multistep process. Begin by closing **iTunes**, and then follow the steps outlined in the sections that follow.

Step 1: Copy Your Library Back to Your Computer

Reverse the steps described previously to drag and drop your library from the external hard disk back onto your computer. You may want to put the library in the same location as the original iTunes library for the sake of simplicity. Refer to the previously mentioned default locations if you need to.

Step 2: Open iTunes and Select the Library

To open the newly copied library, you have to open iTunes in a special way:

1. On Windows, hold down the **Shift** key while you open **iTunes**. On a Mac, hold down the **Option** key. Make sure to keep the key

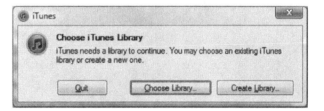

pressed until you see the
small window shown to the
right. If you let go too soon,
then **iTunes** will open
normally.

2. Select **Choose Library** and locate the library you just copied from your external
    hard disk.

3. Click **Open** (Windows) or **Choose** (Mac) to open the iTunes library file.

Following these steps should allow you to restore your iTunes library by opening the file
you just copied from your external hard disk.

The Home Sharing Feature

If you have several people in your home who use iTunes, and they are all connected
together on a home network, then the Home Sharing feature will help you share your
content (music, videos, and more) across your computers and now, for the first time
ever, your iPad or other mobile Apple device. Follow these steps to take advantage of
the Home Sharing feature:

1. Pick the account to use for the Home Sharing feature. All computers and mobile
    devices connected with the Home Sharing feature have to use the same iTunes
    account and password to log in and be connected. You will usually want to pick
    the account that has the most purchased content or the content you would like to
    share across all the computers.

> **NOTE:** New with iOS 4.3: You can now enjoy the Home Sharing feature on your iPad or other iOS
> mobile device (iPhone or iPod touch).

2. Set up the Home Sharing feature and authorize each of the other
    computers. You can get started with Home Sharing much as you can
    with the Genius feature. On your computer in iTunes, click **Home
    Sharing** under the **Shared** heading in the **iTunes** app's Left Nav Bar
    (see Figure 29–21). If you do not see Home Sharing in the Left Nav Bar,
    then from the menu go to **Advanced ➤ Turn Off Home Sharing**, and
    then **Advanced ➤ Turn On Home Sharing**. That should fix the issue.

NOTE: All versions of videos and movies purchased or rented from the iTunes Store are protected by digital rights management (DRM) using FairPlay. However, such DRM-protected content can be played on up to five authorized computers (PC or Mac). Rented DRM content, such as a rented movie, must be physically transferred to one machine or device at a time. Protected music can be authorized on up to five computers, and music can be synced to a large number of mobile devices, as long as those mobile devices sync to only a single computer.

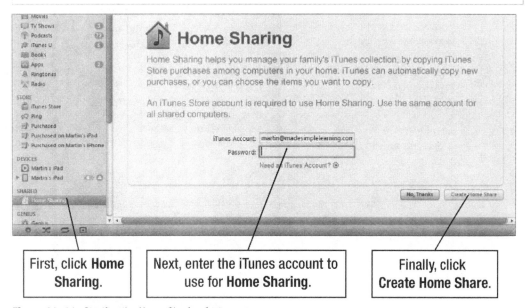

First, click **Home Sharing**.

Next, enter the iTunes account to use for **Home Sharing**.

Finally, click **Create Home Share**.

Figure 29–21. *Starting the Home Sharing feature*

TIP: Check out Chapter 9: "Playing Music" to learn how to enable Home Sharing in the **iPod** app on your iPad.

3. You can control a Home Sharing library on your iPad or other mobile device by following these steps:

 a. Download and install Apple's free **Remote** app from the iTunes Store on your iPad.

 b. Tap **Remote** to start it.

c. Tap **Turn on Home Sharing**.

d. Enter the Apple ID that was used to create the original Home Share to log in.

e. Once logged in, you will see a screen similar to this one, with instructions for controlling **iTunes**.

f. Tap **Done** to close the window.

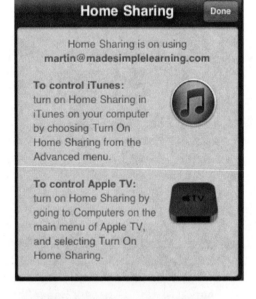

g. Now you will see all libraries on the next screen. In this case, it shows just **Martin's Library**. Tap the library to open it and play the content right on Martin's computer running **iTunes**.

4. Repeat Steps 2 and 3 on every computer and mobile device you want to give access to your home-shared content. Make sure that you use the same iTunes account on every computer; this could be a little confusing at first, but it's important to use the same account. On the other computers, you will probably have to authorize the computer to play content from your iTunes library. The **iTunes** app will notify you if you need to authorize the computer by popping up a window.

NOTE: Up to five computers and mobile devices can be authorized as home-sharing devices.

5. Click **Yes** to continue. Once authorization is complete, you will see a screen showing how many of your five total authorizations have been used up. To learn more about authorizing or deauthorizing computers, see the "Authorizing and Deauthorizing Computers" section later in this chapter.

6. Start enjoying the shared content. Once the Home Sharing feature is enabled on at least two computers, the second computer will then see the shared content underneath the **Shared** heading in the **Left Nav Bar** in **iTunes**. To start viewing, playing, and importing this shared content, click the shared library (see Figure 29–22).

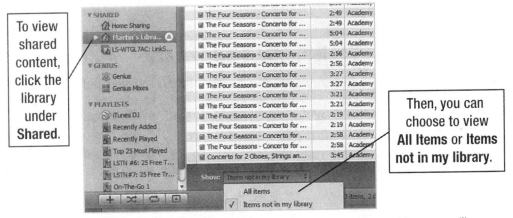

Figure 29–22. *Viewing a home-shared library and filtering to view all items or those not in your own library*

Filtering a Home-Shared Library to Only Show Items Not in Your Library

Once you get up and running with a home-shared library, you will notice that there is a switch at the bottom of the screen that allows you to show only those items that are not in your library (see Figure 29–22). This is a great way to quickly assess what you might need to add (i.e., import) to your library from the shared library.

Two Types of Shared Libraries

You will see two logos in the **Shared** category on the Left Nav Bar of **iTunes**. Each type of logo shows you whether the library is a fully shared library (the **House** icon) or a listen-only type of library (the **Stack of Papers** icon). Table 29–1 describes the differences.

Table 29–1. *Fully Shared vs. Listen-Only Libraries*

Types of Shared Libraries	What This Means
▼ SHARED ⌂ Home Sharing ▶ ⌂ Martin's Library ⏏ Fully Shared Library (the **House** icon)	Martin's library is fully enabled for home sharing—you can view, listen, and import (add) items from this library.
♪ LS-WTGL7AC: LinkS… Listen-Only Library (the **Stack of Papers** icon)	LS-WTGL7AC is a listen-only and view-only library. You cannot import any songs from this library to your own library.

Importing Shared Content into Your Library

When you are viewing a home-shared library, you can listen to anything in that library, as long as your computer has been authorized to do so. If you hit any authorization issues, please refer back to Chapter 3: "Sync Your iPad with iTunes." In that chapter, we show you how to authorize your computers for iTunes.

You can manually drag and drop content into your library, or you can set up the Home Sharing feature to automatically import all new purchases from the home-shared iTunes account.

Importing by Manually Dragging and Dropping

The drag-and-drop method for importing works well if you want to grab a few songs or videos from the shared library. Simply click the songs or videos to highlight them, and then drag them over to your library.

You can also click the songs/videos to highlight them, and then click the **Import** button in the lower-right corner to do the same thing.

Automatically Importing New Purchases

Follow these steps if you want to share all new purchases from the home-shared iTunes account to the library on another device or computer automatically:

1. Click the home-shared library you would like to import from in the Left Nav Bar.

2. Click the **Settings** button in the lower-right corner of the **iTunes** screen.

3. Now you will see a small window pop up that is similar to the one shown to the right. Check off those items to be automatically transferred from the home-shared library into your library.

4. Click **OK** to save your Home Sharing settings.

Toggling Home Sharing Off and On

Once you have enabled the Home Sharing feature, you may want to turn it off at some point. You do this by going to the **Advanced** menu of **iTunes** and selecting **Turn Off Home Sharing**. To turn it back on, repeat the steps described previously by going to the same **Advanced** menu and selecting **Turn On Home Sharing**.

Troubleshooting Home Sharing

Sometimes you may see a "Computer Not Authorized" error, even though your computer has already been authorized on the Home Sharing account. Usually this happens because the content (e.g., song or video) that you are trying to view or listen to from the home-sharing account was purchased by an account other than the home-shared iTunes account. To correct this problem, follow these steps:

1. Locate the person in your home who originally purchased the song.

2. Ask him to authorize your computer. (If you hit any authorization issues, then you'll find Chapter 3: "Sync Your iPad with iTunes" useful; this chapter explains how to authorize your computers for the iTunes service.)

3. Once your computer is authorized, you should be able to enjoy the music or video.

Creating an iTunes Account

If you have already registered for an iTunes account using an Apple ID or AOL screen name, then you need to sign in (see the "Signing into the iTunes Store" section later in this chapter for information on how to do this).

If you want to buy or download free songs, books, apps, videos, TV shows, and more, you will need to acquire them from the iTunes Store. You can do so by following these steps:

1. Click the **Sign In** button in the upper-right corner (see Figure 29–23). If you do not yet have an iTunes account, then click the **Create New Account** button and follow the instructions to create your new account. If you already have an account, enter your Apple ID or AOL screen name and password, click the **Sign In** button, and skip ahead to the "Signing into the iTunes Store" section. This is where you'll enter your Apple ID or AOL account details, if you have them.

Figure 29–23. *The iTunes Store **Sign In** screen, where you can start creating a new account*

2. When you click the **Create New Account** button, you will see a new account **Welcome** screen; click **Continue** to move on.

3. Read and accept the terms and conditions by clicking the checkbox at the bottom of the screen, then click **Continue** to move on.

4. On the next screen, you set up your Apple ID (your login name for the iTunes Store), your password, and your secret question and email preferences. If you do not want email notification, be sure to uncheck the boxes at the bottom of the page. Click **Continue** to move on.

5. On the next screen, you are asked to enter your billing information. Note that you can create a US-based account without billing information. Also, you can enter an iTunes gift card to receive credit, so you do not need to enter a credit card or PayPal account. This screen contains your preferred billing information, which will be used when you buy music, videos, and iPad apps (from the App Store app on your iPad). Click **Continue** to move on. Please note that the contents of this screen may vary slightly, depending on the country in which you are located.

6. Depending on your locale, you may need to verify your county, province, or other local taxing authority. Click **Done**.

7. Now you should see a screen that asserts you have correctly set up your iTunes account. Click **Done** to finish.

Signing into the iTunes Store

If you've successfully created an iTunes account or you already own one, then the wonders of the iTunes Store are now yours to explore! The following sections show you most of the things you can do once you're signed in. But first you need to sign in.

To do this, begin by clicking the iTunes **Sign In** button to go to the **Sign In** screen, where you'll then be asked to enter your Apple ID and password. Alternatively, you can enter your AOL screen name and password.

Getting to the iTunes Store

You can always get back to the iTunes Store by clicking the **iTunes Store** link under **Store** in the Left Nav Bar.

Buying or Getting Free Media from the iTunes Store

After signing in or creating a new account, you will be able to search the store for any artist, album, composer, or title.

To find all the songs by a particular artist, type that artist's name into the **Search** box in the upper-right corner. You could also search by part or all of a particular song's name. Once you press the **Enter** key, you will be presented with all the matching items from the iTunes Store (see Figure 29–24).

> **TIP:** Use the **Power Search** feature shown in the upper-left corner of the main **iTunes** window to further narrow your search. Also note that you can refine your search by using the **Filter by Media Type** box just below **Power Search**. Filter the search by music, movies, TV shows, apps, audiobooks, podcasts, iTunes U, or Ping.

You can then navigate around and purchase individual songs with the **Buy** buttons at the bottom.

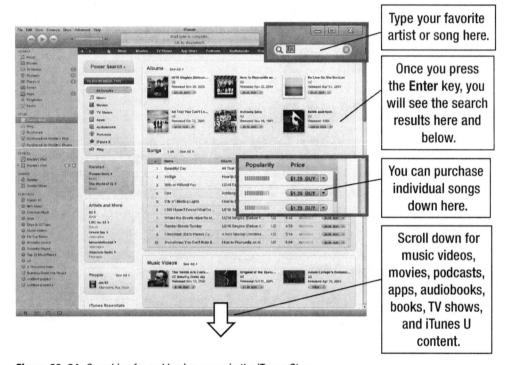

Figure 29–24. *Searching for and buying songs in the iTunes Store*

After you click the **Buy** button, you will need to log in, unless you have previously instructed **iTunes** to keep you logged in for your purchases.

> **CAUTION:** If you are at a public computer or are worried that someone might access your computer and buy stuff without you knowing, then don't check the **Remember password for purchasing** box!

After you log in, you will see a pop-up window if you have just clicked the **Buy** button.

If you don't want to see this dialog box every time you buy something, check the box at the bottom pop-up window that says **Don't ask me about buying songs again**, and then click the **Buy** button.

Now the song, video, or other item you purchased will be queued up to be downloaded to your local library in the **iTunes** app on your computer.

Making Sure All Items Are Downloaded

After you purchase a song, video, app, or other item from the App Store—or if you have just authorized this computer on your account—you should click the **Downloads** link that appears under the **Store** category heading in the Left Nav Bar.

Any items currently being downloaded will show a **Status** bar in the main **Downloads** window. You will see a **Done** status message when the items are completely downloaded to your computer.

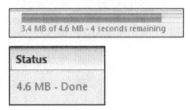

You will need to see a status of **Done** before you can put the purchased item onto your iPad. If you see a pop-up window asking whether you want **iTunes** to download all your purchased items, then click **Yes**.

Redeeming iTunes Gift Cards or App Promo Codes

At some point, you may receive an iTunes gift card or a Promo Code for free apps. Follow these steps to learn how to redeem the value of the card to your iTunes account:

> **NOTE:** iTunes gift cards are country-specific. In other words, a US gift card will only work for a US iTunes account.

1. If you are not already signed in, then sign into your iTunes account by clicking the **Sign In** link in the upper-right corner of **iTunes**.

2. Click the little **Dropdown Arrow** to the right of your iTunes Apple ID where you saw the **Sign In** link, and then select **Redeem** from the dropdown list.

Click this drop down list and select **Redeem**.

3. On the **Redeem** screen, you will need to enter the code from the back of the gift card or Promo Code (see Figure 29–25). You may need to scratch off the silver/gray covering to see the card's code.

4. Click the **Redeem** button.

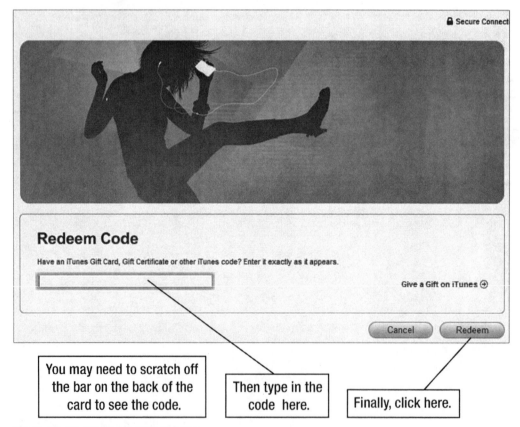

You may need to scratch off the bar on the back of the card to see the code.

Then type in the code here.

Finally, click here.

Figure 29–25. *The iTunes Redeem screen.*

5. To verify that the gift card is being applied to the correct iTunes account, you will need to sign in or re-enter your password.

6. Click the **Sign In** button or the **View Account** button (if you're already signed in).

7. When the gift card has been successfully applied to your account, you will see the total amount of the card in the upper-right corner of the **iTunes** screen, right next to your sign-in name. Now you can use this gift card credit to buy stuff from the iTunes Store.

Getting Your Stuff into iTunes

If you have music CDs, DVDs, E-Books, and PDF files you want to enjoy on your iPad, you will first have to import them into your iTunes library on your computer. We show you how in the upcoming sections.

Importing Music CDs

If you are of legal drinking age, then it's likely that you have a few music CDs in your home library. If you are over 40, that likelihood goes up to 100 percent. So, how do you get all your best CDs loaded onto your iPad? Accomplishing this is a two-step process:

1. First, you must load the CDs into **iTunes**.

2. Second, you must sync or manually transfer those CD songs to your iPhone. (We show you how to sync or manually transfer content with **iTunes** in Chapter 3: "Sync Your iPhone with iTunes.")

In order to import your music from a CD, insert the CD into your computer's CD drive. You may see a pop-up window inside **iTunes** that asks whether you would like to import the CD as shown. Click **Yes** to import the CD.

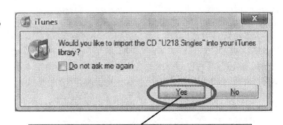

After you insert the CD, you may see this screen pop-up; click **Yes** to Import into iTunes.

If you did not receive this pop-up window, then you can manually start the CD import into **iTunes** by clicking the **Import CD** button in the lower-right corner. Also notice that the CD appears under the **Devices** list in the left column (see Figure 29–26).

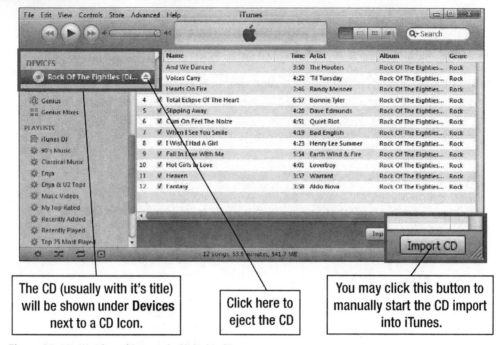

The CD (usually with it's title) will be shown under **Devices** next to a CD Icon.

Click here to eject the CD

You may click this button to manually start the CD import into iTunes.

Figure 29–26. *Working with a music CD inside* ***iTunes***

Importing Movies from DVDs

Some of the more recent DVDs and Blu-rays that you can purchase may have two versions of the movie: one for your DVD or Blu-ray player and an extra digital copy that can be loaded automatically into **iTunes**.

Usually, there will be text on the DVD box that states that there is an extra digital copy for your computer. You can check whether this copy exists by inserting the DVD into your computer's DVD drive and opening **iTunes**. If the digital copy exists, then **iTunes** will automatically detect it and ask whether you would like to import the movie.

CAUTION: Most DVDs or Blu-rays do not provide this extra digital version, which is meant to be loaded and watched on your computer and mobile devices. Standard DVDs or Blu-rays are copy-protected and cannot normally be loaded into **iTunes**. However, if you do a web search for "load DVD into iTunes," you may find some software products (such as **Handbrake**; see http://handbrake.fr) that allow you to *rip* or *burn* your DVDs into **iTunes**. We strongly urge you to obey copyright laws; if you use software like this, you should only use the DVD on your own computer or iPad and never share the movie or otherwise violate the copyright agreement.

Importing E-Book (PDF and iBook Format) Files

If you want to read a PDF file or E-Book (in the industry standard ePub format set by the International Digital Publishing Forum) on your iPad, you will first need to get the file into **iTunes** to sync it to your iPad. There are a couple of ways to get E-Books into **iTunes**. You can use the drag-and-drop method or the menu commands to add files or folders to the library.

The Drag-and-Drop Method

This is a great way to add a single file or just a few files. Follow these steps to do so:

1. Locate the file on your computer.

2. Click and drag that file onto your iTunes library. Let go of the mouse to drop this file into your library. A box will be drawn around your library, as shown in the image to the right. When you see the box, you can let go of the mouse button.

3. Since the file is readable by the **iBooks** app, you should then see the file appear in the **Books** section of your library.

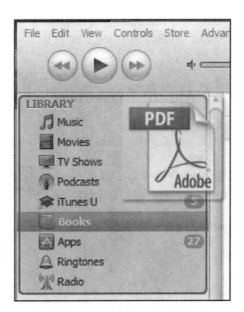

Using Menu Commands

Using menus works well if you have an entire folder or multiple folders of files you want to move into **iTunes**.

> **TIP:** This method works for E-Books and also other content such as music.

1. From the **iTunes** menu, choose **File** and then select **Add Folder to Library** to add an entire folder of content or **Add File to Library** if you have only one file to add.

2. Now navigate to the folder or file you wish to add and click **Select Folder** (or **Open** for a single file).

3. All iBooks-readable files will be added to **iTunes**.

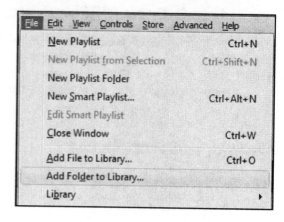

Getting Album Artwork

iTunes can automatically get the album art for most songs and videos; however, if you need to manually retrieve this artwork, follow these steps:

1. Start **iTunes**.

2. Go to the **Advanced** menu.

3. Select **Get Album Artwork**.

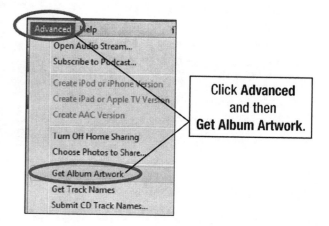

Click **Advanced** and then **Get Album Artwork**.

NOTE: You will need to have an iTunes account already and be logged in for this to work correctly.

Authorizing and Deauthorizing Computers

As mentioned previously, you can authorize up to five different computers to play your iTunes media (e.g., music and movies).

> **CAUTION:** Once you hit five authorized computers, you can deauthorize them all, but only once a year.

Here's a question that you may hear quite often: *Someone else has authorized my computer to play her songs; can I now load and listen to these "authorized songs" on my iPad?*

The short answer is maybe. The answer is no for all songs purchased on iTunes prior to January 2009. It is also no for all songs purchased with DRM protection. These songs are tied specifically to one person's mobile device (i.e., iPad, iPhone, or iPad).

The answer is yes for all songs purchased without DRM protection enabled. Early in 2009, iTunes announced that it would start selling some songs and videos without DRM protection, which means they can be played on multiple iPhones and iPads. Follow these steps to authorize or deauthorize your computer for being able to play songs on your computer and possibly your iPad from someone else's iTunes library:

1. Start up **iTunes**.

2. To authorize a computer, go to the **Store** menu and select **Authorize This Computer...** To deauthorize a computer, go to the **Store** menu and select **Deauthorize This Computer...**

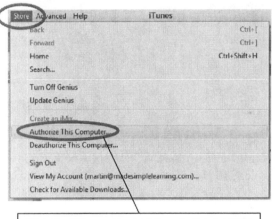

> **NOTE:** You will need to know your iTunes or AOL username and password for this to work.

Click the **Store** menu and then **Authorize This Computer** to enable this computer to play your iTunes media.

3. Enter your Apple ID, or if you prefer, click the radio button next to AOL, and enter your AOL screen name and password.

4. Next, click the **Authorize** or **Deauthorize** button.

iTunes Troubleshooting

In this section, we will provide a few tips and tricks to help you deal with some common issues you might encounter when using **iTunes**. We also have an entire chapter devoted to troubleshooting (see Chapter 28: "Troubleshooting") if you cannot find answers to the problems you encounter in this section.

What to Do If the iTunes Automatic Update Fails

The automatic update may fail if you have the About iTunes.rtf text file open, or you have another related file open that cannot be closed by the installer automatically. If you locate and close the problem file, you should be able to retry the automatic update.

If you see a message similar to the one shown to the right, then you will have to manually install the update. Follow these steps to do so:

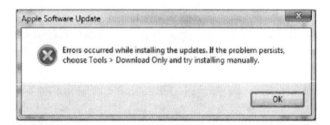

1. From the **Apple Software Update** screen, select the **Tools** menu and then **Download Only**.

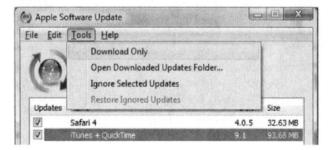

2. You will see the **Download** status screen (shown in the image to the right of step 1). Once the download is finished, a new window should pop up, showing the downloaded files ready for you to install manually (see Figure 29–27).

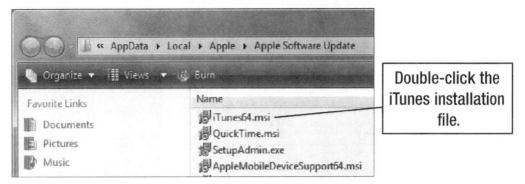

Figure 29–27. *The Apple Software Update manual installation folder (Windows PC)*

3. To manually start the install, double-click the **iTunes** installer file (see Figure 29–27). The file may be slightly different from the one shown in the figure (e.g., iTunes.msi or iTunes64.msi), depending on the operating system on your computer.

4. From here, you need to follow the **iTunes** installation screens.

Fixing the Apple ID Security Error

If you try to log in with your Apple ID, you might receive an error message at the top of the screen that looks similar to this one:

To use this Apple ID you must first login to the My Info Web page then provide additional security information.

If this happens, then you will have to log in to the Apple Store web site, enter a security question/answer, and then add the month and day of your birth.

To correct this error, follow these steps:

1. Open a web browser on your computer and go to www.apple.com.

2. Click the **Store** link in the left portion of the Top Nav Bar, and then hover your mouse over the **Account** link in the upper-right corner to see a dropdown list. Select **Account Information** from this list (see Figure 29–28).

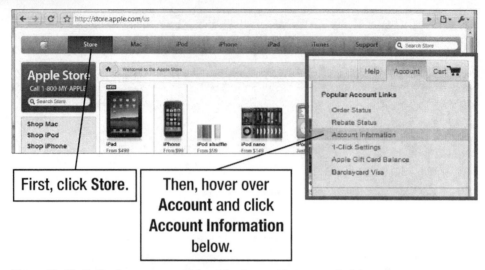

Figure 29–28. *Getting to your account information to correct your security information*

3. If you clicked **Account**, then you will need to select the **Change account information** link from the next screen.

4. Log in with your Apple ID and password (the one that caused the error).

5. Most likely, your security question and answer or your birth month and date are blank. You need to add this information, type your password twice, scroll to the bottom of the screen, and then click the **Continue** button.

You should now be able to use your Apple ID and password to register your iPad.

> **CAUTION:** Apple will never send you an email asking you for your password or asking you to log in and enter your password. If you receive such an email, it is probably a scam. Don't click any links in such an email. If you are concerned about your iTunes account, log in through the **iTunes** app to manage it.

Getting Your Music Back If Your Computer Crashes

The good news is that you'll probably have a lot, or perhaps all, of your music on your iPad. We can't help you get your computer back up and running in this book if the initial reboot isn't successful. However, we can tell you about how you can get your music back from your iPad to your **iTunes** app once your computer is running again.

So, if your only copy of your music, videos, and other content resides on your iPad, iPod, iPhone, or iPod touch, then you need to use a third-party tool to copy your music from that mobile device back into the **iTunes** app on your computer, once you get your computer up and running again.

Do a web search for "copy iPad or iPod to iTunes" and you will find a number of both free and paid software tools to accomplish this task. We recommend using a free trial of any software before purchasing it to make sure it will meet your needs.

This solution will also help if you encounter the problem where all your iPad music is grayed out when you view it from **iTunes**. In that case, you will need to copy all your iPad music to **iTunes**, and then start fresh with the sync or manual transfer steps described in Chapter 3: "Sync Your iPad with iTunes."

> **CAUTION:** Please do not use this third-party software to create unauthorized copies of music, videos, or other content that you have not legitimately purchased.

Index

■N

T

Making Technology Simple

"Turns on the light for features that are not intuitive!"

— Lou

"Easy to follow. I learned a lot!"

— Nicky

"Short & sweet! Definitely recommend!"

— Sandy

"Just what I needed – concise and relevant!"

— Dan S.

"Our BlackBerry users have gained an hour a day in productivity and we've reduced help desk calls by 50% with the Made Simple Learning videos."

— 3,000 Users, Fortune 500 Company

"I would definitely recommend these videos to anyone in a BES administrator or BlackBerry technical support role for any size company!"

— 250 Users, Mid-size Company

"Having the videos right on the Blackberry makes all the difference in the world. I get far fewer questions, and I've heard a lot of the Bold users getting excited that they've "found" new features that are helpful to them."

— 60 Users, Small Company

For You

Get Started Today!

1. Go to **www.madesimplelearning.com.**
2. Purchase any of our video tutorials or guide books right from our site.
3. Start learning in minutes.

What individuals say about our BlackBerry video tutorials:

For Your Organization

Get Started Today!

1. Request a quote by e-mail from: **info@madesimplelearning.com**
2. We set you up with a free trial.
3. Try before you buy.

What corporate customers say:

Videos Now™
3-minute Video Tutorials
About Your BlackBerry®
Viewed on your PC or Mac

Videos ToGo™
Mobile Video Training
About Your BlackBerry®
On Your BlackBerry®

MadeSimple™ Guide Book
Comprehensive yet Simple
with 1,000's of pictures
(Electronic or Printed)

Day in the Life of an iPad 2 User

Sometimes it's easier to learn by watching someone else use his or her iPad 2. The next best thing is to read about it. Follow along here to see how you might best use your iPad 2 in your own personal and work life.

TIME	WHAT I DO WITH MY IPAD 2...	LEARN MORE...
6:30 AM	My **Alarm Clock HD Pro** app from the **App Store** wakes me up with my favorite music from the **iPod** app.	Music – Ch. 9 Bluetooth – Ch. 25
7:15 AM	I sit down at the table for breakfast and read today's edition of *The Daily, The New York Times,* and *The Wall Street Journal.*	New Media – Ch. 26
7:25 AM	I notice some dolphins playing as I cross the harbor bridge, so I stop to take some HD **video** with my iPad 2 because I know my daughter would love to see them. I use the **iMovie** app to add some cool effects to the video right on my iPad 2.	Record and Edit Video – Ch. 17
	When I get to a Wi-Fi hotspot, I upload the video to my MobileMe account.	MobileMe – Ch. 4
7:55 AM	I stop for a break at my local coffee shop and use the fast **App Switcher** to quickly move between apps and check my **Calendar**. I forgot I have a meeting at 10:00 this morning at the new coffee shop in town.	Multitasking – Ch. 8
8:00 AM	I log in to the free Wi-Fi at my coffee shop and upload the video I shot earlier using MobileMe. I email my daughter the link, so she can check it out later.	Record Video – Ch. 17 MobileMe – Ch. 4
8:15 AM	Back home, my iPad 2 automatically connects to my Bluetooth stereo speakers. I'm ready for some different music so listen to my Bruce Springsteen station on the **Pandora** app. With multitasking, I can do other things while the Pandora radio plays in the background.	Pandora – Ch. 9 Bluetooth – Ch. 25 Multitasking – Ch. 8
8:30 AM	At the office, I check my email. I also use **Safari** to browse my favorite web sites.	Email – Ch. 13 Safari – Ch. 11
9:00 AM	I connect my iPad 2 to my computer to sync up all the latest information, music, and videos with iTunes. I use the new **iTunes** Ping feature to see who's going to the upcoming concerts and check out which tunes my friends are buying and recommending. Since I've got the **iTunes** Home Sharing feature turned on, I receive ten new songs that my family members purchased since I last synced.	iTunes Sync – Ch. 3 iTunes Guide – Ch. 29
9:30 AM	I check traffic using **Maps** and find out I need to take my alternate route to my meeting today.	Maps – Ch. 27
9:35 AM	My iPad 2 automatically connects to my stereo Bluetooth in the car, so I can enjoy to a lecture from Boston University I downloaded from iTunes U.	Bluetooth – Ch. 25 iTunes app – Ch. 20

Day in the Life of an iPad 2 User

10:00 AM	My meeting is at a coffee shop with free Wi-Fi so I do a quick **FaceTime** video chat with my friend who also has an iPad 2. I still have time, so I reply to a few emails in the **Mail** app while waiting for my colleague. I speed up my typing because the suggested words are spoken out loud to me by the iPad 2.	Wi-Fi – Ch. 5 FaceTime – Ch. 18 Email – Ch. 13 Typing Tips – Ch. 2
10:10 AM	My colleague is a little late, so I check out the latest from my friends on **Facebook**, **Twitter**, and **Linked In**.	Social Networking – Ch. 23
10:20 AM	My meeting finally starts, and I find out I have to fly to London to visit an important prospect. I use the **Kayak** app to find the best fares. Then I log in to Orbitz.com on **Safari** to book my flights.	Safari – Ch. 11 App Store – Ch. 21
10:30 AM	I use my **Skype** app to place a call to James, my prospective client in London, to discuss the upcoming meeting. With a few more minutes still to spare, I use **FaceTime** to video chat with my daughter.	Skype – Ch. 18 FaceTime – Ch. 18
10:35 AM	I receive an email message from James in London, so I add him as a new **Contacts** entry for easy access during my trip.	Email – Ch. 13 Contacts – Ch. 14
10:40 AM	I add London to my **Weather** and **Accu Weather** apps and see that it will be quite rainy. I better get that rain gear packed!	App Store – Ch. 21
11:55 AM	I'm a little early to lunch, so I play some **Angry Birds HD.**	Games – Ch. 22
12:15 PM	Taking advantage of the beautiful display on the iPad 2, I share some recent shots of my client's artwork using the **Photos** app.	Photos – Ch. 16
1:15 PM	I have a few minutes after lunch and decide to put some of my favorite icons on the Bottom Dock, add a new folder for icons, and change my wallpaper to my client's most recent artwork.	Move Icons – Ch. 6 Wallpaper – Ch. 7
3:00 PM	I snap a picture of my Starbucks receipt and upload it to my **Evernote** app. I can later search for "Starbucks" to find this receipt since **Evernote** changes text in pictures into readable, searchable text.	Notes – Ch. 24
5:00 PM	I rent a movie from iTunes and buy a new book from **iBooks** I've been wanting for the airplane, then head to the airport.	iTunes app – Ch. 20 iBooks – Ch. 12
9:00 PM	Sitting back in my seat on the flight, I first read a few chapters in **iBooks** and then watch my newly rented movie.	View Videos – Ch. 10 iBooks – Ch. 12

A information can be obtained at www.ICGtesting.com
the USA
/00005B/187-222/P